Neither Angels nor Demons

The Northeastern Series on Gender, Crime, and Law
EDITOR: Claire Renzetti

Recent books in this series

Kathleen J. Ferraro, *Neither Angels nor Demons: Women, Crime, and Victimization*

Michelle L. Meloy, *Sex Offenses and the Men Who Commit Then: An Assessment of Sex Offenders on Probation*

Amy Nustein and Michael Lesher, *From Madness to Mutiny: Why Mothers Are Running from the Family Courts — and What Can Be Done about It*

Jody Raphael, *Listening to Olivia: Violence, Poverty, and Prostitution*

Cynthia Siemsen, *Emotional Trials: Moral Dilemmas of Women Criminal Defense Attorneys*

Lori B. Girshick, *Woman-to-Woman Sexual Violence: Stories of Women in Prison*

Karlene Faith, *The Long Prison Journey of Leslie van Houten: Life Beyond the Cult*

Neil Websdale, *Policing the Poor: From Slave Plantation to Public Housing*

Lori B. Girshick, *No Safe Haven: Stories of Women in Prison*

Sandy Cook and Susanne Davies, editors, *Harsh Punishment: International Experiences of Women's Imprisonment*

Susan L. Miller, *Gender and Community Policing: Walking the Talk*

James Ptacek, *Battered Women in the Courtroom: The Power of Judicial Responses*

Neil Websdale, *Understanding Domestic Homicide*

Kimberly J. Cook, *Divided Passions: Public Opinions on Abortion and the Death Penalty*

For a complete list of books in this series, please visit www.upne.com and www.upne .com/series/NGCL.html.

Neither Angels nor Demons

Women, Crime, and Victimization

Kathleen J. Ferraro

Northeastern University Press   *Boston*

PUBLISHED BY UNIVERSITY PRESS OF NEW ENGLAND

HANOVER AND LONDON

NORTHEASTERN UNIVERSITY PRESS
Published by University Press of New England,
One Court Street, Lebanon, NH 03766
www.upne.com

Material from chapter 2 has been previously published in Kathleen J. Ferraro, "The
Words Change, but the Melody Lingers: The Persistence of the Battered Woman's
Syndrome in Criminal Cases Involving Battered Women." *Violence Against Women* 9,
no. 1: 110–29.

Library of Congress Cataloging-in-Publication Data

Ferraro, Kathleen J.
Neither angels nor demons : women, crime, and victimization / Kathleen J. Ferraro.
p. cm.— (The Northeastern series on gender, crime, and law)
Includes bibliographical references and index.
ISBN-13: 978-1-55553-662-6 (cloth : alk. paper)
ISBN-10: 1-55553-662-X (cloth : alk. paper)
ISBN-13: 978-1-55553-663-3 (pbk. : alk. paper)
ISBN-10: 1-55553-663-8 (pbk. : alk. paper)
1. Female offenders. 2. Women—Crimes against. 3. Female offenders—United States
—Case studies. 4. Abused women—United States—Case studies. 5. Sex discrimina-
tion in criminal justice administration—United States. I. Title.
HV6046.F43 2006
364.3'740973—dc22   2006019965

For Kailey and Kyle

Contents

Acknowledgments ix

Introduction 1

1. Blurred Boundaries and the Complexities of Experience 10
2. Irreconcilable Differences: Women's Encounters with the Criminal Processing System 46
3. Negotiating Surreality 71
4. The Social Reproduction of Women's Pain 108
5. Demonic Angels?: Violence against Abusers 158
6. Angelic Demons?: Crimes of Complicity 197

Epilogue 246

APPENDIXES

Appendix A. Pseudonym, Race/Ethnicity, Charges, Relationship to Victim(s), and Role in Offense 254
Appendix B. Abuse of Drugs and Alcohol 258
Appendix C. Women Who Killed Their Husbands/Partners 260
Appendix D. Context of Violence against Husbands/Partners 261
Appendix E. Prior Police Involvement, Children, Work, Abused as Child, and Parental Absence 262
Appendix F. Women Who Committed Crimes against Others 264
Appendix G. A Note on Method 265

Notes 267
References 291
Index 315

Acknowledgments

Neither Angels nor Demons is the product of my twenty-three years of work with women who are both victims of violence and criminal offenders, as well as thirty years in the anti–violence against women movement. It is impossible to name here each of the hundreds of people who have supported my work over these years. Those not explicitly identified should know that I do remember and appreciate their help.

The women who have shared their stories with me have taught me much; I feel honored to have been a small part of their journeys. I hope that this book is faithful to what they told me and that it is helpful to other women dealing with intimate partner violence. Each woman I interviewed expressed the desire to help other women avoid the pain that they suffered; perhaps this book is one way to do that. Naming the defense attorneys who brought me into contact with their clients would compromise the anonymity of the women. These attorneys are some of the hardest-working, most dedicated people I have ever met. They have my heartfelt admiration. Mitigation specialists Mary Durand, Mary Kelly, and Ty Mayberry did a wonderful job of conducting the nitty-gritty investigative work that provided information on women's victimization. They are the unsung heroes in these cases. Over the years, Sue Osthoff and Jill Spector at the National Clearinghouse for the Defense of Battered Women have offered education, resources, and moral support. I am deeply grateful to all of these professionals who dedicate their lives to providing legal support to battered women charged with crimes.

All my friends and colleagues who are currently or were formerly with the Arizona Coalition Against Domestic Violence have been wonderful comrades. I acknowledge Allie Bones, Bahney Dedolph, Danae Dotolo, Yvonne Luna, Sharon Murphy, Leah Myers, Doreen Nicholas, Lynne Norris, Rabeya Sen, and the amazing, indefatigable

Dianne Post for all they have taught me and for the incredible work they do to end intimate partner violence.

Many other activist intellectuals within and without the academy have influenced my thinking as well as provided support for my work. Meda Chesney-Lind, Firoza Chic Dabby, Russell Dobash, Rebecca Dobash, Avery Gordon, Barbara Hart, Michael P. Johnson, Ellen Pence, Stephen Pfohl, Nicole Hahn Rafter, Chiquita Rollins, Andrea Smith, and Elizabeth Stanko continue to inspire me. Claire Renzetti, the series editor, has helped and encouraged me with this book and prior work and also been a driving force behind the growth in scholarly attention to intimate partner violence. Susan L. Miller provided useful comments on the final draft and Phyllis Deutsch, at the University Press of New England, was enthusiastic and helpful at each step of the process.

Most of the interviews for this book were completed while I was at Arizona State University where I enjoyed tremendous support from administrators, faculty, staff, and students. I thank Anne Schneider, my former dean, for her leadership and her faith in me. My colleagues in women's studies gave me the opportunity to learn and teach about women's lives and feminist theory. My thanks to Mary Logan Rothschild for her superb mentoring, and Georganne Scheiner for her friendship. My affectionate appreciation goes to the "Dream Team"— Jane Little, Michelle McGibbney Vlahoulis, and Lisa Schulze—for all their help and for making the job of director fun. My former students/ current friends have helped to develop my work and enrich my life in many ways. Special thanks go to Tascha Boychuk-Spears, Karl Bryant, John Cunningham, Nelta Edwards, Cory Gonzales, Andy Hall, Ria Hermann, Angela Moe, Lucille Pope, Lisa Poupart, and Jennifer Wesely.

I wrote this book in Flagstaff, Arizona, as a faculty member in sociology at Northern Arizona University. My thanks to my new colleagues for allowing me to join what is surely one of the most fun sociology departments on earth. I also thank my chair, Warren Lucas, senior office specialist, Debbie Bell, and office specialist Caprice Schneider for all they do to make my life easier.

For years my dearest friends and family have watched me struggle with the legal cases of the women described in this book. Since our days in graduate school, Lesley Hoyt Croft has always been there to support me when the going gets tough. She spent her precious time attending horrific trials just so I could see a friendly face while I was on the witness stand. M. A. (Peg) Bortner has been a consistent beacon of light throughout my career, personally and professionally. She helped me with every aspect of this book, from the prospectus to the final drafts. Peg provided substantive and editorial suggestions, a retreat in the forest, and enthusiastic support for this book and for all of my work. I don't know what I'd do without her. My friends Butch and Billie Artichoker helped me to find my voice and to use it. My mother and father, Audrey and Joseph Ferraro, and my brother and sister-in-law, Daniel and Georgette Ferraro, have sent love and encouragement from Pennsylvania. I feel very lucky to belong to such a cool, caring family. My daughter, Kailey Johnson, and son, Kyle Johnson, endured my preoccupation (and, sometimes, distress) with work. I thank them both for the boundless joy and love they give me and all that they teach me. This book is dedicated to them.

My enduring appreciation to the mountain, animals, and birds, who remind me gracefully of the beauty that surrounds us. Finally, I express my deepest gratitude to my partner, Neil Websdale. I relied heavily on his scholarly knowledge and understanding of intimate partner violence, his expert editorial skills, and his love. This book would never have been finished without his unfailing enthusiasm, humor, and everyday magic.

Neither Angels nor Demons

Introduction

She is a victim of intimate partner violence, a woman who has been harmed. She is a criminal offender, a woman who has harmed others. Superficially, it seems she is two separate women. The category of victim appears distinct from and incompatible with that of offender. It is impossible to be both at the same time. Victim and offender are binary categories used within law, social science, and public discourse to describe social experiences with a moral dimension. Like other binary categories, each term constitutes reciprocally the meaning of the other.[1] There can be no victim without offending persons or circumstances, and offenders depend on the existence of victims.[2] Also, like other binaries, the victim–offender dualism implies a qualitative hierarchy in which victims are good, offenders are bad. The opposition of victim to offender contributes to the objectification of offenders as those deserving and requiring control. The state is invested with the authority and responsibility to protect and compensate victims and to hold offenders accountable for their harmful actions.

Social evaluation of victims and offenders draws upon cultural narratives of good and bad people that are also mutually constituting. These narratives reflect historicopolitical struggles for dominance among gendered, raced, and classed groups. Narratives about "good women," for example, contain assumptions about sexuality, race, and class. Historically, the madonna–whore binary in the United States defined heterosexual, monogamous, and sexually modest women as good women. Bad women were identified by transgressions of sexual propriety, and were considered impure.[3] This binary opposition was linked with raced and classed "controlling images" of women that portrayed white, propertied women as possessing the virtues of "true women": "piety, purity, submissiveness, and domesticity."[4] This true woman was symbolized as the "angel in the house," the devoted, submissive middle-class wife of the nineteenth and early twentieth century.[5] This angel was not consistent with the controlling images of women of color or working-class women who were defined as highly sexual, physically strong, and impure.[6] The angel's purity was in binary opposition to the embodied labor and sexuality of women who desired or were compelled to work, create, and express themselves sexually. Thus, when Virginia Woolf wrote an address to the Women's Service League in 1931, she described her struggle with and eventual murder of the fictitious phantom, the Angel in the House. Woolf explained that all women writers had to kill this mythical figure of female obedience, passivity, and conformity in order to write their own thoughts.[7]

Angels are often represented as female in art and literature. They symbolize feminine chastity and obedience, and their binary opposite is demons. Demons are commonly depicted as male, with the lead demon, Satan, identified as the evil contrast to a male God. However, women who reject angelic qualities are frequently demonized as monstrous deviations from "real" womanhood.[8] Female demons have the opposite qualities of angels: instead of nurturing men and children, they suck the energy from men through sexual intercourse (the succubus and vampire) and kill children (Lilith, Lamia, and Lilu).[9] In Jewish and Christian mythology, original sin derives from Lilith or Eve who brought evil to the Garden of Eden by disobeying their husband, Adam.[10] Women who transgress patriarchal definitions of femininity threaten the social order and are associated with archetypical female troublemakers.[11]

Binary thinking about victimization and offending, angels and demons, has influenced scholarship, public policy, and activism regarding women, crime, and victimization.[12] When battered women become criminal offenders, people use the moral lenses of good and evil to analyze their conduct. Innocent angels or malicious demons are fictive binary categories that do not live in the complex world of human social life. Nevertheless, these imaginary constructs tap deep emotions that influence our perceptions and understanding. Both the fear of evil and the desire to protect and nourish the good are embodied in images of demons and angels.[13] When we confront the situations of victimized offenders, the temptation to simplify moral complexity is facilitated by available binary codes of good and evil. Is she an angel who did all she could to protect herself and her children from a monstrous man? Or is she a demon who killed for her own pleasure and profit?

The opposition of good and bad women, victims and offenders, as mutually exclusive categories has helped to segregate thinking about and responses to each group. The connections between victimization and women's crime are evident to those with knowledge of women's lives. Incarcerated women, police officers, correctional personnel, and defense attorneys all have experiential knowledge of the links between crimes *against* women and the ways women become participants in criminal activity. On a recent visit to a women's prison, I mentioned to a woman that I was writing a book on the relationship between domestic violence and women's crime. She responded casually, "Oh yeah, almost all the women in here have had domestic violence." This is common knowledge. Yet scholars have only recently begun to focus on the links between victimization and offending. Most of the existing research remains at the abstract level, providing survey data on the proportion of incarcerated women who have experienced violent victimization but no qualitative data on how victimization affected their lives.[14] Official data report that approximately 60 percent of incarcerated women experienced prior abuse.[15] Qualitative studies and informal estimates from those who work with incarcerated women place the figure much higher, from 75 to 90 percent.[16] Childhood abuse in the lives of female juvenile offenders has received more thorough scholarly analysis.[17] Once girls turn eighteen, however, there is little public or scholarly attention to the ways that lifelong victimization influences women's participation in crime.

Lack of academic attention to the nexus of victimization and offending has contributed to what Meda Chesney-Lind has termed the "criminalization of victimization."[18] The term *criminalization* directs attention away from the harm of specific acts and toward the social processes of defining behaviors as criminal. In the United States, policies for responding to social problems, such as poverty, homelessness, drug use, and interpersonal violence have tended to focus on individual behavior rather than social structures. The belief that individuals are ultimately the architects of their own destinies is foundational to the liberal democratic principles of equality and

freedom. At the same time, the individualistic model of human behavior holds people responsible for the failures and successes of their
lives without much consideration of the historical and structural
sources of these outcomes. In the realm of criminality, social control
policy has shifted over the past twenty years from an acceptance of
the social causes of crime to a "get tough" approach that focuses on
holding individuals accountable. This trend includes harsh mandatory sentencing laws, an expansion of the legal control of drug use,
and the introduction of habitual offender and "three strikes" laws
that mandate life imprisonment for third convictions for any felony
offense.[19] The policy focus on controlling the behavior of individuals rather than attending to deteriorating social conditions and opportunities contributes to an environment in which the experiences
that lead people to commit crimes are discounted. It also helps explain the dramatic increases in incarceration that have placed the
United States in the position of incarcerating a greater proportion of
the population than any other nation.[20] By midyear 2004, there were
183,400 incarcerated women in the United States, an increase of
118 percent since 1990.[21] African American and Latina women have
been disproportionately affected by this trend. African American
women were 2.5 times more likely than Latinas and 4.5 times more
likely than non-Hispanic white women to be incarcerated in 2003.[22]

Women are a minority of all criminal offenders and are much less
likely to commit violent crimes. According to national victimization surveys, about 14 percent of violent victimizations are perpetrated by women.[23] At the lethal extreme of violent crime, some four
hundred men and twelve hundred women were murdered by their
intimate partners in 2003.[24] The National Violence Against Women
Survey estimates that approximately 1.3 million women are physically assaulted by an intimate partner each year.[25] The vast majority
of women who are victimized by intimate partners do not become
perpetrators of serious crimes.

We know from surveys that the majority of incarcerated women
have experienced childhood and adult violence. But survey data do
not tell us much about the complicated manner through which victimization is articulated with criminal offending. How is victimization part of the constellation of experiences of women charged with
crimes? What exactly does it mean to a woman to have been raped
by her father, battered by her husband, or assaulted by a stranger on

the street? Does it mean that she views herself as a total victim, unable to make decisions and care for herself and others competently? Does the fact of her victimization render her innocent of criminal offending? How are women's survival strategies compromised by the social context of poverty and racism?

The main purpose of this book is to explore the connections between victimization and offending from the perspective of women charged with crimes. The complex emotions, thoughts, and experiences of women are in sharp contrast to simplistic, ahistorical categories that dominate discussions within academic, criminal justice, and activist communities. As many feminist scholars have argued, language and patterns of thinking reflect social organization, and social organization reflects male dominance.[26] Feminist analyses and activism are not immune from the effects of habits of thought that have been shaped by what Dorothy Smith refers to as "relations of ruling."[27] Struggling to create new language that captures women's experiences and sets them at the center of analysis, we are limited by the conceptual practices of academic disciplines, the law, and everyday life. Marjorie DeVault refers to this struggle as one of translating women's experiences into language that has been constructed to prioritize men's needs and perspectives, inevitably leaving out important parts of women's lives.[28] These translations are thus simplifications and distortions that may advance somewhat the understanding of women's lives while simultaneously creating new fictions that silence important dimensions of women's experiences. Binary thinking is apparent in some of the activist work that has defined intimate partner victimization in abstraction from the larger political, social, and economic contexts of women's lives. In what follows, I shall explain how some of the language we have developed has been used to draw boundaries around victims of intimate partner violence that exclude women who also commit crimes.

Avery Gordon suggests that we loosen the grip of conventional categories of analysis and consider "complex personhood": both the visible, overt forms of power as well as the invisible, covert forms that shape experience.[29] Shifting to a more complicated (less fixed and definitive) discussion of women, crime, and victimization allows for inclusion of contradictory qualities, ambiguous feelings, and confusion. I do not want to translate women's experiences into abstract categories, a typology, or an explanatory model. My goal is to use the stories shared with me to make visible the complex lives of women who are labeled as criminal offenders. I argue that these women, like all people, are neither angels nor demons.

My purpose in detailing the ways in which victimization relates to women's criminal offending is neither to generate a general theory of crime, nor to excuse or minimize the harm women inflict on others. Rather, it is to elaborate the now well known correlation between victimization and offending with details about the contexts and meanings of both victimization and offending in women's lives. These details help expand our understanding of the crimes women commit and counteract some of the stereotypes of criminal women as angry, masculine, vindictive, on the one hand; passive, helpless, and deficient, on the other. As a woman going before the clemency board explained to me: "I don't want to use domestic violence as an excuse. I just want them to understand some of the context for why I did what I did."

The Women and Stories That Shape This Book

In 1983, I was contacted by a defense attorney to assist in a case where a battered woman killed her husband. This was during the first years that courts began to accept expert testimony on the effects of battering in criminal cases.[30] Fortunately, that woman accepted a plea offer and was sentenced to probation. I have heard that she remarried and is doing well. Since that time, I have participated in eighty-nine cases as an expert witness to the civil and criminal courts on the effects of battering. In the majority of these cases, women have been the defendants and their experiences with battering have been a major focus of the defense. In some cases, women were victims and I worked for the prosecution to help explain why they stayed with their abusers or why they refused to assist with prosecution. I have also participated in divorce cases and civil suits by providing testimony on the effects of battering in determining custody or damages.

The forty-five cases selected for this book involved women as criminal offenders. They include thirty-one white women, eight American Indian women, four Latinas, and two African American women (see appendix A). All of the women were heterosexual or bisexual, and their crimes were committed with or against a male intimate partner. I have never been asked to assist in a case involving lesbian partners.[31] I also interviewed two male victims: one charged with homicide of a male roommate; the other, attempted homicide of his female intimate partner.[32] I do not include these cases in the following analysis because my focus is on women's victimization and criminality.

I have included twenty-three cases where women killed or attempted to kill their abusive intimate partners, three cases in which women were convicted as third-party accomplices to the murder of their husbands, one case where a sister killed her brother, and eighteen cases where women were charged with other crimes related to their battering. Their characteristics are described in appendixes A through F. Although other cases in which I have served as an expert for the prosecution or in civil cases have shaped my understanding of intimate partner violence, my focus here is on women who have been charged with criminal offenses. Details describing my methodology are contained in appendix E.

My presentation of quotations from interviews is literal, and I follow DeVault's recommendation for maintaining the integrity of women's statements by presenting them without much editing.[33] The pauses, false starts, repetitions, and asides are included. These stories are not easy to tell, emotionally or linguistically. Although failure to "clean up" quotes renders the text more difficult to read, it is important for readers to appreciate that these stories and the lives they speak of are not clean: they are complicated and confusing.

I wish there were a way to reproduce the sounds of women's voices, the looks on their faces, their tears and laughter. Women's voices and gestures convey so much more than can be communicated by marks on a page. My designation of tears or laughter within parentheses is inadequate to share the texture of our conversations. It is also impossible to reproduce entire conversations. The excerpts I have selected highlight similarities in women's experiences with one another and with all women who have lived in abusive intimate relationships. All who have experienced intimate partner violence will recognize parts of their own lives here. My hope is that this recognition will bring greater understanding of women's experiences and the decisions they made.

It is sometimes tempting to engage in binary thinking about abusive men, and to portray them as monsters, engaged in random terrorism against their intimate partners. Without excusing their behavior, the men must also be viewed as complex persons. Women's enduring love, as well as their depictions of the traumas experienced by the men, locate men's violence within other complicated and ambiguous frames. I was not able to interview the men, so their perspectives on events are absent.[34] There is enormous loss in men's deaths, their suffering, and physical incarceration—as well as in the grief of their parents, children, and friends. The loss and grief are even heavier when innocent strangers or women's children were victims. It is not my intention to diminish the significance of these losses. My effort to tell women's stories and to provide substance and complexity to the knowledge that most women offenders have been physically, sexually, and emotionally abused is undertaken out of respect for *all* of the people involved, their families and communities. My hope is that such a rendering will assist in transforming the current punitive environment to one of greater understanding, connection, and support.

The book thus begins with a discussion of blurred boundaries and the complexity of experience. I examine the ways in which the language of domestic violence and of crime excludes the experiences of women that fall outside the boundaries of the categories of victim/ offender, the battered woman, self and other. Women's efforts to create safety and to understand their situations both make use of and work against these boundaries. Trying to remember, to put into words, and to explain what happened to them often left women feeling frustrated and "nuts." Their narratives and feelings critique the categories that have come to dominate discussions of domestic violence and crime, and suggest the importance of fluidity, complexity, and ambiguity in any effort to document women's experiences. In chapter 2, I describe women's interactions with the criminal processing system. The legal actors held assumptions and images of battered women that contradicted women's experiences. Women found it difficult to be heard and understood by these legal actors. I discuss the notion of "mutual combat" and how it is inappropriate for understanding the experiences of the women in this book. In chapter 3, I develop an alternative to the prevailing notion of the "battered woman syndrome" to delineate the ways in which intimate terrorism destroys and reconfigures the sense of reality held by a woman experiencing battering. Psychic terror and surreal conditions combine with prior experiences of trauma and distrust of mainstream authorities to create situations in which women are dependent on abusers' definitions of reality. Women are then reluctant to violate orders of secrecy and obedience. Chapter 4 examines the notion of a "cycle of violence," or the intergenerational transmission of abuse, by describing women's childhood and early adult experiences. Although many women in this book had direct experiences of parental physical and sexual abuse, more than half did not. Rather, most women had experiences of loneliness, isolation, despair; they lacked a close relationship with either their mother or father or both. The so-called cycle, like everything else in these stories, is much more complex than is suggested in typical discussions of the cycle of violence.

Chapter 5 focuses specifically on women charged with violent crimes against the men who had abused them. One aspect of these cases that has not been described in prior literature is the way the men inhabited women's consciousness before their deaths and continued to haunt them after. This chapter provides insight into manifestations of power—as both direct physical violence and internalized control—that inhabit women's bodies long after the death of their abusers. Chapter 6 describes the cases where women's crimes against others were directly related to abuse by their intimate partners. In most cases, the women were guilty of being in the presence of a violent offender and failing to intervene or report the crime. These cases include those where women's children were killed or abused by their partners and they were thus charged with the same crimes as the actual offenders: murder or physical and sexual assault of a child. The epilogue reiterates my critique of the artificial binary of victim–offender as applied to women. I argue that a more complex, nuanced understanding of intimate partner violence will contribute to a public policy less focused on control and "accountability" of individuals than on developing social conditions that promote safety, hope, and well-being for women, children, and men.

1 ～ Blurred Boundaries and the Complexities of Experience

The social movement to end violence against women has challenged many of the conventional binary categories defining social realities. What was once viewed as a private matter is now considered a social problem. Violence that was accepted as "moderate chastisement" in the nineteenth century is now a crime, both legally and in popular opinion.[1] As these categories have shifted, the boundaries circumscribing "normal" and "acceptable" behavior have been modified. The ways in which these categories are defined not only *prescribe* behaviors, they help to *constitute* what people take for granted as true and real.

Our efforts to describe experiences of intimate partner violence have helped to create new vocabularies. Like many aspects of women's experience, there was no specific language to capture the forms of violence in intimate relationships prior to the emergence of the anti–violence against women movement in the mid-1970s in Western Europe and the United States.[2] It is difficult to think about experience when there is no language to describe it, or when the language available is inconsistent with one's experience.[3] For example, Raphael Lemken developed the term *genocide* in 1943 to describe the systematic efforts by the Nazis to destroy groups of people based on their ethnic heritage, sexual orientation, or physical or mental disabilities.[4] Lemken's creation of this term influenced people's conceptions of the Holocaust and other genocides and facilitated the development of international human rights law dealing with genocide. To describe women's experiences of male violence, scholars and activists developed the terms "sexual harassment," "stalking," "domestic violence," "femicide," "marital rape," and "intimate partner violence," thus helping to shift public views of behaviors and experiences that had always occurred but were absent in discourse and policy.

Our knowledge of social phenomena is negotiated through conceptual practices that are saturated with power.[5] What we know is shaped by the way social relationships are organized and by our location in the social hierarchy. Over the past thirty years, feminist scholars have worked to reveal the masculinist biases in knowledge and to offer alternatives. Some of this work (for example, standpoint and postmodern feminism) has been critical of the notion that knowledge is ever objective, universally true, stable, or predictable.[6] From this perspective, simply adding "women's voices" to the mix of information about the social world does not address the ways in which all knowledge is fundamentally structured by power.

Standpoint feminists adopt the epistemological position that one's location in the social order shapes one's perceptions and understanding of the world.[7] Standpoint feminists include a range of epistemological stances and do not represent a unified position apart from the view that all knowledge claims are tied in some way to social location. Some standpoint feminists, like Sandra Harding, Nancy Hartsock, and Patricia Hill Collins, have argued that women's lives, particularly marginalized women's lives, offer a unique, more valid perspective on domination than do the lives of privileged people. Patricia Hill Collins explains:

> A Black women's standpoint and those of other oppressed groups is not only embedded in a context but exists in a situation characterized by domination. Because Black women's ideas have been suppressed, this suppression has stimulated African-American women to create knowledge that empowers people to resist domination. Thus Afrocentric feminist thought represents a subjugated knowledge. A Black women's standpoint may provide a preferred stance from which to view the matrix of domination because, in principle, Black feminist thought as specialized thought is less likely than the specialized knowledge produced by dominant groups to deny the connection between ideas and the vested interests of their creators. However, Black feminist thought as subjugated knowledge is not exempt from critical analysis, because subjugation is not grounds for an epistemology.[8]

Collins's work has helped scholars attend more carefully to the ways that the experience of domination shapes knowledge. She, along with others, emphasizes that all standpoints are situated and that "no one group has a clear angle of vision."[9] Subjugation and marginalization do not ensure the production of "truth"; they do, however, often lead to the development of new knowledge that challenges the dominant perspective. *Subjugated knowledges* is a term first used by Michel Foucault to describe knowledges "disqualified" by those higher in the hierarchy of authority.[10] Collins and other standpoint feminists have adopted the term to refer to knowledge that emerges from the experience of domination and the struggle for recognition and social change.

There are also scholars who are more wary of the reliance on women's experience as a grounds for knowledge. Joan W. Scott, for example, explains how appeals to the authority of experience obscure the ways that our knowing and our subjectivities are shaped by language, history, and political processes. When we rely on experience as the foundation for knowledge without consideration of these processes, we treat the individual as someone who exists outside history, language, and politics. Scott does not suggest abandoning "experience," but cautions us to be more careful and analytical about the ways that experience is constituted: "This entails focusing on processes of identity production, insisting on the discursive nature of 'experience' and on the politics of its construction. Experience is at once always already an interpretation *and* something that needs to be interpreted. What counts as experience is neither self-evident nor straightforward; it is always contested, and always therefore political."[11] Scott and other feminists influenced by postmodernism encourage a political engagement with "women's experience." This means that "women's experience" should not be viewed as authentic truth against which other knowledge claims can be measured. Rather, experience needs to be analyzed in terms of the sociohistorical processes that shape how women define and interpret their lives.[12]

Women's experiences of male violence have formed the basis for activism and scholarship. As the movement to combat violence against women has progressed, the diversity of women's experiences has become more apparent. Without a political analysis of these experiences, it is possible to develop knowledge that replicates existing power hierarchies. Activism in the absence of theory is dangerous. A growing number of activists are documenting the problems that have emerged as a result of policies that developed with the encouragement of many people in the anti–violence against women movement.[13] For example, improvements in police and court responses to battering were one of an array of needs identified by activists in the early 1970s. By 1990, however, the criminal processing system became the primary focus of activism and funding.[14] Women's needs for housing, health care, income, transportation, education, and childcare were submerged in the focus on treating domestic violence as a crime.[15] As I shall discuss throughout this book, the criminal control model excludes the needs of many and is directly punitive to significant numbers of women.

I examine the ways that knowledge, power, and experience operate in the lives of women who are both victimized by intimate partner violence and who commit crimes of their own. These women occupy two social locations that are ordinarily viewed as dichotomous and mutually exclusive: victim and offender. But this artificial dichotomy represents only one of the ways that the lives of women spill over the boundaries of popular and legal discourse.

Women's experiences with intimate violence and crime do not fit neatly into legal or social science categories. The categorical boundaries between victimization and offending, physical assault and emotional abuse, fear and love, past and present, truth and lies, woman and child, self and other blur together in the lived experience of everyday life. These categories are all socially constructed, both shaping and being shaped by broad historical and cultural trends, individual experience, social policies, and legal decision making. The specific content of categories varies across cultures and time, changing with shifts in economies, technologies, resources, and ideologies. Some change is gradual and relatively consensual, such as shifts in the definition of "childhood" that occurred in Western Europe between the seventeenth and twentieth centuries.[16] Other change is more conflictual and violent, such as changes in the social acceptability of same-sex intimate partners. Both accommodation of change and reinforcement of tradition occur, often simultaneously, as people negotiate the categorical boundaries of everyday life.

The Language of Intimate Partner Violence

The language that we have adopted to think about violence and abuse in intimate relationships focuses our perceptions of which actions are included in our definitions, the significance of these terms, and what steps we should take.[17] As the boundaries of acceptable interpersonal behavior in intimate relationships have shifted, the techniques of social control have expanded. A new vocabulary has emerged that creates expectations and assigns responsibility. The terms "domestic violence," "intimate partner violence, "battered woman," and "batterer" are all recent additions to popular language in the United States, dating from the 1970s.

The social construction of "intimate partner violence" is an example of how categories are constructed, reinforced, and then treated as if they were naturally occurring phenomenon that existed prior to human processes.[18] Both individual behavior and the harm it causes exist apart from social constructions of their meaning. But the processes of identifying those behaviors and harms, labeling them, and prescribing interventions are social constructions. It is possible to forget and hide the social aspect of these processes and to view the human behaviors as facts; sociologists call this process "reification."[19] Many of the categories related to intimate partner violence have become reifications of people's lived experiences. According to popular conceptions, battered women have low self-esteem, are passive and weak, and perhaps have "learned helplessness."[20] Such women are deserving of sympathy and support, but may also be disparaged for poor choices and submissive acceptance of violence. Women who do not conform to these expectations of a "real" battered woman have a difficult time convincing people that they have been battered and that their partners' abuse terrified them and caused them to be complicit in criminal acts.[21] When women who are battered become labeled as criminal offenders, they face the struggle of translating their experiences into language that transcends the conventional categories of intimate partner violence. This struggle is both internal and external. Women must confront the categories of thought that they and the people with responsibility for helping or punishing them share about intimate partner violence.

The new language of intimate partner violence developed through interaction among individual women seeking help, grassroots activists, institutional actors, scholars, and politicians. From the beginning of the anti-violence movement, the varying political and ideological commitments of these groups resulted in struggles over appropriate language. The best-documented struggles surrounded the issue of gender neutrality.[22] Feminists argued that gender-neutral language, such as family violence or spouse abuse, failed to signal the critical role of patriarchy and male dominance in perpetuating violence. They used the terms "woman battering," "wife abuse," or "violence against women" in preference to language that left the sex of perpetrators and victims in question. People also raised concerns about focusing on "marital" violence, as many cases involved intimate partners who were not married. The term "domestic violence" gained prominence by the 1980s, enshrined in the titles of state and federal coalitions (the National Coalition Against Domestic Violence and the National Network to End Domestic Violence), and in legal statutes. In the late 1990s, the language of "intimate partner violence" emerged as a corrective to the image of battering as a phenomenon limited to co-residing couples and heterosexuals. This currently preferred language focuses on the sexual and emotional link between abusers and abused persons and is inclusive of same-sex partners, dating partners, and former partners.

The terms "battering," "batterer," and "battered woman" have also been problematic. This language emphasizes the physical aspects of violence. It tends to reinforce the view that intimate partner violence is nothing more than physical assault directed at a spouse or intimate partner. The context of intimidation, degradation, isolation, cruelty, and threats is obscured when language focuses on physical violence. Yet this is the language that dominates domestic violence discourse. Michael P. Johnson has developed an analysis differentiating between intimate partner violence that does not involve coercive control (situational couple violence) and violence that is one technique in a repertoire of control strategies (intimate partner terrorism).[23] This important distinction, however, has not yet altered the pervasive tendency to view intimate partner abuse as a single, homogeneous phenomenon.

Knowledge of intimate partner violence depends on language that is saturated with judgments. The social meaning of "violence" changes over time and across cultures. For example, the use of physical punishment in order to control the behavior of wives was both legal and socially acceptable during the nineteenth century in the United States and England.[24] Women were defined as the morally inferior wards of their husbands who were thus given authority to control them. The same behavior in 2005 is grounds for arrest and prosecution. The behavior is the same, but the social definition and response has changed.

The anti–violence against women movement has focused primarily on physical violence as opposed to the symbolic and emotional violence that women deem much more damaging. When we speak of "intimate partner violence," in legal, social science, and lay terms, people distinguish between "hitting, kicking, and beating up," and making derogatory comments, ignoring a loved one's need for attention and respect, or engaging in emotionally frightening or damaging behavior. Men who physically beat their wives are subject to legal interventions, even if those interventions are light and sporadic. Men who denigrate their wives' appearance, performance and abilities, flaunt marital infidelity, monitor and control their wives' actions, and scare them with aggressive driving, angry verbal outbursts, or other frightening behaviors are rarely subject to criminal sanctions. Women who eventually seek help almost always say that emotionally abusive behaviors hurt more and are more difficult to repair than actual physical assaults.[25] When I interview women about their experiences, they spend much more time talking about the ways in which their partners hurt and terrified them emotionally than about physical violence. As Beth expressed it, "The physical abuse doesn't hurt. It doesn't. I don't feel pain any more. It's the emotional shit that he'd do to me." But these nonphysical assaults are separated off from bodily harm in the dominant discourses on intimate partner violence.

We also separate violence perpetrated by individuals against other individuals from violence perpetrated by groups against groups. Corporate crime and preventable malnutrition and disease result in death and suffering for millions of innocent people annually. In the southwestern United States, more people die each year trying to cross the border from Mexico into the United States than die from intimate partner violence.[26] If they are thought of at all, these more indirect, impersonal forms of bodily harm, even death, are considered unfortunate consequences of legitimate enterprise, the necessary costs of capitalist production and maintaining *geographic* boundaries. They are not conceptualized as the deviant behaviors of individuals operating outside the established bounds of nonviolent human interaction, despite the enormous toll they exact. The victims and perpetrators are not analyzed in search of childhood traumas, mental illness, substance abuse, or genetic flaws that would explain their behaviors.

The collective culpability implied by group harm prohibits attribution of guilt to a specific individual. Who should be prosecuted for the exposure and dehydration deaths of immigrants trying to cross the border? The categories of guilt and innocence depend upon individualized conceptions of justice and responsibility. It becomes technically difficult to identify perpetrators, bystanders, and victims when harm is perpetrated by groups against groups.[27] It is easier to focus on individual men who assault women and individual women who are abused. When individual women become violent or criminal following months or years of their own victimization, the boundaries between victim and offender are blurred. The determination of responsibility, guilt, and innocence is confounded.

The broader paradigm of understanding associated with the modernist project shapes the language used to describe intimate partner violence.[28] Within this paradigm, there is faith in the capacity of social scientists to adopt the methods of natural scientists to define and measure the behavior of humans accurately and objectively. Scientific observers can produce valid, objective knowledge of society by adherence to the scientific method. The social facts produced by scientists are also viewed as relatively stable, fixed truths that mean the same thing to different people in a diverse range of settings, and the same thing to the same person across various circumstances and times. For example, there is an assumption that when people indicate they were "beat up" by an intimate partner they are all describing the same type of experience and could all be categorized or "coded" in the same way. Other aspects of their identities, such as their childhood experiences of physical abuse, could be coded as easily and correlated with this category and then used in causal models attempting to explain intimate partner violence. Most social scientists and some natural scientists have challenged and revised these epistemological assumptions about our social lives that were components of the positivist paradigm. A great deal of social science, however, continues to reflect their influence.[29]

In the realm of intimate partner violence, modernist assumptions about the clarity and fixity of social categories have implications for research and policy. Prevalence and incidence studies, for example, define intimate partner violence in a way that permits accurate

counting of cases and of "variables" that can then be correlated with
both victimization and perpetration. The Conflict Tactics Scale
(CTS), developed by Murray Straus and Richard Gelles, is the most
common tool used to measure intimate partner violence. The CTS
and revised CTS2 list behaviors used to resolve conflicts, ranging
from "discussed the issue calmly" to "used a knife or gun"; people
are asked which behaviors they have used in their relationships.[30] A
line is drawn between verbal and physical aggression and between
minor and severe violence to determine instances of violence.[31] It is
necessary to operationalize intimate partner violence through links
to specific actions in order to measure it. The data produced through
these studies have been essential to raising public awareness and
garnering support. Astoundingly, even in the 1970s many people believed that intimate partner violence was rare; the surveys that documented violence in a significant proportion of relationships challenged this belief successfully.[32] But the success of the research has
consequences for perceptions of intimate partner violence. The process of operationalization transforms amorphous, complex human
experiences into codable categories that take on a life of their own.[33]
The definition of violence and the variables associated with it create
what we accept as knowledge. That is, the actions of scholars and activists do not simply *describe* the facts of intimate partner violence;
they *create* those facts by deciding what counts and what does not
count as the truth of intimate partner violence. I do not mean that
there is no physical and psychological suffering within intimate relationships apart from this definitional process. I do mean that the
messy, complicated, shifting meanings of suffering undergo a transformation as they are forced into the categories consistent with the
new truth of intimate partner violence.

The Battered Woman

One example of how language, or discourse, shapes knowledge is the
way the term "battered woman" has influenced individual women's
and general public opinion about the experience of violence within
an intimate relationship. This term developed during the early 1970s,
when the contemporary battered women's movement took shape,
and was meant to describe women who were physically assaulted by

their current and former intimate partners. The development of language that identified violence in intimate relationships and the gendered nature of this violence was important in challenging the complacency that surrounded violence in the home. In 1970 there were no shelters for battered women, policies instructed police officers *not* to arrest men for assaulting their wives, and social scientists were silent on the topic.[34] A review of articles in the *Journal of Marriage and the Family* did not locate a single article on marital violence between 1939 and 1969.[35] Language that identified women's experiences was empowering; it also, however, contributed to cultural understandings that have not been helpful for all women.

The term "battered woman" focuses on victimization and suggests an *identity* as victim rather than a set of experiences.[36] The victim identity is stigmatized in a culture that stresses individual responsibility, strength, and assertiveness. There is disdain for those who overemphasize their victimization: for example, the popular phrase "get over it," and the media's attention to "victim feminism" and feminist "whining."[37] Popular pundits argue that the nation has succumbed to a culture of victimization that shifts personal responsibility onto external forces and undermines the moral fabric of the country.[38] Cultural imagery of victims of abuse portrays women victims as mentally ill (say, suffering post–traumatic stress disorder), damaged, and helpless.[39] "Ideal victims" are also meek and distraught, innocent of provoking their victimization, and possessing a body that symbolizes these qualities. Young, white, middle-class, attractive (but not overtly sexy) women embody cultural notions of deserving victims.[40] Konradi found that rape victims whose cases were going to trial were well aware of these images and consciously presented themselves in conformity with them as a strategy for successful prosecution of their rapists.[41] Women performed both "appearance work" (purchasing clothing that projected the image of authentic victims), and "emotion work" (displaying emotions they thought juries required of victims). The rape victims interviewed by Konradi made strategic use of victim imagery to help convict the men who raped them, but images of victims as "damaged" are themselves damaging to women. Cultural expectations and evaluations of female victims may distance women from accepting a self-definition as victim.

Angelic women may conform to public imagery of victims, but

few women actually view themselves as totally pure and innocent prior to victimization—or permanently damaged and defective after. If involvement with the criminal processing system forces them to consider their experiences as "battering," they are drawn into a process of remembering and self-definition that reflects cultural constructions of victims as defective. The women I interviewed struggled with remembering events in their relationships, as well as with issues of responsibility, blame, and pathology. Women's narratives often reflected cultural stereotypes that something was wrong with *them* because they were abused by their partners.

Mona's narrative exemplifies the difficulty of forcing experience into narrow legal categories, as well as her own resistance to the label "battered woman." Mona was a twenty-five-year-old, working-class Italian-American woman who grew up in New York City. She was feisty and funny, and our interview was filled with both laughter and tears. Mona's account of her marriage included many descriptions of emotional and financial abuse as well as physical assault. Her husband was a methamphetamine addict and dealer who moved in with his eighteen-year-old girlfriend during the first year of his marriage to Mona. Both women became pregnant with daughters at about the same time. He moved back and forth between households, but did not pay the bills. Mona and her daughter lived without electricity or hot water. He had choked her on several occasions, thrown her against walls and across rooms, punched her in the face, and pistol-whipped her. After she moved in with her parents for protection, he stalked her and police found a shrine with her picture surrounded by machetes in his room. Her husband accidentally shot and paralyzed her father while attempting to shoot Mona, but she could not "picture" herself as battered. After the shooting, he was released on low bail and continued to stalk and harass Mona. She went to his apartment to tell him to leave her alone, and he again assaulted her, repeatedly hitting her in the face. Mona escaped to her car where she had a loaded handgun and shot her husband. He sustained minor injuries, but Mona was charged with attempted murder. She explained her reaction at the scene:

MONA: The detective said, "How many times were you battered before?" I said, "Does this matter to you?" I didn't know they were considering me battered. He said, "Yes," that mattered. I said, "Well, I guess I was battered before." He said, "When?" I said, "I don't know." He was kind of telling me it was going to help the case, but I didn't know what to tell him. I didn't think I was really what they call. . . . They put me down as a battered woman. I didn't know who they were referring to. I said, "Who's battered?" I asked one of the cops there. They said, "You're the battered victim." I was like, "I'm battered?" I couldn't imagine.

KATHLEEN: You couldn't think of yourself that way?

MONA: No, never was I a battered woman. That sounds . . . I still really wouldn't consider myself really "battered." Maybe "mentally tortured" or "married a bad man" but "battered" is so . . . like a picture of a coma or, I don't know what picture. I just never pictured *me*. Like Farrah Fawcett in *The Burning Bed*, she's battered. She looks battered.

At the scene described above, Mona's face was severely cut and bleeding from being hit by her husband. A detective tried to elicit information from her that would help explain why she took violent, defensive action. His efforts to document prior abuse in a legalistic fashion, however, did not make sense to Mona who rejected the label "battered woman." For Mona, the "picture" of a battered woman was the image she held in her own mind about what constituted a "real battered woman." She focused on what could be seen, and the "picture of a coma" or the terrified, thin, blond, white victim portrayed by Farrah Fawcett, was incompatible with her own self-image as a strong, self-sufficient woman with a good sense of humor. Mona's focus on the visible image of battering reflects the modernist idea that visibility is the most reliable evidence of "truth."[42] Only physical assaults produce this evidence, and people expect battering to be reflected in a face and body that is bruised, bleeding, and broken. Mona said she did not realize that she was battered because she did not look in the mirror to see her injuries. Despite the extreme emotional and physical violence she endured, and the shooting of her father, she did not think of herself as battered.

Mona was a small woman, about one hundred pounds, who went to her violent, drug-dealing husband's apartment with a loaded gun in the car. Why would a woman who was terrified of a man deliberately seek him out? This question was raised about a number of women in this book who had been severely abused yet continued to have contact with their male partners after separation. The men that women seek out are not strangers, but are men they have loved, shared their lives with, and who are the fathers of their children. Even the most extreme abusers are only violent a small portion of all of the time spent with their partners. Women may be afraid of their abusive partners, but continue to perceive them as part of their intimate circle. Past experience of abuse, however, will lead women to take precautions, such as carrying a weapon. This is not the action of someone who is completely "helpless," as the concept of "learned helplessness" implies. It is the action of someone who is afraid but still believes the person they married or shared an intimate relationship with is someone they *can* talk to, or *must* talk to. Mona's decision to visit her husband reflected her continuing view of herself as someone who could resolve her own problems and protect herself. The detective's label of "battered victim" did not fit with her own self-image.

None of the women in this book described themselves as battered women. Although I was interviewing them to help explain the role of victimization in their criminal offenses, none of the women focused on physical assaults. Many forgot to mention violent incidents that were documented in police or medical records. While some people—especially prosecutors—have noted the possibility that women will *exaggerate* experiences of abuse in order to gain a more lenient response from courts, my experience and that of others has been that women routinely *minimize* physical abuse.[43] Minimization is one strategy for surviving in a violent relationship.[44] It also commonly causes difficulty in remembering the trauma of abuse.

Another reason that women were reluctant to define themselves as battered was the lingering hope that their relationships would improve. Some women said they still loved their violent partners, and others expressed a desire to preserve positive memories of the "good parts" of their relationships.

Boundaries Between Good Parts and Bad Parts

For most women (not all), the abuse was also mingled with positive experiences. This combination of abuse and nonabuse did not follow a routine pattern, such as that described in Lenore Walker's "cycle of violence" model. Walker describes battering relationships as following a cycle of tension building, acute battering, and loving contrition, also called the "honeymoon" phase.[45] Women did not describe such a cycle, and very few women indicated that their partners apologized for the battering, or even acknowledged that they did it. One woman (Dorothy) used the phrase "like a cycle" to refer to the pattern of her partner leaving and her accepting him back, but no woman described the discrete components of tension building, acute battering, and contrition portrayed in Walker's model. Instead, there were "good parts" to the relationship that women wanted to preserve. The term "battered woman" seemed inappropriate as a self-descriptor because it focused the woman's identity on the bad parts. Dorothy, who killed her husband said, "I miss him, you know, the good parts, you know, I think about. I always want to remember the good parts . . . mostly it was bad, but there was some good parts. And that's the one I like to remember."

Marjorie DeVault has argued that "good parts" is a shorthand term that women use to capture the emotionally satisfying aspects of their domestic lives. These satisfying aspects serve as the impetus for engaging in the mundane drudgery of domestic labor.[46] For most women, the "good parts" were the companionship and love they shared with their partners. It was disturbing and confusing to them that they continued to hold these feelings despite their partners' violence and abuse. They judged themselves: "I still do love him, sometimes I think I'm crazy, after all the things that I went through, all the pain" (Crystal). And they suspected that others judged them as well: "I think sometimes that people think I shouldn't love him, but I do, not like I used to, but I do" (Jane). Despite these judgments, women recounted the "good parts," and wanted me to understand that their partners were not "all bad." Teresita described how she felt about her boyfriend when they first fell in love:

> I fell in love with him. He was like the world. He did everything to make me happy. What I'm saying is, like, he was like my friend, but then my boyfriend. Something like you need in a relationship, like a friend and a boyfriend. It was like he was the world, he was like the king. You know. Primo this, Primo that, . . . Oh yes, Primo. It was like that good for awhile, until then he started beating me. And he didn't started beating me, it's been about a year after I had the twins.

Teresita struggled with ambivalent feelings of love and hate toward Primo after the death of her baby, the crime for which both she and

Primo were charged. I discuss her story and the relationship between intimate partner violence and harm to women's children in chapter 6.

Dianne also expressed ongoing feelings of love toward her abusive husband whom she was charged with killing during a violent confrontation. She felt tremendous loss over his death; as she tried to describe their relationship, she was overwhelmed with sadness:

> We were pretty close (*crying*). He was my best friend, you could say. He liked to go to the horse races, he liked to gamble. We used to go to Laughlin a lot, and to the ponies, he liked ponies, of course I did too. Then he taught me how to golf, and that was fun. He was into sports, he loved sports, which is great too, 'cuz I love football, and so did he, we watched football together and stuff, on Sunday, nobody worked, just laid around, ate ice cream, naked, and watched movies and stuff. . . . I seen more in him than anybody else did (*crying hard*). Everybody else thought he was a bad person.

Dianne's sorrow over the loss of her best friend and her ability to see "more in him than anybody else," are aspects of "battered women who kill" that are rarely addressed in media or academic accounts.[47] It is difficult for people to reconcile high levels of control, violence, and degradation with friendship and love, and it is also hard for women who experience these contradictions to understand their partner's behavior and their own reactions. Because violence was unpredictable and inexplicable, women found the mixture of good and bad parts of their relationships particularly distressing. Nicole used the term "struggling relationship" to describe the mixture of love and fear she felt toward her partner: "I wanted to get away from him even then, but then he would treat me real nice, and then I was just so much in love with him. I thought I was. And so everything would be okay, and it was a whole, kind of a struggling relationship all the way through. I would wanna leave, and then I wouldn't wanna leave, and then everything would be okay, and I was just so much in love with him."

Although psychological labels have been applied to this ambivalence, such as the battered woman syndrome and traumatic bonding, these labels suggest that women's emotions are pathological or deviant. Women frequently share these public interpretations and express the sentiment that "something's wrong" with them. Mona, who did not think she was a "battered woman," explained that she did not want to try to remember all the abuse she experienced, even though it would help explain her violent actions. She thought the abuse indicated that something was wrong with *her:*

MONA: I just don't want to have to remember and then realize who I was with, because *there's something wrong. There's something wrong with me.*

KATHLEEN: Why do you think that?

MONA: Because you just don't stay with a person who does that to you. You just don't.

Women sometimes asked me if there was something wrong with them. My own constructions of normality and responsibility are apparent in my responses. For example, when I asked what she wanted to happen next, Katy described her desire for freedom and peace and her feeling that *she* should have been the one to solve the problem of her partner's violence:

KATY: (*crying hard*). Getting away from him, I'd like to be able to have a life for myself, to take a deep breath and have some freedom. Sometimes I wish he were dead. He used to scare me so bad that I couldn't breathe, and my mouth would be dry, and I'd be so terrified, I wouldn't know what to do. . . . I gave and gave and gave, and he expected it, he demanded it.

KATHLEEN: Yeah, but he's a sick person.

KATY: It's not normal?

KATHLEEN: No, what's normal is to reciprocate.

KATY: But that's my problem, I should've been able to get out of it.

The sense of being "in love" with a man who is also terrifying and cruel creates a struggle. In retrospect, women judged their love and commitment as pathological, misguided, or naïve. Romantic scripts of being in love do not include ambivalence, and certainly exclude terror. Women desired relationships that conformed to these romantic scripts, and men provided some confirmation that this was possible. Having fun together, feeling uniquely understood and connected to another person, and sharing sexual intimacy were "good parts" that endorsed women's feelings of love and commitment. The "Jekyll–Hyde" phenomenon described by so many women challenged their love and commitment and contributed to their personal sense of pathology. These women judged themselves harshly, feeling they *should* have known better, been able to get out, or rejected the "good parts" that sustained their commitment to relationships. Their self-judgments—despite their own experiences of death threats, severe violence, stalking, and the ineffectiveness of outside interventions—mirrored social prejudices that women can "just leave" violent relationships. Like several other women, Katy owned the house her boyfriend shared with her. "Leaving" not only meant confronting his threats to kill her but also relinquishing the home she had worked so hard to obtain.

Not all women described this struggle. For some, fear and terror dominated their relationships; they no longer (if they had ever) felt there were any "good parts."[48] The designation of psychological labels is an artificial attempt to impose order and consistency on experiences that are an ongoing struggle "all the way through." Good and bad are not clear, binary categories that alternate in predictable cycles. Rather, they are confusing components of relationships that are meaningful in ways difficult to explain or understand.

The notion of a cycle, with predictable components, is a popular paradigm within the culture of the United States. Cycles of poverty, abuse, violence are often invoked by those wishing to demonstrate the predictability of future problems based on measurement of discrete elements of existing problems. Cycle models depend on simplification of these elements and emphasize the dichotomous categories discussed in the beginning of this chapter. In chapter 4, I critique the popular *intergenerational* cycle of abuse model. The model of the cycle of violence within relationships is widely popular and taught by graphic handouts in many intimate partner violence trainings. This model oversimplifies the nature of violent relationships.[49] Most women described good parts and bad parts of their relationships (although, again, some saw no good parts). They did not, however, describe a cycle: *all* aspects of their relationships were confusing and unpredictable. Moreover, as Mary Ann Dutton has pointed out, control is being exercised over women during the good, "honeymoon" phase, as well as during the acute battering incident.[50] And as Sarah Buehl argues in her oral presentations, a break in violence and deliberate cruelty can hardly be equated with the romance, love, and affection associated with honeymoons.[51]

Boundaries Between "Normal" and Abusive Sexuality

The definition of "normal" sexuality is also a political process that varies over time and location. Foucault argued that discourses on sexuality did not assume a coherent form until the seventeenth century in Europe when prescriptions for sexual behavior took shape, particularly within the Church.[52] Perceptions of normality in sexual behavior exhibit tremendous variation. Within the context of an abusive relationship, definitions of normal sexuality depend on a struggle between women's emotional and bodily reactions, what they believe is expected of them, and men's desires for sex. Women who had experienced childhood sexual abuse found the negotiation of sexuality in abusive relationships particularly problematic.

Few women volunteered information about sexual abuse without being asked. Obviously, feelings of shame and embarrassment restricted spontaneous recollections of sexual violence, but some women did not define unwanted sex as abuse. Ronnie, for example, thought that her displeasure at her husband's practice of having sex with her while she slept was a consequence of her own disordered sexuality. She thought there was something wrong with her because she did not like this practice. Forced to perform oral sex on her father as a child and raped by a stranger as she walked to school at age fourteen, Ronnie viewed her dislike of sex while sleeping as a response to these earlier assaults. She was very surprised when I told her that this was not a normal practice between husbands and wives, and that many people would define it as rape.[53]

Many women said that they became repulsed by sex in their relationships because the violence and emotional abuse destroyed the pleasure they initially felt with their partners. They would acquiesce to sex in order to placate their partners and avoid arguments or violence.[54] Angie said, "I don't even like sex," and only participated in sex to comply with her boyfriend's demands and avoid a fight. Danielle said that her husband told her he had affairs with other women because she was frigid. But she viewed her lack of interest in sex as a result of his abusive and neglectful behavior:

> He said I was frigid. How can I not be frigid? And I would tell him, "You don't even show me any affection, except when you wanna sleep with me at night, and then I'm everything?" I'm sorry, I can't just "Oh,

okay." I need to feel love, and it got to the point it was sad because I knew when I had to have sex with him that night 'cuz he'd come home and he'd kiss me. And it was like my clue, and it would just, after a while it just would turn my stomach.

While some women just gave in to their partner's sexual requests, other women were forced to participate in painful or degrading acts. Forced sodomy was mentioned by four of the twenty-four women who killed, tried to kill, or were charged in the third-party murders of their abusers, and by one woman charged with a violent crime against another woman. I did not, however, push women to talk about things that they seemed reticent to address, so the prevalence of forced sodomy may be higher than indicated in the interviews. This form of abuse was a particularly painful memory for women who did discuss it, and always resulted in silence and weeping. Other forms of sexual violence committed by abusers included putting objects inside women's vaginas, punching women on their vaginas and breasts, making videotapes of sexual activity and threatening to sell them or show them to others, asking women to have sex with other men, raping a woman while she was handcuffed to a motorcycle, urinating on a woman, selling a woman to a fellow gang member, making sexually explicit, degrading comments in front of women's children, forcing fellatio for hours at a time, and, in one case, raping a woman while fondling their eleven-year-old daughter. One woman reported that she was forced to perform fellatio on her partner for ten hours. When she was questioned about the accuracy of this memory, she said, "Well, it *seemed* like ten hours!"

Twelve women reported sexual abuse while they were children or teenagers, ten by adult men and two by adult women. As far as the women knew, only two of the people who sexually abused or assaulted them throughout their lives were incarcerated as a result. Both of these men had abused other females, both young girls. One was the father who fondled his daughter while raping his wife; he was only prosecuted for the assaults on his daughter, which also included rape. The woman, Marcie, was also charged with failure to protect her daughter from abuse (discussed in chapter 6). The other man sent to prison had separated from his wife when his four daughters were very young. Left alone with his children, he began sleeping with his eldest daughter and fathered a child by her. He lived with her and his other daughters until his granddaughter/daughter was three years old, at which time the child's mother reported her circumstances to a high school teacher. The daughter that I interviewed, Salina, the second oldest, could not remember any sexual abuse by her father and was confused and upset when I asked her about the incest. She was surprised to be told that fathers sleeping with their daughters is not a "normal" activity. She was devastated by her father's incarceration. Like Marcie, Salina was charged with failure to protect her children, but one of Salina's children was murdered. At age twenty-one, she was sentenced to life in prison for her boyfriend's murder of her two-year-old daughter and the aggravated assault of her five-year-old daughter.[55] These women's stories substantiate the arguments offered by Chesney-Lind, Bortner and Williams, and Gaardner and Belknap, that the criminal processing system often fails to protect young women and girls from sexual victimization, but holds them accountable when their own behavior results in harm to others.[56]

Another pattern described by several women was men's insistence on having sex with them following a beating. Women were angry and upset that men thought they could use them sexually after beating them, and initially tried to stop them. Eventually, they gave in because they believed there was nothing they could do to stop them. Teresita described this pattern with her boyfriend, Primo:

> You know, so it's, like, after he got done beating me it was sex time. Yep, it was like that all the time. I mean there would be times where I wouldn't let him, and he'll say that if I didn't give it up, he'll just take it from me. You know and I'll tell him that's rape. You know what I'm sayin'? And he's like, "It's not rape, you're my baby's momma, how is that rape?" You know I'm like, "If you say no, it's rape, Primo." He'll be like "No, like I said, I'll just take it from you, you're my baby's momma, I can have sex whenever I want it." You know, so it's just like I mean, I look at him with disgust. There will be times where I got to the point where I'm like I didn't want to fight with him anymore, where I just let him do what he wanted. I'll just lay there with tears comin' out of my eyes and you would think that he would stop, but he didn't.

Primo's belief that he "can have sex whenever" he wants it violates the basic boundary between consensual and coercive sexuality. His patriarchal attitude that Teresita owed him unlimited sexual access because she had given birth to his child had been traditionally supported by legislation that excluded marital rape from criminal statutes. This legislation only began to change in the 1980s; in many states, marital rape is still a less serious offense with more stringent evidentiary requirements.[57]

Beth also reported that following beatings, her partner Matt would insist on having sex with her. She told him that it was impossible for her to feel sexual desire for him after he assaulted her, but he forced himself on her. She tried to avoid him, but he usually prevailed:

> That night Matt raped me. I don't care what anybody says, if you don't consent to sex, it's rape. He did not own me. He had no right to take me. He would wake up in the morning and he would just take me. I would not consent to him. Or he would get up and I wouldn't get up until he was gone. He'd turn up everything in the house. He'd turn up the TV, turn up the stereo, slam the door, anything to get me up and I wouldn't get up. I was afraid to move. He'd walk out and he'd go, "I know you're awake, bitch." I wouldn't get up until I'd hear the truck start. Then I would get up and son-of-a-bitch if he wouldn't come back in the door.

Unlike Ronnie, Teresita and Beth were clear in their own minds that they were being raped. But they were unable to prevent it on their own, and never reported it to the police. For Teresita, prior efforts to obtain police assistance produced nothing but anger in Primo and, like other women, she did not know how she would support their five children without him. Beth's continuing love of Matt and belief that she could help him overcome his addictions deterred her from calling the police.

Boundaries between Self and Other

Descriptions of violent events were intertwined with the relationships women had with others, particularly their children, as well as their partners. Concerns for their own physical safety were linked directly with desires to protect their children from abuse and from becoming orphans. Describing brutal behavior from their partners was also problematic for some women who not only wanted to "remember the good parts" but to preserve their deceased partners' memories without exposing their children and extended families to gruesome accounts of violence. Decision making during the relationship reflected women's efforts to balance their own needs with those of their families. Although outsiders may have evaluated these efforts as deficient, even criminal, for women partnered with violent men, negotiating safety for themselves and their families was an ongoing concern (and particularly true for women who were financially dependent on their abusers).

In addition, many women would have been ashamed or embarrassed to tell other people about their victimization. Women who partnered with violent men against the warnings of their parents, family, and friends felt that they had "made their own beds" and now had no one to blame but themselves. Revealing the abuse would only confirm their poor judgment and diminish them further in the eyes of their families. For women who did not want to end their relationships, discussing the abuse with their families generated conflict when they were encouraged or even ordered to leave the man.

Recollecting memories of physical abuse was difficult for Mona, and she did not want people, especially her family, to know what she was going through in her marriage. Sadness and fear were her most prominent memories, and both were linked closely to her love and concern for her daughter. After confronting her husband at his girlfriend's apartment and telling him she never wanted to see him again, she returned to her parent's home:

> I went home. I cried when I told my mother. I cried. You know what my mom said? "Maybe it's the best thing." I said, "I know it but I'm still sad." There's something sad about it but I don't know what. I wish I did know why I would cry over something like that. I should be happy but I'm not. I was happy when I left but then the other side of me was really . . . When I would have to tell anybody, I would go about it in any way I could. I know that everybody knew he wanted to kill me and that's bad, but now I wonder why he wanted to kill me.

Mona expressed ambivalence about leaving her abusive husband but recognized that he was serious about killing her. Fear for her own safety was related to her worry that, if she were badly injured or killed, her daughter would be more vulnerable to a dangerous father and she would not be there to provide protection. She also worried about the impact on her child of witnessing violence, and she strategized her responses to violence based on protection of her baby. Boundaries between her own physical safety and the well-being of her child were blurred and intertwined—as was true of most mothers. Abusive partners used women's connections to their children to keep them from leaving: they threatened to kill women, kill children, take custody, kidnap the children, or impoverish women so they could not meet children's needs.

> MONA: My head had hit something, it was the side of a wall, I think, or door or something. [He] hit me up side the head and it knocked out my jaw or something. I asked if he thought this was good for Roseanna to see. "I know you don't care about me," I said, "but have something for the baby. Don't let her see me get beat up." I used to care about that. She loves her mother. She does love me. She'd say, "Momma, Momma, Momma . . ." And, I knew. I wouldn't fight back any more because I knew if I fought back it would get worse and the worse it got, the worse it was for her. . . . When I was out of sight is when she would flip. Otherwise, she would be okay but once I was out of her sight, she used to like just scream for me. That's when I would come out. I could hide from him. I was able to learn how to hide because I'm small. I could sneak into a place that he couldn't get into.

While Mona worried about the effects of violence on her child, and the possibility of her own death leaving her vulnerable to abuse, Jane was told explicitly that if she tried to leave her husband, she would have to watch him kill their daughter. Jane recalled the threats her husband made to keep her from leaving: "I knew if I confronted him [about his lies], he'd kill me. He told me, 'If you try to leave me, first I'll take Chelsea [their daughter], and make you watch me kill her, and then I'll kill you.' I didn't know it at the time, but he was saying the same thing to Chelsea. I don't know why I didn't know. I feel like it's all my fault."

The deaths of children as a result of intimate partner violence and familicides is not carefully documented; thus it is impossible to know how often children are killed by battered women's partners.[58] Threats to kill children usually occur in the context of ongoing intimidation and violence; women take them seriously and adapt their behavior to protect their children. For other women, concerns for the well-being of their children revolved around economic survival and dependence on their violent partner for income. Marcie's husband did not threaten to kill anyone, but made her believe that she would lose her seven children if she reported his abuse of her and their daughter:

> They're [prosecutors] looking at why I didn't report him while he was out of the house, when he was at work or went somewhere, why I didn't pick up the phone and make a call. But he had my mind so wishy-washy that I was just trying to keep my family together. I was just trying to protect the children and keep the father in the home. Because he told me that I wouldn't be able to take care of the kids and I would get them taken away from me. Because I could not work. And so he was the only provider I had.

In Marcie's case, her failure to "pick up the phone and make a call" formed the basis for criminal charges of sexual abuse of her daughter. The county attorney wanted to hold her criminally responsible for failing to protect her daughter from her husband's sexual abuse. I discuss her case in greater detail in chapter 6, but mention it here to illustrate that women's responses to and recollections of abuse cannot be extricated from their relationships to others for whom they care.

Many women said that they thought about committing suicide as the only way out of their situations; three (Ronnie, Danielle, and Nicole) had made serious attempts. Other research has documented the high prevalence of prior domestic violence in cases of women's suicides and suicide attempts. Evan Stark and Anne Flitcraft report that of the 176 suicide attempts by women they studied, 29.5 percent were battered women and 22.2 percent had at least one documented incident of domestic violence.[59] For the women I met, love and concern for the vulnerability of their children if they were to die prohibited them from following through with suicide. Jane explained:

> There was one time I thought about shootin' myself. In fact I had the gun in my mouth, and I was gonna' pull the trigger, and then I thought about Chelsea havin' to be raised by him, without me there, and it stopped me. Several times, I came close to doin' it, but every time I thought about her. I thought about doin' a lot of different things. I thought about taking medication, but somethin' stopped me every

time. To me it was the only solution. But I think Chelsea would've
really gotten it bad, because I wasn't there to protect her.

After Leah shot her husband, she reloaded the shotgun and intended
to shoot herself. But when her five-year-old son said, "No, Mom,
let's go," she shot the gun off in the air. After the deaths of their
abusers, many women indicated that they wished they had died instead of their partners (see chapter 5). Yet the link to their children,
the desire to protect them from both their father's abuse and the pain
of losing a mother, prevented women from following through on
their suicidal thoughts.

Several women also mentioned ways in which they protected
their husbands and lovers, during their relationships and even after
their deaths. They did not want people to know about men's violence, due to feelings of shame and concern for their partners' repu-
tations. In part, women did not want children to think badly about
their fathers. But some women also felt a sense of loyalty and commitment to their partners that was inconsistent with adopting a self-
definition as battered. Teresita describes why she did not want to tell
anyone about her abuse:

TERESITA: I didn't want nobody to know.
KATHLEEN: Why not?
TERESITA: I don't know. I didn't want people to think that I was living this
    horrible life. I wanted people to think that my life was good. That he was
    a good person. Because I knew he was. You know, and it's like I wanted
    people to see that. I didn't want people to see that he beated me. You
    know 'cause I didn't want him to get hurt either. You know what I'm
    sayin? So it's like I never told anybody. I kept thinking that things will
    get better, things will get right. But it never did.

For Danielle, her loyalty inhibited her willingness to discuss her
husband's abuse, even while she was on trial facing life in prison or
the death penalty. She spoke about her concern about the impact on
her sons of watching their father's violence, but also emphasized her
consistent support of Tony, her husband:

Tony was hitting me and Danny come in and jumped on his dad and
said, "Stop it, stop it." When it was over and the boys were huddled
around me, Danny just looked at me and said, "How much more are
you gonna take, Mom?" and I said, "What?" and he said, "When are

you gonna make him stop?" I didn't know he knew (*crying hard*) and right then something inside of me went, "I gotta stop it because I can't let them," I wasn't worrying about me, I says, "I can't let them think that this is okay, he's gotta know that you don't get hit, my boys gotta know that you don't hit women." You know? And I remember, Danny was yelling at his dad and his dad said, "You don't talk to me like that. You're almost a man, and you don't understand," and I remember, Danny looked up and said, "If bein' a man's bein' like you, Dad, I'd rather be a queer." And I said, "Danny, don't talk to your dad like that," and still, no matter what, I always protected Tony. I wouldn't let the kids talk disrespectful to their father, 'cuz that's your father, no matter what.

While she wanted to shield her sons from the impact of observing their father's violence, she also wanted to protect Tony from their disdain. Her son's intuitive grasp of the relationship between normative masculinity and violence against women was pushed aside by Danielle. She focused on her son's suggestion that being "queer" was better than being a wife beater rather than on the disrespect Tony displayed to all of his family. Later in the interview, as Danielle told me she did not want to testify, she said: "I don't wanna fight anymore, and I don't wanna get up and I don't wanna tell everybody what kind of person Tony was. They want me to testify, I don't know if I can (*crying hard*). I don't want my family to know what I went through and I don't want his family to see what kind of person [he was], and there's not anything anybody can do about it. He's not here to defend himself."

Danielle was not really "there" to defend herself either. She was not able to give a lucid account of the abuse she experienced at Tony's hands, although others did provide that testimony to the court. A marriage counselor to whom Tony had admitted the abuse and who had seen Danielle with a black eye, described Tony as a "monster." When the prosecution pushed me to identify the ways in which Tony sexually abused Danielle, she became hysterical and crawled underneath the defense table, curled into a fetal position and cried uncontrollably. She did not want these details of her private life aired in public, and she did not want to be reminded of what she suffered. Ultimately, after one hung jury, evidence of battering was determined to be irrelevant, as Tony had been murdered by a third party while living in a separate house and Danielle had planned to move in with him the following day. Her case is described more fully in chapter 5. Here, it is important to understand that even when women are on trial for their lives, they are sometimes reluctant to adopt the language of victimization or to sever their own defense from defense of those they love.

Negotiating Resistance and Compliance to Men's Commands

These relationships demonstrate complicated patterns of repression and resistance. Men lashed out with physical and psychological violence when women transgressed their always shifting expectations for service, obedience, and loyalty. Some of these expectations reflect cultural notions of gendered behavior. For example, service of food and drink to men by women is a pattern in many cultures. The linkage of women and food service is also influenced by class, with upper-class people expecting hired help to perform this job. For all of the women in this study, male partners expected to be served food and drink.

Women attempted to fulfill these expectations, even when they rejected most other aspects of conventional femininity. For example, Sarah was a "biker chick," an exotic dancer who was involved with a series of men who belonged to an outlaw motorcycle gang. Sarah found straight society and law-abiding men boring. She resisted gendered expectations for women's sexual modesty and sobriety, yet she complied with the subservient role of servant to the biker gang. Few people would have described Sarah as an angel, but within the biker subculture, she was as subservient to men as the Victorian angel in the house. She prided herself on adhering to the men's demands for "respect," and rationalized being beaten for not being strong enough. After her third lover died, from an overdose, she earned the reputation of a "black widow" and was shunned by the biker community:

> I blamed myself for it. I coulda done this, I coulda done that, if I'da been a little bit stronger, you know, he didn't beat me that bad, I deserved it, I'd get drunk and talk back, or I didn't show the respect that I should have, to his brothers. It's a big respect thing with those bikers. I would sit at a poker table for twelve hours. I'd sit one chair be-

hind where everybody sat. Anytime anybody pulled a cigarette out the cigarette was lit. I knew when there was this much left in a beer can, and it was replaced, you know. I was a trained dog.

Phyllis did not view her husband's demands as legitimate, but her resistance to them resulted in severe physical punishment. She described how he made her take off her clothes and feed him while she was naked as a way of degrading her:

> I don't know what he was on, but he got it in his head that I would leave him, and when he come back, he took off alla my clothes and threw 'em out the window, so I couldn't leave him, and he was tellin' me (crying) to feed him and everything, and so, and I didn't know if they [his friends] were gonna walk in any moment, I'm still naked, but I opened up a can of soup and brought it to him, and he wanted me to feed it to him, he was just trying to degrade me, and I started to feed it to him and after a couple of bites, I thought, fuck this, and I threw the hot soup in his face and I took off runnin', naked and everything, and I ran outside and he chased me down and he caught me of course and he brought me back in and he started chokin' me, and I wasn't gonna let him choke me out again, he'd done it so many times, and so I started pullin' his hands away from me and he got mad because I'm too little to be overpowering him, you know, so I was actually that scared, so he stomped me (crying hard), my temples were swollen out and bruised, I had a boot print on the back of my neck, on my chest and my arms.

Phyllis did not acquiesce to her husband's demands, but she was physically unable to protect herself. If his friends had not returned and called 9-1-1, he may have killed her. She lost consciousness and was hospitalized for two days.

Other women spoke of "just accepting it," deciding not to resist, trying to comply with demands, and not question his authority. Crystal explained how her husband spoke to her when she returned from an errand for him to the neighbor's:

> He said, "Did you get fucked by him before he gave the pump to you?" I didn't talk to him, usually when he starts sayin' those things, I don't bother him. If I say something, I'm gonna get a punch in the face or a kick. So I just told him to hurry up and pump up the tire, breakfast is on the table for you. He said, "It better not be cold." It seemed like he

wanted everything perfect. He would, if the food was cold, just throw the whole plate at me, and I would stand there with food comin' down my face, and he would say, like, "EAT IT!" and I would do that, 'cuz he's standin' right there, and if I don't do that I would get a beating. I tried cheering him up, calling him "hon," "please don't say that," in Navajo.

Several women described having plates of food thrown at their faces when the food did not meet the arbitrary, shifting criteria set by their partners. Not only does throwing food or drink at a woman cause physical harm and degradation, it demonstrates disdain for the acts of nurturance and love involved in the preparation and service of food. Her offering is rejected, and she is forced to clean up the mess. Jane recounted another incident of thrown food: "He would call and say this is what I want for dinner, and I would fix it. One time he called, and he wanted spaghetti, and I didn't have regular noodles, I had those shells, and he was so mad about that he took and threw that hot spaghetti on me and made me just stand there with that boiling hot spaghetti on me and fix him something else."

Again, the physical violence involved in throwing a drink or a plate of food at a woman cannot be separated from the psychic violence she experiences. Repeated experiences of these random acts of violence led women to decide not to challenge their partner's authority, or, in some cases, to speak at all. Jane described how she decided to conform her talk to her husband's desires: "There's been times when we'd be sitting there having a conversation about anything, and maybe I didn't agree with him, and he'd haul off and smack me one. I got so I didn't express my opinion, I found out how he felt about it, and that's what I'd say. It was just easier." Dorothy described how she pretended to be asleep while riding in the car so that she would not be accused of flirting:

Wherever you go, you know, you can't even go around the corner and you'll be accused of something. And then you can't even look at somebody walkin' down the street or road, and he'll get mad at you, tell you, "Get your goddam eyeballs back in your eyes." You know, stuff like that, so, wherever I used to go, I used to just go to sleep. Once we start goin' down the street, I'll just lay back and close my eyes, and sleep, or just pretend to sleep, half the time, until we get to where we're going.

These strategies helped women prevent violence, but simultaneously constricted their freedom and confidence. When women acquiesced and spoke or behaved as they believed men wanted them to, violence could be deferred. Their acquiescence, however, was never a permanent solution: their partners inevitably became enraged and accused them of imagined infidelities, imperfections, and disobedience. Although women tried to negotiate resistance and compliance, they could not control how their partners interpreted their actions. Women thought they were adhering to men's rules, but men attributed meanings that were beyond women's intentions. Dianne described her inability to understand why her husband always thought she was cheating on him:

> He was always accusin' me of messin' around with somebody else, like all the time, I mean, I couldn't even look at men, if I was drivin' down the road, and just happened to glance over, thought I'd recognized somebody, "Who the hell was that? One of your boyfriends?" He was just, if I was five minutes late from work, I was screwin' somebody, and that just drove me crazy. It seemed like the harder I tried, the worse he'd get. Why is that? I never understood it.

The physical and psychological impact of these acts reinforces larger patterns of male dominance that have shaped intimate relationships for centuries. The expectations for service, combined with punishment for real or imagined transgressions, draw individual men and women into re-creating historical axes of domination. When men assault women for not showing proper respect, serving pasta shells instead of spaghetti, or being a little slow delivering a drink, they are establishing control over an individual woman. Criticizing women's eye movements, suspecting infidelity if they only *looked* at someone walking down the street, reinforced the belief that the women were their sexual property. As sexual property, they had no right to look at other men, and certainly not to talk to or spend time with other men. By punishing women's transgressions of the rules they set, men are performing masculinity in a manner that re-inscribes patriarchy. When women acquiesce to men's demands and decide to "just accept it," they may avoid some abuse, but they also participate in upholding male privilege. When they directly challenged a demand, as Phyllis did above, or as Mona and Monica did below, they were punished with severe violence. As women adapt to the threat of violence, they become accustomed to ignoring their own moral compass and obeying commands. Commands may eventually involve women in committing illegal or immoral acts, rather than being victimized. In chapter 6, I explore the consequences of this pattern.

It is interesting that women's accounts so rarely linked violent outbursts to arguments or conflicts; the primary quantitative scale for measuring intimate partner violence, the Conflict Tactics Scale, relies on questions about methods used to resolve conflicts.[60] For most women, for most instances of violence, there was no conflict being resolved. The violence directed against them could more aptly be termed an "intimidation tactic." That is, violence was used to reinforce a man's position of authority with regard to women's conduct and to demonstrate the punishment that would accompany disobedience. For example, Katy, who was prosecuted for buying her boyfriend's drugs, explained that his unprovoked attacks helped establish his sense of superiority: "I never could understand why he'd hit me, I could never figure it out, or why he flipped out the way he did, I really couldn't and that's so dumb. He didn't have a reason. That's why he never stated a reason, he just wanted to beat up on somebody to make himself feel, I don't know what, to reinforce his own, who knows what, it's sick."

On the other hand, some women knew exactly what triggered a specific violent attack. Mona described her husband's threat to "blow my head off," because she complained of the drug dealers around the house.

> Like the time he threatened to blow my head off and it was in front of Rosie [her baby]. This was right before I left him this last time. Matter of fact, it might have been one of the last times I ever saw him before he shot my dad. The electricity was turned off and we were fighting. He was hanging around this notorious drug dealer and I did not want these people around Roseanna or in my house. I could get arrested. He said, "You tell them to do a blood test." I said, "So, I don't do drugs, I just sell them. That's what it's gonna look like." I didn't want these people around her so I would leave all the time and drive around.

Mona was exactly right; many women are convicted of drug offenses because they are in the same house or vehicle used for drug deals.

This conflict was actually prescribed by the law that requires women to be aware of criminal activities taking place in their house and near their children and to stop and/or report them. As discussed in chapter 6, men's need to secure women's complicity in their crimes was accomplished with violence and threats in various forms. Again, Mona's husband's threat in this situation was less a tactic of conflict resolution than of intimidation. In other cases, the conflicts conformed more closely to conventional marital disputes over household chores, children, and money, similar to the conflicts described by Straus and Gelles.[61] As reported by Dobash and Dobash, conflicts that lead to violence often reflect notions of masculine entitlement to women's unquestioning obedience.[62] Women who violate this expectation are subject to physical punishment that is sometimes extreme. The same request described by Danielle below that preceded her husband's "episode" of violence, "Get me a drink," was denied by Monica, a working-class white woman, with severe consequences:

> I come home from work, and I was tired, and I wanted to lay down and take a little nap before I made dinner, and he was drunk and I wanted to lay down, and first of all, he'd taken like a fluorescent light bulb and hit me over on this side of my head in the bedroom, and he said, "Get up and get me a beer," and I said, "Kiss my ass." You know, I'm not gonna do that, and then he threw the beer bottle at me, and of course I was crying tears, I got up and went to the shower and washed out the glass, you know, the fluorescent light bulbs, they explode, and I had a little bit o' blood on this, this was on the right side o' my head, so, I could see glass on the bed, and I was like, the hell with you, so I went to the living room and laid down, and he goes, "I want you guys out o' here when I get back." I went to the couch and laid down and, then he came back like two hours later, and then I don't know what happened, but I woke up and the next thing you know he like, picked up a pipe wrench, I never said anything to egg him on, he'd been drinkin' whiskey and beer, and I don't know exactly how it started, but then he picked the pipe wrench up and he just started hitting me. I've got still, like, an indentation on my left leg, and a scar from where he hit me there, and he hit me several times on my head.

Monica and Mona did not passively acquiesce to their husband's demands. They resisted, both criminal activity and prescribed domesticity. Yet the level of their resistance could hardly explain the ferocity of their husband's responses, and Mona was left wondering, "Why did he want to kill me?" Monica knew the initial reason for her husband's throwing a beer bottle at her, but did not "really know what happened" when he returned later and began hitting her with a pipe wrench. She could only remember being hit, screaming, and bleeding. Despite the arbitrary nature of men's violence, women still tried to make sense of what happened by examining their own behavior, particularly when they felt others were hurt as a consequence of their inability to control their partner's violence.

Why?

CRYSTAL: The closer home got, seems like I could just feel that pain, and that chill goin' through my body. And I remember I kept telling him, "Hon, why, please don't hurt me when we get home. Please, what did I do?" I kept begging him, I said, "Why? why?" I don't know what was goin' through his head. He didn't try to talk, he kept on being mad.

In trying to make sense of their experiences, women often said they thought about why their partners abused them. No woman said they *deserved* the abuse, but some did think if they had tried harder to meet men's demands they could have controlled the violence. They learned men's rules and what things would trigger violence. Most women also said that there were violent incidents that they could not predict or explain. They struggled to understand what they did that apparently made their partners so angry, violent, and cruel. Simultaneously, they described the arbitrariness of the abuse and the accusations. Kim Lane Scheppele makes the case that a woman participates in "stories of self-blame and complicity" in cases of sexualized violence because she recognizes that "her own story of abuse requires, as a matter of cultural legibility, a prominent role for herself as the reason for the abuser's conduct and also a knowing judgment of what such a role would mean about herself in the eyes of others."[63] Developing stories of self-blame also help women restore a sense of control over their lives: if I don't do X, that caused me to be hurt, then I won't get hurt again.[64] When I asked women what led to the abuse, what preceded a violent incident, most said they had no idea. Finding the words to express their experiences was also difficult. For example, Danielle, convicted of first-degree conspiracy to commit the murder of her husband, explained:

DANIELLE: That's what I started calling 'em, just an episode. I didn't know how else to label it because it was like turning on a light switch. It would start and it would be over. And I'm just sittin' there, like, I don't even know what happened! And, so, they were episodes.

KATHLEEN: And what did he do in the episodes?

DANIELLE: That's when he'd become—*violent!* Like I said, it would be like a light switch. He'd come in, everything'd be fine, and he'd say, "Can you get me somethin' to drink?" "Yeah, okay," I'd get up and walk in the kitchen, get somethin' to drink, and in that amount of time, come back, "Here you go," and he'd throw it in my face. What'd I do? *I mean, what did I do?* [her emphasis] I didn't get it fast enough, I guess. I mean, it got to the point I didn't even question what I did any more. I just accepted it. I would just accept it.

Danielle used the term "episode" to describe her husband's outbursts because they seemed to begin and end arbitrarily and be unconnected from anything she did. She used the phrase, "I mean," as a gesture toward clarifying, trying to help herself and me understand what had happened. The unpredictability of her husband's violence was reflected in many women's accounts. Women described being awakened by being hit, being hit for an innocuous statement, for accidentally looking at a man walking down the street, or for getting a phone call from someone who dialed the wrong number. Women relayed these apparent catalysts for men's violence in order to explain that they could not predict or control it. But they also frequently offered possible explanations: "maybe I didn't get it fast enough," "maybe I didn't cook right for him," "I have to blame his mother and his sisters a lot, 'cuz his mother was a prostitute." These techniques for rationalizing their partner's abuse helped them to think about their situations as at least partially explicable rather than completely random.[65]

Jane's husband had a pattern of raping women, then coming home to beat her. After learning from a family member that he had probably raped another woman, she waited with a loaded gun for him to return home, and shot and killed him as he got out of his car and ran toward her:

I blamed me, and I still feel sometimes like it was my fault that he did things to other people. What was it about me that made him want to hit me? I don't think I was the terrible person he said I was. Someone would call and get the wrong number and just hang up, and I cannot tell you how many times I was thrown against walls for that. Or driving down the road and somebody honked, that's supposed to be my boyfriend. Or walkin' down the street, someone says, "Hi," and he asks, "How long have you known him?"

Although men's use of physical violence, accusations of infidelity, and emotional abuse seemed unjustified, uncontrollable, and inexplicable, women did not want to think of their partners as complete monsters, or themselves as *only* victims. They searched for reasons to explain what happened, why their partners were so cruel, and why they stayed. As Dorothy, charged with the stabbing death of her husband, said, "You get so scared, he threatens all the time, you don't know when you're gonna be hit, or when you're gonna be kicked. I probably had my bad points too. Maybe I irritated him, maybe I didn't cook right for him, or somethin'." The label "battered woman" did not help women understand their situations, and the term's focus on physical violence was at odds with their memories. Organizing their narratives to focus on abuse as part of their criminal defense was difficult because the abuse was "so much," intertwined with daily expressions of disdain, mistrust, and threats of punishment.

Unruly Women

The binary opposition of angels and demons is replicated in the opposition of "real" battered women and women engaged in "mutual combat," and other "unfeminine" conduct, such as drug abuse, prostitution, and other forms of criminality. "Real battered women" are portrayed as being overcome by their partner's violence and abuse. Sympathy is reserved for such women who must also adhere to feminine prescriptions for good mothering, sexual fidelity, and sobriety. Women who fight back, do not protect their children from their partner's abuse, have affairs, or abuse drugs or alcohol—unruly women— do not fit comfortably within the cultural construct of the battered woman, and are likely to have a difficult time accessing the resources that have been developed for battered women.[66] Women of color and immigrant women are particularly disadvantaged in this regard.[67]

The notion of "the battered woman" has been useful in some contexts, such as criminal trials, to assist in describing the effects of being terrorized by an intimate partner. Simultaneously, the creation of this category has contributed to the dilution of complexity and diversity in the experiences of women and added to the view that scientific expertise is able to determine the truth of women's lives. Women who are strong and resistant to male dominance and prescribed domesticity are not easily recognized as belonging to this category of pathetic victims, this "picture of a coma." The development of a category of "battered women" to describe women's experiences reflects dominant, conventional notions of femininity that reinforce those notions and draw boundaries around certain kinds of women who conform to these notions. While racist conceptions of femininity complicate this categorization, the narrowness and contradictions within expectations for "pure victims" exclude most women, particularly those who participate in violent crimes.

The tenuous boundaries between victim and offender, love and fear, and self and other described here challenge the knowledge that has developed in the field of intimate partner violence. Much of that knowledge is incompatible with the ways that women experience their lives and the desires they have for love and safety. What women who have experienced intimate partner violence and who also commit violent crimes say about their lives does not represent the "truth" that should replace previous ideas. It does represent a more complicated and situated knowledge that can complement and revise the rather rigid categories and analyses that have come to dominate public policy toward and scholarly research on intimate partner violence.

In the following chapter, I examine how these dominant images and ideas influence the response of state agents to women. The disjuncture between women's lived experiences, the expectations of official agents, and the requirements of the criminal processing system produce irreconcilable differences between women and the law.

2 ⚬⚬⚬ Irreconcilable Differences: Women's Encounters with the Criminal Processing System

Living in a situation that defies conventional categories and boundaries creates obstacles to communication with official actors in the criminal processing system. Women seeking help often feel that they are misunderstood or expected to behave in ways that are incompatible with their own knowledge and needs. The criminal processing system, including police, prosecutors, defense attorneys, and judges, requires victims to meet certain expectations in communicating their complaints.[1] These include prompt reporting, consistency over time, corroborating evidence, a clear timeline of events, and a commitment to follow through with prosecution.[2] These criteria do not simply reflect individual preferences or biases of criminal processing actors, but the evidentiary requirements for successful criminal prosecutions.

There have been statutory changes in these requirements that recognize the circumstances of female victims of sexualized violence. For example, the requirement for corroborating evidence of sexual assault has been abolished in all fifty states. Also, the statute of limitations for bringing charges of child sexual abuse has been extended or eliminated in many states. In some states, there is no statute of limitations for the most serious sexual assaults regardless of age. Since the early 1980s, all states have expanded police power to arrest in domestic violence cases without witnessing the crime or requiring victims to file complaints.[3] The implementation of these changes, however, has been challenging. The construction of women's credibility in cases of intimate partner violence continues to rely on ideas about victimization that are inconsistent with women's experiences.[4]

Delays in reporting, ambivalence about prosecution, lack of corroborating evidence, and inability to produce a clear timeline of events still undermine the credibility of women's reports.[5]

The Inaccessibility of Women's Experiences to State Agents

In some cases, women's experiences are so at odds with those of their interrogators that the officials simply cannot understand what is being said. It is difficult for outsiders to understand women's perceptions that nothing can protect them or keep abusers away. With all the publicity surrounding changes in laws and resources for victims of intimate partner violence, it may appear that anyone who wants out of a violent relationship can obtain help and protection. Women's experiences of persistent abuse, stalking, and harassment following separation or divorce are sometimes incomprehensible or suggest exaggeration or fabrication to people who have never had such experiences.

For example, as discussed in the previous chapter, women sometimes express confusion over their continued support for a violent partner. The ongoing relationships between women and their abusers are thus commonly perceived as mutually desired, as women's "going back" to their abusers. A transcribed interview with a woman whose ex-husband was being prosecuted for sexual assault, kidnapping, and aggravated assault reveals how she was worn down by constant abuse and the failure of police to protect her.[6] This twenty-nine-year-old, low-income Mexican American had known her ex-husband since they were both thirteen years old. They married at age nineteen and had three children together. She was five feet four inches and weighed one hundred pounds; he was five feet eleven inches and weighed 240 pounds. She divorced him after many years of physical abuse, but he kept returning, breaking into her home, raping and beating her, and refusing to leave. His defense attorney tried to suggest that she could have prevented contact by refusing to allow him in her home or by calling the police:

ATTORNEY: He moved in without you agreeing to it?
WOMAN: Yes, without me agreeing to it.
ATTORNEY: What did he do?

WOMAN: He just came in through my window and moved in. He came in the middle of the night through my window and we argued, we had a fight like always, and he said he was staying and he stayed.

ATTORNEY: Did you call the police?

WOMAN: They wouldn't listen to me. He's always coming in through my windows in every place I've lived and he's always come to fight and he's always stayed on his own. I've never asked him to move there, never asked him to move after my divorce.

ATTORNEY: You mean he would just come in and live in your house?

WOMAN: Yes.

ATTORNEY: And you wouldn't say anything?

WOMAN: It didn't matter if I said anything. He wouldn't listen anyway.

In this exchange, the attorney questioned the woman's claims of victimization and attempted to portray the relationship as mutual. If she did not want him there, why wouldn't she call the police or just tell him to leave? She tried to explain that her opinion had no relevance to her ex-husband or to the police. A person living in a well-protected, middle-class home may have a hard time imagining that an unwanted intruder can simply enter through the window and insist on staying. In low-income housing with flimsy or absent locks, no window screens, and hollow doors, forced entry is quite simple. Men who are determined to continue a relationship with a woman they abuse are not often dissuaded by being asked to leave.

This woman experienced forced sex on a routine basis, and even more frequent physical assaults. Pressed by his attorney to give an exact number of cases, she estimated that she had been raped one hundred times and assaulted one thousand times. The attorney assumed that since they had three children together, she had believed his stories of love and promises to change at some point.

WOMAN: He would say he would leave his girlfriend, he wanted to marry me and, it's a routine, it's, I've, it's . . .

ATTORNEY: It's a routine?

WOMAN: It's a routine with him.

ATTORNEY: But uh, this has happened before? How many times?

WOMAN: Oh, gosh, I can't even remember. I can't even think of . . . with the sixteen years that I've known and been with him, um, twice a month for maybe ten years.

ATTORNEY: Okay, that's where he'll tell you he'll leave whatever girl he's with at the time and come back to you?

WOMAN: And beat me and . . .

ATTORNEY: And then leave and then come back, and it's like a broken record?

WOMAN: Right.

ATTORNEY: Now, in the past you have fallen for that line?

WOMAN: No, it's, uh, he's very persistent and I get very tired . . . and the law doesn't protect me.

ATTORNEY: You had, I mean in the last sixteen years you said you got beat at least twice a month?

WOMAN: Yes.

ATTORNEY: And you have three kids from him?

WOMAN: Yes.

ATTORNEY: So, I assume that you have given in or believe what he has said to you?

WOMAN: No, I haven't. I haven't believed what he's ever said to me.

ATTORNEY: Why is it then that you go back to him?

WOMAN: I don't. He ends up going in through my window and he moves into my house.

This woman tries to describe her exhaustion and her inability to keep her abusive partner away from her and her children. But the attorney "assumes" that she "gave in" or "believed what he said." Like so many outsiders to violent relationships, he wonders why she "goes back," while she tries to explain that she never went back or believed her husband. It is difficult for the attorney to accept that for sixteen years her husband repeatedly forced his way into her home and her body. He interrogated her about efforts to use the criminal processing system to keep him away.

ATTORNEY: You normally wouldn't complain [to police] that he had sex with you against your will?

WOMAN: No.

ATTORNEY: Why not?

WOMAN: My mind was tired. I just couldn't take it no more. I just didn't want to hassle with it, I just wanted him out of my life, that was it. If it was possible to take him out of my life right now, I would even drop everything. That's what I told him before, if it was possible.

ATTORNEY: Well, what I'm getting at, if someone was physically assaulting me over and over again, it would seem logical for me to go to the police and say "this guy is just hassling me. I want him locked up and the key thrown away."

WOMAN: I did that and they didn't do it. Or they would hold him for twenty-four hours and that would be it. He would be out the next day.

In this exchange, the attorney attempts to critique the woman's efforts by describing what *he* would have done, what would "seem logical" for him. The woman maintained that she tried this approach and it did nothing to deter her husband's abuse. Later in the interview, she said she had called the police more than twenty-five times since her divorce. She had also filed orders of protection, but he ignored them and the police would not arrest him.

ATTORNEY: How many times have you been to that court to get orders of protection?

WOMAN: Around four or five times.

ATTORNEY: And you know what an order of protection does for you?

WOMAN: Yes I do. It doesn't do anything.

ATTORNEY: What do you mean it doesn't do anything?

WOMAN: I know what an order of protection stands for.

ATTORNEY: And when he would come around, you wouldn't call the police?

WOMAN: Yes, I would.

ATTORNEY: And the police wouldn't do anything?

WOMAN: No, they wouldn't.

ATTORNEY: Not even after you showed them the order of protection?

WOMAN: They were afraid of him.

ATTORNEY: The police?

WOMAN: Yes.

ATTORNEY: Well, why?

WOMAN: Because when he's upset and everything like that he's pretty wild.

ATTORNEY: Well, he, did he, has he beaten you before?

WOMAN: Has he? Yes.

ATTORNEY: How many times?

WOMAN: Over a thousand.

ATTORNEY: Over a thousand?

WOMAN: Yes.

This woman's negative experience of using the order of protection to try to prevent her ex-husband from forcefully entering and occupying her home is similar to other women's accounts. The orders are designed to provide a legal mechanism to prevent abusers from harassing victims by stipulating no contact at various locations, depending on the specific order. Perpetrators who violate the orders may be arrested, jailed, fined and/or ordered to counseling, even if they do not commit any criminal acts. In some cases, these orders facilitate women's efforts to separate from abusers and remain safe. For many women, however, the order is simply a piece of paper that means nothing to their abusers and is not enforced by police.[7] This woman tried to use the legal system to protect herself, but found it worthless. Her estimate that she was beaten "over a thousand" times again suggests the problem of communicating abuse in legal language requiring specific dates, times, and places. It was not until her ex-husband nearly killed her that felony charges were filed against him. She eventually dropped charges and moved out of state with her children, saying she was just exhausted with trying to keep him away.

Women's Expert Knowledge

Women have knowledge of their partners that outsiders do not. For example, Danielle knew what an order of protection would mean to her husband, and it would not mean he should leave her alone. She had expert knowledge about her husband that informed her view of how he would respond to outside intervention. Charged in the third-party murder of her husband, Danielle told me that after she was arrested, an officer asked why she didn't just get an order of protection:

> I says, "Well, let me see. Remember that woman at Metrocenter [shopping mall]? She put an order of protection, did that save her life?" I says, "a man like Tony, I woulda served him with a piece of paper saying he couldn't be around me, I wouldn't be around today for that paper to mean anything because that would've been an insult to him, that would've been disrespectful to him, that would've been a slap in his face because I took something that was private and let it be known public."

Survey data from the National Crime Victimization Study indicates that the most common reason (25 percent) given for not reporting assaults by spouses is that it was a "private matter."[8] This coded response, however, does not reveal women's intimate, detailed knowledge of how their partners would respond to making the matter public. Danielle's knowledge of Tony's perspective on private matters meant that *she* felt an order of protection would be a death warrant, not that she agreed that their problems should remain private. Survey data do not allow readers to know the process by which women's knowledge of their partners is translated into a codable category. The most common code (29 percent) was "some other reason" that includes "did not know why they didn't call the police." It is possible that women's ambivalence about reporting prohibits providing a clear-cut answer that can be coded in survey research.

As part of my study of the police response to intimate partner violence, I and two of my students, Kathryn Seeley and Kimberly Bauman, interviewed fifteen women who had called the police for help.[9] Most women defined the police as "professional," but did not think calling the police helped to end their abuse. They believed their partners were fully capable of killing them and that there was little they or anyone else could do to deter them. One woman, who had been married for twenty years and divorced for more than five years, explained the mix of emotions that inhibited her from prosecuting her ex-husband:

WOMAN: I wouldn't want to be responsible for putting him in prison that if he keeps on, he's going to jail, you know. But it won't be over an assault charge. It will be over disobeying the order of protection . . . and that's simple, a little jail or fine, or something like, you know, cruisin' time. Of course I've always known that if I had him put in jail, he would come back and kill me.

INTERVIEWER: You think so?

WOMAN: Oh yes.

INTERVIEWER: Is that why you wanted the assault charge dropped?

WOMAN: I don't know. I don't know if it was that or if I just didn't want him to go to prison. I don't know. I'm not afraid to die and I got some medical problems. It's not that, I don't want to die, you know. I don't continue to put up with his crap. I've gotten more mad now and I don't . . . it's not right, you know. If I feel like having him put in jail, then I'll have him put in jail. I'll take my chances. I'm taking them anyway.

This woman's description of her feelings is typical of the ambiguity many women express about their abusive partners and ex-partners.

Women want to be safe, want violence to end, but often feel ambivalent about participating in their abuser's incarceration and about the effectiveness of such actions. Some women simply stated that they did not know anything that would stop their partners. One woman, who had been married for nineteen years and abused the entire marriage planned to get a divorce once her children were grown. However, she was quite certain that a divorce would not end the abuse.

INTERVIEWER: Do you think you'll be happier then?

WOMAN: Yes, if he will let me be free. I don't know if he would. Even if I get a divorce, he wouldn't let me go free.

INTERVIEWER: Why do you say that?

WOMAN: Because he told me lots of times that he won't ever let me be free.

INTERVIEWER: Have you thought about moving away?

WOMAN: No matter where I go.

INTERVIEWER: Have you thought about getting an order of protection that you can get from the judge where if he comes around, he can be arrested for coming in?

WOMAN: I wish you knew my husband, he's . . . oh.

INTERVIEWER: It wouldn't work?

WOMAN: No, it wouldn't work.

INTERVIEWER: Why?

WOMAN: He's a snake, you know. He goes all over the place. He knows his way. Okay, he would go through the kids to get to me. He'll have to. I know it wouldn't work.

INTERVIEWER: Do you know of anything that would help?

WOMAN: No. I don't know of anything that would help.

The possibility of permanent incarceration of her husband did not even enter this woman's mind. That would only occur in the most extreme circumstances: her death. In most cases, even the most serious assaults that result in permanent damage are punished with sentences no longer than fifteen years. And men are able to continue harassment and violence even from behind bars, through men they hire or have influence with on the outside.[10] Her statement, "I wish you knew my husband," communicates the intimate knowledge women have of the ways their partners would respond to outside intervention. It is this knowledge that is often disregarded when women are encouraged to call the police or get an order of protection. Research that documents the pervasiveness of "separation assault" and domestic fatalities that occur when women try to leave abusive partners now validates women's expert knowledge.[11] Yet women continue to struggle with questions from others and from themselves about why they did not leave or pursue intervention.

The Law as Enemy

For other women, the legal system is an unknown territory that is potentially as harmful as their abusive partners. Women who are in the United States without legal documentation face language and knowledge barriers as well as threats of deportation if they report their abusers.[12] The Violence Against Women Act (VAWA) enacted certain protections so that immigrant women could gain protection and remain in the United States, but these protections are not guaranteed. Many immigrant women do not know about VAWA, or about the laws of the United States more generally.[13] Applying for protection is a complicated process and women must prove that they or their child have been battered and that they are of good moral character before being granted a visa. The cultural obstacles to publicly identifying an abusive partner are formidable for many women.[14]

Before VAWA, in 1988, I worked with a woman who was a migrant farmworker from Mexico. She did not speak English and lived in the shacks (without telephones) provided by farmers for workers in rural Arizona. Her husband molested their daughter and she was charged with failure to protect her child from abuse. The law that holds nonabusive parents responsible for the conduct of abusive parents was unknown to her. She believed she had handled the problem herself by warning her husband never to touch their daughter again and making certain he was never alone with the child. However, he abused the little girl while her mother slept, and the child reported the abuse to an aunt. The aunt reported to CPS (child protective services), and both parents were charged. The county attorney indicated that he wanted to make an example of this woman, to teach the migrant community what could happen if they did not report abusive parents to authorities. Fortunately, the public defender assigned to her case realized that the abuse she suffered from her husband could mitigate her failure to report. The judge at her initial appearance agreed that the woman had done all she could, given her circumstances, and was more valuable to her daughter at home than in jail. Charges were dropped.

Many low-income women are fearful that if the police are notified of their own abuse, child protective services will remove their children. The presence of an abusive man in the household raises questions about children's safety. Investigations of the "co-occurrence" of child and spouse abuse in the same household range in estimates from 30 to 60 percent of cases.[15] The links between adult intimate partner violence and child abuse have become the subject of research and policy over the past decade. The "Greenbook Initiative" is a nationwide effort to coordinate responses between the multiple criminal processing and social service agencies that may have contact with an abused woman and her children.[16] The initiative recognizes the potential harm to children living in households where intimate partner violence takes place, but also the punitive damage to mothers and children of separation based solely on the mother's victimization. In 2004, the U.S. Court of Appeals for the Second Circuit upheld an earlier decision in *Nicholson v. Williams* that New York City's Administration for Children's Services must not remove children from their mother's care solely on the basis of her own victimization.[17] Despite this ruling, child protective agencies responsible for the well-being of children often require that women terminate abusive relationships in order to maintain custody of their children.[18]

Failure to ensure the absence of abusive adults in the household places children at risk. I have worked with seven women prosecuted for the violent crimes against their children committed by their abusive intimate partners. Four children died at the hands of violent husbands or boyfriends, and three of their mothers are currently serving life sentences for these deaths. The other woman is serving ten years to life. These cases are discussed more fully in chapter 6. Child protective services had been involved in three of these cases and returned children to homes where violent men continued to live.[19] There is no guarantee that intervention by child protective services will reduce the danger posed by women's intimate partners. In fact, while women are held criminally responsible for the crimes committed against their children by their husbands or boyfriends, child protective services are not legally responsible for returning or leaving children in the custody of violent caregivers after intervention.[20]

Women know that their lives and mothering will be closely scrutinized if child protective services are involved and there is a possibility that they will lose custody.[21] The child welfare system is much more likely to view poor women of color as inadequate mothers, and children of color are vastly overrepresented in the foster care system.[22] This fear of CPS intervention is another reason that women of color are hesitant to call the police for protection. As an African American woman in my study with Angela Moe explained, she would not call the police for protection from abuse because that would bring CPS into her life: "What the (Southwest City) police had been doing is taking both people to jail, and so I was terrified of calling the police because I didn't know what would happen to my children because I had nobody to take them, so if I had called the police on him, they would have taken both of us to jail, they would have taken my children to CPS, and in foster care, and it would've turned into a nightmare."

Women are also reluctant to report their partner's abuse to authorities or to friends and family because of the historical and contemporary social context of violence against people of color by whites in positions of authority.[23] Histories of colonization, genocide, slavery, and ongoing oppression influence women of color's confidence in relying on the law for protection.[24] The contemporary context is one of increasing surveillance and control, particularly over marginalized communities.[25] The responses of African American women to their partner's violence are rooted in the historical and current demonization and violent oppression of black men and white disregard for the unity and integrity of black families. The African American community has traditionally provided the protection to women that the authorities would not. Reporting violence by partners to the police is felt not only to be a betrayal of that individual man, but also of the larger community. There is also an accurate perception that the victims are as likely to be arrested as the men they're reporting.[26] Recent research by Andrea Ritchie documents police brutality toward women of color when police intervene for domestic violence.[27]

The term *people of color* obscures some of the unique historical and contemporary processes that affect each marginalized group within the United States.[28] White authorities, including slave owners, soldiers, police, social workers, and legislators, have violated the integrity of families of marginalized groups in varied ways. African

American children could be sold away from their families in the antebellum era, while American Indian children were forcibly removed to boarding schools through the 1970s.[29] Children of low-income European immigrants to U.S. urban areas were removed from their families by such white organizations as the Children's Aid Society and sent to work for rural farmers in the Midwest.[30] Today, inner-city African American women confront a context where their male children have a higher probability of going to prison than to college.[31] These historical and contemporary experiences of oppression suggest that many women of color do not view the criminal processing system as a neutral agency of protection. Indeed, many women in communities of color view the anti-violence focus on policing as a distraction from the structural issues of oppression they face.[32] Yet some data indicate that African American women are *more* likely to call police in cases of domestic violence than women in other racial/ethnic groups.[33] Despite distrust of the police, fear of condemnation from the community, or retaliation by the abuser, the police may be the only resource that is available.

American Indian women living on reservations, on the other hand, engage with tribal police rather than non-Indian officers for most instances of intimate partner violence. The fear of racist reactions from non-Indian police officers is diminished, except for major felony crimes, which are under the jurisdiction of the FBI.[34] McGillivray and Comaskey describe the frustration of First Nations women living on reserves in Canada in being unable to receive help from either Canadian or tribal police.[35] Native women reported that either nothing would be done to help them or they would be blamed for their own victimization. They also faced child custody problems, as they were prohibited from removing their children from reserves. The American Indian women I spoke with expressed similar views. None were worried that reporting their partners' violence to police would reinforce negative stereotypes about American Indians, and most had their partners "thrown in" jail by tribal police several times. Some women did indicate, however, that there were community repercussions as a result of reporting their husband, with his extended family spreading gossip and turning against her. Two of the American Indian women I interviewed had been beaten up by their partners' relatives for reporting them. Women also felt there was little the tribal police could or would do to protect them from further abuse.

There is tremendous variation in living conditions among American Indian communities, from the small Mashantucket Pequot tribe in Connecticut that operates one of the most successful casinos in the nation to the Lakota nation in Pine Ridge, South Dakota, where approximately 61 percent of the population lived below poverty level in 2000.[36] On some reservations, the unemployment rate is 85 to 90 percent and housing conditions are stressful. In 1990, some 20 percent of households on reservations lacked complete plumbing facilities, compared with one percent of U.S. households overall. On the Navajo and Hopi reservations, about one-half of households lacked complete plumbing.[37] The significance of these "neighborhood characteristics" is different for American Indian people than for other groups in the United States: many tribes consider their homelands part of their identities and have no desire to move to more economically prosperous areas. As Roberta Blackgoat, a leader of resistance to the forced relocation of Navajos from Big Mountain, Arizona, said, "Our way has no word for relocation."[38]

The American Indian women I have met who have been victims of intimate partner violence have had much more difficulty escaping abusers than women from other racial groups. Reticence to leave their homes on the reservation makes moving away from abusers an unattractive option. For many of the American Indian Nations in the Southwest, land and homes are held in women's names and inheritance is matrilineal. While this is a source of power, it is also a compelling reason to stay put on one's land rather than flee an abusive partner. It is also significant that large parts of the reservations are rural with undeveloped roads and few telephones. Even if police intervention is desired, dialing 9-1-1 is not an option. Tribal police cover huge amounts of territory, so it may take hours for a woman to find a working phone, contact an officer, and have someone arrive to protect her. Also, police brutality by tribal and urban police has been widely documented and discourages women's calls to police.[39] Extended clan relationships may mean there are more relatives to help protect a woman and her children and provide resources; they may also mean that the abusive partner's relatives will shield him from arrest or prosecution. The importance of extended family relationships also deters women from moving away from their homes. Serious assaults and rapes are under the jurisdiction of the FBI. All of the issues of fear and mistrust of police that exist in other communities of color are multiplied by the historical relationship between many tribal members and the FBI. For these and many other reasons, American Indian women face unique barriers to escaping violence.[40]

The Latinas I spoke with did not mention concern about public perceptions of Latino men. They indicated that they refrained from calling the police because of their partners' threats and retaliation for occasions when they had called. Some also had negative experiences with police, either being arrested themselves or having no action taken against their abuser, or both. One Latina, married to a white man, had been arrested for domestic violence and so was hesitant to call the police again. Two Latinas were heavy drug users, as were their partners (one Latino, one African American), and police intervention only resulted from calls made by other people. Again, one of these women was arrested for domestic violence, and she had no desire to involve either the police or child protective services in her life. The one other Latina woman never called the police. This particular woman did not seem able to register mentally the danger to either herself or her children. Her story is described more fully below under the pseudonym Salina. The conflict between the needs of women of color for protection from abuse and the larger context of discrimination against people of color in the criminal processing system is being addressed by scholars/activists like Andrea Smith, Andrea Ritchie, and Beth Richie, as well as by grassroots organizations like INCITE! and Sista II Sista.[41]

Another issue that limits low-income women's ability to rely on police intervention is crime-free housing policies. Beginning in 1996, President Clinton devised the "One-Strike and You're Out" policy to combat gang and drug activities in public housing. These policies encourage local public housing authorities to establish policies that evict residents when anyone in their households engages in crime. Similar policies have been adopted in private housing complexes. When police arrive at a residence in response to intimate partner violence, managers and landlords may initiate eviction processes. This eviction may occur even though the resident is a victim rather than an offender, even when people other than the victim call the police, and even when the offender does not live on the premises.[42]

Victims, Offenders, or Mutual Combat?

Since the adoption of mandatory and presumptive arrest policies for domestic violence in many cities in the 1980s, the proportion of women arrested for violence against their intimate partners has increased. Many women are arrested for "mutual combat" based on physical appearances at the crime scene that belie the larger context of domination and terrorism in the relationship. One of the unintended consequences of efforts to increase arrests for intimate partner violence has been an increase in arrests of women, many of whom are abused by the "victims," their husbands and boyfriends.[43] Meda Chesney-Lind has recently reported dramatic increases in arrests of women for intimate partner violence: from 12.9 percent to 21 percent of those arrested for domestic violence between 1992 and 1996 in Maryland; a 91 percent increase between 1991 and 1996 in Sacramento (while arrests of men fell 7 percent); and in California, arrests of women went from 6 percent in 1988 to 16 percent in 1998.[44] She also notes that a Canadian study by Elizabeth Comach et al. found that in 1995, "58 percent of all violent crime charges against women were for partner violence," and that "in 35 percent of the intimate partner violence cases involving women, the accursed [*sic*] woman had actually called the police for help."[45] Shamita Das Dasgupta reports on participants' comments at a seminar held by Praxis International in 1999. Participants from Montana and North Dakota estimated female arrest rates of less than 10 percent and 12 percent, respectively, but Vermont's estimate was 35 percent and Orem, Utah's, 20 percent to 40 percent.[46] Susan L. Miller describes the conflicts that have emerged as a consequence of incident-based arrest policies that assume a gender-neutral approach to domestic violence.[47] The women included in this book represent cases from the early beginnings of the mandatory arrest phase of police response (1984) to the current context in which twenty-one states mandate arrest for intimate partner violence.[48]

Arrests of women for intimate partner violence are particularly problematic when women later commit serious acts of violence in self-defense, such as murder or attempted murder. Then the prior arrest is used to demonstrate that "violence went both ways," and her claims of being abused and afraid are not believed. Two of the women I interviewed, Lisa and Beth, had been arrested on charges of intimate partner violence prior to being charged with manslaughter and attempted manslaughter. The proportion of the total group of women arrested for intimate partner violence is small, but this low arrest rate is partially a reflection of the lack of police involvement in these cases. In twenty-five cases (55 percent), police had never intervened in the relationship (see appendix E). As discussed above, some women expressed the view that the police could not help and would only make things worse.

Lisa, a working-class Latina, was forty-two at the time she shot and injured her white husband. Beth was a white, working-class woman, living with a white man. She was twenty-nine when she killed him with a knife. Both men had also been arrested for intimate partner violence. Lisa's husband spent a year in prison for assaulting her; Beth's boyfriend was arrested for assaulting two prior girlfriends and incarcerated for failure to pay child support. Lisa and Beth both took plea bargains. Lisa received a six-and-a-half-year sentence for aggravated assault. Beth served seven of a ten-year sentence for attempted manslaughter. The prosecution portrayed both women as violent and vindictive, and their prior arrests contributed to this image. Their complicated histories illustrate the elusive boundaries between victimization and offending.

Beth's father died when she was two years old and her mother remarried a man who physically abused her and her children. Beth witnessed numerous incidents of violence by her stepfather against her mother and two older brothers. When Beth was thirteen, her twenty-three-year-old boyfriend raped her and left her tied to the bed. She never reported the rape. At fifteen, she began dating a much older man who was involved in organized crime. When she was seventeen, Beth and her girlfriend agreed to serve as prostitutes at a party arranged by this boyfriend and his uncle:

BETH: My friend and I went and prostituted ourselves at a bachelor's party, and when my mom returned from Hawaii, all of her bills were paid. I paid off all her debts, her credit cards, her car, her rent was paid for four months, so she didn't have to work two jobs any more. And that's something, I don't know why, but I carry that around with me. And every man that I've ever been with, I feel that if I don't tell them, I feel dirty, like I'm hiding something, so, I feel like I'll always bear that cross. I still haven't told my mother to this day.

KATHLEEN: She didn't ask you where you got all that money?

BETH: She did, and I just told her that I wasn't gonna tell her. I wouldn't. The man that I was with at the time, I had access to anything I wanted. I had access to anything.

KATHLEEN: Did he set it up, the mafia guy?

BETH: His uncle did. And to this day, Chris doesn't know. His uncle forced me to have sex with him, and his dad tried to get me to have sex with him. I don't know, I guess in my own mind, everything was okay 'cuz I didn't know any better, but I look back now, and I think wow, what a slut. . . . I'm not one of those women really into money or material things, I just want somebody who will love me for me. That's it.

Beth had several physically abusive relationships with men, as well as two relationships she described as nonviolent. One of the men she dated, whom she described as nonviolent, obtained an injunction against harassment against her when Beth "keyed" his truck, scraping the paint with her key. She also scratched and struck him as they argued in the street. On another occasion, this man called the police when Beth came to his house at midnight and threw a beer bottle at his door and at the vehicle of the woman who was with him. These events occurred three years before the homicide. Despite the doctors' prediction of infertility, she had a son with one of her abusive partners, but they never lived together after the baby was born. Her son was six years old at the time of the homicide, and Beth had sent him to the neighbor's apartment to ask her to call 9-1-1.

Her year-and-a-half-long relationship with Matt was extremely volatile and they both abused alcohol and methamphetamine. She had received medical treatment for injuries sustained when Matt raped her with a beer bottle about four months prior to the homicide. She had also been treated for a urinary tract infection caused by repeated "body slamming." Matt was very jealous, constantly accusing her of affairs with other men; he made her quit her job because he was jealous of her boss. Two of her female neighbors corroborated her accounts of abuse. However, these same women also reported to detectives that Beth had told them she would kill Matt if he continued to abuse her. The police report written when Beth was arrested for intimate partner violence indicated that "she said that she just wanted Matt to leave or she would kill him." This statement, in conjunction with the neighbors' statements, combined to convince the probation officer, prosecutor, and judge that Beth premeditated Matt's murder. When Beth described to me the threat she had made to kill Matt, she emphasized her need to protect herself and her son: "I told him [the officer], 'If he comes after me to hurt me and my baby I will do anything, anything to protect myself and my son. This man is not going to hurt me anymore. If I have to protect myself and kill him to keep me and my son safe, I will."

One evening after they had been arguing and drinking vodka, Matt struck Beth and ripped off her dress. He then locked himself in their bedroom. Beth said she wanted to get in the bedroom to retrieve a pillow and blanket; she also said she began to worry about Matt because no sound was coming from the room. She used a screwdriver to try to unlock the door, and when that failed, she got a large butcher knife from the kitchen. She knelt before the door, trying to pry open the latch when Matt flung open the door and lunged at her. The knife plunged into his chest and he staggered out into the hallway. Beth began to scream for help and to administer CPR (cardiopulmonary resuscitation) as he lay bleeding on the stoop. When the police arrived within minutes, they found her screaming, trying to give Matt CPR. She said his last words to her were, "Don't worry about it, Beth. It will be all right." The knife went five inches into his thorax and he was pronounced dead at the scene by the fire department.

Although evidence of battering was introduced to argue for a mitigated sentence, Beth maintained that Matt's death was an accident rather than the result of self-defense. Police detectives argued that the nature of Matt's injury was inconsistent with an accident and that significant force was required for such a deep wound. The county attorney offered her a plea agreement to the charge of *attempted* manslaughter, and Beth accepted this offer. The assumption of premeditation and prior acts of violence, however, led to the imposition of the presumptive term of ten years, rather than the mitigated term of seven.

Clearly, Beth is "no angel." Whether she killed Matt intentionally or accidentally, she had used violence against him and others on prior occasions, abused alcohol and drugs, had stalked a previous boyfriend and destroyed his property, and violated an injunction against harassment. She told people, including police officers, she would kill Matt if he continued to hurt her, and she used profanity when questioned by police in prior offenses. Beth was not a demon, either. She had watched her mother and brothers brutally assaulted by her stepfather and had been hit by him as well; she was raped by a number of men, beginning at age thirteen, physically abused by four different boyfriends, and beaten, body slammed, and raped with a beer bottle by Matt. A psychiatrist diagnosed her as severely depressed and suicidal while she waited in jail to be sentenced. As Dasgupta has argued, Beth's violent action cannot be ripped from the entire context of her life and examined under the narrow lens of legal definitions of "self-defense," without obscuring the ways in which her actions related to many years of abuse by others and by the specific victim of her violence.[49] The larger, sociocultural factors of poverty, lack of parental care, dependence on a violent stepfather for economic survival, and gendered expectations for care of her mother, her son, and her boyfriend also shaped the ways Beth negotiated the violence against her.

Lisa also had one prior arrest for intimate partner violence, as well as two convictions for driving under the influence of alcohol. The domestic violence arrest was for breaking a window in her home after she was locked out by her husband, Brian. Her three children were inside the home, and both she and Brian were drunk. She endured seven years of physical, sexual, and emotional abuse, and Brian had spent a year in prison for assaulting her. She shot him when she believed he was molesting their two-year-old daughter, resulting in minor injury to his shoulder. Her one arrest for domestic violence contributed to the sentencing judge's perception: "This was not one-sided as presented by the defense. The abuse goes both ways."[50] When I asked Lisa about prior police involvement, she described her own arrest:

KATHLEEN: Did you ever call the police when he was beating you?
LISA: Yeah. There was that one time that he was arrested. But the police had been to our house so many times. One night they even took me.
KATHLEEN: Did they arrest both of you, or just you?
LISA: Just me. And like, after that, every time the police would come to the house, they would always ask me to leave the house, or I would volunteer to leave the house or something, just to keep peace, I would leave, so nothing would happen.

The judge listened to my testimony about battering and Lisa's fear, but announced he had seen much worse cases and felt this was more a case of mutual combat. Lisa's injuries included two concussions on separate occasions, and Brian had forced her to have two abortions. She is a fundamentalist Christian and abortion is against her religious beliefs. She told me she viewed them as "baby killing," and she was deeply hurt and angry that he had coerced her to abort. With three young children to care for, she believed Brian's threats to leave if she had another and that no one else would want her. She had also been subjected to forced sodomy and bound with duct tape while he planned how to dispose of her body. Brian's only injury was a scratch on his face. Like other women, Lisa had a difficult time providing a linear narrative and emphasized emotional over physical abuse. She only recalled the following incident after several hours of talking, as I was preparing to conclude the interview:

> Brian taped me up, he taped my feet up, taped my hands up and had me sit on the bed . . . then he tied me up and stuff and then I had a go pee, he took me to the bathroom, hobbling, to go pee, and wiped me and everything, and then took me back to the bedroom and then he said he was trying to figure out a way to kill me and dispose of my body, again. And, in our trailer, he put an addition, and he cut a floor thing in the corner, and it's all dirt down there, so, I guess that's what he dug that for, he was gonna bury me under that, under the house. Oh God. He was gonna dig that out because he made it big enough where he could stand there too with a shovel, which he never started diggin' anyways, but he had a light down there and everything, you know the light, he had it to where he could see and stuff, he was gonna dig a hole under the house, under that addition, so I guess where he could kill me and bury me. He was trying to figure out how to kill me, how to dispose of my body, and since I was too fat and he couldn't carry me or take me somewhere or something, I don't know, I guess he was just gonna bury me there. So then, finally he took the tape off me, and it leaves, duct tape leaves gooey stuff, and I had that on for a time.

Like many other women, Lisa kept saying, "you must think I'm crazy," as she relayed her story. She wrote me after the interview and said, "When I was talking to you I felt like it was someone else's life. I can't believe I endured all that. Then I thought, God, does she even believe me? But in my heart I know you do." Lisa's use of drugs and alcohol, including two convictions for driving under the influence of alcohol, contributed to the court's perception that she was not a battered woman but a participant in marital violence that "went both ways." Her drug and alcohol use did add to her problems, and will be addressed more fully in the next chapter. The sense of unreality she expressed was exacerbated by drugs, but was shared by other women who never used drugs or alcohol.

Abby, who did not use drugs or alcohol, felt that she did not really know her husband of eighteen years. After she killed him, she learned that he was drinking much more than she knew and was probably using drugs as well: "Where was my mind? You know, to let him to take control of another person like that, my confidence, and you know, I was just insecure of everything." Looking back, women found it incredible that they endured years of abuse, and knew it was difficult for outsiders to understand what they had been through.

Tough Women

The cultural image of "the battered woman" as helpless and passive contributes to perceptions that "tough women" cannot be victims. Images of battered women as helpless and pathetic make it difficult for judges and juries to understand how strong, competent women can be dominated by an abuser and fear for their lives.[51]

Dianne's case is an example of this dilemma. Dianne was a thirty-seven-year-old, working-class white woman married to a white man. In chapter 1, I described Dianne's feelings about losing her husband, her best friend. She was a physically strong woman who earned her living cleaning houses, and she enjoyed hanging out in bars and playing pool. She was gregarious and many witnesses testified that everyone who knew her liked her. Seven witnesses also testified to her husband's brutal, aggressive personality, his constant drug and alcohol abuse, and extreme possessiveness and violence toward Dianne. One witness testified that he had never seen anyone beaten so badly as Dianne, that her face was so swollen he could not recognize her. This witness, along with several others, reiterated Dianne's own statements that she stayed with him because she loved him and saw more good in him than other people did. The prosecutor in the case tried to portray Dianne as a tough woman who could defend herself physically, and as an "outrageous flirt" who could "hold her own."

In her interviews with me and other witnesses, the prosecutor tried to elicit testimony that would counter sympathetic victim imagery of Dianne. For example, one witness who had known both Dianne and her deceased husband James, described how James berated Dianne's clothing and called her a whore. The prosecutor tried to direct the witness, but he would not agree with her view:

PROSECUTOR: Can I ask you something? When he would do that with her and be verbally abusive with her, what would she do?

WITNESS: "Oh, James, you're full of shit, you don't know what you're talking about." You know, Dianne was really calm. You know, Dianne'd be calm until he'd smack her and then she'd smack him back. I never seen her do anything to him, you know, it was always him doing it to her, and then she would fight back.

PROSECUTOR: She could probably hold her own, though.

WITNESS: Well, she tried. No, not, well, I don't think she could hold her own, but she was pretty tough, she's a pretty tough girl, you know.

PROSECUTOR: Strong, physically strong.

WITNESS: Ya', well, she's got courage. She's got a heart, you know, she would try . . . up to a point, you know, and then he'd overpower her. Was all you could see, you know, was two black eyes and a bloody lip, you know, her arms out of whack or, you know, she's got gravel up her back.

The witness testified that Dianne had "courage" and "heart," and the prosecutor tried to use this as evidence that she could not be battered. The witness, however, refused to construct Dianne's violence as equal to her husband's and to acquiesce to the prosecutor's view of her as able to "hold her own."

In the prosecutor's interview with me, she built a hypothetical scenario and asked me if women whose husbands were pathologically jealous typically engaged in flirtatious conduct: "Let me ask you this: Built into that scenario [of abusers' pathological jealousy] is it also typical for the woman, knowing that her husband, her mate, tends to be jealous, to go out and flirt absolutely outrageously with everyone in sight when they're in a social situation? 'Cause we have a lot of testimony that she did that too."

The prosecutor used testimony from the victim's family that she was an "outrageous flirt" at the only social event in which they had ever observed her and from friends that she was "friendly and outgoing" to argue that Dianne could not have been a battered woman.

The prosecutor was suspicious of my objectivity as an expert, but she nonetheless framed her question as if I could answer: "Is it typical?" Of course this question could not be answered productively without questioning the validity of the testimony that Dianne went out and flirted "absolutely outrageously with everyone in sight." Without first evaluating the accuracy of this statement, a "no" answer would cast doubt on Dianne's status as a battered woman; if I answered "yes," I would then have to explain why a woman would intentionally provoke jealousy if her husband was violent.

Both the prosecutor and I were engaged in constructing the "truth" of battered women in general and Dianne's experience in particular. The prosecutor thought Dianne was too tough, strong, and flirtatious to be a battered woman. I thought that the testimony about outrageous flirtation was a distortion drawn from a family's grief. It is difficult to imagine a similar conversation about a man's behavior. Would he flirt outrageously with everyone in sight if he knew it would make his female partner violently angry? Would being tough undermine his credibility? The topics of flirting, "holding her own," and fearing for her life at the hands of her husband are topics that draw on conventional images of femininity. In addressing them, both the prosecutor and I reinforced those images and forced Dianne's life into these preexisting categories, although we differed in how we thought it fit.

Dianne took a plea to manslaughter and evidence on the effects of battering was introduced at sentencing for mitigation purposes. The final sentence of five years, with probation rather than incarceration, reflected a consideration of the impact of battering and Dianne's perceptions of imminent threat. But the argument of self-defense was not adequate to drop charges; that is, without her plea, she would have risked trial for manslaughter and a ten-year prison sentence.

Fighting Back

Most women did try to fight back against their abusers, and none found this an effective means of controlling his violence. It usually only made men angrier and more violent.[52] Angie, for example, described herself as a "fighter," and said "I wasn't going to let him see

I was afraid of him," but her boyfriend was much stronger than she and overpowered her. Phyllis also said that letting her husband see her fear only made him angrier and more violent, so she tried to sound tough and fight back:

> One time we was fightin' and he stopped to drink a beer and he wanted me to stop so he could take a leak, and when he got out, I gassed it and I was gonna leave him, and I kept lookin' in the rearview mirror and I saw him standin' there and I felt sorry for him, and my dumb ass turns around and goes back. And he just gets in the car calmly and he reaches back there and he grabs a hammer, and he hit me in the head with it, right there, and I put my hand on it and I saw blood, and I had this thing about not showing him, lettin' him see me be scared, and I was trying not to let him see that it would make him go off worse, that pissed him off, for people to be scared o' him, so I said, "look what the hell you done to me. Now I'm gonna have to whip your ass," and I got a handful o' blood from my head, I only did that because I was so scared, and he just started laughin', he thought that was the funniest thing, and I blacked his eye one time, 'cuz I tried to defend myself by kickin' him, 'cuz he was sorta attackin' me and I was on the passenger side, and I knew I couldn't fight him off, and I started kickin' him and I had bruises all up and down my leg and I gave him a black eye, and he thought that felt so good, I mean, that felt good to him, and he was really like proud o' me for standin' up for myself.

Women who "stand up for themselves" are often viewed as equal participants in a battering relationship. Evidence of women's prior use of violence is often used by prosecutors to suggest that they were not really battered women, but women engaged in mutual combat, as described in Dianne's case.

Michelle described how her friends told her to fight back against her boyfriend's abuse and the consequences of her efforts:

> I don't think there was ever a time I'd try to hit him back. I remember one time I tried to hit him back, you know because right in front of my friend, I got beat up one time, and my nose was broken. We were in the bathroom and they told me, you better not let him, she was just telling me I was just lettin' him beat up on me. I wasn't trying to defend myself. She told me that he knows you're scared of him, that's why he keeps doing that to you. She always used to talk to me, because I show

so much fear that he keeps doing that to me. She told me, "stand up for yourself if you don't wanna take this beating, you have to fight for yourself." So, one time I did that. I hit him back (*laughs*), I tried to hit him back, but that's when I got beat up worse.

Women did not passively acquiesce to being assaulted, but they also could not control partners through their own use of violence.[53] The notion of mutual combat may be appropriate for some relationships. Where levels of violence are very low and not aimed at establishing control, both men and women may engage in violent conduct.[54] There are also a few cases where women *are* able to match or even surpass men in strength, viciousness, and terrorism.[55] In none of the cases examined here, however, did the violence described fit the reciprocity implied by the phrase "mutual combat." The complexity of women's experiences and feelings are not easily reconciled with the evidentiary demands of the criminal processing system.

On the other hand, women also report experiences of presenting clear, unambiguous requests to police officers, prosecutors, and judges that are not met. Domestic violence victim advocates responded to women's complaints about lack of response and follow-through in domestic violence cases by pressing for consistent, equal protection for battered women. Mandatory and presumptive arrest policies, expanded arrest power, and no-drop prosecution policies are reactions to the knowledge that women's requests for protection were often not met.[56] The irreconcilable differences I have described are not a rationale for rejecting the criminal processing system as a resource in toto; that suggestion is neither responsible nor realistic.[57] It is imperative, however, that police, prosecutor, and judicial interventions be informed of and responsive to the diverse needs of women. The question remains, of course, of how to achieve this balanced response.

In the next chapter, I examine the ways that women's perceptions of the world are influenced by experiences of intimate partner violence. The behaviors of some batterers, especially those who are mentally ill or drug addicted, challenge women's basic assumptions about everyday life. Women become entrapped in worlds that are terrifying and chaotic. In the surreal worlds constructed by abusive partners, trust and safety are elusive and women may engage in actions inconsistent with their own moral values and desires.

3 ⸺ Negotiating Surreality

I don't trust anyone, yet. I used to basically trust the good of people or, even more basic than that, I believed that my reality was other people's reality. In other words, even though there's variations on the same thing, that if I perceived the world as such, they see the world as such and that's not necessarily true. And the older I get, the more I see that this is very untrue. As a matter of fact, it's even a fallacy and if that is the case, which I believe it to be, then there's reason to be frightened. There's a lot of twisted people in the world.   —Belinda, raped and beaten by her fiancé

Trust in other people and the belief that "my reality is other people's reality" are basic foundations for identity and positive social interactions. The ability of people to enjoy life and succeed in economic, educational, and interpersonal pursuits depends upon satisfying the basic human needs for security.[1] Our sense of security and trust is built upon the meanings we construct with other people. We know who we are, what to expect from others and what is expected from us based upon the accumulated experiences of everyday interactions. Sociologists, especially ethnomethodologists, have demonstrated the ways in which people converse and interact based on these taken for granted expectations and the interactional problems that result from rule infractions.[2] We know how much physical space to grant each other, what type of eye contact is appropriate and how to take turns in conversation. Culture, social class, and gender, racial, and ethnic group membership shape these everyday assumptions. Granted, people hold widely varying perspectives about such important things as religion, politics, and morality. But we expect that most people with whom we interact have basic shared assumptions about social reality and that we belong to communities of shared understanding. This expectation allows us to move more or less comfortably and unconsciously through our social worlds, knowing that other people share our beliefs about traffic signals, personal space, and basic social etiquette. Violations of these common codes of behavior are punished by legal or social reprimands. We also have a common expectation of truthfulness about mundane aspects of identity. When acquaintances tell us what they do for a living, where they're from, and if they are married or have children, we generally accept their account without suspecting fabrication. We base our interactions with one another on the assumption that information about biographies and everyday events are fairly accurate representations of people's experience even if each person has a slightly different interpretation. It is disturbing to discover falsifications in self-presentations. It is particularly upsetting to learn that close friends or intimate partners distort, exaggerate, or misrepresent their past and current activities.

Women who survive intimate terrorism often describe ways in which abusers manipulate their perceptions of events ranging from routine, everyday occurrences to entire biographies. At the everyday level, women talk about "mind games" that involve challenges to memory and perceptions that undermine women's confidence in their abilities to know what is real. Often, this manipulation involves ways that violent or abusive events are recalled and represented. Abusers tell women that they were not pushed down, they fell. Their bruises are not from being hit, but from bumping themselves as they tried to move away. Subtly and gradually, women begin to doubt that their physical experiences provide reliable sources of knowledge about their world. Recollecting verbal exchanges and feelings is also complicated by an abusive partner's revisions of events. Abusive men attempt to place all blame for problems on the woman, which often involves accusations of behavior that never occurred, particularly false accusations of infidelity. Some men also create false identities and biographies. Discovery that one's intimate partner has fabricated the details of his life or has violated basic shared understandings creates a strong sense of betrayal and a feeling that one is living in an unpredictable and dangerous world. As Belinda said, "There is reason to be frightened."

In this chapter, I focus on women's negotiation of surreality and how this nightmare state contributed to their crimes. Women described the loss of confident belief in what they thought was safe, sure, and true. The sense of unreality that developed in many relationships also influenced the memories women constructed of crimes. All of the women indicated some sense of confusion and betrayal by their partner's actions. Only some women, however, described the devastating and terrifying experience of having their basic views of the world turned upside down. Eleven of the forty-five women (24 percent) described how their partners spun tales of superhuman powers, conspiracies, or spiritual connections that undermined their own ability to know what was "really going on," and to act on their own free will. Three of these women killed their abusive partners, and the others participated in crimes against others at the direction of their abusers. Two of the women who killed their partners, Doreen and Anne, were placed on probation. The other women served prison sentences ranging from two years for purchasing marijuana to life for first-degree murder.

Physical assault by an intimate partner is a startling, visceral betrayal of a sense of shared communication. The belief that you are in a loving relationship with someone who cares about your well-being is shaken when that person physically assaults you. Belinda's faith in a fundamental shared reality among human beings was shattered by her experience of being violently raped by a man she believed loved her. Her trust in basic human goodness that allowed her to form relationships and feel safe in the world was obliterated. She believed there are "a lot of twisted people" who have no qualms about inflicting pain and suffering on others, even those to whom they have declared their love. Physical brutality is only one dimension of the process of destroying a person's faith in the reliability of their perceptions and, as discussed in chapter 1, is supplemental to the more painful and common experience of emotional and mental abuse. For some women, violations of shared assumptions are mundane, such as broken promises and widely varying expectations. Most women in abusive relationships report their partner's lack of interest in their thoughts and dreams or in sharing domestic tasks and projects. In other words, abusive relationships are usually one-sided, with the abusive partner making decisions and assuming the rest of the family will comply.[3] It is also very common for men to accuse women of flirtations and affairs that have no basis in women's actual behavior or desires. Breaches of shared assumptions and disrespect for a partner's opinions are destructive to intimacy and problematic in any relationship, but are not cataclysmic disruptions of women's trust and security. They may, however, form the background for more dramatic violations of shared meaning as the relationship progresses. The process of moving from the mundane to the fantastic is mediated by violence, threats, and fear; it is not simply a matter of differing perceptions but of a violent imposition of one person's perceptions on the other. Women lose their sense of knowing what to expect. Jennifer described this as feeling like "I wasn't really anywhere" and Chris said it was like "living in the Twilight Zone."

Women's ability to negotiate the surreality of violent relationships reflects personal biographies and resources. For women with histories of betrayal and abuse from multiple caregivers, violent behavior and mental manipulation by an intimate partner may be experienced as a continuation of normal instability. In the next chapter, I examine the relationship between childhood and adult experiences of abuse. The sense that the world is a safe, secure, and loving place is not shared equally by all women who encounter intimate partner violence. The past shapes expectations and reactions to the present. Also, women whose worldview is shaped by their own mental illness or drug or alcohol abuse face more complicated obstacles in dealing with the delusions and fabrications of partners, as will be discussed below.

For all women whose partners created alternative versions of reality, however, it was difficult to establish a solid sense of truth. Men's claims of superhuman powers, links with secret agencies, imaginary persecutors, and fabricated identities challenged women's abilities to separate fact from fantasy. Both fact and fantasy are social constructs that allow people to live together with a semblance of predictability and safety, as well as pleasure in creating stories and dreams. It is hard to know whom and what to believe when a family member or intimate partner routinely violates the boundaries between these constructs.

The Social Context of "Truth"

Individual-level constructions of facts take place within a larger social context that includes historically developed ideas of what "really happened." All cultures have repertoires of stories that describe origins, values, and current status within the world. These stories tend to legitimate reigning power structures and the organization of social life. In the United States, there is a dominant story about the founding of a nation by people in search of freedom who were dedicated to the principles of liberal democracy. According to this story, military aggression by the U.S. government has been and continues to be determined by these principles and dedicated to the spread of democracy and freedom globally.

At the same time, there are many counterstories that describe ways that the U.S. government has violated these principles domestically and abroad, in the past and today. The genocide committed against Native peoples that continues into the twenty-first century, slavery that was transformed to institutionalized racism, extensive corporate and political corruption, and foreign intervention to secure economic benefits challenge the stories about "what really happened" and continues to happen.[4] In 2005, the basis for war in Iraq and the torture of prisoners at Abu Ghraib and Guantanamo Bay were sites of debate about the "truth." Memoranda between high-level officials and photographs of torture provide documentary evidence that the war in Iraq was not about preventing Saddam Hussein from developing weapons of mass destruction. They also provide evidence of torture that violates international human rights law and the high-level authorization of these techniques.[5] Despite all this evidence, George W. Bush, Tony Blair, and Donald Rumsfeld continue to maintain that the war was a response to information about weapons of mass destruction, and that incidents of torture were the result of a few "bad apples" rather than official policy. People in the United States and Great Britain must struggle with how to decide the "truth" about their government's actions in the face of official statements that boldly contradict documentary evidence.

For marginalized groups, the discrepancy between official statements and the behavior of government officials is nothing new. Discrepancy is the social context in which many people have had to negotiate their relationship to dominant cultural stories.[6] In the contemporary context, not only marginalized and disenfranchised groups, but large segments of the population now face a contradiction between the "official story" and all the eyewitness, textual, and photographic information about what is "really going on." This context is one in which appeals to the truth, and to "knowing better" than to follow illegitimate or illegal orders of an authority, are particularly problematic. At the social level, many people seem unable to respond to the situation of political actions that are discordant with cultural stories of freedom and democracy. Yet at the individual level, where there is much more direct pressure to accept an abusive partner's views over one's own, women are expected to "know better" and to defy commands that violate their perceptions and moral commitments.

Reality?

My exploration of women's negotiation of surreality is not a philosophical inquiry into the nature of "reality." I do, however, subscribe to the belief that social reality is an accomplishment of human perception and interaction rather than a set of objective "facts." Women who experience intimate partner violence define "reality" within the context of a social world that is terrifying to them because it violates basic expectations about other people and the assumptions by which women order their lives. Deliberate falsifications, delusions, and mental manipulation within an intimate relationship not only undermine trust in the predictability of the world and reliability of one's perceptions; they complicate moral decision making. Knowing right from wrong depends upon knowing truth from lies, fact from fiction. Women who are in abusive situations are isolated from other people who could provide counternarratives to the stories constructed by abusers. When these stories focus on the danger of other people and threats if women disobey, women may be convinced that their own moral compass is misguided and they must follow the course set by the abuser. As Myrna said, "My husband is what you call a persuader. He can practically persuade anybody into doing anything." He was able to persuade this nineteen-year-old woman with no prior criminal involvement that robbing a bank was the best way to get money for their baby. Her own instincts told her this was a stupid and immoral act, but the combination of isolation, physical violence, and constant mental pressure convinced her that he was right.[7]

This persuasion is not that different than the persuasion that occurs at a social level to encourage people to adopt the perspective of those who wield political power. Mass media information is scrutinized and limited to stories that validate the stories told by government officials.[8] Although alternative accounts are available to those who pursue them, the majority of people, isolated by their demanding jobs and families, depend on the mass media for news. Most people do not have direct access to the perspectives of people in other countries because of language, spatial, and information barriers. People also feel insecure because of actual physical assaults, such as the bombings of September 11, 2001, and threatened assaults, such as the now discredited reports of the existence of chemical and biological weapons in Iraq. Isolation and fear, like Myrna's isolation and fear, then persuade people that those in positions of authority, must be obeyed and *should* be obeyed. People who question the statements of the president or the secretary of defense risk being labeled as unpatriotic or even threatening to the security of the country. Because most people are not sure what the "truth" is, and because questioning authority is risky and potentially costly, most people are persuaded to acquiesce to the "official story."

Women who violate the law because of beliefs about their abusive partners are often vilified in the popular press because they "should have known better."[9] When innocent people are injured or killed, we want to be able to assign moral culpability to those who contributed to those losses. It appears that women should be able to separate their own actions from anything their abusive partners tell them. Certainly women vary in terms of their ability to assert themselves against the demands of a partner, both in terms of individual women's reactions in various situations and in differences among women. But resisting the demands of someone who threatens you and your loved ones and who consistently denigrates and denies your own view of reality is not easy.

Women's Agency and Patriarchal Authority

People's capacity to act on the basis of their personal values, beliefs, and goals rests on social arrangements that limit restrictions on freedom and offer a minimum level of subsistence. The basis of a liberal democracy is a political structure that maximizes the possibilities for people to act on their "individual judgment, uncoerced and unindoctrinated, rather than on established authority in determining matters of truth and morality."[10] The high value placed on individual autonomy within liberal democracies correlates with a need for egalitarianism and a legal structure that supports individual rights. Since the founding of the United States, of course, there has been a tension between the ideals of liberal autonomy and egalitariansim and the realities of racism, sexism, and classism. The gradual erosion of legally based inequalities since the mid–nineteenth century has eliminated some of the most glaring legal barriers to egalitarianism. However, the ideological and structural bases for inequality remain.

The term *patriarchy* has fallen into disuse in the domestic violence discourse of the 2000s, and in feminist and gender studies more generally. The idea that we are in a "postfeminist" era where patriarchy no longer exists is embraced across a wide spectrum of political adherents. Among people who endorse the ideals of feminism, there is rejection of totalizing portrayals of patriarchy and the race, class, and sexuality biases of earlier versions of feminism. That is, patriarchy is not viewed as a single, coherent force that gives all men power over all women. Particularly among many young people, the terms "feminism" and "patriarchy" suggest doctrinaire or dogmatic positions on sexuality, appearance, and expression inconsistent with their own playful and subversive explorations.[11] At the other end of the political spectrum, people who yearn for a return to "traditional values" blame feminism for what they view as a disintegration of the moral fabric of the country. Some authors have argued that women have been harmed by feminism and now desire a return to a prefeminist era.[12] There is no question that some aspects of second-wave feminism were essentialist and exclusionary or that many of the traditional barriers to gender equity have fallen. Contemporary feminism is critical of any notion of "woman" that assumes that there is an essential, inherent quality that defines all women in opposition to all men. Postfeminism fails, however, to recognize the many ways that patriarchy continues to influence social life in the twenty-first century.

Patriarchy is a "system of social structures and practices in which men dominate, oppress and exploit women."[13] Many scholars have debated the ways that patriarchy does and does not operate through various systems and social locations.[14] Most agree that patriarchy does not operate monolithically; that is, there are multiple sites of rupture and resistance to patriarchy and there are factors other than gender that shape its manifestations. That does not mean, however, that patriarchy has disappeared and is no longer relevant for analyzing intimate partner violence. Russell Dobash and Rebecca Dobash differentiate between the structure and ideology of patriarchy.[15] The *structure* includes all those hierarchically organized institutions that subordinate or exclude women. The inclusion of token women in powerful positions within institutions, such as secretary of state or CEO of major corporations, does not nullify the overall pattern of male preference. In the 2004 national elections in the United States, women were 15 percent of elected members to Congress, an all-time high.[16] Women are no longer *excluded* from political participation in the United States, but their representation is far below their majority position in the population (51 percent). Women may also hold positions of power yet continue to uphold traditional patriarchal ideology.

The customs and ideas that legitimate male dominance constitute the *ideology* of patriarchy. These ideas include biologistic notions of the proper spheres of activity for each sex and males' inherently greater capacity for leadership; social notions of appropriate family responsibilities; and religious teachings about male and female roles. Traditional patriarchal ideology in culture and religion dictates that men should be the economic providers and authoritative heads of households while women should provide emotional support and domestic service. Patriarchal ideology is also multifaceted and appears differently depending on the culture and circumstances in which it operates. It is present, however, in any culture where it is assumed that men are the natural and appropriate leaders and women their natural, appropriate followers and helpmates.

In spite of the transformation of both patriarchal structure and ideology over the past one hundred years, they continue to inform people's beliefs and actions. Women's agency, their ability to craft life decisions consistent with their "uncoerced, unindoctrinated" beliefs and needs, is enacted within a context of patriarchy. Again, patriarchy is not the only context for enacting agency: transnational capitalism, racism, and homophobia all affect people's agency. Here, however, I am concerned with *women's* agency particularly vis-à-vis their male intimate partners.[17] Women employ multiple strategies of resistance to try to fashion intimate relationships that meet their needs and are consistent with their morality. Women try to respond to partners' requests, seek outside help for themselves and their partners, leave the relationship, make demands on the abuser, and gather resources to change their situations. Their responses, however, are also constrained by structural possibilities and internalized values. When police and courts fail to follow through with help, when income is too meager to establish an independent household, and when employers fire women because their partners are too threatening, the structure of patriarchy limits women's options. The ideology of patriarchy is at work when men expect obedience to their demands and the undivided attention of their wives and children. Similarly, when women accept men's demands for service, focus all their hopes for intimacy on an abusive partner, and protect their partner and themselves from outsiders' condemnations of marital failure they are acting in accord with patriarchal ideology. Their acquiescence may be a strategy for altering their vulnerable position but it reflects, nonetheless, the influence of patriarchal ideology on their relationships. The historical legacies of patriarchal legal structures are relevant for appreciating the contemporary laws that govern women's conduct.

Femme Couverte *and the Doctrine of Coverture*

Legal traditions in the United States were developed from the British Common Law that defined women as legal subordinates to men.[18] For the most part, up until the 1840s, white women's legal status was determined by their fathers and husbands. The doctrine of coverture meant that the legal existence of women was subsumed under that of their husbands in marriage. "Femme couverte" meant the married woman was covered by the man in law. In terms of criminal liability, coverture was presumed to protect women from prosecution when crimes were committed under order of their husbands or even in their husband's presence. According to Friedman, the married woman was "under certain obligations of obedience, affection, and confidence toward her husband. In return for this, the law allows her this indulgence, that, if through constraint of his will she carries her duty of obedience to the excess of doing unlawful acts, she shall not suffer for them criminally."[19] Statutory and case law through the nineteenth century recognized the "duty of obedience" expected of wives and thus excluded certain crimes committed by wives from prosecution. In practice, however, this protection was rarely implemented. Certain crimes, such as infanticide, abortion, and prostitution, were never excused on the basis of coverture, nor were most other crimes. According to one study of Pennsylvania criminal trials, a "woman seemed almost never to be the recipient of leniency because of her alleged legal subservience to her mate."[20]

Although courts rarely extended leniency based on women's "duty of obedience," these laws reflect a generally held belief that it was customary for women to obey their husbands. By the beginning of the twentieth century, courts rejected even superficial adherence to this custom. Instead, courts made explicit reference to the "equality" of modern marriages and made decisions that portrayed earlier notions of coverture as "barbaric." These decisions can be found in cases involving specifically female crimes, such as "scolding," as well as cases of female victimization, such as marital rape and domestic violence.[21] The doctrine of *femme couverte,* or coverture, eroded with the passage of Married Women's Property Acts between 1840 and 1900 and was considered archaic by the 1970s in most areas of law. The formal law now defines women and men as equal with regard to moral and legal responsibility. There are situations, however, in which a person's responsibility for criminal activity may be diminished.

The legal concept of "duress" defines situations in which people commit crimes because of pressure and threats made by others. In many states, duress cannot be claimed as a defense for murder. In some states, in some cases, proof of the existence of duress may reduce the criminal charge or the sentence.[22] The law assumes "free will" on the part of defendants, and only in cases where there is an immediate physical threat can defendants rely on the argument that their free will was overpowered by someone else. For the crime of murder, the courts and legislatures generally have required that people risk their own lives rather than take the life of another person under orders from someone else. Because women in abusive relationships are viewed as voluntarily choosing to be in those relationships, their situation is analogous to people who choose to belong to criminal gangs. They cannot claim duress if they are voluntarily members of a group or relationship known to involve violence.

It could be argued that gang membership is not completely voluntary, as some young people live in communities where gang participation is integral to socialization.[23] It is clear that many women in violent relationships cannot be defined as completely willing, voluntary participants. When a woman believes that she will be killed if she tries to leave, or if her abuser imposes himself in her life regardless of her efforts to separate, their continued relationship is not voluntary. Voluntariness, or choice, is located within the context of the relationship as well as the larger context of people's lives. The larger context is layered, ranging from the sociohistorical conditions structuring a specific location to the microdynamics of a family situation.

The context in which women's agency is played out includes cultural scripts about appropriate female behavior, economic, legal, and political resources, and individual biographies. These are all influenced by women's race/ethnicity, class, sexual orientation, and physical abilities. As discussed in chapter 2, women in marginalized communities face substantial obstacles to reporting intimate partner violence and establishing safety from abuse. Most women in the United States balance decisions about their own lives against the needs of dependent children, and often the needs of dependent elders. For some women, biographies of childhood physical and sexual abuse, neglect and abandonment frame their ability to "know better" than to comply with their abusers' orders. Their experience of being forced to engage in behaviors they fear and hate at the direction of people who are supposed to care for them influences adult reactions to abusive men (as I shall discuss in chapter 4). In order to reject the demands of abusive partners and act on their "free will," women negotiate these structural, relational, and personal contexts.

Mind Games

Women use the term *mind games* to refer to the ways that their partners undermine their confidence in their own perceptions. Florence Rush describes the process through which women's perceptions of sexual abuse are denied and reconceptualized as fantasy as "gaslighting," based on the classic film *Gaslight*.[24] In this film, a criminal (played by Charles Boyer), intentionally tries to drive his wife (played by Ingrid Bergman) mad by tricking her into doubting her own perceptions. When men deny their abuse, or try to convince the woman *she* was the one who was abusive, they encourage women to replace their own views of reality with those of the batterer. Their efforts are often enhanced by the collaboration of other family members and by legal and criminal justice actors who do not believe women's accounts.

As an example of her husband's mind games, Teresita described how her husband tried to provoke a false confession about sexual infidelity from her:

> He will use, what is that called, reverse psychology, basically on me. Like he'll make me believe what he's sayin', when I know it's not right. Like so therefore, say I went to Wal-Mart or something, and I got this and that. And he would be like, "Don't lie to me. I heard that you just talked to this one dude, why are you lying about it?" And I'm like, "what the hell you talking about?" He would be like "Teresita, you didn't just meet no guy at Wal-Mart that you were just talking to?" I'm like, "No, what the hell you talkin' about?" He's like, "Don't lie to me! I just talked to home dude." I'm like, "No, oh my God." Then I'm thinking "Who would I talk to at Wal-Mart?" Like I'm trying to seriously think. He's like, "Come on Teresita, do I have to describe the way he looked?" And I'm like, "So what, you stalkin' me?" He be like, "Don't worry about if I'm stalkin' you, like I said, I got tabs on you!" You know, see, see what I'm sayin'? Then, I'll be like, okay, "What are you talkin' about?" He be like, "See, you fuckin' did, see, you did!" And then I'll get my ass kicked. And I'm thinking, "Oh my God!" Like, and I'm knowing I didn't talk to nobody. And he'll get me to the point, "Oh my God, he's really going to call the dude." He's like "I'm callin' him right." I'm like "No, no, no." And he will just get me and say, "See, you're lying, you're lying about something." I mean that's what he used to use on me, and I used to cry. Like, how is he doing this?

Efforts to distort women's perceptions were usually combined with denigrating comments about women's intelligence and incompetence.[25] Doreen, whose story is described below, was blamed for a tire blowout on a long trip because she wanted to be home in time for Thanksgiving. As discussed in chapter 1, women were punished for serving the wrong food, not serving it fast enough, and/or for some rule infraction they could not understand. Men also demanded that women "take care" of any problems they had: running out of alcohol or drugs, not having enough money, or having their car break down. For example, Phyllis described Billy Bob's expectations that she take care of his problems:

> His truck needed something, and it was like my fault, and he was like, "You better figure this out, or I'll whop your ass," and I was scared of him, and I said I'd do whatever, and I walked all the way to his mother's house, and that was several times, and I had helped him pay off a bunch of his debts and buy this huge big car hauler thing, and it was always runnin' out o' gas, and he'd tell me, "You need to do something, you need to take care of it," and finally it just got so bad, I had no control anymore, no control of my life, or what was goin' on or anything, and I lost my job.

Women who held jobs while they were with abusive partners often lost them or were forced to quit.[26] Beth's boyfriend convinced her that he would pay the bills so she could stay home and take care of her four-year-old son. She wanted to be a stay-at-home mom and was thrilled with the offer. Once she was unemployed and dependent on his income, however, she realized that she was in a vulnerable situation:

> He's very jealous of anyone who looks at me. He'll say, "What the fuck you lookin' at?" He made me quit my job. I didn't realize then but I've had a lot of time to think [in jail]. He made me quit my job. He was like, "I know you've had a really hard time. You've supported [your son] on your own since he was born. You've got a new car payment. Don't worry about that. I'll take care of everything. Why don't you stay home with your kid? Make sure he's ready to go to kindergarten." That was the best thing anyone could have told me. I was like "Okay. I can stay home. I can be a mom. I love to cook. I could do what I wanted to." It was a blessing in disguise, but when I think back to it, it was just weird. It just didn't fit, but at that time I didn't care. I knew that he loved me. He would come home from work and I'd have dinner ready and have candles on the table and all that stuff. I had my hair done. I had my makeup on. He'd walk in the door and he had been drinking and he'd say, "Where the fuck have you been? Why are you dressed?" Not even look any further than me, you know. I was just like, "You're unbelievable."

Meeting the demands of their partners often conflicted with the needs of their employers, and women were fired. As Lloyd documents, women's employment threatens abusive partners' control and they engage in multiple tactics to undermine women's labor force participation: they turn off clock alarms, disable cars, disappear when relied upon to care for children, and harass women at work until they are fired.[27] Women then become more isolated and more economically dependent on their abusers. For women like Phyllis, drug and alcohol abuse also led to unemployment and to a tenuous grasp on "reality."

Drugs, Alcohol, and Mental Illness

Women who have no prior experiences of victimization or current drug or alcohol problems become disoriented when their partners try to convince them that their perceptions are wrong or demonstrate through actions that nothing is safe or certain. The use of illegal drugs, especially crystal methamphetamine and crack cocaine, makes it even more difficult to know what is "real." There is acrimonious debate among those studying and responding to domestic violence about the role of drugs, alcohol, and mental illness in men's use of violence. On the one hand, some argue that although there may be a correlation between drugs, alcohol, or mental illness and the use of violence against an intimate partner, these factors do not *cause* violence.[28] Many people, especially women, who have problems with chemical dependency or mental illness, do not inflict violence on their intimate partners. People who hold this view argue that drugs, alcohol, or mental illness are excuses for individual men's use of violence; when we focus on them, we divert attention from the more structural sources of domestic violence that encourage and justify it. When men are high on drugs or alcohol or experiencing paranoid delusions they usually do not violently attack people randomly, but direct their aggression at people close to them.[29] The choice to beat up their intimate partner rather than their boss or a burly man in a checkout line suggests that men *can* control their violence, even when their judgment is impaired by chemicals. Jacobson and Gottman measured the physiological reactions of couples engaged in heated arguments. They found that one group of men maintained internal calmness in the heat of vicious verbal attacks on their partners. They dubbed these men "cobras" because of their cold, controlled dispositions prior to striking.[30] Their other group of abusers, "pit bulls," did lose control in the sense of having elevated heart and perspiration rates. These men still are in control of where they direct their violence. The notion that men who are abusive to their intimate partners lose control has been rejected by most scholars and practitioners in the field as an excuse that disguises the ways that men deliberately select intimate partners as targets for both physical and emotional abuse.

On the other hand, many people who do clinical work and some who conduct research observe the frequency with which drug and alcohol problems accompany domestic violence; they argue that these problems must also be addressed in order to help families and end violence. The issue of the co-occurrence of chemical dependency and mental illness, or dual diagnosis, among both abusers and victims has also become a topic of increasing concern among service providers.[31] These bureaucratic categories are abstract ways of defining complex experiences for purposes of policy and practice.[32] Here I am interested in how women defined their own and their partners' involvement with drugs and alcohol, their perceptions of mental illness, and how these affected their own abuse and participation in crime.

Of course, intimate partner violence is not limited to families with chemical dependency or mental health problems. This does not mean, however, that these factors are irrelevant to understanding the dynamics of domestic violence, particularly in the more extreme realms of intimate terrorism. Many of the women in this book describe men whose personalities were dramatically altered by addiction to methamphetamine or crack cocaine.[33] Women's reactions to intimate terrorism were also affected by their own drug use, which often developed after the onset of violence in their relationships, either voluntarily or at the insistence of their abusers. Some women described men whose delusions and behaviors seem to fall within the realm of serious mental illness, although most were never diagnosed or treated. It is not possible to think about the ways that intimate terrorism undermined women's sense of self and reality without examining the use of drugs and alcohol and the possibility of mental illness in their partners.

Of the forty-five women in this book, twenty-eight (62 percent) had intimate partners who regularly used illegal drugs, most commonly crack cocaine and/or crystal methamphetamine, sometimes called crank (see appendix D). Fourteen (31 percent) of the women also used crack and/or crystal. Only two women were using these drugs prior to their involvement with their violent partners. Four women described how their partners introduced them to drugs and encouraged them to use. Two women were injected with drugs by their boyfriends. Sarah described her first experience with being "shot up" by one of her many abusive boyfriends:

> I was Jack Daniels drunk, and he stuck a needle in my arm for the first time, and I did that for about six months. And so, I just, I had no veins, I couldn't dance for a living, 'cuz I was too skinny. It was cocaine, and bathtub crank he used to make out of inhalers. Mmmm, lovely stuff. He used to knock me around, I was screwin' everybody, doin' drugs without him and stuff. I don't make a good junkie, okay? First off, I can't watch anybody give me a shot or anything, you know? I never learned.

Women spoke of taking speed to keep up with their partners and to please them. Although some women became addicted and developed a strong desire for the drug, most had initially begun use as a way to deal with a partner's violence and emotional abuse.

Almost all of the men abused alcohol, either in combination with drugs or alone, and twenty-two of the women did so. Defining what drug or alcohol "abuse" means is not straightforward, and what is abuse to one person may be unproblematic consumption for another. Two of the women I interviewed referred to a twelve-pack of beer as "a drink." "Drug abuse" can mean smoking an occasional marijuana cigarette or staying up for two weeks shooting methamphetamine. It is not possible to analyze the connections between drug and alcohol abuse and domestic violence without consideration of the continuum of meaning attributed to substance abuse. The same definitional problems apply to mental illness, as the process of defining someone as "mentally ill" depends on many factors that have nothing to do with a person's perceptions and behaviors.[34] Two of the men were clinically diagnosed as seriously mentally ill, according to their partners, without any use of illegal drugs. Many of the women (nineteen) were taking prescription antidepressant medication at the time I met them, but in all but one case this was in response to depression following their crimes. None of the women were diagnosed with serious mental illness either before or after their crimes.

There are only five cases of the total group in which drugs or alcohol did not play a significant role in the crimes committed. In most cases, high levels of consumption of alcohol and/or drugs influenced men's perceptions and actions in general, not only in terms of their intimate relationships. Women who were addicted to crack or crystal all felt that the drugs had ruined their lives and taken everything from them. Nicole, for example, was in a good marriage and had two young children; she blamed drugs for her divorce and involvement with a violent man:

> I will never touch drugs again. I've been exposed to it in here, and I won't, you know, I'm not takin' drugs again, I hate them, I hate them because of what I went through (crying) you know because you lose your priorities, my priorities weren't my kids, it was drugs, you know. . . . A lot of things he [her boyfriend] said weren't true, and the people get so bizarre when they're on drugs, they really do, and weird things happen, they really do.

I describe Nicole's bizarre experiences in chapter 6, and it does seem that heavy drug use influenced her own and her abuser's crimes. Phyllis also described how drugs affected her behavior. She had never stolen anything, yet, when she became addicted to crack, she started writing bad checks and stealing from her mother.

The effects of drugs, alcohol, and mental illness on people's perceptions vary depending on the person's social location. For example, although paranoid delusions of persecution are common among people who are heavy users of amphetamines, these delusions take different forms and produce different responses among people, particularly along gender lines. Delusions of grandeur or persecution reflect historically and culturally situated ideas about gender, race, and class. Men who were delusional, either due to heavy drug use or mental illness, reflected these ideas in the form of their delusions. White men often thought they were involved in secret conspiracies, had superhuman powers, or were God. None of the American Indian men shared these specific delusions about themselves. Their delusions were more focused on the imagined infidelities of and persecution by their intimate partners and, in one case, their "special powers." Women also abused drugs, but their delusions focused more on their male partner's omnipotence rather than their own powers.

Women's drug usage made it more difficult to critique and reject men's delusional stories, but even women who did not use drugs or alcohol were sometimes drawn into men's fantastic accounts.

The Social Context of Delusions

For both men and women, delusions and reactions to them reflect cultural beliefs. Among Western European people, particularly those with Christian or Jewish backgrounds, there are strong associations among divinity, authority, and masculinity. In these religions, God, Jesus, the prophets, and the patriarchs are males and the Bible and Talmud define men as the legitimate moral authority of families. When men claim divine power within their intimate relationships, women evaluate these claims within this cultural context.[35] Among American Indian cultures, divinity is not limited to masculine figures; in many cases, female figures are viewed as the source of creation. Many spiritual beings do not have a sex, or combine both sexes.[36] American Indian women did not say that their partners thought they were God, and this may reflect the absence of a belief in the superiority of masculine divinity in their cultures. Similarly, positions of authority in political and military organizations in most cultures are generally held by men. Stories involving political or military intrigue, such as being a government spy, invoke these gendered roles and expectations. When men tell their partners that they are God, a vampire, a secret agent, or a renegade gang member, they are drawing on culturally and historically developed myths and scripts that link masculinity with supernatural and political power. Dianne's husband believed he was God and he had chosen her to help him accomplish certain tasks on earth. His beliefs were related to ingestion of hallucinogenic plants:

> When I got back from visiting my family, I went to a friend of mine's house before I even seen anybody, and she said, "Have you seen Ted yet?" I said, "No, why?," and she said, "Well you'll see, somethin's not right," and I said, "What do ya' mean?" and she said he'd been down, livin' on the beach, and eatin' some kinda' jimson weed, or somethin', and he thought he was God, I mean (*starts crying here*), and he really honestly believed he was, and he'd tell me such wild stories that . . . if I'd come down and talk to him, you know, I'd say, "You're on some-

thin'", and he'd say, no he wasn't, that he'd chosen me to do this and that, and so I mean, he wasn't right, you know.

The Academy Award–winning film *A Beautiful Mind* illustrates the influence of gender, race, and class in the development of delusions and people's responses to them. The film is an adaptation of the biography of mathematician John Nash and his wife, Alicia Nash, and their struggles in dealing with John's schizophrenia and hallucinations. In the early years of John's illness, Alicia shared John's belief that he was working for the government in Cold War efforts to break Soviet codes. As a white male intellectual at an elite institution, it is not unthinkable that he could have been participating in these activities. Viewers of the film are also drawn into this illusion, and only gradually become aware that the government man in black and other figures in John's life are hallucinations. Alicia's recognition that her husband is not under surveillance and not working for the government is hindered by the plausibility of his stories and their consistency with his class, gender, and racial locations. The film allows viewers to share in the ambiguity and confusion Alicia experienced when discovering that John's perceptions did not match those of anyone else. Wives of schizophrenics and men who develop elaborate fabricated identities for other reasons, such as drug-induced paranoia and criminal intent, experience these feelings of ambiguity and confusion when their husbands' realities conflict with their own.

Responding to Delusions

Yarrow et al. interviewed wives of schizophrenics about their responses to their husband's mental illness.[37] They analyzed women's coping processes and how women progressed from viewing their husband as a "well man" to a "man who is mentally sick or in need of hospitalization." This research tells the other side of the story of "becoming mentally ill" provided by Szasz, Scheff, Laing, and Smith.[38] The work of these scholars illuminates the social processes that transform people's troubled relationships into psychiatric diagnoses. Their focus is on the nexus between people's lived experiences and professional discourses of mental illness. Yarrow et al. and I emphasize how women respond to behavior that contradicts their own perceptions of the world around them. The appearance of delusions and unusual behavior is threatening to a relationship, and women attempt to normalize, minimize, and balance acceptable with unacceptable behavior, and deny that the behavior is a problem. Yarrow et al. recount behavior by husbands that is bizarre and threatening, including physical assaults. In the mid-1950s context of their research, these assaults were not defined as domestic violence and received no sustained discussion in their analysis of wives' coping strategies. The resistance of women to defining their husbands' behaviors as "mental illness," even when men stopped going to work, heard voices, believed they were victims of extraterrestrial conspiracies, and became violent, illustrates the problematic nature of confronting mental illness in an intimate partner. Even after men were committed to mental hospitals, being shuffled into institutional definitions of "mental illness," one-fifth of the women interviewed still did not define their husbands as "mentally ill." Because so much of everyday life with an intimate partner involves shared and negotiated meanings, women attempt to make sense of unusual and bizarre behavior by making excuses and trying to understand their husbands' actions. Women do not immediately assume that their husband is hallucinating or delusional, but rather frame their behavior as worry or stress and a temporary lapse. These rationalizations are similar to women's reactions to their partners' violence.[39] Women rarely define the first instance of violence as "battering," but instead rationalize violence as not truly harmful, not the man's fault, or a sign that they need their wife's help rather than blame. Making sense of the strange is part of negotiating a relationship. It is complicated by men's use of violence and threats that seriously constrain women's ability to challenge their partners' views and behaviors.

The sense of betrayal engendered by physical violence is usually overcome by an ongoing desire to maintain the relationship and the abusive person's claims that the event was anomalous, would never happen again, was the woman's fault, and other rationalizations. The patterns of men trying to convince women that violence is not a grounds for rejecting the relationship are well documented and familiar.[40] So, this violation of shared communication assumptions is confusing but not usually sufficient to end the relationship. The reasons for this are complex and varied, depending on women's past experiences, their current resources, the overall character of the current relationship, and the level of danger they perceive.[41] However, rarely is the violence itself the only violation of assumptions of honest communication. The kinds of fantastic illusions constructed by abusive men may extend to every aspect of their identities.

Soul Mates and God

The fantastic identities constructed by abusive men are often correlated with supernatural powers and mystical connections to intimate partners. Abusers attempt to convince their partners that they are "soul mates,"destined to be together. The soul mate relationship bestows unparalleled compatibility and symmetry of personalities so that the partners are described as a "perfect fit," "my other half," or "the only one who can really know me." This view of the intimate partner is promoted by modern and contemporary views of romantic love that emphasize both the preordained and complementary halves conception of marriage. Love songs, films, novels and religious imagery normalize the soul mate mythology so that people who refer to their intimate partners as soul mates may be viewed as hopeless romantics, but well within the realm of normalcy. It is the soul mate model, however, upon which obsession is based. Those who stalk and murder partners who try to reject the soul mate paradigm display the extreme consequences that inhere in the logic of lovers who were "meant for each other." Yet the pattern of obsession is not random but is linked to gender. When men commit intimate homicide or homicide/suicide they are motivated most commonly by vengeance for rejection and the belief that "if I can't have her, nobody else will." The same motive is rarely present in female-perpetrated intimate homicides.[42]

For abusive men, the soul mate paradigm is also often accompanied by delusions of grandeur. They convince women that they have supernatural powers of clairvoyance that allow them to know exactly what their partners are thinking at all times. Julia, charged with the kidnap, sexual assault, and robbery of a teenaged girl, asked that I turn off my tape recorder when she talked about her partner, Bobby. She told me that he knew when she had negative thoughts about him, and that she would be in trouble if she said bad things about him to me. Her attorney gave me a photograph of Julia with severe bruising all over her face, inflicted by her partner, and she was facing a twenty-year prison sentence for the crimes he committed, but she told me that she still loved him. Prior to turning off the tape, she described his ability to control people and how she became one of the women he controlled:

> He had a deep spirituality, and there's certain things that he can do. He's really perceptive to people. I remember seeing him with, like, girls surrounding him, and they were all just not doing anything, but just surrounding him, and they would do whatever he said. He'd be like, "Go clean this," and they would do it. "Do this," they would just do it right away. I was like, wow, what the hell is this guy's deal, that he's got all these girls doing everything that he wants them to do? He had an amazing ability to manipulate people, and hypnotize people. Girls would just call him up, wanting to come over and suck his dick, as he would like to put it. I am like, why? How? I am still not seeing the attraction to this guy. But gradually I became one of those people. I don't know how it happened. And he would tell me, too, when I got really deep into the relationship, "I am gonna destroy you, I am gonna destroy you." And I said, "Okay, go ahead."

He also told her that when she disobeyed or hesitated in obeying him that it upset the other people around him, to whom he represented God. Her disobedience disturbed their faith and their relationship with God. His "deep spirituality" and godlike status are obviously at odds with his heavy drug use, and sexual abuse and rape of women, but to Julia, and some of the other women under his sway, Bobby had the "power" to see into their minds and hearts. While both Bobby and Julia were incarcerated, she received letters from some of the girls telling her to "be strong" and remember they were all one big family. The girls encouraged Julia not to testify, to protect Bobby from prosecution. The control he established over other people, male and female, and the portrayal of the people around him as a family is reminiscent of the Manson "family," although fortunately the crimes Bobby and his followers committed were not so heinous as those of the Manson "family."[43]

Chris, charged with counterfeiting, also reported that her husband was surrounded by young girls who obeyed him and had sex with him in exchange for drugs: "One of the businesses [they owned] was video rooms, so there was lots of little teenyboppers and he would have his pick of these girls. Some were as young as twelve. He was also buying the drugs to get to these girls. That gave him some control over them or whatever. I just couldn't understand it." Like Julia, Chris could not understand the apparent power her husband, Rex, had over young women, but was also incapable of escaping his control. Rex was also a methamphetamine addict. His belief that he was being pursued by the Secret Service, the Mafia, and gangs of African American men began with an actual event, but spun into an elaborate conspiracy:

> See, Morgan [co-defendant] got turned in because of an informant. The informant didn't like him, and he told the Secret Service that Rex was involved in it and that's why Rex thought they were following him around. It obviously turned out to be nothing. Anyway, because he was being followed around, he swore up and down they were after him and that they were going to kill him. He knew that they were going to kill me to hurt him. He fabricated a story and a half. That's how I knew he went crazy. Black gangs were involved with it and the Mafia was involved in it and they were after him. He would never leave the house and he wouldn't let me leave the house without a tape recorder in the car. There was nothing on these tapes, but he imagined it. He heard voices on there. I mean, he'd hear a whole conversation on there and he swore up and down that they were after him and somehow they had convinced me to prostitute for them and I was only doing it to save his life. They told me that if I prostituted for them, they wouldn't kill him. The whole thing struck me as absurd. Nothing was going on at all. I was staring at him in disbelief. It was like I was in the Twilight Zone. No amount of talking to him could convince him, even his own parents. At first, you kind of believed him, not everything, but he really thought he stumbled across something. We thought he was really sincere, but once the things started involving tapes that weren't there (*tails off*). We'd watch a video and he'd swear he'd hear some message being sent to him. So he was hallucinating all around. It was scary.

Chris went to a family services agency twice to try to get mental health treatment for Rex, but he threatened to kill her if she continued with the process. Like many abusive men, Rex also blamed Chris for the abuse, even explaining to social workers that her bruises were the result of his efforts to prevent her from hurting herself when *she* went crazy. The most extreme example of this reversal of blame process that I observed occurred in the case of a man who strangled his live-in girlfriend to death. His defense was that she strangled herself with a towel, and her thrashing around while he tried to help her caused the bruises covering her entire body. He was convicted of murder and sentenced to sixteen years for second-degree murder. For Chris, threats by Rex, as well as his refusal to acknowledge his problems, caused her to give up seeking help from agencies or police. Chris's crime was committed with Rex's friend Morgan, after she finally escaped from Rex. Seven years of physical and mental abuse by Rex contributed to the ease with which Morgan established control of Chris and forced her to participate in his counterfeiting scheme (discussed in more detail in chapter 6).

In some cases, men also claim extraordinary powers of healing. Hedda Nussbaum's failure to obtain medical care for her abused, dying daughter was partially based on her faith in Joel Steinberg's magical healing abilities.[44] While these claims sound fantastic from an outsider's perspective, they are woven into the fabric of daily interaction in ways that make them seem plausible. They are demonstrated in minor, but convincing ways that construct men's omniscience and power for the women who love them.

For Anne, not only was her abuser's identity falsified; he also convinced her that her own identity and that of her two children would be obliterated and reconstructed by the secret government agency of which he was an employee. Within a period of a few months, Anne became the captive of her boyfriend whom she eventually shot and killed in self-defense. She was originally charged with first-degree murder but accepted a plea offer to a lesser charge and was placed on probation.

Anne's prior unsatisfactory relationships with men and her current unstable financial and emotional position contributed to her attraction to this apparently kind, stable man. She was working as a bartender, in the process of divorce, and raising a nineteen-year-old-son and six-year-old daughter when she met Bruce. He quickly moved in with her and spun a tale of conspiracy and threats to her life that made it impossible to escape. His version of his biography included that he was a born-again Christian and a minister in the "New Hope" ministries. He said he had recently retired from the Alcohol, Firearms and Tobacco (AFT) agency, where he was an undercover officer. He also told her he had cancer and diabetes. She took him to weekly hospital appointments, but now believes he did not have cancer. Although she had not felt threatened by anyone prior to meeting Bruce, he insisted that it was best that he move in with her "for her own safety." It was difficult to follow Anne's story because of her confusion and crying. When I asked if she could describe what the relationship was like, she said, "It wasn't normal. It just wasn't normal." He was with her "24–7," their phone was disconnected, and he would not let her use pay phones or her pager. When I asked if she was ever out of his sight, she explained: "There was supposedly a hit, he said there was a hit put out on him by this accountant, and at that point, supposedly, twenty-four-hour surveillance had started. And from the beginning he told me like that my house, the phone was bugged and my house was bugged. . . . That's all we talked about twenty-four hours a day, guns and weapons and what was going to happen." Their life revolved around the fantasy that Brian constructed about his relationship with the AFT and their plan to either move her and her children to another country under new identities or kill her and the children:

> He told me some things after he'd been there for a while. He told me more involved things about what he did workwise for AFT, for the government, this type of thing, more involved type thing, and then, the overall relationship, there was an initial break, early on, because there were some things that he did, actions, and he came back and told me that I knew too much, that things that he had told me had basically consummated our relationship forever, that there was no getting out alive, because of the things he told me, that I knew too much. Most of the relationship was, it wasn't a normal relationship. It was like being a hostage or a prisoner type of thing.

He made her quit her job and told her that they were under twenty-four-hour surveillance. Their apartment was bugged, and he would insist that they go to bars to talk where there were no hidden microphones. According to Bruce, the AFT was arranging for their transfer to another country, her name had been changed, and they had been married.

> He said that my son would be drugged, so that he wouldn't know where he was going and wouldn't be able to tell where he was going. That they would come in the middle of the night and do that, and that it would be fast, that Aaron would be scared for a little while until the

drugs took effect and then he said that there would be a month spent here in the U.S. somewhere while they did things to make them forget, not to let them know certain things and to make them think like he was their dad and give us a whole different life, and if I didn't cooperate that they would kill my little girl, if I freaked out, that they would get back to me, and he kept telling me, "Don't lose it, Anne, just don't lose it," that it would just be worse.

Each day, she would dress and go to a bar where she was supposed to meet the agents responsible for her transfer. Day after day she went through this charade and no one ever came. Then Bruce disappeared for three days, and Anne thought that maybe he was going to leave her alone. She went to court and got an injunction against harassment and stayed with her mother.[45] While only her mother was at home, he set their trailer on fire. Her mother escaped and Anne went back to court to report what happened. On her way home, Bruce appeared in a car next to her and ordered her to pull over. For twenty minutes, he threatened her and told her he was going to make her watch him kill her children and would finally kill her. When he got out and came toward her car, she shot him with the gun her estranged husband had given her for protection from Bruce. She drove into a convenience store and asked the clerk to call for help.

Apparent links between law enforcement and her abuser exacerbated Anne's confusion in this situation. After she filed the injunction, Bruce seemed to have copies of the police reports, reciting details he could not have known without these documents. A police officer that took a report for violation of the injunction indicated to Anne that Bruce was well known, worked undercover, and was indeed a dangerous person. At the time we spoke, Anne was still very unclear about who Bruce really was, whom he worked for, and how much of the surveillance he described really existed. Her car had been stolen, her mother's trailer was vandalized and the windows of her brother's truck were shot out. Although Bruce was dead, Anne was still terrified and confused about who was harassing her and her family.

Anne's experience was extreme, but not unique. Five other women said that their abusers told them they were undercover law enforcement agents or linked to violent gangs. The suggestion that men were part of large, covert, violent organizations, legal or illegal, reinforced their demands for isolation, secrecy, and control. As if part of a giant conspiracy plot, women were convinced that they were under constant surveillance, not only by their abusers, but by the men in organizations of which they were part. These capillary networks of patriarchs extended men's reach and ensured women's isolation and entrapment. Women were afraid to use the phone, talk to their friends or relatives, or try to escape. As Anne explained: "It was just survival by that time [at the end], it was just trying to get through days and trying to survive each day and trying to stay alive each day. I found it safer not to talk. I wasn't allowed to say anything or to talk, or I didn't dare talk, I wasn't allowed to talk, I was allowed to answer questions."

Toward the end of Bruce's life, his grandmother told Anne that he had been diagnosed as paranoid schizophrenic. She begged Anne not to let Bruce know her address or phone number. Bruce was not just fabricating lies to scare Anne. He believed he was being followed. Other men developed delusions through excessive use of methamphetamine that led to paranoia, especially when used heavily over several days. Like other forms of delusion, paranoid fantasies may be connected to actual experiences of threat, surveillance, and harm. Men currently engaged in illegal activities and those who had had prior combat experience became paranoid, in part, because of things that had happened to them and their friends. Women involved with drug dealers knew there was a realistic concern over safety, so when men told them they needed to carry guns for protection, that their house was being watched, or their phones tapped, women were not sure how much was true. Some men began to believe their wives or girlfriends were part of the conspiracy against them and the constant criticism that is typical of battering relationships expanded to include accusations that women were trying to "get them."

Like Anne, Doreen shot and killed her husband, Sam, with the gun he gave her to protect herself from "them." Sam's paranoia was drug-induced, and described in a letter his best friend wrote to Doreen's attorney to assist with her defense:

Sam was becoming a very disturbed man. He told me he was having real problems with his employer and financially going downhill. He then turned back to drugs to cope with the situation. He would totally go off the wall on just about everything I tried to say to him. He was getting even farther from reality. I tried to explain to him the emotional and physical stress he was causing his family and, if he did not try to get his act together, he would probably lose his family. He said, no way would Doreen leave him because he took her to the woods one day and said he put a gun to her head and told her if she ever thought of leaving him, he would blow her away. He said she was petrified of him and he had control of her. I could not believe what I was hearing. When we had them over to our home, he verbally abused Doreen to a point where I thought he was about to punch her out. It was that night I realized he did have total control of her and she was deathly afraid of him.

Doreen wrote an account of their "vacation" that described Sam's paranoia and abuse. He used and sold "crank" during the trip, and drove around aimlessly, afraid that people were after them. After staying awake for a week, Sam insisted that Doreen and their two daughters accompany him on a vacation, driving across the country. He made the family sit in the car while he loaded and unloaded things, telling them they were just about ready to leave. Doreen wrote:

He took us all to a local motel one night because he was afraid someone was going to come after him to kill him and our phone was disconnected and he had to leave and he didn't want us to be at risk. He *insisted.* As usual, we weren't out by checkout time and an entire day was wasted before we got back home. At one point, the children sat in the car for two hours with me in there off and on thinking we were going to leave any time. It was another two days or so before we actually left. He got himself so worked up and paranoid that he wanted to hurry and leave. He wouldn't go inside the house unless I stood guard outside with a gun and made sure nobody came around. He was wearing three or four guns on his person and kept his shotgun handy. The man never slept the entire time, although he kept saying he needed to.

Sam also insisted that Doreen carry a gun in her purse for protection. On the night they returned home, he began arguing with her again in their bedroom and again told her he would kill her. She took the gun out of her purse and shot him fatally. Doreen was charged with first-degree murder, but accepted a plea to manslaughter and was placed on probation. She remarried and is living a safe and happy life with her daughters.[46]

Men's paranoid fantasies were even more difficult to unravel and escape for women who had experienced sexual victimization throughout their lives from multiple perpetrators. These women had been told lies about their abusers and the abuse from a young age (described more fully in chapter 4). For all the women, the discontinuity between their expectations and experiences with abusers created confusion. When they tried to describe their relationships and their crimes, they had difficulty piecing things together in a coherent narrative. Their experiences were not coherent, but were fragmented and surreal.

Memories of Abuse

The topic of memory is a contested arena, and there have been acrimonious debates concerning the nature of trauma memories, particularly memories of childhood sexual abuse.[47] As perceptions of current experiences are filtered through socially constructed, historically situated categories, memories also reflect the cultural context of the person remembering. People's memories are colored by their age and gender as well as their unique biographical relationship to events. Even people from very similar situations, such as siblings, recall past events with different tones and emphases.[48] This is especially the case in recollecting traumatic events, such as violence between family members.

Identity is constructed through the process of remembering and telling one's story to a witness. Retelling the past not only represents personal history, but also helps to define who a person is and how she came to be that way. Each time that a memory is shared with another person, the past gains new meaning in the present. Narratives of the past are not a photographic reproduction of what has occurred, but an account that draws upon the full range of people's experiences and capacities. The dichotomy of past and present is a fiction that conceals the mutually constituting nature of our memories of what happened and what we report. People constitute their identities through memories, and people who witness memories become part of this process. In the case of trauma memories, the events do not take complete shape in consciousness until they are recalled and retold. As Dori Laub points out, "[M]assive trauma precludes its registration; the observing and recording mechanisms of the human mind are temporarily knocked out, [they] malfunction. The victim's narrative does indeed begin with someone who testifies to an absence, to an event that has not yet come into existence, in spite of the overwhelming and compelling nature of the reality of its occurrence."[49]

The literature on trauma memories describes gaps concerning events that dramatically challenge a person's sense of reality and identity. Witnessing homicide or other atrocities, experiencing bodily violence, or being forced to commit a violent act are experiences that many people are unable to assimilate to their normal consciousness. The experience of severe trauma threatens people's sense of psychic integrity, of a reliable and safe world. It is common for people to dissociate from a traumatic event so that recollection of details is difficult. The psychological term *dissociation* describes a "defensive disruption in the normally occurring connections among feelings, thoughts, behavior, and memories, consciously or unconsciously invoked in order to reduce psychological distress."[50] While dissociation helps to preserve an individual's psychological identity by "splitting off" the traumatic event, it also interferes with memory. Less dramatic forms of psychological defense also occur with trauma. Active efforts to avoid thinking about traumatic events explain some of the forgetting reported by survivors.[51]

Like other victims of trauma, women did not recall violent incidents with clarity or linearity.[52] The narratives of their abuse were filled with side stories and sometimes explicit efforts to move the story away from abuse. Women spilled soda, asked for cigarette breaks, begged me to answer my telephone, anything to move the conversation away from abuse. Physical violence was interwoven with psychic abuse and women resisted efforts to extract the physical assaults from the ongoing fabric of their relationships. Yet descriptions of specific, discrete incidents were required by police and the courts to document a history of victimization prior to their own offenses. Doreen, for example, was kicked, punched, held at gunpoint, forced out of the car and left stranded on a deserted highway. She was told that she and her daughters would be killed. But in her written account of her relationship, she began with, "Mental abuse was the predominant factor in our relationship. He was into mind games," and she composed five handwritten pages detailing his mental abuse of her. Many women explained that their physical injuries healed, but the psychic injuries remained painful. The nature of psychological abuse is described in detail in chapter 1

Mona, who rejected the label "battered woman" also did not want to remember the physical abuse she suffered. She felt overwhelmed by the memories, and could not remember details or form a coherent timeline. Feelings of shame and sadness also colored her memories because she believed living with an abuser demonstrated that something was wrong with her. When she took her baby to the doctor, he asked how she sustained bruises to her face and throat, and she would not confide in him:

> He knew that my face had been knocked up, but I never looked in the mirror until afterwards so I never knew what it looked like. I just didn't know. *They want me to remember things that I remember part of and I feel stupid because I don't remember some parts of it. I try to make myself remember and I do get flashes of things, but I can't sit down and remember everything. There's so much. There's so much that I don't want to remember.*

I have added emphases to Mona's statements regarding both the difficulty of remembering and her sense that something is wrong with her. Mona conveys the sense that the abuse she suffered was pervasive—"so much"—and much more complex than a discrete battering incident that she could identify with times and dates. There were specific incidents of physical violence, but these merged with the daily experiences of her husband's verbal assaults, economic abuse, infidelity, abandonment, and drug dealing. She "felt stupid" because she could not remember everything that happened.

The inability to remember specific events or to produce a chronologically accurate, linear narrative was distressing to women; they often commented that they felt like they were "nuts," "stupid," or "going crazy." Women often say, "You must think I'm crazy," after telling me their story. For example, Mona's narrative jumps around and she dwells on nonviolent issues, including a lengthy discussion of her wedding night. As an only daughter in an Italian family, she was given a huge wedding and wore a beautiful gown. Her husband never told her she looked pretty. "Maybe he didn't like the dress." He became angry with her and her many relatives, smashed cake in her face, called her a "cunt," and left the reception without her. She laughed when she explained that she drove to the Circle K to buy cigarettes dressed in her wedding gown. Despite this inauspicious beginning, Mona accepted his apologies the next day and moved in with him.

Like many survivors of trauma, unremarkable events triggered memories of the abuse and made her feel like she was going crazy:

> See, I don't know why I get so many things mixed up. I don't know why. That's what's driving me nuts more than anything. I sometimes think I am nuts if I can't remember because the things I remember just pop in my head at the stupidest moments. Like that 9-1-1 show that was on yesterday? All of a sudden I remembered something because of that 9-1-1 music. These things just pop in my head. When you don't have a car, you can't leave. Frankie cracked up my car too and he stole my notary seal. He just did . . . *it doesn't end. It doesn't end.* He had four different accounts. All my money went to his accounts. He never spent it on me or Rosie and I was always working.

Mona believed there was "something wrong" with her for not leaving her husband sooner. The levels of her husband's physical violence, his stalking and threats to take her daughter and to kill Mona, and her own efforts to leave were minimized as she criticized her inability to end the relationship. She blamed herself for her father's injuries (accidentally shot and paralyzed by her husband) because she "didn't leave sooner." Many women conveyed this sense of self-blame and deficiency: "Something is wrong with me." In contrast to the argument that "victim feminism" excuses women for poor choices, women were not content to blame others for their problems. Instead, they struggled to understand why their relationships failed, why their partners were violent, and why they stayed.

Monica also expressed difficulty in reconstructing a serious assault by her boyfriend. She was charged with failure to protect her children from his abuse, and needed to explain her fear of him. She recalled her injuries and a few things that were said, but could "barely remember" the details. While she sat in jail on charges of failure to protect her children, prosecution for his assault of *her* had never gone forward:

> I mean, *I barely remember what happened,* you know, *I remember getting hit in the head several times, I remember him screaming at me, I can't remember what he was saying, he kept hittin' me,* on my

whole left side, they thought my left shoulder was broken, I mean, my whole left side was really, it was really messed up, 'cuz I was trying to defend myself, but I was on the couch, up against the wall, when he was doin' this, he told my daughter to go call my mom to come pick us up, but then he goes, "If you go out that door, I'm gonna kill your mom," I remember hearing him sayin' that. Oh yeah, I'm sure she saw it all, I was screamin' at the top o' my lungs, "Stop it, stop it." He ended up leaving and, after he left, blood was pourin' down the side o' my head, like a water faucet. I ran out next door, I was in tears, I was frantic, I got blood gushin' out the top o' my head, I can't see. The police called forensics out, he had beat me so bad. They took pictures of all this. To this day, I'm waiting, willing to help the state press charges.

Following this event, Monica married her boyfriend. She said that somehow she thought this would make things better. The day after their marriage, they were both arrested. It is extremely difficult for outsiders to understand women's willingness to continue in relationships with men who have caused serious physical injuries; I address this question directly in chapter 5. In the context of their own criminal defense, inability to construct a clear narrative of abuse and the return to an abuser following severe assault undermine women's credibility. Even when the physical abuse is well documented and undisputed, women's allegiance to violent men contrasts with their victimization. People cannot understand continued love for a man who is so dangerous and cruel. Without an appreciation of the consequences of abuse, return to a violent man signals voluntary immersion in a criminal environment and, thus, legal culpability.

Phyllis was eventually convicted of first-degree murder and sentenced to life in prison (her situation is discussed in chapter 6). Photographs taken when she was arrested showed a terrified, battered woman with swollen facial features and hair missing. The image in the photograph looked nothing like the attractive young woman I met approximately six months after her arrest. Medical records, police reports, and witnesses all verified that her husband, Billy Bob, had severely abused her. Yet she continued to be in love with him, returned to him repeatedly, and still loved him after they were both apprehended and awaiting trial. She described a particularly bad beating and her return to Billy Bob:

I woke up I was in [town's name] in his mom's apt. and I was sittin' on a couch and the officer, he started comin' in the door with another officer, and they said, "Phyllis, what's goin' on?" and it's like I just snapped all of a sudden and I looked up, and I was like "how did I get here and whose clothes do I have on?" You know, I didn't know what happened, and he started askin' questions and Billy Bob kept talkin' over me and he just kept tellin' me to shut up and I wouldn't and he said, "Come with me, Phyllis," so he took me outside and Billy Bob come out, of course, and I um, passed out, and I started goin' and they set me down, and he called an ambulance and he handcuffed Billy Bob and everything, he was gonna put him in the car, and Billy Bob started gettin' outa the handcuffs and everything, so they slammed him up with his arms and his feet up together, and they put him back in there, and the ambulance come, and I don't really remember the ambulance ride or anything. And I don't remember nothin' for like two or three days and later I come to on my mom's couch, 'cuz every time I would come to she would pop a pain pill in my mouth and finally I was like "No, wait," and I said, "What am I doin' here and where's Billy Bob?" and she said, "You don't remember what happened?" and I said, "No," she said, "He's in jail," and then it started comin' back to me, you know, and I was like, "Is my car over at Faye's?" his mom's, and she's like, "Yeah," and I said, "Will you take me to get it?" and she says, "No, I sure won't!" so I took off walkin', and I could barely hold my head up, but I walked all the way over there, which was, maybe a mile, you know, walked over there and got my car and drove straight to see him at the, they had him in prison by then.

In spite of her own pain and injuries, she was worried about her assailant/husband, Billy Bob. Her continued allegiance to him eventually put her in the situation where she participated in actions that resulted in the death of two innocent people.

Like a Dream

Survivors of childhood sexual abuse, torture, and rape all refer to a sense of unreality and fragmentation when recollecting their experiences. The sense of unreality, or being in a dream, was mentioned by all women who had participated in violent crimes. For some women who killed, there was a complete blockage of memories, an inability to recall the actual event that resulted in death for their partners, children, or other people. Michelle, a thirty-year-old, low-income American Indian woman, killed her abusive husband by hitting him in the head with a pipe while both were very drunk. She could not remember much about the fatal incident: "He hit me, he missed me, maybe he was too drunk. It's hard to remember. I remember arguing with him. I don't remember if I had that pipe in my hand. I don't remember how I picked it up, or why I picked it up." Michelle's loss of memory was confounded by her alcohol intoxication. But other women who killed their partners or other people without any use of alcohol or drugs also described a blank spot in their memories at the point when fatal injuries were inflicted. This is consistent with other women's accounts of blocking out the memory of killing their partners.[53]

Women who were present when their partners killed someone else described the feeling of being in a dream. Nicole, a forty-year-old, working-class white woman, witnessed two separate murders committed by her boyfriend and is serving a life sentence for the second. In both cases, she felt as if she were watching from above the scene, and used the term "dissociated" to describe her mental state during and after the murders.

> It wasn't real, the whole thing wasn't real, and I just put it back. The whole thing didn't happen. . . . After he killed the second guy, I couldn't function right. They were all so mad at me, because I would just be staring off into nothing, and a couple times I would just sit down and cry. I don't know exactly why, but I couldn't say why he had done it, and I know I was sittin' there talking to [co-defendant] and I was just crying and crying, and a couple times I remember just being outside the shop, and just sittin' there staring, I don't understand why.

Nicole's ability to "just put it back" dated to early childhood when she was sexually molested by an uncle and a stepfather over many years. Because she could not control the abuse, she tried to pretend it was not happening. As an adult who felt trapped with a brutal murderer, she experienced disorientation and depression, but could not come to grips with the reality of what she had seen: "And another thing, too, when I say I would go into a dissociative state, I think it was more or less after the first killing, in order to be there, to live with him, I kind've like put that out of my mind, like it didn't happen, and that's how I was able to function with him, and then when he did it again, and there was so many people around, it was hard, I don't know, I didn't know what I was gonna do." Nicole's failure to report the murders or to escape from the murderer was the basis for the charges of first-degree murder brought against her. Her story is described more fully in chapters 4 and 6.

Extreme physical violence, fantastic stories of superpowers and conspiracies, and the perception of constant surveillance create a netherworld where reality is illusive and safety seems impossible. In this surreal context, women begin to doubt their own perceptions and their ability to distinguish fact and fantasy. Women's use of alcohol or drugs exacerbates the confusion created by partners who are delusional or intentionally manipulative. Negotiating surreality involves the challenge of determining the validity of one's own perceptions in a context of the bizarre and frightening behavior and stories of abusive partners. Memories of abuse and coherent narratives of their experiences are disrupted by the trauma of their own victimization or witnessing violence against others. Women's biographies of childhood victimization contribute to adult perceptions of the untrustworthiness of the people who are supposed to love them as well as their own ability to ascertain truth. In the next chapter, I explore women's childhoods in greater detail and describe the matrix of domination that was the context of their involvement with an abusive intimate partner.

4 ⟿ The Social Reproduction of Women's Pain

The family is a complex environment in which pleasure and pain, sorrow and joy, pride and resentment permeate the atmosphere and affect children as much as specific words and deeds. Pain is socially reproduced by intimate partners and family members in ways both subtle and direct, intentional and unintentional. There may be dramatic instances of violent behavior that stand out in memory, but our experiences in families are richly textured and ethereal. Categorizations of families, such as "dysfunctional," "fragile," or "abusive" fail to capture this complexity. Physical violence is only one component of a plethora of painful social situations localized in the family.

One of the most popular accounts of the causes and consequences of intimate partner abuse is the cycle of violence or intergenerational transmission of abuse model. There is a commonsensical and scientific basis for the widespread belief that childhood abuse leads to adult problems, including violent behavior, increased chances of victimization, drug and alcohol abuse, and criminality.[1] Women's childhood experiences with abuse, neglect, and trauma shape their reactions to abuse as adults. And adult experiences of trauma influence women's perceptions of safety and their trust in themselves and others. What is less obvious and more complicated to unravel is how children's experiences in families are linked to broader social dynamics that transcend the intentions and limitations of individual parents. In this chapter, I explore women's childhood experiences and how they relate to their adult relationships and crimes. I argue that the emotional and physical pain inflicted by family members on children and adults is deeply embedded in complex structures of feeling that are linked to larger social contexts.

Structures of feeling, as articulated by Raymond Williams, are the patterns of emotions, tastes, and desires of a group of people that are formed by the material circumstances of the group.[2] They are subjective feelings that permeate lived experience.[3] This concept mediates between a strictly economic view of subjectivity (i.e., that class position determines personality characteristics), and a psychological or social psychological view that focuses only on individual qualities or interpersonal experiences.

Our standard categories for measuring privilege and disadvantage—race, class, and gender—are relevant for understanding the context of women's pain. They fail to capture, however, the ways that pain transcends specific social locations and permeates lived experience. Social privilege may insulate people from the most damaging aspects of contemporary culture, such as homelessness, rampant street crime, and lack of adequate nutrition and health care. But privilege cannot erase the ways that power is deployed in everyday life, especially within the family. When violent behavior is attributed to the "cycle of violence" or the "intergenerational transmission of abuse," complex structures of feeling are collapsed into discrete, modular units. The ethereality of violent experiences and their influence throughout life cannot be reduced to a modular analysis.[4]

The larger contexts of culture, time, and place influence the manner in which relationships with family members and intimate partners affect us. Physical injuries, sexual abuse, and neglect of basic needs are injuries that result from specific actions or inaction by family members. Other invisible injuries are hidden by their more subtle, ambiguous, and contingent links to the impersonal forces of the economy, culture, and politics. When Chris describes her father as giving her "no encouragement whatsoever"; Michelle explains that "I was mostly lonely by myself"; and Sheila says, "I didn't feel like she loved me," they are describing invisible injuries inflicted by parents. In each case, these parents were consumed with their own problems and did not provide daughters with the attention and affection they craved.

Women's adult pain is linked to their childhoods, but through complicated webs of emotion spun by the circulation of power. Angelic and demonic imagery symbolizes the polarities of this power. Notions of good, angelic women and bad, demonic women disguise the complex links between women's choices and the deployment of power. When daughters feel lonely and unloved and as young women are "swept off their feet" by a violent, abusive man, they align with structures of feeling about romance, masculine power, and overwhelming passion. They are not simply making bad choices or replicating the behavior of their parents. Their desires and efforts to fulfill dreams are shaped by their childhood experiences, and these experiences are infused with power.

The direct and brutal expression of power in acts of physical violence and sexual aggression is visible and startling, and thus easy to identify as a source of pain. In contrast, the structures of feeling are deeply embedded in people's desires. People's needs for recognition, meaning, and connection to others are channeled and restricted by larger social structures, particularly economic and labor structures. The social control of desire cuts across race, class, and gender boundaries and is also influenced by these axes of domination. These boundaries cannot be transformed by parenting classes, batterer intervention programs, or any intervention that focuses solely on individual attitudes and behaviors. Counseling, education, and support groups are important and helpful ways for individuals to improve their lives and change their relationship to others and their communities. Individual-level changes on their own, however, do not alter larger structures of the economy and culture. The social reproduction of women's pain proceeds through structures of feeling about the self, relationships, and the possibilities for creating meaningful, fulfilling lives that are intricately linked to these larger structures.

In this chapter, I critique the popular notion of a cycle of violence and argue that this model is an oversimplification of women's experiences of pain. It fails to link violent acts in families with their social context and subtle structures of feeling. Women's descriptions of childhood illuminate the ways that the qualities of the advanced capitalist economy, the patriarchal culture, and colonization and racism infuse the microlevel interactions in their families. These qualities shape the environments in which men and women enact intimate relationships and parenting. At the same time, parents and partners reproduce the pain of these qualities in their everyday interactions with each other and their children.

The "Cycle of Violence"

What is the impact on children of parental abuse and neglect? Do demonic parents create demonic children? Do abused children become sociopathic violent offenders without remorse for the pain they inflict on others? Or do they become adult victims, seeking out abusive intimate partners? These images are widespread in popular media and advocacy work, as well as scholarly research. "Breaking the cycle" has become the mantra of the anti–violence against women movement, a sound bite to motivate intervention and funding for programs. The depiction of intimate partner violence as a cycle, however, limits our understanding of people's complex lives and fails to capture the pain and struggle that most families experience. The model is individualistic and modular and therefore inadequate for addressing the macrodynamics of power that infuse family life.

The "cycle of violence" model is used descriptively in advocacy and education, and more systematically in social science research. Within the advocacy and education communities, the "cycle of violence" is often invoked as the rationale for intervention: "we must stop the cycle of violence." It is connected with a plea for "prevention" programs, often couched in the homily about pulling babies from the river. Prevention is equated with the wisdom of going upstream to restrain the person throwing the babies into the water rather than rescuing them downstream. Effective prevention would eliminate the problems of responding to intimate partner violence after it occurs. The metaphor is inappropriate because intimate partner violence does not emanate from one identifiable source that, if eliminated, would prevent future violence. Prevention and treatment programs focus on individual attitudes and adjustment. These programs may be positive and helpful but, like drug prevention and treatment programs, they operate at the individual level and cannot address larger structural issues.

Social science research on the cycle of violence is often not specific about the nature or direction of violence being discussed. In some research, experiences of direct victimization are combined with observation of violence, violence against mothers is not differentiated from child abuse, and emotional and physical abuse are included with neglect and with sexual abuse. Some research refers to "intragenerational" cycles of childhood experiences leading to adolescent and then adult problems. Other research describes "intergenerational" cycles of abuse being transmitted from adult perpetrators to child victims who then become adult perpetrators. In public policy and advocacy materials, the cycle of violence is often invoked without clarification of its meaning and components. Academic research examining the "cycle of violence" sometimes delineates these factors carefully, and occasionally employs control groups of people who have not been officially defined as abused.[5] Even with careful attention to forms and frequency of abuse, victimization, and observation, and the use of control groups, "cycle" model research does not provide much information about the context and meaning of people's experiences. It depends on the same assumptions of categorical clarity discussed in chapter 1. That is, the application of cycle models to human experience presumes that there are clear-cut boundaries around experience that allow people to categorize life events so accurately that they can be counted and correlated statistically with other events. From this perspective, it is possible to separate experiences in a dichotomous fashion between abuse/not abuse, criminal/noncriminal, child/adult, sexual/nonsexual and use the resultant "data" to explain future behavior that is also simplistically defined, usually through official records or formal, self-report questionnaires. The idea that "abuse begets abuse" sidesteps the slippery, context-specific definitional processes involved in deciding what counts as abuse and appropriate responses to it.[6]

The cycle of violence holds intuitive appeal and remains a popular explanation despite the paucity of supporting evidence. Even within the discourse of statistics and causality, the percent of the variance explained by childhood abuse is often very small.[7] Yet scholars and advocates frequently report that the "transmission" of violence from generation to generation has been demonstrated empirically and amplify the relevance of parental violence to adult behaviors.

The individualistic focus of the cycle of violence model subordinates political analyses of the family, the society, and the distribution of resources to analyses of pathological behaviors within individual families.[8] It is consistent with the myth that intimate partner violence is a classless phenomenon rooted in the pathologies of individuals rather than the pathologies of the culture.[9] Like individualistic approaches to other social problems, the cycle model segregates "bad" families from "good." Identifying these "bad" (fragile, dysfunctional) families then offers the hope of predicting and controlling behavior so that the problem of intimate partner violence can be controlled without altering the basic arrangement of social resources, responsibilities, and rewards. People's childhood experiences with abuse influence their adult behaviors, often in destructive ways. But extracting specific abusive events from the larger context of people's lives hides the links between individuals and their social contexts.

The women I met worked to eliminate the oppressive aspects of their parents' lives and behaviors toward them. Their efforts to construct meaning and love as adults sometimes reproduced the pain of their childhoods, as they became victims of abuse and perpetrators of crimes. They did not, however, simply model violence or victimization, but confronted the same problems that their parents struggled to overcome: loneliness, overwork, bad relationships, poverty, addictions, illness and death of loved ones.[10]

Memories of Childhood Pain

As mentioned in the introduction, surveys of incarcerated women indicate high levels of prior victimization. Yet identifying and defining childhood abuse depends on how well women recall events from their childhoods. The problem is not only one of accuracy of memory, but of how memories are constituted and valued. As discussed in chapter 3, the topic of memory is a contested arena and there are significant costs to defining childhood experience as abuse. These costs hold true for most people, as Lillian Rubin discovered in her interviews with working-class families. Her interviews uncovered stories of childhoods where the "dominant memories . . . are of pain and deprivation—both material and emotional" but people felt ashamed and guilty about criticizing their parents and minimized their childhood problems.[11] Adults risk alienating family members and undermining their own credibility when they recall childhood pain in opposition to the positive memories of parents and siblings.[12]

When women are facing prosecution for felony charges or serving prison sentences, they need the support of anyone who cares enough about them to give it. For women who still have family members who are involved in their lives, it is not the best time to focus on the childhood abuses inflicted by parents. As Jennifer said, "My life has suddenly gotten too serious" to think about whether her stepfather abused her. She needed both the emotional and financial support he provided as she went through various hearings and served her prison sentence. For some women, support by parents had disappeared long ago (if it ever existed), and they elaborated on the emotional, physical, and sexual abuse they suffered as children. Other women told stories that revealed pain and deprivation, but couched them in terms of a "normal childhood." For these women, the absence of *severe* trauma equates with "normality."

Not every woman went into detail about her childhood. Some interviews, particularly during my first few years of talking to women about crime, focused only on their present circumstances. As I became more aware of the relevance of childhood experiences, I began each interview with a request that women tell me about their childhoods. Six of forty-five women did not provide information about their childhoods. Of the thirty-nine who did, seventeen (43.6 percent) described being abused as children. Sexual assault and abuse were described by twelve women (31 percent). The offenders included strangers, stepfathers, biological fathers, stepbrothers, a biological brother, friends of brothers and stepbrothers, a cousin, boyfriends, a coach, a friend's father, a female babysitter, and an aunt. Most women who experienced sexual abuse reported more than one offender. All women who said they were sexually abused as children were penetrated vaginally. Penetration was with fingers, penises, and objects. Eleven women (28 percent) described physical violence from their caregivers, and six women (15 percent) experienced both physical and sexual abuse. The physical violence included hitting with boards, punching, slapping, and beating up. One woman had her hands pushed down on a hot stove by her mother while her stepfather held her feet. No caregivers were ever punished for the abuse they inflicted on these children, although one was incarcerated for the repeated sexual assault of another daughter. Only four women were removed from parents' care by a protective agency. Four women reported witnessing physical abuse of their mothers by their fathers or stepfather. One woman was left on the side of the road by her mother, and three women were given by their mothers to other relatives. Seven women never met their fathers who abandoned their mothers before they were born or shortly after.

Twenty-two women (56 percent of thirty-nine) said they had not observed violence in their homes or been physically or sexually assaulted prior to their abuse by a boyfriend or husband. Emotional abuse was described by all of the women mentioning childhood abuse, and by two women who did not report any physical or sexual violence. Eight women described extremely close, loving relationships with one or both parents, but two of these had lost one or both parents to death. Other women who did not report violence described homes where their parents were unavailable because of overwork and/or illness.

There is, thus, a range of childhood experiences, from nonabusive, loving families to abandonment and tortuous violence. There is no clear-cut line from childhood to adult abuse that explains how women become entrapped in violent relationships. Several themes do emerge from their stories, however, that suggest the ways that childhood experience influenced their adult lives. These themes include physical, sexual, and emotional abuse and abandonment, but in conjunction with other complex conditions as well. Women's descriptions of childhood loneliness, estrangement, boredom, and sadness illustrate the limitations of a narrow focus on abuse as a precursor to adult victimization.

More than half of the women who discussed their childhoods did not identify childhood abuse as part of their biographies. Some women may have tried to portray a more positive image of their childhood, and some may not have defined as "abuse" behaviors that would be included in formal survey research. All but a few women, however, described childhoods filled with struggle and pain even if they defined this as "normal" or "average."[13] It is this more ethereal childhood experience that is missing from theories that focus on the deficiencies of individual families.

Gender, Race, Class, and the Impact of Childhood Abuse

Analyses of the impact of various forms of neglect and abuse generally do not address gender, race, and class systematically, historically, or politically. Scholars studying the cycle of violence who have paid particular attention to social location do not analyze the *intersections* of various aspects of social identities or their political constructions.[14] That is, groups of abused and nonabused people are compared by gender, or by race, but the manner in which gender and race and other factors combine to influence lives is not evaluated. Few scholars in this field consider the relevance of social class, and its intersections with gender and race, in terms of the official recognition and labeling of abuse, delinquency, and adult offending. Even with matched control groups that represent various racial/ethnic, gender, and class identities, the political context of these factors is almost always absent from analyses.

The fairly consistent report that "abuse begets abuse" does not reflect consideration of the ways that abuse is filtered through gender, race, and class locations. For example, Cathy Spatz Widom found that about 8 percent of abused and neglected girls became chronic violent offenders, nearly three times the rate of nonabused girls.[15] Yet this statistical finding does not help to explain why girls are so much less likely to be arrested for violent offending than boys or why such a small proportion of girls who are victimized become violent themselves. The reasons for women's lower rates of violence compared to men are complicated, and there is debate about the contribution of biological factors to these difference.[16] Unless one adopts a strictly biological view (difficult to sustain in light of the research), there are social and cultural factors that influence the gendered effects of childhood trauma.

These studies also fail to take into consideration the larger cultural context in which abuse, violence, and crime are defined by agencies of social control. As Meda Chesney-Lind has pointed out, the increases in official rates of girls' violent behavior are largely an artifact of changes in statutory definitions and arrest practices.[17] These changes and practices have a different impact on girls in marginal locations than on economically privileged girls. The so-called cycle of violence does not draw public or scholarly attention to the multiple, intersecting factors that shape experiences within families and the behavior of youth.

The categories of gender, race, and class cannot fully explicate the complex, invisible structures of feeling that permeate family life. These axes of domination, however, are important dimensions of life that influence the availability of material and emotional resources within families. Among the women I interviewed, social class played a large part in how childhood was experienced. Forty of forty-five women (89 percent) were from poverty-level or working-class families. Social class influenced the kinds of resources parents could provide to children and the compromises they faced. Most of the women who were sexually abused by males within their childhood households felt that their mothers could not confront the abuser because of the family's economic dependence on him. One woman indicated that the aunt who took her in, and whose son abused her, was the only person available to provide a home and food. Most working-class and low-income women felt that their options for independent living as teenagers were limited to low-waged service work, sex work, or being supported by an intimate partner. Even women who described their parents as loving and supportive were denied opportunities and care because of the long hours and exhaustion of hard-working parents.

Class intersects with gender and race in the matrix of domination that shapes the texture of pain within families.[18] American Indian women described childhood pain that was shaped by the long-term impact of colonization on Indian communities. Native women who had very close, loving relationships with their parents nevertheless moved away from their parents' home and lifestyle. It is difficult for young people to chose a traditional lifestyle in remote areas of the reservation where there are few options for earning money. Moving to reservation towns to find jobs and housing with modern conveniences, women lost daily contact with parents and with traditions that defined and supported family life. Crystal, for example, had a close relationship with her parents before her marriage. Her parents spoke their native language, not English, and lived traditionally, far from any towns. They did not have running water and heated their home with a wood stove. It was difficult to raise children in this manner, to get them to school and social activities. Crystal moved to a reservation town with her husband where she had no help and support from her family. Neither she nor her husband could find regular jobs, so they were always worried about money. Her husband's violence and abuse isolated her from extended family members who could have supported her but were intimidated by his violence. Her tribe's tradition of women's power and matrilineal authority were undermined by the influence of Christian missionaries and European culture. Crystal believed her role in life was to serve her husband. She became entrapped in her violent marriage because of her lack of economic alternatives, her fear, and continuing love for her husband. I describe her story in more detail in chapter 5.

Other American Indian women recounted childhoods filled with the pain of abandonment, neglect, and loneliness. As emphasized elsewhere in this book, such parental failures cannot be attributed solely to "bad" parents. They are manifestations of the social problems resulting from years of federal government policies that undermined the self-sufficiency and sovereignty of American Indian nations.[19] I discuss Michelle's story below as an example of the socially situated pain of American Indian children.

I also interviewed five women who were raised in middle-class homes with many advantages.[20] Four are white and one is African American. Their privileged class locations did not insulate them from the criminal processing system, although all but one had private legal counsel.[21] People assume that private counsel will result in more lenient outcomes for defendants, but that was not the case for these women. Their sentences are not different from the other women: one is serving life for the murder of her husband, one is serving a ten-and-a-half-year sentence for manslaughter of a stranger; one got a three-year sentence plus extended probation for her role in the sexual assault of a stranger; and two received probation, one for manslaughter of her husband and one for aggravated assault against her boyfriend. One of these women, serving time for manslaughter of a stranger, has been denied clemency despite completing her college degree while in prison and having a very clean disciplinary record. Their backgrounds and current resources do seem to equip them to deal with incarceration through obtaining relatively interesting work in prison and continuing self-improvement efforts.[22]

My perceptions of the influence of class on children's experience of intimate partner violence are also informed by my work on custody cases. Middle-class women are much more likely to seek an expert witness to assist in custody battles than are working-class or low-income women. Most women without extensive financial resources cannot even afford basic legal representation in divorce.[23] Free legal services are sometimes available for divorce, although the wait is long, but there is no free legal assistance with custody. In these cases, I see horrific violence and psychological abuse and manipulation of women. I also see, however, the resources available to middle-class women and their children. They employ play therapists, provide private lessons, and take their children on fun vacations. In one case, a woman hired a male coach to provide guidance and a "role model" for an adolescent son. They are able to hire a private attorney, often with financial assistance from parents, and an expert to explain their experiences of abuse. These individual-level resources may not change the structures of feeling generated by the larger culture and by the abuse they witness at home, but they do enhance children's lives. They may also, however, simply be part of the bourgeois focus on developing children's cultural capital discussed below, substituting for the caring involvement of extended family members.[24]

The intersections of race, class, and gender in children's experiences within families cannot be unraveled apart from detailed analyses that consider the particular histories of various groups. As discussed in chapter 2, the term *people of color* disguises the specificities of a diverse range of cultures, often suggesting that the experiences of inner-city African American and Latino communities can be generalized to people with dramatically different histories, cultures, and contemporary experiences, such as American Indian people living on rural reservations. Class and gender also intersect with race, ethnicity, and nation to generate unique problems and opportunities for people.

The Politics and Economics of Childhood in the United States

The concept of childhood is socially and historically mediated.[25] The modern view of childhood as a protected sphere of innocence and dependency emerged among the middle classes in Europe during the seventeenth century. As the modern concept of childhood developed, the middle class separated their children from lower classes in order to prevent "contamination."[26] In the contemporary United States, children are separated according to their parents' wealth and race/ethnicity. The class hierarchy and racial segregation determine the resources available to children in terms of health, education, and the structure of leisure.[27]

Annette Lareau argues that there are distinct forms of child-rearing based on class that have a strong influence on children's life chances. Middle-class parents focus on organized activities to develop children's talents and abilities. Working-class parents adhere to a "natural growth" model that allows children more unstructured, free time but also depends on stricter discipline and expectations of deference to adult authority.[28] Different parenting styles impart differential advantages to children, with middle-class children obtaining the skills for professional and occupational success and working-class children developing strong familial and social networks. Scholars such as Bourgois, Hays, and Kurz who have focused on more marginalized communities, describe how both of these advantages are denied in many families struggling with basic survival.[29] Children in these communities spend a great deal of time alone, are exposed to drugs and violence, and often enter the underground economy as adolescents. Specific experiences of parental abuse occur within this broader context that is structured by shifting economic relationships.

Social class plays a major role in determining the life chances and experiences of children and youth. Social class is the single best predictor of children's health and educational status. For example, low-income children are 1.6 times as likely to die in infancy as children born to families with incomes above poverty level.[30] Health differences related to social class continue through the life span and are intersected by gender, race, and ethnicity. African American men have a life expectancy eleven years shorter than that of white women (sixty-nine years compared to eighty years).[31] With regard to education, the United States is increasingly moving to a tiered system in which wealthy children receive premier educations in private schools and low-income children attend poorly funded, overcrowded, dilapidated schools. Children from the poorest families are six times as likely as children in more affluent families to drop out of school.[32] The structurally determined opportunities for children's good health and quality education influence their experiences throughout life.[33]

The political and social construction of childhood and the resources available to children and parents are essential considerations in understanding how childhood deprivations influence adult lives. The social reproduction of women's pain in families is filtered through the political organization of childhood. Children are deprived of basic care as well as the energetic attention and loving involvement of adults when parents are pushed to the margins of economic and social existence. In this context of deprivation, physical violence is only one aspect of a plethora of socially situated painful experiences that are intergenerational.

Patriarchal Disarray

It has always been a struggle for working-class and low-income men, immigrants, and men of color to succeed in the white, middle-class role of family breadwinner. But the economic transformations of the past twenty years have dramatically reduced the opportunities for men to be the sole provider within their families.[34] Philippe Bourgois refers to the shifts in patriarchal authority and earning power as "patriarchal disarray."[35] Women have not replaced men as primary wage earners in most two-parent families, but for many working-class and low-income families, neither mother nor father can secure the necessary resources on their own. In 2004, both husband and wife worked in about half of married-couple families, and seventy percent of mothers with children under eighteen participated full-time in the labor force.[36] Women of all social classes participate in waged labor at high rates, reflecting both their desire to work and financial need. For working-class and low-income families, men's loss of access to jobs with living wages, and the increase in families' reliance on the wages of women have shifted gendered power relations. It has also contributed to the frustration, depression, and rage that many men express toward their loved ones.[37] The violence that men inflict on their partners and children is, in part, a reaction to the shame and anger men feel when women provide the income that they cannot. This does not excuse their violence; it contextualizes it.[38]

In families in all social classes, the roles of mothers and fathers have been influenced by changes in the economic structure. Middle-class, dual-earner families are harried and overburdened, and spend much of their parenting time transporting children to their various "cultivation" activities. Working-class, dual-earner families are not only exhausted by their waged labor, but constantly worried about their precarious financial situations. Within the lower-income sectors, parents focus energies on survival and protecting children from street crime, drugs, and gangs. But mothers and fathers do not face identical challenges to parenting.

Historically, mothers have borne the greatest responsibility for providing for their children. Although the white, middle-class model conventionally prescribed males as breadwinners and females as caregivers, most women have had to provide both financial and emotional care to their families.[39] Linda Gordon's detailed analyses of the development of social welfare policies provide many examples of the struggles of low-income single mothers to care for their children and the disdain shown to mothers who worked outside the home.[40] The contemporary situation, in which single mothers must struggle to support their children emotionally and financially, is shaped by historically developed economic relationships. During the second half of the twentieth century and into the twenty-first, industrial production has been automated and globalized. The industrial jobs that were the foundation of the working class through the 1960s have been eliminated or transferred to other countries; their replacements are low-waged, service-sector, and part-time jobs without benefits or union protection. Jobs available to those without postsecondary education, such as food service or phone sales, generally neither pay adequate wages to provide the basic needs for a family nor offer benefits. Whether families are headed by one parent or two, those without advanced training and education must work long hours, evenings and weekends, often combining more than one job, to support their children.[41] Because of historical policies of exclusion and oppression, people of color are most adversely affected by these trends in the labor force.[42]

This larger economic and political context is relevant to understanding the impact of violence within families on children and how it influences their adult experiences—the so-called cycle of violence. Economic stress and overwork deprive family members of material and emotional resources to provide nurture and care to their children, their partners, and themselves. Stress and overwork do not *cause* intimate partner violence; they are part of the context in which structures of feeling are generated and material and emotional resources are constricted. In the vast majority of cases, it is mothers who bear the greatest burden of meeting the needs of their children. As one of the divorced mothers in Demie Kurz's research said, "I have no time for friends and no time for myself. I am last on the list."[43]

Many mothers must choose between staying in abusive relationships with men, leaving children home alone while they work, committing minor property or drug crimes, relinquishing custody, or moving into overcrowded and temporary shelters.[44] The harsh economic realities faced by single mothers translate into problems of meeting the physical and emotional needs of their children.[45] As mentioned above, membership in the middle class serves as a buffer, but is no guarantee of security.[46] The social reproduction of pain occurs in homes where mothers' exhaustion, worry, and links with violent men mediates their relationships with daughters. Mothers' boyfriends may provide added income, assistance with transportation, and care of children, but they may also be physically and/or emotionally abusive to mothers and to their children. It is not *only* the experience of physical, sexual, and emotional abuse from mothers' boyfriends or husbands that contributes to the social reproduction of pain. Girls also experience loneliness, isolation, boredom, and lack of guidance from caring adults. Some see their brothers abused; others are brutalized by their brothers. Several women described physical and emotional abuse and neglect by their mothers or female caretakers.

By the time they become teenagers, young women are anxious to get away from home and to find someone who shows them attention and affection. Older men are often eager to provide a refuge that appears more attractive than their homes. If men are also abusive, "hard living," and/or abandon the girls, their alternatives are limited.[47] They do not have a home to return to, an education to obtain a good job; many times they have a child or children to care for. Although they may still be legal "children" themselves, they then become the mother with too little money, too few resources, and too many demands to provide the care their children require. Sometimes, the easy escape and anesthesia offered by alcohol or drugs becomes another obstacle to meeting the demands on them; often, their abusers *insist* that they join them in alcohol or drug use. Women then are in an adult abusive situation similar to that they observed and feared in childhood. They do not model victimization, seek out an abusive partner, or believe that violence is an expression of love. They are reproducing the pain of their mothers through the social matrix of educational, occupational, and relational deficiencies overlaid with the destructive consequences of alcohol and drug abuse.

The experiences of childhood pain described by the women I met are diverse, but revolved around four main themes. The themes that emerged from women's childhood memories include (1) loneliness, loss, and alienation; (2) physical and sexual abuse; (3) parental overwork, exhaustion, and absence; and (4) maternal emotional distance and paternal abandonment.

Loneliness and Women's Relationships with Parents

A common theme in all the women's stories was their father's physical and/or emotional absence and a loss of their mother's care, through her overwork, physical or mental disability, substance abuse, or death. As the literature on childhood sexual abuse describes, most women were more judgmental and angry toward their mothers than toward the men who actually abused them as children or as adults.[48] Some women were appreciative of their parents' efforts, but still described their relationships with their mothers as distant and cold. Most women did not blame their mothers, but could not turn to them when their relationships became frightening and difficult.

Dianne represents the dilemmas faced by the children of working-class women even in the absence of abusive men. Dianne's close relationship with the husband she eventually killed was described in chapter 2. The second-youngest of seven children in a white, working-class home, she took care of her father when she was twelve and thirteen while he was dying of cancer. She did not blame her mother for lack of emotional support but simply said they were "not very close." Dianne explained:

DIANNE: My dad's been dead since I was thirteen. He was back there (Pennsylvania) when we moved out to New Mexico and they found out he had cancer, so in several months, I moved back there with him, and they didn't expect him to live for more than a year, and he lived for two or three years. . . . He was kinda goin' senile, and at that time I didn't know that he was in a lot of pain, but he was.

KATHLEEN: And you had to take care of him?

DIANNE: Not really. He made sure we was takin' good care of.

KATHLEEN: He took care of you, you felt like—.

DIANNE: Oh, yeah.

KATHLEEN: Were you pretty close to your dad?

DIANNE: Yup, I loved my father very much.

KATHLEEN: How about your mom? Do you get along with her?

DIANNE: Oh, I get along with her fine, I'm just not that close. I mean, I love my mother and everything, but, she worries so much about everything.

KATHLEEN: I'll bet. I'll bet she's worried about you. Okay, so you had a pretty close relationship with both of your parents?

DIANNE: Mmhmm, yeah. My mother was always workin' her tail off just to support us seven kids, so I really didn't see that much of her.

KATHLEEN: You never had children?

DIANNE: No . . . I'm glad I didn't now.

KATHLEEN: Yeah, in a way, at least you don't have to worry about that right now. Concentrate on yourself. Are you workin' right now?

DIANNE: (*Laughs.*) Yeah, I'm workin' my tail off. I work hard every day [cleaning homes].

Dianne did not describe any abuse in her childhood, and felt very close to her father until he died. Nothing in her childhood led her to expect violence from her intimate partner, to view it as inevitable or as a demonstration of love, and that is not how she described her relationship. She was with her abusive husband for six years before she killed him in self-defense. They lived in small towns, far away from any family support, and Dianne was not able to turn to her family about the abuse. Her distant relationship with her mother was shaped by their class locations, in which her mother "worked her tail off" to support seven children. She saw very little of her mother when they lived together, and Dianne moved away at age twelve. Typical of low-income families, a young daughter was assigned to care for a dying parent and younger siblings as her mother worked to support the family. In no case did women describe brothers taking any responsibility for parental or sibling care. Dianne also describes *herself* as "workin' my tail off," and is glad that she had no children to suffer through the consequences of her husband's death and her murder charges. She was worried about missing work to attend court hearings, as she depended on each day's pay. Dianne's life circumstances reproduced the social location of her mother, both working long, hard hours for basic survival. Dianne's father was loving and she felt very close to him, but his death left Dianne on her own. Her husband did not ease the burdens of her economic location, but did provide the friendship and love she felt her parents could not provide due to early death and overwork. Unfortunately, this love was accompanied by extreme violence and jealousy that eventually led Dianne to shoot him in self-defense.

Richard Sennett and Jonathan Cobb developed the concept of "the hidden injuries of class" based on their interviews with working-class men about their family experiences.[49] A separate analysis of interviews with women was planned but never completed. The work of Lillian Rubin, Beverly Skeggs, Carolyn Steedman, Michelle Tea, and Janet Zandy offers insight into working-class women's experiences of class and explores the relationships between class relations, identity, and structures of feeling.[50] The injuries described by these authors are hidden because they lie in structures of feeling about self and the world, rather than officially identifiable and codable behaviors, such as delinquency or crime.

The model developed by Sennett and Cobb did not address gender, but it is useful for examining how parents' position in the class hierarchy affects their relationships with children and their children's perceptions of the social world. Their analysis demonstrates how personal pain may be passed from father to child through the structures of class relationships rather than the personal pathologies or deficiencies of parents. They uncovered injuries of class that were based on people's relationships to labor and economics, and the psychological wounds of class society. The working-class men they interviewed felt ambivalence toward social class mobility and toward their children. These men sacrificed their time, energy, and personal desires to provide the material resources their children required to become educated and "cultured" in the sense of acquiring the habits of the middle class. They wanted their children to be "upwardly mobile" and have better lives than their own, but they knew that such mobility would leave them behind. They expected their children to show respect and gratitude for their sacrifices, but they were often repaid with rebellion and disdain.

Children viewed their fathers' sacrifices as motivated by a desire to control them, more than a selfless expression of love. When children did move into middle-class professions, fathers felt uncomfortable in the presence of their children's colleagues and friends. Their children's success was a mixed blessing, as the "culture" they obtained was foreign to their fathers. Men viewed middle-class professional work as somewhat of a scam rather than real work. They wanted the benefits of this scam for their children—especially their sons—but knew that participation in the scam involved disrespect for their own work and values. Their good intentions toward their children were thus complicated by their social class positions. Sennett and Cobb referred to the emotional distress caused by this ambivalent relationship as one of "the hidden injuries of class." These hidden injuries serve as psychological motivation for men to continue their roles in production and consumption as a way of healing a "doubt about the self." Their analysis is summarized in the following passage:

> Class society takes away from all the people within it the feeling of secure dignity in the eyes of others and of themselves. It does so in two ways: first, by the images it projects of why people belong to high or low classes—class presented as the ultimate outcome of personal ability; second, by the definition the society makes of the actions to be taken by people of any class to validate their dignity—legitimizations of self which do not, cannot work and so reinforce the original anxiety. . . . *the psychological motivation instilled by a class society is to heal a doubt about the self rather than create more power over things and other persons in the outer world.*[51]

In a class society, the binary categories of angels and demons are articulated through personal ability. Those who succeed in achieving middle- or upper-class status are on the side of the angels, having demonstrated their ability, sobriety, and hard work. People who live in poverty are demonized as having cultural and behavioral deficits. Even people who succeed in the class competition, however, struggle with anxiety that can never be fully resolved about their worth. Sennett and Cobb's analysis helps explain why men spend most of their time laboring for others at jobs that are unfulfilling in order to consume products that they have no time to enjoy, and that are quickly replaced by new needs. They are attempting to secure a lost sense of dignity through socially prescribed consumption.

Diagnosing psychological motivations is a complicated business, and the either/or terms in which Sennett and Cobb framed their analysis obscure the ways in which efforts to "heal a doubt about the self" are linked with, rather than opposed to, efforts to "create more power over things and other persons." People who use psychological, physical, and sexual violence against the people who love them are exercising power over them. Many of these abusive people have deep doubts about themselves and are dependent on the people they abuse for a sense of mastery and power.[52] The concept of "hidden injuries" helps draw attention to the psychological pain inflicted by class society. These injuries, however, are compensated not only through work and consumption patterns, but also through interactions with others, particularly within the family.

The pain that is passed from mother to daughter reflects the hidden injuries of class through structures of feeling that include loss, exclusion, and resentment for desires left unfulfilled. Mothers' experiences of the world of work and of relationships as difficult, disappointing, and dangerous are communicated to daughters through the tone in their households, the stories they tell, and the advice that they give. All but one of the women in this book remained within the same lifestyle and social class as their mothers. Many felt pity for their fathers and resentment toward mothers who were unable to offer the kind of support for which they yearned. A hidden injury of class society that is often overlooked is boredom.

Bored beyond Belief

In 1963, Betty Friedan published *The Feminine Mystique* and identified the malaise of housewives who were devoting themselves to domesticity. She referred to this malaise as "the problem that has no name."[53] Friedan's work resonated with the experiences of many women and was a significant catalyst in the emerging women's liberation movement. Since its early success, however, Friedan's work has been criticized for its middle-class bias and failure to recognize the travails of working-class and poor women who could not afford the luxury of being stay-at-home moms.[54] But boredom knows no class, race, or gender limits. Many of the women in this book stayed at home with young children and did not work outside the home, or only worked part-time, even though their partners made little or no money. Eighteen women (40 percent) did not have jobs. Of the American Indian couples, two men held paying jobs and only one woman worked outside the home, cleaning houses for other people. This is reflective of the high levels of unemployment on the reservations.[55] Other women worked as waitresses, bartenders, exotic dancers, or maids. Several women had jobs they enjoyed: a hairdresser, medical technician, nurse, and electronics processor.[56] But these women were the exception. Most of the women who worked held service-sector jobs with few or no benefits and little opportunity for promotion or skill development. Even these jobs provided some sense of purpose and connection to the world outside their relationships. Danielle's husband earned a middle-class income in his job as a car salesman, but she had worked throughout their marriage whenever finances became tight. She described how her husband, Tony, would make her quit whenever she started to find success in a job: "My oldest was a baby and I hated to go to work, I mean she was a *baby* baby, but we needed the money. Then right after we got up on our feet, I had to quit. With Tony, any time I got to working someplace where I started improving, I had to quit. I don't know if he was afraid, I don't know what it was, I really don't. Every time I'd start to be a success at something, I had to stop it."

Danielle became extremely bored once her children were all in school. Her husband did not like her to work, but she eventually took a job at Wal-Mart that she did well at and enjoyed. She described taking the job because she was bored: "It's just like, I didn't have anything to do. You can only clean so much and there's nobody home to get anything dirty and now, or after the kids were in school, I'm sitting there going—(silence, rolls eyes, and drums fingers on table)." Her husband always told her she was stupid and did not know what was going on in the world, but at work she found that her opinions were solicited and valued. It irritated Tony when her boss called her at home for information, and she tried to explain that it was not for romantic purposes, but for work-related communication: "He [her boss] respects me as a person. He respects my opinion when it comes to business. And he [Tony] just couldn't or wouldn't accept the fact that somebody respected what I had to say." Unfortunately, Danielle's success at Wal-Mart was later used by the prosecution in her trial to argue that she could not have been a battered woman because she was assertive with customers at work.[57]

Some women discussed the value of having an identity outside the home and apart from the batterer's negative definitions. Yet these jobs provided neither the economic resources nor the personal satisfaction that would constitute a "career."[58] That is, some women found low-wage work rewarding, and they depended on it for their own and their children's survival. But it was not work that engaged their passions and creativity. Only three women talked about their educations and work as important, enriching experiences that they wanted to further if and when they escaped the criminal processing system. The rest of the women focused on romantic relationships, religion, or drugs and alcohol to escape the boredom and tedium of their lives.

Five women left adult intimate relationships with nonviolent men that they found boring. Women said the men were "too nice," or that they "just couldn't see spending the rest of my life with him." In part, their boredom was due to marrying at a very early age to get away from home, then later realizing that they had never had an opportunity to have fun and be independent. Lisa was married at seventeen after dropping out of school in eleventh grade. She was the middle child in a working-class Latino family of seventeen children. They lived in a small town in rural Oklahoma, and she described her childhood as "average": no big traumas, but obviously no big opportunities either. She was married to her first husband for fourteen years and they had two children. They got along well; there were no problems, and he was supportive of her during her trial for attempted murder of her second, very abusive husband. I was able to meet him at her sentencing hearing that he attended for moral support. When I asked why she left her first marriage, she replied: "Well, 'cuz I felt like I didn't get to date, and I wanted to get my own place, and I did get my own place, and I had my own car, and my own job and I just wanted to be single for a while. And then I met Brian [second husband] and then—(sighs, shakes head)." Instead of being single and enjoying some freedom, Lisa had three more children with Brian and suffered the extreme physical and emotional abuse described in chapter 1.

Phyllis also left a nonviolent husband whom she described as an alcoholic and a workaholic:

> If he had any free time, he was workin' on an engine somewhere at somebody's house, and I worked too all week long, and I wanted my family with me on the weekends. And I was just gettin' aggravated because he would go do his thing, my kids would go do their thing and here I am watchin' movies and barbecuing by myself and I thought, you know what, I'm gonna go look up some of my old friends, and that's when I ran into Billy Bob (her co-defendant). I know we always loved each other, but we shoulda loved each other from afar. We both talked about it, and it was just selfish to get back together again, we just hurt too many people and it ended up hurtin' us in the end.

Billy Bob was the man who beat Phyllis into unconsciousness (described in chapter 1), and her co-defendant in the murder of a camper. If she had not reunited with Billy Bob, it is extremely unlikely that Phyllis would be spending the rest of her life in prison for murder.

Marriage as the Way Out

Almost all of the women in this book married or became intimately involved with men as a way out of their parents' homes. Some were married with a child by the time they were sixteen. Young women in working-class and low-income families often view marriage as the only route to independence from their natal families.[59] Even the women who did not get married legally moved in with boyfriends and had babies at a young age to get away from their parents. Danielle regretted her decision to drop out of high school and marry at sixteen. I also interviewed her father who confirmed that they tried to talk her into waiting, but she would not be deterred:

> I mean I totally look back now and see that I got married too young, but at the time nobody could have convinced me otherwise. I think I had my mind set, I wanted to get out of the situation I was in, and I look back now, and I was perfect for Tony because he wanted to get somebody that didn't know anything and groom them to be the kind of wife he wanted them to be, and I was a willing participant. Because he wanted something, and I wanted something, and (*claps hands*) it just came together, and after the kids, that's why I stayed.

Like other women discussed below, Danielle did not have a close relationship with her divorced mother and wanted to get away from her. Danielle's mother introduced her to Tony and encouraged their relationship because Tony was financially stable.

Women who grew up in extreme poverty with little parental involvement married or moved in with a man as soon as they were old enough. Leah, an American Indian woman, was abandoned by her mother when she was two years old and was placed with her grandmother. Her grandmother could not take care of her, and she was sent to boarding school. Her school records indicate that she was a "promising young lady," but they expelled her for sniffing glue when she was fifteen. She was sent to live with her mother who had remarried and begun a new family. Obviously, Leah did not feel close to this woman who had abandoned her as a baby, and she took the first opportunity to move out. She became pregnant at sixteen and moved in with her boyfriend, the man who beat and abused her for twelve years before she killed him.

But poverty and abandonment were not the only contexts in which women dropped out of school and married at young ages. Phyllis described her childhood as very happy and loving. She is a white woman, raised in a small, southern town where poverty was the norm. Her mother devoted herself to her three children and her father was a stable, caring man who worked delivering bread. Phyllis said she loved school as a child, and math was her favorite subject. Nevertheless, she dropped out at age fifteen and got married to her first of four husbands. She was only thirty-two when we met and she was on trial for first degree murder:

KATHLEEN: Okay, so then you dropped out of school when you were fifteen?
PHYLLIS: Yeah, I got married and moved to Oakdale, and we kinda went back and forth, and I was gonna go to a private school and I started working so I could pay for it, and he was into drugs really heavy, and he played electric guitar in a little rock band, and he would get my money and go spend it on pot and stuff when I was workin', and I was still real young, I was just stupid lettin' him, and then I would leave him, we'd get in an argument or somethin', I'd leave him and go back home, and then he'd come there and then we'd get in an argument and he'd go back, or he'd talk me into goin' back, and it was just a back and forth thing for like about three years, and in that time period when we were split up one time, is when I met Billy Bob. That's my husband now [and co-defendant], and the first time, I was like maybe about sixteen, and that's when I met him and we dated for close to a year. I was still married to Randy, I kinda held onto that marriage thing 'cuz that way I couldn't get married again (*laughs*).

Phyllis knew that marriage was probably not the best decision for her, particularly marriage to the violent and destructive Billy Bob. Nevertheless, she married and divorced one man after another, and had two children.

It was often an experience of sexual abuse or assault, at home or by a stranger, that preceded a young woman's pregnancy and decision to leave home. Teresita, a working-class Latina, was close to her parents and loved school, but she was raped by a stranger when she was fourteen. The rape was reported but never prosecuted, and Teresita did not receive any counseling to deal with her assault. The following year, she fell in love with Primo, as described in chapter 1, and dropped out of school. She wanted to be part of the "cool crowd" he belonged to: "Yep, yep, I dropped out of school. I was just trying to follow the crowd, 'cuz the people at that time were cool that he hanged with. So I tried being with that little crowd, I tried to be a little grown up. It didn't all work out." Teresita had five children, including a set of twins, by the time she was twenty. She and Primo were both addicted to crystal meth and Primo spent his days using and dealing, seeing other women, and playing video games. It was not the "cool" world that Teresita was looking for when she moved in with him, but she was trapped by his violence and the need to care for five small children. I discuss her situation more fully in chapter 6.

Girls who were sexually abused within their own homes were even more likely to become pregnant and move out as soon as possible. Ronnie, a middle-class, African American woman, was sexually abused by her biological father from age four to twelve, and then raped by a stranger at age fourteen. Her father was a highly respected professional and activist in the civil rights movement, and Ronnie did not think anyone would believe what he was doing. He also threatened to harm her, her sisters, and her mother if she told, so she remained silent. Like Teresita, she did not receive counseling and she told me that her mother did not believe she was raped. She accused Ronnie of fabricating the rape to cover up her sexual activity. In fact, Ronnie was attacked from behind by a stranger on her way to school and had a concussion from having her head banged against the sidewalk. Like so many women in this book, Ronnie was also the caretaker in her family, providing care of her diabetic mother. She finished high school, but married her violent husband when she was seventeen. Ronnie wanted to be a forensic psychologist and completed three years of college before her husband insisted that she drop out and follow him on his move to another state. Her dreams of having a career were submerged in her violent marriage that lasted nineteen years, and she had four children before her husband divorced her. She was working as a mail carrier when I met her, while she was on trial for stabbing her boyfriend.

Sarah's sexual abusers were her stepfather and his sons. It was her mother's instability, demand for care, and emotional abuse, however, that drove her into an early marriage:

My mom was a basket case, and my ex-husband, who I love dearly, still very close, he knew that I needed to get out o' that house. And somehow or other, it had come up about me being molested, or something. And she told him, "Oh, it probably never even happened. She's

just crazy. It's probably just an excuse for actin' the way she does."
And so, he was like nineteen, and he said, "Marry me. I don't care
whether you love me or not, but I want you to be able to get away from
her and be able to grow, have some peace. You can't live like that."
He's a wonderful guy.

Sarah only stayed with this man for a few months before leaving him
for a more exciting life with a motorcycle gang.

Most of the women had been good students and reported that they
loved school. They played sports, took music and dance lessons, and
went to church. I was provided with school records for many women,
and they are filled with comments indicating that as young girls
they were bright, energetic, and eager to learn. Three out of forty-five
women had disciplinary problems in junior high school, including
fights with other girls and using drugs. The other forty-two did not
have problems in school or out, so far as I could tell, and had not been
in trouble with the law. As mentioned in the introduction, for most
women, the serious felonies they were charged with when I met
them were the first crimes of their lives. These women did not fit
the image of violent criminals depicted in works like Jessica Pearson's and Deborah Baskin and Ira Sommers's.[60] They were girls who
were diverted from their educations by a desire to get away from
home, establish independence, and be loved by a man. Their stories
of giving up on school are not that different from the stories of girls
described by Mary Pipher.[61] Pipher's work focused on white, middle-
class adolescent girls, but her finding that adolescent girls lose self-
esteem and begin to fashion their identities to appeal to boys also
applies to the working-class and poor women of all races described
here. For the women in this book, dropping out of school, becoming
pregnant and marrying, or moving in with a boyfriend had disastrous
consequences. In place of the autonomy and love they sought, they
found dependence on a violent, often criminal, man.

Alcohol and Drugs to Heal Hidden Wounds

In the last chapter, I described the ways that alcohol and drugs contributed to the confusion and ambiguity women experienced in their
adult intimate partner relationships. As I indicated, the ways that alcohol and drug abuse are connected to violent behavior against loved

ones are complicated. Neither alcohol nor drugs cause a person to become an abuser. In many families, however, substance abuse exacerbates neglect, emotional abuse, and physical violence.[62] Women who talked about their parents (thirty-nine of forty-five) often spoke about the role of alcohol in their parents' lives. No woman indicated that her parents used illegal drugs. Twelve women (31 percent of those who spoke about their parents) felt that alcohol had played a very negative role in their childhoods. Eight women attributed the physical abuse they suffered as children to parental alcohol abuse, and four women were removed from their mother's custody due to alcohol abuse for at least portions of their childhoods. Parents' alcoholism left them unable to provide love and affection to their daughters, and sometimes resulted in role reversal where women felt they had taken care of their mothers or fathers rather than being cared for. Most of these women described their own involvement with alcohol, beginning at around age twelve to fourteen.

Michelle did not view her childhood as abusive, but spoke of her feelings of loneliness growing up in an alcoholic family, and turning to alcohol herself at age fourteen. She was the youngest of nine children in an impoverished American Indian family, and the only child left living with her alcoholic mother after her father left to live with another woman. Her father died when Michelle was eighteen years old. Michelle had no memory of being held or praised by her mother, or of her mother ever providing guidance or support. She explained how she started skipping school to try to keep her mother from drinking:

MICHELLE: I remember every one of my family were drinkin' when I was growin' up. I didn't like that. I didn't like my family drinking. I was the youngest. If my mother was out there drinkin', I would come home and nobody was home. At times I would be there by myself alone, and I would go to my neighbor's house. I was mostly lonely by myself. Because my older brothers and sisters were startin' their own family, or out drinkin', my mom was out drinkin', my dad was out livin' with another woman. So, mostly, growin' up I was mostly by myself. My sister and my aunt used to take care of us sometimes. She would be there to cook for us.

KATHLEEN: And then you came down here [Phoenix] to go to school?

MICHELLE: Yeah. In the first year I came down here, I was suspended. I started drinkin'.

KATHLEEN: Is that when you first started drinkin'?

MICHELLE: Yeah. Whenever they went out drinkin, I drank with them. At times I would think, "I don't wanna' do this, I don't wanna' drink anymore." They tried to stop me from drinkin', but . . .

KATHLEEN: You were only about thirteen years old?

MICHELLE: I was about fourteen when I started drinkin'.

KATHLEEN: When you were a child at home, was anybody ever violent to you, or hurt you physically?

MICHELLE: Physically? Physically, not that I remember. My mom was never, yeah, she was [would] yell at me at times because I didn't wanna go to school at that time. When my mom was drinkin', I didn't wanna go to school. I wanted to protect her, get her to stay away from drinkin'.

KATHLEEN: You thought if you stayed home you could get her to stop drinking?

MICHELLE: Yeah. She would even walk me to school. That's when I started taking off from school. Well, I don't think I really was abused at home.

Michelle met her first husband at age fourteen when she was in Phoenix at boarding school, and they began to drink together. She became pregnant and dropped out of school in the ninth grade and moved back to the reservation. That relationship ended and she had two other children. Her youngest child died of sudden infant death syndrome at three weeks of age, and she gave up her second youngest for adoption due to her alcoholism. She was married to the father of her first child when she became involved with her second husband, with whom she had another child. He was also an alcoholic and was physically, emotionally, and sexually abusive; they were together for six years. Michelle killed him by hitting him over the head with a pipe when they were both very inebriated. She did not remember the event; he would not have died from the blow had he not been so drunk that he choked on his own vomit. Michelle was sentenced to treatment and probation after pleading guilty to manslaughter in federal court.

Michelle's story is illustrative of the ways in which the social reproduction of pain in families is intertwined with historically situated social relations. Michelle, her mother, her husbands, and her children are members of an American Indian nation that has been colonized for the past two hundred years. As a consequence of colonization, traditional ways of living together and meeting needs have been disrupted. Their reservation is rich in natural resources and cultural practices have been preserved, but there is also a 60 percent unemployment rate and one of the highest youth suicide rates in the nation. At the time that Michelle was in junior high, students were sent to boarding schools in Phoenix, as there were not adequate schools on the reservation. With a background of loneliness and estrangement from her family, the pressure to drink with peers at boarding school was strong and the attraction of studying and staying in school was weak. Without a high school diploma and with four children by the age of twenty, Michelle became an alcoholic even though she did not want to and tried to stop drinking. Despite her dislike for her mother's way of life, she was in very similar circumstances, as were other women who described a lack of parental care.

Sheila was the middle child of three in a white, working-class family. Her family's economic circumstances were more favorable than Michelle's and she grew up with a mother and her mother's boyfriend present, yet she was even more estranged from her mother and more immersed in alcoholism and drugs. Her biological father died of cancer when she was fifteen, but she did not see much of him after her parents divorced (when Sheila was two). Her mother's live-in boyfriend raised Sheila, and he died of cirrhosis when Sheila was a young adult. Although she described her childhood as "normal," her mother, father, and "stepfather" were all alcoholics, and she had a very conflictual relationship with her mother: "She wasn't an exceptionally loving parent. She would be there if you needed her, but I tended to stay away from her. We always had a personality conflict. I never felt like she liked me. I always felt I was in her way. She was always letting me know my brother was more important. I didn't feel like she loved me."

When Sheila was eleven, her mother reunited with Sheila's father. She forbade Sheila from having any relationship with her "stepfather"; that is, her mother's boyfriend who had raised her and whom she loved and felt closest to. The loss of her "stepfather" was devastating, and Sheila started drinking at age fourteen. By the time she was sixteen, she was drinking a half a fifth of whiskey every day, often going to school drunk; nonetheless, she was able to graduate. She married at age eighteen to get away from home and had two children. During this period, she was sober, but very unhappy with her relationship and her lifestyle. After six years of marriage, she left her husband and he got full custody of their children, allowing her only one month of visitation each year. This marriage was not abusive. She spent a year in college, but dropped out after her divorce and started dancing in exotic dance clubs. Like Sarah, Sheila's dancing career led to her involvement with bikers, alcohol, and methamphetamine.[63] Her alcohol and drug usage jumped to a fifth of Jack Daniel's and a quarter-gram of meth each day. During this period, she met the man she eventually shot as he broke into her home in the middle of the night. He was a biker who regularly abused her physically and had several other women in his life. She tried to end their relationship and began to see another man. When he broke into her home, she believed he was going to kill her, and she shot him. Fortunately, he was not badly injured, and she was placed on probation for this, her first criminal offense.

For Bonnie, a nineteen-year-old, white, working-class woman, her parent's alcoholism was linked to their physical abuse of her. She described constant drinking and fighting and being "beat up" by her parents. She left home at fifteen, and while taking a course in corrections at a community college, began correspondence with a man in prison. Her initial contact was the result of a class assignment. Between prison visits and letters, she fell in love with this man. He set her up with a prison buddy who was released before him. This man conned her into driving him to two bank robberies. She was arrested and charged when the second robbery went awry and he shot and killed a woman while trying to steal her car. Bonnie claimed she did not know the man was robbing the banks as she waited for him in her car, but the court did not believe her. Bonnie entered into a plea agreement for armed robbery and received a ten-and-a-half-year sentence, enhanced for dangerousness. This was her first criminal offense.

Child Abuse in the Lives of Women Offenders

For the seventeen women who experienced physical, emotional, and sexual violence in their childhoods, the violence had a significant and long-term influence on their adult lives. But this influence was more complicated than a simple "modeling" of the behaviors they witnessed between parents or that were directed against them as children. The explicit violence they experienced occurred within contexts of loneliness, isolation, abandonment, and instability. All but two families described as violent were poor or working-class, not only measured by income but by the drudgery and limited opportunities emblematic of poverty and working-class life in the United States. For these women class was manifested in the nature of their relationships with their parents (particularly their mothers) and the options they saw available for work and intimate relationships. Gender shaped the ways in which they negotiated the restrictions of class. Race also complicated the experiences of childhood violence, as women from marginalized racial minorities faced additional obstacles to finding safety and happiness.[64]

Beth's crime was described in chapter 2. She spent seven years in prison after pleading guilty to attempted murder/manslaughter in the death of her live-in boyfriend. Beth's problems with her mother and stepfather were typical of relationships in which women described their mother as childlike and in need of care. Like Michelle's, Beth's mother was also an alcoholic, and Beth used alcohol and drugs from a young age. She felt she took care of her mother rather than the reverse, and she left home at age fourteen to escape her abusive stepfather. She experienced a series of violent relationships with men, including the father of her son, until she met Matt. Beth described her care of her mother:

BETH: My mom was a single mom, my dad died when I was two, and my mom raised all three of us kids by herself, and she started drinkin' real heavily, she drank a lot when my dad died. And I left when I was fourteen, and I kind've, the roles got reversed, I was the mom. We always tease each other still, it's like who's the mom, who's the daughter, 'cuz I always had to take care of her.
KATHLEEN: Are you the oldest?
BETH: I'm the youngest and I'm the only girl.
KATHLEEN: Oh, okay.
BETH: So, I always did everything for her. I seemed to always strive to get better, and get out of the house and do things to help her, and I don't know, I guess, somehow I grew up too fast. I was out of the house by the time I was fourteen. . . . I get angry with my mom. My mom told me, she goes, "Well, if you didn't have such a shitty attitude you wouldn't be in there." [jail]. I says, "No, if you would have been my mother, I wouldn't be here. If I wasn't *your* mother and I wasn't so busy trying to look out for

you, maybe I would have had a normal childhood and a normal life." I feel really bad that I told her that but I think it's the truth.

The theme of a father's death and a daughter as caretaker to a sick or alcoholic mother pervades these stories. In Beth's case, the man her mother married after her father's death was extremely violent and was the motivation for Beth to leave home at age fourteen:

BETH: She remarried when I was four, and he was really abusive. He had a paddle that was over twelve inches long and about two inches thick. And it had holes in it and we could actually hear it whistle. I was not hit by the paddle, because I was daddy's little girl. I had two older brothers that were beaten pretty bad.

KATHLEEN: Did you ever see him?

BETH: Yeah, I stood between them, he'd chase my brother, and I'd stand between them. He hit my mom. He hit her so hard one day that he busted all her dentures and cut her mouth wide open. And then when I got older, that's when he started on me, 'cuz then I was no longer daddy's little girl, and I didn't sit on his lap, I had an opinion of my own. He was the type of dad that would bring me home something every single day . . . then he started hitting me, because I got mouthier.

While most abuse was committed by adult males, several women described abuse by female caretakers. As a child, Luisa was severely abused emotionally and physically by her mother and sexually abused by a female babysitter as well as an older male. She was one of two daughters her mother had before marrying and having several more children. Luisa is Mexican and very light-skinned. She believes her light color and resemblance to her biological father was the basis of her dark-skinned mother's hatred toward her. Her mother inflicted beatings with a wooden paddle, a belt, "anything she could get her hands on, or if she couldn't hit you, she'd throw something." Luisa's mother was the person described at the beginning of the chapter who pressed her daughter's hands down on a hot stove while her husband held Luisa's feet. Luisa's hands blistered so badly that she was kept indoors at her grandmother's house for a week, but no outside agency ever intervened in the family. School officials called in child protective services to question Luisa and her mother when Luisa appeared at school with severe bruising all over her body. Luisa's mother said she had fallen, and the investigation was closed.

Beyond the physical abuse, however, Luisa said her mother's hatred and emotional abuse caused her the most pain, and that the scars from that will never go away. Her mother never hugged her or told her she loved her, never took her to the doctor or dentist, did not celebrate her birthday, and gave away the presents her biological father sent for Christmas. Luisa was a "sports addict" involved in soccer, volleyball, and track, but her mother never went to see her play. When she made her mother gifts for Valentine's Day or Mother's Day, her mother threw them in the trash. She constantly told Luisa that she was a "mistake," and she would put her in an orphanage if she did not behave. Luisa was also sexually abused by a babysitter and by her stepfather's father, and Luisa's mother used her victimization to further punish and stigmatize her. She would not allow her to sleep on sheets, but spread rags over the bed for Luisa to sleep on.

At fifteen, Luisa intentionally became pregnant so she would get thrown out of the house for good. She lived with the baby's father for a short time, then moved in with her sister. She had six more children, including a set of twins, by several men. I read through fourteen police reports for domestic violence committed against Luisa by a series of abusive male partners. She could not remember about half of them as her life was so filled with violence. As with so many other women, the criminal processing system did not move to protect her, and child protective services intervened but did not effectively protect her or her children. The system finally acted when one of her children was killed by her boyfriend. Luisa is serving a life sentence for first-degree murder in her son's death.

Several women described histories of maternal neglect and abandonment that began in infancy and was due to their mother's alcoholism. For three American Indian women, social services stepped in on several occasions to remove them from their neglectful households. Leah, discussed above, suffered abandonment by her mother, then neglect in boarding school, and at fifteen was finally returned to her mother's care. Carrie's mother was an alcoholic, and frequently left her children alone for long periods of time. Her father and older brother were both killed in separate, alcohol-related accidents, and two siblings were born with fetal alcohol syndrome. By age two, Carrie was registered as a possible child abuse victim after admission to the hospital with pneumonia. When she was five, her mother left her and her siblings alone for two months, including Christmas.

The family was finally evicted by the tribal Housing Authority for her mother's failure to supervise her children, and they all moved into a small hogan. Here she was routinely beaten and verbally assaulted by her older brother. Carrie was also raped by her brother's friend. At fourteen, she gave birth to her daughter and dropped out of school. Despite her mother's abandonment and failure to provide protection from her brother's abuse, Carrie described her relationship with her mother as very warm and close.

Emma was sent to live with a grandmother after her mother's death. Her father is an alcoholic who regularly battered Emma's mother. From the age of two, Emma was shuffled between relatives and boarding schools and finally became pregnant and started living with a man at age fifteen. When I met her at age thirty-nine, she had given birth to twelve children and had lost custody of all of them. These three women, like Michelle (discussed above), had extraordinarily abusive and neglectful childhoods. It would be easy to generalize from their stories and reaffirm the negative stereotypes about American Indians and alcoholism. There is no question that alcoholism is a problem among Native people, as it is among other groups in the United States, particularly among young people.[65] Smith cites the disturbing statistics that reflect the overall health problems among American Indians, including a much lower life expectancy than the national average and extraordinarily high rates of death by disease, suicide, and accidents.[66] These health problems, however, are not primarily the result of individual bad choices or lifestyles; they reflect more than five hundred years of colonization and government policies that exploit and punish American Indian people. It is also important to note that three of the eight Native women in this book described very close relationships with stable, loving parents.

Sexual abuse was reported by twelve women. Women described being sexually abused by fathers, stepfathers, brothers, stepbrothers, uncles, grandfathers, an aunt, coaches, family friends, a babysitter, and strangers. Sexual abuse by men in their households was associated with the absence, mental health problems, alcoholism and drug abuse of mothers, and their financial dependency on abusive men. For some women, sexual abuse was part of their earliest memories; for one woman (Salina), it was such an integral aspect of family life that it was difficult for her to define as abuse. Most women described their mothers as too frail to bear the knowledge of their sexual abuse, or as completely absent from their childhoods. They had not revealed their torment until they were older and, in some cases, not at all. Only one man of all the men who had abused women during their childhoods was ever prosecuted for his sexual abuse. Women learned that men had protection based on their financial usefulness to mothers. Like Beth and Dianne, women who were sexually abused by family members left home early, typically with older men who were often abusive—sexually, physically, and emotionally. Women who were placed with other relatives because of their mother's alcoholism or drug abuse felt trapped when family members were sexually abusive. Carol, a low-income American Indian single mother of five explained her problems while being raised by her aunt:

> I couldn't talk to her [aunt] about anything. Her son, he would try to get into my pants and stuff. Every time that he would try those things, it was real hard, I wouldn't really do anything to defend myself because one time, I tried defending myself and I got in trouble for it, 'cuz I had hurt him, I hit him, and I beat him up, actually, and I got in trouble for it. And when that happened, I knew I was trapped. So, when that happened, I just left it alone.

Carol felt that she could not defend herself from her cousin because she depended on her aunt for room and board. She entered boarding school at age sixteen, where she met and married her violent husband. She quit school, which she found boring, and went to trade school to learn carpentry. Carol was never able to pursue a career, however, because she was trapped in a violent marriage with four children by the time she was twenty-five. Almost all of the women in this book sought protection and love in romantic relationships at a young age. For women who were sexually abused as children, however, the choice of an intimate partner never met their expectations and ended in divorce. For these women, there were generally a series of abusive partners that led up to their crime.

Sarah's victimization began in childhood at the hands of her stepfather and his sons, and continued through a series of abusive men until she was arrested for armed robbery. Her parents divorced while her mother was pregnant with her. She believed that her mother blamed her for all of her problems, and also felt that she took care of her mother rather than the reverse:

Yeah, it was all my fault. See, my mom hada remarry my father. (*In a singsong manner*) My father used to beat my mother, and she divorced him, and then a week after the divorce was final, she found out she was pregnant, and so, "for the love her unborn child, she sacrificed the family," . . . bunch o' shit if you ask me. I've about had it with her throwin' her shit in my face (*laughs*). So, she stayed with him for about four years, and couldn't take it anymore and moved to Arizona, and I'd see him occasionally in summers and stuff.

Like other women described above, Sarah became a caretaker for her mother. When she was in sixth grade, her mother read Sarah's diary and discovered that Sarah was being sexually abused by her step-father and his sons. Sarah came home and found her mother in a panic attack and drove her to the mental hospital:[67]

KATHLEEN: You were like eleven years old, twelve years old?
SARAH: Yeah, I've pretty much been raisin' my mom all my life. She's a bas-ket case. Then, she wanted to know details, what he did, why he did it, when he did it, how he did it, you know, and it was like, sorry I didn't take movies for you. I just refused to talk about it, you know?

Sarah also resisted talking to me about her childhood and adult vic-timizations. She was very funny, laughed a lot, and admitted that was her way of covering her pain:

SARAH: I think my mom knew what was goin' on. I mean, she left me with her boyfriend's son once, and I told her I didn't wanna be left with him 'cuz he was nasty, and she didn't believe me. She said, "Oh you're just goin' to bed anyway, shut up and lay down, we'll be back in a few hours." (*Said in nasty voice*): "I don't know, in my generation, that stuff didn't go on." Yeah, right, it's a new breed, mom (spilled her soda). . . . I liked the other conversations better (*laughs*).
KATHLEEN: I know. I know, it's hard to talk about.
SARAH: If I'd done more talkin' about it at a younger age, maybe I wouldn't be where I am today (*laughs*). I know I sit around and joke about all the problems in my life, and I figure if I'm jokin' and laughin' about 'em, I got 'em handled. Yeah, right (*laughs*).
KATHLEEN: Well, it's one way to deal with it . . .
SARAH: Nah, it's one way to *not* deal with it.

As an adult, Sarah exhibited many behaviors that could lead one to categorize her as a demon: she drank up to a fifth of whiskey a day, was involved with a series of outlaw bikers, worked as an exotic dancer, was shot up with crank by her boyfriend, and eventually was convicted of armed robbery involving a threat to a child. As she indicates, she liked to joke and laugh and presented herself as a "tough broad." By looking backward a few years, it is easy to understand how she developed this veneer of toughness and rebellion. She was sexually abused from age eight to twelve, and served as the caretaker for her emotionally fragile mother. Instead of receiving comfort and protection from her mother or other caring adults, she was forced to assume responsibility for meeting their needs. I don't know whether Sarah was an angel at age eight, but I know her adult behaviors should not be judged without consideration of the pain of her childhood. When I met Sarah, her only desire was to stay out of prison and be a good mother to her own daughters.

Several women described the fantasy life they developed in their childhoods. Two of these women said that living in a fantasy world protected them from the devastation of their loneliness and abuse.[68] Jennifer's situation is described in chapter 5. She was an isolated young woman whose parents divorced when she was young; at nineteen, she had lost her mother to cancer. In treatment for depression and alcohol abuse, she had recalled memories of childhood sexual abuse by her stepfather, but was uncertain whether these memories were accurate or imagined. She was certain, however, that she had been molested by both her swim coach and her best friend's father. She also described a lonely childhood and her common retreat into fantasy:

JENNIFER: I think I've always (*laughs*) to me I've had them [fantasies] for a long time. . . . I've never been real social with other people, never had many friends. At least in high school, to go to a reunion, I wouldn't know anybody there, in four years, I basically danced every day after school.

KATHLEEN: You were in your own world.

JENNIFER: Right. Very much so, to the point where I was in like a fantasy land. It really was.

Jennifer felt that her immediate attraction to her co-defendant, Jared, and her willingness to follow his lead was related to her lack of assertiveness and retreat into fantasy. In retrospect, while awaiting sentencing in jail, she viewed Jared as a dangerous, deranged, and manipulative man. But for an unfortunate period she was able to believe his tales about being soul mates, connected from a past life. Her attraction to and belief in Jared's lies facilitated his control over her and the situation that resulted in her long-term incarceration for manslaughter.

Salina's situation, recounted in chapter 1, established a pattern of denying the realities of child abuse that occurred in her childhood and adult households. She was still deeply immersed in fantasy and denial of what was going on around her. Growing up under the strict rules of her father, Salina was never told the reason that her mother left her four daughters. Their father was an alcoholic, a Vietnam veteran who was diagnosed with PTSD (post–traumatic stress disorder). He forbade them to have friends or to visit with other relatives. "Your sisters are your friends," they were told, and they made up elaborate fantasy games to entertain themselves. When I met Salina, I had already read the documents about her father's incarceration for the long-term sexual abuse of her oldest sister. Salina did not spontaneously mention this when I asked her about her childhood and her relationship with her father, so I probed for information. I am including a lengthy segment to illustrate Salina's difficulty with articulating what happened and her feelings of guilt for not protecting her sister:

KATHLEEN: Well, I read that your older sister (S: Oh, yeah) had some problems with your dad.

SALINA: Um, let me see, that must have been when she was little (K: Mmhmm). Oh. Um. Let me think. I don't remember. You know what? It was strange. Um, did they sleep on the same bed? (K: Mmhmmm). That was normal? (K: No). Oh my gosh! It's weird, 'cuz I think we probably grew up thinking it was (K: Yeah). (*She starts crying.*) I don't know, I didn't know, um. Like, when she took her high school, she took it through a course. (K: mmhmm, at home?) and (*crying, then laughs*) oh, I don't know, just, not asking questions. I don't think I really knew, I just never wanted to know anything. You know, then later on, I think, in years, I don't know, it was kind've brought up, I guess, or something. And then, I don't know, it was just kind've like, "don't ask questions," and so I never really looked into or thought about it, 'cuz I didn't wanna know, and then, well, later on, it's kinda like you don't know, but you just never pay attention. 'Cuz she was like, she had to stay at home for our high school, and then she had a baby, she had [child's name], and, well, we knew she didn't have a boyfriend. I don't know, I think I kinda', you suspect, and then you just don't, I don't know, what did I think? And she stayed home, she did her high school at home.

KATHLEEN: I guess she didn't talk to you about it, huh?

SALINA: She, I don't, you know, I don't think she ever, I don't, I know we kinda', I don't know if I knew. I don't know if I just block it, I don't know if I'm better off that way. I mean, now I think about it, there's ways, but you grew up like that, you grew up not sayin' anything, and I grew up more to where, I could not, that's how I protect myself, I don't wanna know anything. And what else? I know. There started to be like tension, my sister wanted to work and stuff too. She wanted to do things too. So she did get a job, and she worked, and I think my dad rode his bike with her every day, you know, separate bikes, he was real protective of her, made sure she'd come home, and then when, I thought, I didn't think, I don't know, how weird, did they? Okay, never mind. I know I talked to my sister a couple nights, like two weeks ago. I don't know. I felt bad (*crying hard*).

This lengthy quote illustrates how confused and naïve Salina was in her understanding of the incest committed against her sister. Salina lived with this incest from the time she was a toddler until her father was arrested when she was seventeen. By that time, she had been living with her niece/sister for three years. She described the night her father was arrested as the worst day of her life.[69] She did not recount any incidents of her own abuse by her father, and I do not know if she repressed this knowledge too or if her father limited his abuse to the eldest. This is not an uncommon pattern, and threats to move onto younger children are often used to maintain the victim's silence and compliance.

When Salina's boyfriend began to abuse her own daughters physically, she was unable to intervene and protect them. She is serving a thirty-five-year sentence for first-degree murder of her child, due to her failure to prevent or disclose her daughter's death at the hands of her boyfriend. Her boyfriend accepted a plea to child abuse and received a twenty-four-year sentence. When she was incarcerated, she was already six months pregnant by her boyfriend, and gave birth while in jail. The baby was adopted by her younger sister. The tragedies that surrounded her did not seem to sink into her awareness, and she told me, "I like to be happy." Letters she sent to a friend during this time are covered with drawings of smiley faces, suns, and flowers; they focus exclusively on her relationship with God. In these letters, she refers to God as her father: "It is the most wonderful feeling to know that we have a Father that loves us beyond human understanding and He wants what is best for us." She writes over and over how much she has to be thankful for. The letters were written less than a year after her daughter was murdered.

Nicole remembered much of her childhood sexual abuse and related it to her adult problems (her situation is described in chapters 3 and 6). Her first experiences of sexual abuse were hazy in her memories, but her older sister clearly recalled the abuse of both girls by their stepfather. She spoke with me on the phone about how Nicole would wake up screaming, and confirmed Nicole's memory of sleeping in six pairs of underpants, hoping to deter him. Nicole's sister said she hated her stepfather and blamed him for Nicole's predicament. Nicole described her memories of him and her efforts to resist his abuse:

NICOLE: I just didn't want to be around him, and other times, I would just glare at him, and I just couldn't stand him—and he wouldn't let us date, wouldn't let us have any guys over, we couldn't have guy friends, and of course we didn't wanna have girls over to the house, and we had discussed it among ourselves, and we thought the reason (*sighs*) well, we knew that mom depended on him to support us, so we didn't wanna tell mom, I don't know. We were tryin' to protect her, or something, I guess.

KATHLEEN: She didn't figure it out, huh?

NICOLE: She says that she doesn't remember a lot from her whole life. I guess she blocks out a lot too. I can block out a lot o' stuff too, when things happen. . . . I remember he had his hands on me or something, I'd think, *this is not me.* He never penetrated me with his penis, but with his fingers he did, but you think, this isn't happening, this isn't happening, and you just, *it's just not real.* And after a while, I had a string hooked up, so I could close my door, thinking that was gonna stop him (*laughs*). When I did tell him off was after we moved back to Yuma, and I was like a freshman or sophomore in high school, and she asked me why I hated him so much, and I said, "Mom, he sneaks in my bedroom at night." And then she told me that her stepdad had done that to her too, so my grandpa had done that too.

KATHLEEN: Did she do anything about it?

NICOLE: She divorced him. I don't know—my sisters said that they went to her a long time ago and told her, but I don't know if they did, because when I told her, she did divorce him.

KATHLEEN: What was your relationship like with her?

NICOLE: We weren't very close, we've never been really close, my mom and I. You know I call her every week now. She's always been real distant, she made clothes for us and stuff like that, she was just real quiet. She set rules, like, I would get in trouble for things I didn't even do, and bein' grounded, all the time grounded, for things I didn't do. . . . I was eleven or twelve, I started sneaking out, and I became what you might call promiscuous.

KATHLEEN: With boys your own age, or older guys?

NICOLE: Older guys.

KATHLEEN: Men, or older teenagers?

NICOLE: Men and teenagers—what were they interested in an eleven-year-old girl for, thinkin' about it now, of course back then, I thought I was pretty cool. I mean, I don't know how we'd do it, I mean, I would sneak out and, well, my sisters' friends arranged my first sneak-out date, because this guy had saw me. He thought I was really cute, so they arranged it, and I lost my virginity, and I was so eager to do it, I don't know, I think, when I was in medium security, for the first six months here, I went to some classes that they have for incest survivors, and the reason, they said a lot of times when you do something like that, it's not common, but it's not uncommon to be promiscuous. And so I didn't feel so bad.

Nicole was also sexually molested by her uncle. The group counseling she received in jail was the first help she ever received to deal with her childhood sexual abuse. She believes that her meth use, described in chapter 3, was related to her efforts to hide the pain of her childhood while carrying on a conventional life as a suburban housewife and mother. She also describes how the sexual abuse was "not real" to her, that the child being molested was "not me." This self-protective response was similar to the reactions to the murders she witnessed. As described in chapters 3 and 5, Nicole continued to live with her abuser after he committed a brutal murder in her presence. Although she found herself crying and staring into space, she responded as she did to her childhood sexual abuse: "I didn't tell anybody, and I know, I can't, it was not real to me."

Salina and Nicole represent the effects of child sexual abuse on women's development as described by Herman.[70] Herman did not focus on women's criminal offending, but explicated the developmental processes of adaptation to sexual abuse that shape women's adult behavior. The impact on adult intimate relationships is consistent with Salina's and Nicole's stories:

> The survivor has great difficulty protecting herself in the context of intimate relationships. Her desperate longing for nurturance and care makes it difficult to establish safe and appropriate boundaries with others. Her tendency to denigrate herself and to idealize those to whom she becomes attached further clouds her judgment. Her empathic attunement to the wishes of others and her automatic, often unconscious habits of obedience also make her vulnerable to anyone in a position of power or authority. Her dissociative defensive style makes it difficult for her to form conscious and accurate assessments of danger. And her wish to relive the dangerous situation and make it come out right may lead her into reenactments of the abuse. . . . Many survivors have such profound deficiencies in self-protection that they can barely imagine themselves in a position of agency or choice.[71]

Girls' fantasy life and dissociation helped them survive situations where no one protected them from abuse. As adults, however, women's fantasies clouded their ability to recognize the danger around them and to act decisively to protect themselves and others. In Salina's case, she obeyed her boyfriend and drove him to the place where he disposed of her baby's body. He lied to the police and said her baby had disappeared. Although she knew this was not true, she became very confused, repeated the story to the police, and thus participated in the attempted cover-up of the murder. She requested a polygraph because she was no longer able to discern the truth for herself. The polygraph indicated that she was lying. In her discussions with me and the mitigation specialist, she explained that when she realized there was something wrong with her baby, "I felt like I died. I saw myself dead with her from a distance. I felt like I was on the outside of everything." As described above, Salina continues to maintain psychological distance from the tragedies in her life. In contrast, Nicole is much more aware of her losses and the loss she has caused others. Her tears flow freely as she discusses her two children and her sadness that she will miss their entire childhoods while in prison.

Other women did not rely on dissociation or fantasy to cope with their childhood victimization. They engaged in both caretaking and perfectionist behavior, achieving success in school and work. Herman describes this as a result of efforts to please and placate abusive parents.[72] This may be true for some survivors, but for others, their accomplishments are achieved *in spite of* their uncaring parents and to please themselves.[73] Chris was such a woman. Growing up in the white middle class, she was the youngest of two daughters. Her mother died of heart disease and her father turned to alcohol when her mother became sick. After her mother first had her stroke, her father became physically and emotionally abusive to Chris and her mother. Despite the relative economic and social privilege of her family, she lost the care of her mother at age thirteen and became responsible for all domestic labor until her father remarried when she was twenty-five. Chris displayed both the "empathic caretaking" and excellence in school that are often observed in female victims of child abuse. She had a four-year degree in medical technology and a successful career. At age thirteen she assumed the responsibilities of caregiver to her entire family. She received no emotional support from her parents, and felt that she had been denied a childhood and a social life because of her role in the family. She described the dramatic shift in her life after her mother became ill:

I had to take the role of cooking, cleaning. I literally couldn't boil water. After that he became alcoholic and became abusive towards her and me. The relationship degenerated. . . . Here he was my father and he probably figured he was going to be there for me and he's the one who fell apart. Both him and my sister did. It was like they didn't even want to face reality. I was only thirteen and I needed some comfort too. I never received it. Even when I asked for it, it was like "Leave me alone. I don't want to be bothered." That's when the big rift started.

Chris's father was not sexually abusive, but her first sexual experience at age seventeen was rape by a family "friend." Following the advice of a friend, she never reported her rape to police or her family. She kept the rape and her father's abuse to herself and stayed at home caring for her mother. Her father denigrated her abilities and was not supportive of her desire to attend college. She went without his approval and continued to care for her mother while working and going to school. Chris described how her father's opposition and abuse spurred her desire to excel:

CHRIS: He [her father] didn't want me to go. He said, "Well, your sister didn't go and she did fine." Well, I'm not my sister. He fought me tooth and nail against going. He gave no encouragement whatsoever.

KATHLEEN: So how did you pay for it?

CHRIS: I paid for it. I worked.

KATHLEEN: You worked and took care of him and went to college?

CHRIS: Yep. Full time. It wasn't easy, but I think I was more determined because he was against me. You know, I could have done really good and gotten excellent grades, but under the circumstances I couldn't devote 100 percent. Instead I got good grades. Instead of A's, I got B's and A's. That's still not bad but to me that wasn't enough. I felt like I had to get straight A's. . . . He didn't help one bit and there were times that I almost felt like quitting just because of the no encouragement that I got. It was always "It's a waste of time. Why are you doing it?" Years later he would always tell me, "I'm glad you went to college and you have a college degree. At least if you get married, you know you can take care of yourself." It's like "Hey, no kidding. That's what I was trying to tell you." I don't doubt that he loved me but it just was not the kind of relationship I would have wanted. You need a parent to always encourage you. You want their approval but it got to the point that I didn't really care about his approval. It was just what I wanted. I was hoping that he would be happy with what I did but if he wasn't, then that's too bad.

Chris was physically abused by her father, but like the other women described above, the failure of her father to provide support and approval were her main disappointment. She turned to a boyfriend to provide the love she did not receive from her father, and this man physically and emotionally terrorized her for years, as I described in chapter 3. After eventually escaping from him, she became involved with another violent man who coerced her involvement in his counterfeiting scheme. Chris was white, middle-class, college-educated, and financially independent, but she also became ensnared with violent men who convinced her to participate in criminal activities. Clearly, class privilege does not always insulate young women from other sources of pain, including parental illness, death, alcoholism and abuse.

In describing the childhood abuse women experienced and its effects on their adult lives, I am not suggesting that the abuse *caused* either their crimes or their violent relationships. It is easy to slide into the assumption that childhood abuse is the major factor leading to women's crime. As discussed above, this is an individualist, apolitical approach that ignores history and context. Nevertheless, childhood abuse does *contribute* to the ways that individual women respond to violence from their intimate partners. It is vital that this contribution be recognized and understood, particularly within the context of criminal law. When women go along with their partners' criminal activity, fail to protect their children from abuse, or commit crimes at the direction of their abuser, backgrounds of abuse and neglect help prosecutors, courts, and the public understand their complicity.

The Social Reproduction of Mothering

Chodorow employs psychoanalytic and objects relations theory to explain how mothering is reproduced across generations.[74] My focus is on the *social* relationships that influence how women mother their children. For the women in this book, the ability to mother their children was compromised by their relationships with violent men. Thirty of the women had children, and as discussed in the previous chapter, their children were integral to their identities. The absence of their mother's care and love propelled many women into relationships with men. Yet these men then became threats to their own children and often were the reason that women could no longer be with their children. All women who were mothers began to cry when they spoke of their children. Being forcibly separated from them was the most difficult part of incarceration.[75] Teresita, who was only twenty years old, talked about the pain of being away from her four remaining children: "I mean I miss them sooo much. Just not being able to wake up and have them there and saying, 'Mommy, I love you,' all the time. It's like, nobody will ever know how much it hurts inside, to get your kids taken away from you."

Sarah, who was on her own recognizance pre-trial, was worried that her mother or her ex-husband would get custody of her two daughters if she went to prison. The mother, whom she described as a "basket case" when she was a child, was still hostile to Sarah and hit her in the face when told she could not testify in court:

> She's nuts, she's absolutely nuts. So, I'm not leaving my children to her. I'm not leaving my children to that drug-addict [her ex-husband] in that sick, sick, twisted household. I am not giving my children to the state. My children need me, and that's the way it's gotta be, and then I will do anything and everything, you know? Otherwise, I would go out here right now, and I'd walk in front of a truck. Because I would rather have my children think I was dead. They could go on and find another mommy, and not be stewing over me in prison. You know what I mean? Instead of worrying about mommy sitting in prison (*crying hard*). Well, I'm not going. They're gonna have to shoot me in the back. I'll do whatever they want me to do, but I'm goin' home to my children, 'cuz they got nobody else to go home to.

Sarah was sentenced to three years in prison, and her children were sent to Ohio to live with her sister.

Seven women were able to keep their children because they were sentenced to probation. Three women's children were with ex-husbands who had not been abusive or involved in their crimes in any way. Two of these women had already lost custody of their children to their ex-husbands prior to their crimes. Children of three women were placed with the mothers who had abandoned their own daughters in childhood but were deemed suitable caregivers for their grandchildren. Violent husbands had custody of the children of two women. Lisa's three young children were originally placed in the custody of the husband she shot because of her belief that he was sexually molesting their young daughter. Within weeks, he abandoned them, she relinquished custody, and they have been adopted.

Carol's two children were with the father who had abandoned the family to live with another woman in another state. In the cases of five women, their nonabusive parents took custody of their children, and sisters took custody in two cases (Salina's baby, born while she was in jail, went with her sister; the older child, with the biological father). Two women had children placed with the parents or siblings of the abusive husbands they had killed. Shanna's brother-in-law was ordered by the sentencing judge to bring her son to visit her in prison once each month, which he has done for the past fifteen years. Shanna's son was three when she entered prison and is now eighteen, and she reports he is doing quite well and they have a good relationship. Danielle's oldest son enlisted in the military and was sent to Iraq. She sees her daughter, youngest son, and grandchild on prison visits. Only one child, Carrie's infant daughter, was placed in foster care as the only available relative, Carrie's mother, is still an active alcoholic. Jane's daughter was raised by her grandparents. Today, Jane is out of prison, directing a shelter for battered women, and is reunited with her grown daughter, who is attending college.

It is impossible to know how these children will develop, and each has his/her own traumas to endure. The children who witnessed their mother's abuse, or the murder of their father, stepfather, or siblings have a difficult and troublesome past to overcome, and most have received no counseling or professional support. I only interviewed one child, Danielle's seventeen-year-old daughter, and that was during her mother's trial. The daughter had already been convicted of writing bad checks and had a baby of her own to care for. At the time we spoke, she was angry and bitter toward her deceased father and his family, and could not comprehend that her mother would be spending the rest of her life in prison. Although many women were motivated to protect their children from abuse and to be good mothers, their desires were compromised by the violence of their partners and their participation in crimes. As many women endured motherless childhoods, their own children are left to struggle with the loss of their mother's care.[76]

Conclusion

These women did not say that men show love by beating their wives, that they think domestic violence is normal, or (for most) that abuse in childhood led to their own violence or victimization. Instead, they described situations in which adults abandoned them, they were lonely and anxious to escape households where they were expected to fulfill adult responsibilities. As young women eager to gain acceptance and love and to be considered attractive by males, they often formed relationships with men as a mechanism for leaving home. Some parental abandonment was the result of the unavoidable distress caused by death, illness, or divorce. In many cases, parents' use of alcohol prevented them from providing the attention and care their daughters craved and eventually sought from men. The theme of daughters assuming the role of caregiver, either for their mothers, fathers, or for other siblings, is prevalent in many of the women's backgrounds. As caregivers, they learned to submerge their own needs for pleasure, support, and achievement to the needs of others in their families. As adult women in relationships, acceptance of their obligations as caregivers contributed to subservient obedience to violent partners, often to the extent of facilitating or committing crimes as a way of serving men and attempting to gain their approval.

There was also horrific violence and sexual abuse directed at young girls. My own outrage over the physical and emotional abuse inflicted by caregivers demands that I acknowledge that these people caused immediate and long-term damage to innocent little girls. When the evidence of abuse is so vivid and shocking, it is tempting for me to view these families as the primary or sole source of women's adult problems, to adopt a "cycle of violence" model. There is other evidence, however, that draws me away from this simplistic explanation. What I have sought to demonstrate is the complexity and ethereality of family relationships and their relationship to social factors outside the bounds of individual families. Women's loneliness, thwarted dreams, physical and sexual abuse, and assumption of caregiver roles were mingled with love, commitment, and gratefulness to their parents. Their childhood disappointments were also linked to the lack of social and community support for terminally ill parents, low-income parents, and alcoholic parents. In the few cases where child protective services intervened, they left girls in abusive homes without resources for either parent or child. When parents were incapacitated or absent, daughters were assigned domestic tasks consistent with traditional gender roles. People simply assumed that daughters were appropriate domestic servants and, in some cases, sexual partners for adults. Most of the women viewed marriage, rather than education, as the best way out of a bad family situation. The one woman, Chris, who persisted in college did so against her father's wishes and without his support. She succeeded in spite of the painful conditions of her childhood, but this success was shattered by two violent and manipulative male partners.

These families certainly had serious problems, but women's lives could have been different had the social context of these problems included a sense of communal responsibility for children. Communal responsibility does not simply mean government intervention or larger welfare checks. In some cases, money was not the problem. Communal responsibility for children means creating a social environment that privileges their well-being and development. Real "prevention" would focus on creating social institutions that foster growth, respect, and joy. Instead, the social reproduction of pain has continued for many of the women's children as their mothers are incarcerated. Ironically, their children are often placed with the relatives who contributed to women's loneliness and entrapment or with the families of their violent partners. The women are locked away or, in a few cases, placed on probation. But the social conditions that led to their crimes are left undisturbed.

In the previous chapter, I discussed the experiences with violent men that undermined women's sense of secure links to a predictable world. Childhoods filled with loneliness, disappointment, and parental alcoholism and abuse established a background in which bizarre and violent behavior from an intimate partner was often accommodated. As children, accommodation to undesirable behavior by family members and others helped them to survive until they could leave. Leaving violent partners, however, was never easy, even once women had made the decision to do so. The social reproduction of women's pain described in this chapter formed the background in which women confronted intimate partners who threatened their lives and their children's lives if they failed to follow orders or tried to escape.

Women had hopes and dreams of creating loving family units and were reluctant to relinquish these dreams.[77] Some women became deeply committed to men who promised the love, affection, and affirmation that was lacking in their childhoods. When those promises fell through and the realities of violence, emotional abuse, and criminal behavior took their place, women did not want to relinquish their hopes for love.[78] In the next chapter, I discuss situations in which women killed their abusive partners. Neither love nor fear is extinguished by the death of men who continue to haunt the imaginations of the women they tormented in life.

5 〜 Demonic Angels?: Violence against Abusers

It's driving me crazy now, staying there, the same room. I took the bed down, moved most of the stuff out, but it's still there, memories are always there. Sometimes I'll walk around and look around and feel like he's there, he's still out there, and, you know, like it goes through my mind, "he's gone, he's gone" and that's when it gets to me sometimes.
  —Dorothy, stabbed her husband to death while he was attacking her, sentenced to probation.

Women's use of lethal and near-lethal violence against an intimate partner is unlike most other forms of interpersonal violence. It almost always takes place within a context of ongoing victimization and is unplanned and unintentional; women feel enormous grief and regret as a consequence of their actions.[1] Of all the crimes committed by battered women, the killing of abusive partners has received the most scholarly, media, and activist attention.[2] These crimes grab public attention because they are dramatic and tragic. Despite this attention, women are far more likely to be *victims* than perpetrators of intimate partner homicide. In 2002, men perpetrated 81 percent of spousal homicides and 71 percent of boyfriend/girlfriend homicides.[3] Intimate partners kill about three to four percent of all male homicide victims, but about one-third of female victims.[4] Women are much less likely than men to commit homicide, but when they do, their victims are most likely to be family members.[5]

In this chapter I describe the situations that led to killing or using deadly weapons against an abusive partner and the aftermath of violent events. Women who kill their intimate partners are scrutinized by criminal processing agents and the general public in terms of their motivations and character. They are not automatically demonized, but their innocence or guilt is evaluated in gendered terms regarding the appropriate behavior of women and wives.[6] Like female victims of sexual violence, battered women who kill are analyzed in terms of their "moral purity" as a victim of male violence prior to their fall into criminal homicide.[7] Legal justification of their offense often turns on perceptions of their innocence prior to their use of lethal violence.

Of the forty-five women in this book, nineteen killed their partners and seven women shot or stabbed their partners, but did not cause death. The difference between women who killed and those who used deadly weapons was not a matter of their level of fear or intent to harm, but rather the unintended physical consequences of their actions. The women and their partners who did not die were simply more fortunate because their gunshots or stab wounds were not fatal.[8]

I never met a woman charged with the death of her abusive partner who had *wanted* to kill him. Some had fantasized about his death, or even told someone else they wanted to kill him, because they knew no other way out. One woman admitted that she held a gun pointed at her sleeping husband for an hour, but could not bring herself to pull the trigger. To a prosecutor, telling a friend that "if he touches me again, I'll kill him," and having fantasies of his death represent premeditation. From women's perspective, they were not serious intentions but desperate thoughts in a situation of hopeless entrapment. For some women, their partners' death was a horrible personal loss. Despite the violence and abuse, they loved them and mourned their death. Other women had stopped loving their partners, if they ever did love them, and simply wanted the abuse to stop. They killed their partners in a situation of immediate threat in order to protect themselves. The loss of life at their own hands was a tragedy they mourned, but their grief did not include the sense that they had killed their one "true love." They felt safer after his death, although many continued to feel his control.

Situated Transactions in Intimate Partner Homicide

In the field of homicide studies, scholars have examined the interactions between perpetrators and victims that produce lethal outcomes. Researchers have viewed homicide as an interactional event where victims "precipitate" violent actions through provocative behaviors or statements or by failing to capitulate to offenders' demands.[9] The transactions that occur between participants in a violent confrontation reflect the "historical roots" of conflict within the specific relationship and in the broader culture.[10] For women who kill or who use sublethal violence against their partners the historical roots of their actions most often include ongoing abuse.[11] They evaluate immediate threats based on this history. All of the cases in this book involved a history of violence and abuse by the male victim against the woman who killed or assaulted him. The reason I knew about these cases is that their attorneys believed that prior domestic violence was relevant to their defense. Unlike general studies of homicide, my sample only includes cases involving intimate partner violence. I cannot use these cases to contribute to discussions about the proportion of female-perpetrated intimate homicides that were preceded by the woman's abuse by the male victims. I certainly do not presume that all women who kill their intimate partners have been abused. I use these cases where abused women have killed to help explain *why* the women felt so trapped in the relationships, *how* they perceived threat, *why* they resorted to violence, and *how* their actions affected them and their families.

The history of violence in these relationships shaped women's construction of meaning of behavior that might appear innocuous, or at least not life-threatening, to outsiders. For example, when Angie's boyfriend asked her if she was afraid to die, she answered no. This question could be asked of an intimate partner in a nonviolent relationship without appearing sinister. Angie's boyfriend, however, had previously threatened to kill her; they had separated and reconciled several times. At the time he asked the question, he had been drinking and using drugs. His question was preceded by a verbal tirade in which he told her he didn't "have to take this shit." They were alone in the bedroom, and he assumed a menacing body stance. Because his question did not intimidate her, he moved on to comment, "Maybe your grandma should be afraid." Angie was devoted to her grandmother and said she would have done anything to protect her. When her boyfriend made a threatening comment about her grandmother, Angie panicked and pulled out the gun they kept in a dresser drawer. Absent knowledge of her relationship with her grandmother *and* her boyfriend's history of violence against Angie, his statement would not appear immediately threatening. Angie, however, believed that it was. In the struggle that ensued, Angie shot her boyfriend, causing minor injury. She did not intend to shoot him, only to scare him and let him know she would not allow him to hurt her grandmother. Angie was sentenced to probation.

Second, the violent history of abusive men led women to interpret threatening statements as much more serious than they would have been without this history. Women knew the men were capable of inflicting severe violence and, in some cases, knew they had killed other people. When men said, "You're going to die, bitch," or "How would you like your ass kicked?" women did not perceive this as an idle threat, but as a promise.

Third, women developed nuanced knowledge of men's facial expressions, tone of voice, and body language. They knew when he was in a particularly bad mood. Many women referred to the strange look that came over their partners' faces or into their eyes that made them look "evil" or "like somebody else." For example, when Beth returned from a trip to the grocery store, she found her boyfriend transformed into something dangerous: "I come back and I think that Matt turned into something like the devil. I don't know what happened to him. He didn't look . . . he looked distorted. He looked really bad." From previous assaults, women knew that these looks signaled a serious beating or death. As Dianne commented, "I knew he would never let me leave that house alive."

Finally, women made connections between other events and assaults against them. One woman, Jane, knew that if her husband sexually assaulted another woman, he would come home and beat her. Often men's use of drugs or alcohol, or their suspicions that a woman was seeing someone else, were excuses for violent assaults against her. If women were late getting home, or knew their partners had consumed large amounts of drugs or alcohol, they could predict an assault. For example, Dawn knew that information about their impending mortgage foreclosure would result in a serious beating.

In previous studies of homicide, researchers have argued that the boundaries between offender and victim are fluid and tangled. One person may initiate a violent conflict but become the victim in the situation.[12] In most of the cases discussed here, the female offender began as the victim of her partner's physical, sexual, and psychological abuse, then used violence as a *defense* rather than an *offense*.

David Luckenbill argued that homicides occurred when offenders felt they had to take violent action to counteract affronts to their self-image, even if these affronts were unintended or unknown to the victim.[13] Most women did not knowingly initiate affronts to men's self image. Although women occasionally "talked back" or even hit back when they were being abused, in most cases, they were intimidated by their partner's violence and tried to control his violence by "not saying anything." Women were aware that their partners attributed malicious intent to them, especially sexual infidelity, although most were at a loss to understand why. They went to great lengths to placate their partners. The violence men inflicted was used to punish, control, and degrade their partners, not to "save face." When women responded to the "provocation" of their husband's threats with the use of lethal or sublethal violence, they were not attempting to "save face"; they were attempting to save their lives.

Situational Contexts and Penalties for Crimes against Abusers

There were three main contexts in which women used lethal or sublethal violence to protect themselves: reactions to imminent danger, proactive violence, and involvement of third parties.[14] The contexts and women's behaviors are detailed in appendix D. The most common situations were immediate, life-threatening confrontations in which women killed or used sublethal violence to protect themselves.[15] Eight women killed their partners in such a context, and all but one of them either received a sentence of probation or had the charges against them dropped. The other woman, Dianne, received a five-year sentence for manslaughter, but only served two-and-a-half years. Two of the women who used sublethal violence were in life-threatening situations. The charges were dropped against one; the other received probation. In six cases, women were not in a situation of immediate threat. They used proactive violence in a situation they believed would end in severe violence against them unless they took the initiative to protect themselves. Three cases resulted in death: of these, one woman was sentenced to nine years, another to eight and a half (both for manslaughter), and the third woman is awaiting sentencing. In two cases where the men survived, women were placed on probation. The third, Mona, received a five-year prison term. Three women were convicted for their part in a third-party murder: Danielle, Shanna, and Eve. They were each convicted for conspiring with the man who actually committed the murder of their husband. Danielle received a life sentence; Shanna, eighteen years; and Eve, twelve-and-half years. Danielle's sentence was the same as that of the murderer: life. A third co-conspirator in this case was only sentenced to three-and-a-half years. Shanna's sentence was three years longer than the murderer's, and the man who actually killed Eve's husband was released and not prosecuted. All three women claim that they did not know their husbands would be killed, and the evidence linking them to the actual murderers varies. I discuss these cases below.

In two cases women's violence was proactively aggressive outside a context of immediate threat. Ronnie stabbed her boyfriend when he arrived home and went to hug her. She was not afraid at the time, but was angry at his physical and economic abuse and the problems he had created in her life. Ronnie was experiencing extreme mental anxiety and disorientation as a result of the combination of physical and psychological abuse, prescription medication, and street drugs. I describe her situation below. Lisa's case and the violence that Brian inflicted on her was described in chapter 2. She went to the home she had shared with Brian and shot him because she believed he was sexually abusing their two-year-old daughter. She had tried to enlist the help of the police department, but no one believed her complaints. In their small, rural town, her husband had powerful connections. Brian obtained an order of protection to keep her away from the house, although he expected her to continue cooking, cleaning, and meeting his sexual needs. When she shot him, she had lost any hope of finding safety for her child or herself. Lisa is serving a six-and-a-half-year prison term after pleading to aggravated assault (enhanced for dangerousness).

Ronnie stabbed, but did not kill, her abusive boyfriend when he showed up at her apartment because she believed he had stolen her debit card and was just using her for money. He had assaulted her in the past, and also set up her sexual assault by his drug connection. She was extremely agitated and distraught because her ex-husband had taken custody of her children and removed all her belongings from her apartment. Within the previous few days, she had also used crack and prescription antidepressants; the drugs left her disoriented and anxious. Ronnie had also been abused by men throughout her life: by her father, by a stranger, and by her husband of sixteen years, as discussed in chapter 4. She was standing outside her apartment when her boyfriend drove up in her car, approached her, and tried to appease her with a hug. Ronnie does not remember plunging the knife into his stomach, but remembers suddenly seeing blood and hearing him scream, "The bitch stabbed me." When police arrived and placed her under arrest, they tape-recorded her angry and obscene ravings about her boyfriend's physical and mental abuse.

In two cases, women claimed that their lethal actions were accidental, although the courts did not believe them. Rhonda ran over her husband with a truck; Beth stabbed her husband as he lunged at her (described in chapter 2). Rhonda was sentenced to five years for negligent manslaughter, and Beth was sentenced to ten years on a plea to attempted manslaughter.

Finally, for three cases (Michelle, Tina, and Cindy) it is impossible for me to determine the context of men's deaths. All three women had been abused by their partners, and that fact was not disputed by the prosecution. The question was how the abuse related to the death of their partners. Michelle's case, discussed in the previous chapter, involved a fight with her husband, but her recollection of events is so clouded by alcohol that nobody knows exactly what happened the night her husband died. The medical examiner indicated that the cause of death was asphyxiation on his own vomit rather than the blows inflicted by Michelle. Michelle was placed on probation.

In another case, Tina crashed a party her boyfriend was throwing and shot him in his garage. He was married and had been trying to end their affair, and she pursued him. There were 9-1-1 tapes that recorded his threats to kill her on another occasion, but no one knows what happened in the garage that night. The case occurred about the time that the film *Fatal Attraction* was popular, and the press dubbed Tina the "Fatal Attraction Killer." Her pursuit of a married man was the focus of the media and the prosecutor, and the violence she endured was barely mentioned. She is serving a life sentence for first-degree murder, and has been denied clemency.

Finally, Cindy described a late-night confrontation with her husband in their home, but maintains that she did not kill him. She says that she knows who did, but she will not divulge that information. A great deal of evidence points to her, and she is serving a sixteen-year sentence for second-degree murder.

Women's Feelings About Abusers

Women who killed or used nonlethal violence against their partners vary considerably in terms of their feelings about their abusers. Of the twenty-six women who killed or used sublethal violence against their partners, all but four were terrified and believed he was going to kill them or have them killed. Two women were not afraid of their partners: one claimed his death was an accident; the other claimed she had no part in his murder. Two other women were afraid, but not terrified of their partners. Of this group of twenty-six, only seven were not living with their abuser at the time of the violent event. Danielle was planning to move back in the following day. One woman, Abby, was planning divorce, and her husband's discovery of this led to the conflict in which he died. The high proportion of women who killed and who were living with their partners raises questions about how and why women remain in relationships where they are terrified; I address these questions below.

Eight women who killed their abusers were still very much in love with them, wanted the relationships to work, and miss them. Five of them said they would still be in the relationships if their partners were alive. Eleven women were no longer in love with their partners, were terrified of them, and felt safer after their deaths or their own incarceration. None of the women who used sublethal violence against their partners indicated they were still in love with them.

Anne's relationship with the man she killed was short-term, about three months, and she described it as "not normal." Her initial attraction to him faded very quickly, and she felt that he forced himself into her life. Once he had moved in with her, she could not get him to leave her alone. He told her outrageous stories (described in chapter 3), and repeatedly threatened her life and her children's lives. Anne did not feel love for this man, but only fear and confusion.

The other seventeen women who were not in love with the men they killed or assaulted had either become involved with their partners at very young ages or lost their feelings of love over the course of years of abuse. Women who became involved with their partners at ages fifteen or sixteen said that they stayed in the relationship because of their children, economic dependency, and depression. Some women had lost feelings of love because their partners abused their children, had blatant affairs with other women, or were drunk or high most of the time. Two women indicated they had never been in love

with the men who hounded them until they agreed to become intimately involved. These women felt they had always been dominated
by their partners and simply did not know how to get away from
them.[16]

Expert Testimony on Battering and its Effects

Unlike cases where battered women's children are killed or women
commit crimes against strangers, women who kill abusive partners
are more understandable and sympathetic, as they resemble traditional self-defense cases. Over the past twenty years, traditional self-
defense law has been influenced by the anti–violence against women
movement and feminist lawmakers.[17] Their work has helped to shift
the legal definitions of appropriate responses to a violent attack in
the context of intimate partner violence.

Many women are still imprisoned for killing their abusers. According to the National Clearinghouse for the Defense of Battered
Women, approximately two thousand women are in prison for killing an intimate partner, one-third of incarcerated female homicide
offenders. Of this group, "at least 45 percent and perhaps as many as
97 percent" were abused by their victims.[18] But the courts and the
public have begun to recognize that a woman who has been battered
by her partner has a different perception of his lethal potential than
most people would have of an assailant. The "reasonable man" standard that was used by courts to assess the justification for use of
deadly force for self-defense has been expanded to include the perceptions of a "reasonable battered woman." By 1996, all fifty states
accepted expert testimony on battering to help explain why a
woman used lethal force rather than simply leave a violent man.[19]

The use of expert testimony on the effects of battering in criminal
trials has changed since it was first introduced in the early 1980s.[20]
Early testimony relied heavily on the "battered woman syndrome"
and the work of Lenore Walker in describing the characteristics of
this syndrome. The limitations of the syndrome language have been
thoroughly documented.[21] The notion of a syndrome psychologizes
the effects of battering by focusing on certain psychological effects
to the exclusion of the broad range of social, economic, and psychological problems resulting from battering. The inclusion of the term

learned helplessness to describe one aspect of the syndrome also creates an expectation for general subservience and passivity that often is not descriptive of women who survive violent relationships. Generally, the word "syndrome" suggests a malady that it is possible to diagnose; but of course, there is not one, unique response to battering.

For a decade, scholars and activists have urged legal actors to discontinue use of the term "battered woman syndrome," but it persists. Every attorney who contacts me to assist with clients who have been battered refers to the syndrome. Legislators and attorneys have argued with me that it's "just semantics," and "battered woman syndrome" is easier for people to grasp than "battering and its effects." I believe that the language we use shapes understanding, and that the "battered woman syndrome" perpetuates views of women as sick. It is also an inaccurate description of what we know about the effects of battering and should be discarded.[22]

By 2006, knowledge of the effects of battering on women's own violent behavior toward their abusers reflects thirty years of research. We know that many factors influence women's perceptions of their safety and alternatives in a violent relationship: her economic dependence on the abuser; prior history of victimization; the reactions of friends, family, and children to her abuse; results of prior help seeking (especially from the police); levels of physical, sexual, and emotional abuse; abusers' threats to kill her, her loved ones, her children, himself (if she tries to leave); women's own abuse of alcohol and drugs (both prescription and street); immigration status; cultural values regarding divorce and abuse; and hope that the abuser will change.

Evidence on the effects of battering has a contradictory impact in cases where women have killed or used violent force against an abuser. It may help a jury or judge to understand the context in which a woman acted and her perceptions of danger and options for escape. This understanding can support a self-defense argument or mitigate the seriousness of her use of violence. At the same time, demonstrating the violence and degradation inflicted by an abuser may reinforce the perception of a woman's *motive* to kill. All may agree that a defendant was battered by her partner, but argue that she should have left the relationship and obtained legal protection. She should not have resolved the problem by using violence against him. Explanations of the ways that batterers systematically destroy women's perceptions of alternatives, and often continue to harass and threaten, even after the woman has physically moved away, *should* help juries and judges understand the restrictions they face. The perception of women's actions depends on many factors apart from her experience of battering (described in chapter 2). Women who have been violent in the past, used drugs or alcohol, and expressed jealousy over their partners' affairs with other women, do not often gain the same sympathy as women without these characteristics. The use of evidence on the effects of battering is particularly problematic when a woman has already left the relationship or when a third party commits the murder. In these situations, it is more difficult for outsiders to understand her perception of imminent threat as she no longer shares the same household, or was not present at the time of his death.

Why Does She Stay?

I'm so sick and tired of hearing, "Well, why didn't you just leave? Why didn't you just walk away?" Well, until you've been in my shoes, you ain't walking anywhere. There is no way out. He took away my car. He took away my financial independence. He took away everything. I had to depend on him for everything. —Beth

Many activists and scholars have critiqued appropriately the excessive concern with women's reactions to abuse. Asking "Why does she stay?" rather than "Why does he abuse?" or "How can we end abuse?" tends to contribute to victim-blaming attitudes that deflect attention from perpetrators.[23] In the context of women's crimes, however, this question is pivotal. When women kill or attempt to kill their abusers, or when they commit other crimes, the reasons that they remained in the relationship must be explained. Of nineteen women who killed their partners, only four were not living with them at the time of the man's death. Of seven who shot or stabbed their abusers, three were no longer living with them. The resort to lethal violence must be explained within the context of the multiple factors that keep women living with men who threaten their lives. For women who were *not* living with their abusers, their violent, sometimes lethal, assaults require explanations of the factors that led them to believe the men would kill them. As mentioned at the outset, the use of information about prior abuse when women kill helps to explain their actions, not excuse them. In the following sections, I describe the situations women faced prior to and in the immediate context of the use of deadly force against their abusive partners.

Getting Trapped

Women living with abusive intimate partners often develop a sense that escape is impossible. As discussed in chapter 1, this sense of hopelessness leads women to thoughts of suicide as well as homicide. In Neil Websdale's analysis of domestic homicides, he notes that in most cases (83 percent), women who killed their partners were still living with them and had no plans to separate. He notes that "most women who killed were backed into a corner and could not escape. Their entrapment was acute and intense."[24] Women are entrapped at multiple levels: physical, social, and psychological. Abusive men are not egalitarian, rational partners who accept women's requests and decisions. When women say they want a divorce or want to separate, most abusive partners let them know that they will not allow it. As described throughout this book, threats to kill women if they try to leave are common, and are often accompanied by graphic demonstrations of the intent to follow through. Women have guns held to their heads, are driven to remote places and told they will be killed, and are beaten for even suggesting separation.

In some cases (described in chapter 2), men continue to stalk, harass, and invade women's new residences even when women have been able to move out and away. As one woman expressed it, "Even if I get a divorce, he wouldn't let me go free. . . . No matter where I go. . . . I know it wouldn't work. . . . I don't know of anything that would help." Men's physical abuse and threats to kill establish realistic fears that efforts to escape are dangerous. The vast majority of violent relationships do not end in homicide; when women *are* killed, however, it is more likely to occur during or after separation.[25] There is some evidence that even thinking about leaving increases women's risk.[26]

There are also social and economic factors that trap women in violent relationships. Women's relatives and friends may not be willing to harbor her from her partner because they are afraid of his violence or because they are unable or unwilling to provide economic support to the woman and her children. They may focus on the positive aspects of the relationship and minimize the abuse and danger. Four women spoke about the ways their abusers manipulated their parents and tried to portray the women as the problem. Danielle, for example, explained how she knew she was trapped when her father sided with her husband:

> All they [her parents] did was just sing the praises of Tony. And how do you, you know, go to somebody and burst their bubble, "No, it's not like that, this is how it is." And I remember one time my son had called my dad, that's the time Tony had beaten me with the phone, and my son called my dad and my dad come up there. And my dad had always said, if anyone ever hit his daughters, you know, and so when I knew my dad was coming over, I was almost like, okay, my knight in shining armor is coming and then when he gets there, and the whole side of my face was full o' blood and both my boys were hovered around me, for my dad to look at me and say, "What'd ya' do?" (*starts crying*). At that point I knew, I was alone. I mean, and Tony was still there with the phone saying, "Do you wanna call the cops?" and he'd hit me in the head with the phone, "Call the cops."

Shanna explained to me that her husband would call her mother and tell her what a bitch she was. "I believed it. I thought I was a bitch and I deserved to be hit." Teresita also explained how her boyfriend, Primo, would tell her mother that *she* [Teresita] was the problem:

> You know, he made it to where, that nobody would ever believe me. I had nobody, and you know sometimes when I'll call my mom and cry like he was hitting me, he would get on the phone and take it from me and while he was hitting me he'll tell my mom, "She's over here trippin' like, 'she's hittin' on me,'" havin' my mom believe him, you know, so right there I see like no one isn't ever gonna believe me, you know. If he can get my mom fooled, he can fool anybody else. So, it was like I was trapped in this house thinkin' that I had nowhere to go. And it was like it's scary to live in that situation, and just lookin' at your kids and thinkin' like, "I'm stuck."

Women were also trapped by their economic dependency on abusive partners. As Beth said, being "totally dependent" on a man limits women's ability to walk away from a violent relationship. For women with small children and few marketable skills or experience,

the prospect of trying to live independently from abusers was daunt-
ing. Most men who were killed or injured were not bringing much
money into the household, but some women still believed their
chances of economic survival were better with the men than without
them. In other cases, women were the primary earners, sometimes
working two jobs, and economic dependence was not the problem.
Sheila, for example, owned her own home, and wanted her partner to
move out, but could not get him to leave. Even women who owned
their homes or were the primary renter and earned more money than
their partners were stuck because their abusers refused to move out.

Psychological entrapment also influenced women's perceptions
of their alternatives. As mentioned above, seven women were still
very much in love with their partners. These women held onto romantic dreams and hoped that they could help their partner overcome the problems that led to his violence. They did not want to end
their relationships. Because there were "good parts" of the man they
loved and of the relationship, women clung to their hopes and their
commitment. Other women who were no longer in love were entrapped by the psychological mind games men played: making them
believe they would lose custody of their children, that *they* were to
blame for the abuse, that no one else cared about them, or that the
men's putative superhuman powers prohibited women's escape.
Men's threats about taking custody or women's inability to survive
on their own had a basis in reality; thus women were convinced they
were insurmountable obstacles to escape.

No Exit

When women killed their partners, they believed that there was
nothing else that would protect them. Unlike the popularized image
of battered women murdering sleeping men, most women who killed
did so in the context of an immediate threat to their lives that they
could not escape.[27] Anne's story of killing her boyfriend as he approached her car was described in chapter 3. Seven other women who
killed were responding to immediate threats to their lives.

Sue was the first woman I met who had killed her husband. She
was a thirty-year-old, white, working-class woman who was in her
second abusive marriage. Her husband had been physically assault-

ing her and emotionally abusing her since their marriage two years before his death. The abuse had escalated to severe levels; on several occasions, he had placed a loaded gun in her hands, put his hands over hers, and said, "I should have you kill me." On the night of his death, he came into their house and woke her from a deep sleep. He first started to hit her in the face and scream obscenities at her. Sue did not know where the gun came from, but suddenly he placed a gun into her mouth and threatened to blow her head off. He then forced the gun into her hands, pointed it toward himself and pulled the trigger. She ran to the neighbors to call the paramedics for help, but her husband was already dead when they arrived. She was charged with manslaughter, and accepted a plea with a stipulation to probation. Sue did not serve time for her husband's death, but she does have a felony conviction on her record and had to comply with probation for several years. At sentencing, the judge ordered her to perform service in a battered women's shelter and also told her that she could not enter into an intimate relationship for at least a year. Several years later, she remarried and was living a peaceful, crime-free life.[28]

Lynne had two lodgers who observed the extreme violence and abuse by her husband. They were not able to protect her, but were able to confirm her reports of abuse when she was charged with his murder. She was a forty-eight-year-old, white, working-class woman who had been married to her second husband for several years. He was an alcoholic who kept an arsenal of loaded guns close at hand and had begun beating Lynne on a regular basis. Lynne had almost no free time, working as a maid during the day and a bartender at night, but he believed she was seeing other men. He offered her friend three hundred dollars to tell him whom she was seeing so he could "blow him away and her too," and had left a death threat on her windshield saying, "Daddy's going to kill you." At the point of his death, he was drinking two quarts of vodka a day, plus beer. Lynne had given up on calling the police; they had been to her home on fifteen separate occasions and he was only arrested once. He was ordered to attend a batterer's intervention program, and he bragged to everyone that he duped the counselors, who were "idiots." It certainly did not reduce his abusiveness. On the night of his death, Lynne walked into the house after finishing her evening job. He pulled his gun out of the sofa cushions, pointed it at her, and said, "You're gonna' die, bitch."

That is the last thing Lynne remembers, but she somehow got the gun and shot and killed him. She was originally charged with manslaughter, but charges against her were dropped after evidence of her battering and self defense was introduced. The judge explained to me that because Lynne held the gun and her husband did not, she should have walked out the door instead of shooting him. The grand jury, however, decided not to indict her.

Men's fascinations with and easy access to guns and threats to kill women with them are strongly correlated with women's death by intimate partner homicide. Jacquelyn Campbell et al.'s research on factors associated with femicide found that "women who were threatened or assaulted with a gun or other weapon were twenty times more likely than other women to be murdered."[29] In combination with unemployment, extreme jealousy, prior threats to kill, and women's separation from their abusers, the availability of weapons dramatically increases women's risks of lethality. For Sue and Lynne, the guns men intended to use against them became the source of their own self-preservation.

The presence of other weapons also increases the risk for lethality. Dorothy's common-law husband, Barney, trapped her in their bedroom and threatened her with a knife. They had been drinking with Dorothy's teen-aged sons, and Barney became angry with her.

He started slappin' me, pullin' my hair, and I told him to stop it. And I told him "I'm gonna go back out there." And he said, "No, you and I are gonna talk," and we got into a fight, and then all of a sudden I saw that he had a knife in his hand. And I told him to stop it, you know, I kinda got scared, our waterbed was, the bathroom was this way, and I came, and I tripped over the bed, and then, he went that way, I went that way, we did that for a while, then he started throwin' things, sayin', "I'm gonna cut your this, I'm gonna cut your that," but I didn't wanna scream, because of the kids in there, hoping that, you know, he usually does snap out of it. I kept hoping that he would.

And then, finally, I just figured, well it's gonna happen like with that gun, that he'll come to his senses, just put it down. Then I was shakin', I was scared, and cryin', so I said, "Go ahead then," he had things all knocked down (*pause*), then somehow, I guess, either I took the knife from him, or he dropped it, I know the knife was on the floor (*crying harder now*), so I picked it up, and I think he took it back from my hand, I don't exactly remember what happened, but all I know is the knife was in him, and he was staggerin' that way, and when he died, not right then, when he fell, I went out and I told my son to come on in. I said something, "he's stabbed," and to get the ambulance, to send the kids, or somethin' like that. So, I guess, he told the kids maybe to go. I remember I was just sitting there, and my son was shaking me, telling me to snap out of it. The ambulance came, those guys came, and they were talkin' to him when he was on the floor. And then they took him, and either my son went with them, or he followed them, but by the time he came back, he told me that Barney, they couldn't do anything for Barney.

Crystal also stabbed her husband in a confrontation where she believed she was going to be severely beaten or killed. Her husband, Tom, had been in a foul, threatening mood all day. Tom was an extremely abusive man, physically and emotionally.

I used to go through, all the four-and-a-half years that I went through pain. And even at night, even if it was snowing, I would try and run with my kids, middle of the night, without my shoes. There were times that he would find me, and drag me all the way back to the house with my hair, and there I used to get the worst of it (crying hard). My kids, they seen me with him, what he used to do to me. He would just start hitting me, cussing at me, and start beating me up, and that continued, and when I was carrying my son, when I was pregnant with him, he kept on with that, and he used to always kick me around with his boots, one of those, steel toes boots, times that he used to tell me to undress and he would continue kicking me all over, and when I would try to run, try to get out of the house, get away from him, he didn't care what it was, he would use it on me, especially my ankles, and from that I still have a lot of scars (shows me).

He would use his knee to like jump on me, on my back, when I was pregnant with my son, he would use his knee, and there was always bruises all over my body, 'cuz he used to kick me around then a lot, my butt, most of the time he used to beat on my side, it would just be black and blue. And the year [child's name] was born, he was only five, six months, he would use steel, uh, a steel on me, and he broke my arm (she shows me deep indent on arm where it was broken). And they did surgery in Gallup, New Mexico, I was taken over there, scheduled for surgery, and I went through it, and that kept on, and scars on my face that he gave me when he used to just sit on me and beat me. And there were times when he used to come home drunk, and he burned me with cigarette butts, just hold my arm down, have his knee on my chest, and just burn them (*sighs and cries*). One day, that he used the hose on me, and he just kept usin' it all over my body, and I remember I blacked out because of the pain, and I thought I lose my thinking, I guess, and I remember, I guess he got scared, he poured cold water on me. That's when I snapped.

Tom was also psychologically cruel to Crystal and her children. He only referred to her as "bitch" or "whore," and she said "it just seemed like my name to me." He accused her of having sex with her father, brother, his friends, any man walking down the street, and told her in front of her son, "One day you're gonna' fuck your son." He tore her clothes off in front of her children and beat her with a broom and a hose. He constantly harassed her oldest son, who was from another marriage, and would grab the food the boy was eating and jam it down his throat. Crystal said that she and everyone else in town were too afraid of Tom to challenge him.

On the day she killed him, he told her repeatedly, "You know what you're gonna get when we get home, bitch," and despite her pleas, she could not talk him out of his anger. They spent most of the day trying to make their car work so they could travel to get money back from people who owed them. While she drove, he cursed her and punched her in the face. She was able to jump out of the car at a stop sign and escape with her daughter. Unfortunately, her son was still strapped into an infant safety seat in the back seat of the car. Crystal flagged down a ride and was able to get in touch with a friend. Her friend helped her locate a police officer, after many hours of trying, who accompanied her to her apartment to get her baby, as well as food, diapers, and clothes for the night. While she was in the apartment, she also retrieved a knife for protection. After the police officer left, Crystal's friend decided she needed to stop in for just a moment to see another woman who lived in the same complex. It was then that Tom reappeared:

I could feel him around there. I could really feel the pain of like when he's beating me up—the hurt and the pain. I was afraid, I was scared (*now crying again*), and I went to the kitchen, drank the water, and I don't know why, I opened the drawer where all the utensils were. And the knife was there, and I picked it up. But I didn't think that I would stab him. I went back to the car, it seemed like he would jump out from the corner, and I held that knife for protection. I said, "Well, let's go" [to her mom's house]. But no, she wanted to stop at Jessie's to ask her something. She got off, and as soon as she got off, I locked the door. The knife, I just threw it on top of the dashboard, and I forgot it.

We were sitting there, and I saw him coming, when she was halfway to the door. And he came, tried opening door, and he said "Bitch!" He yelled and started banging on the window. He came around, and he banged on the top, and I remember he said somethin', and I rolled down the window, I don't know why, about so much (*indicating about five inches*) and he grabbed my hair, and pulled my head so hard against the window, and he was trying to grab the other side too, and I kept pulling away, and he kept saying "Remember you're gonna get it, you're gonna die, bitch, whore, bitch," and I grabbed that knife, and I just went like this (*shows stabbing motion while looking other way*), and I remember he goes "Ahhh, ahhh," and he got away, and I was holding my baby, and I put him on this side, and I couldn't open the car door and he staggered away.

In Tom's case, Crystal's stab wound might not have resulted in death had medical help been more available. As it was, it took nearly an hour for an ambulance to arrive and it was too late.

I remember I said, "Hon, hon," and I didn't know I hurted him (*crying hard*). I started running after him. He ran this way, then that way, then he fell. He was face up and he was trying to mumble something. "Hon, I didn't mean to hurt you, where did I hurt you?" and that's when he took his last breath. I was screaming for help, someone to call the ambulance. It took almost an hour. They pulled me away from him. It was just like a nightmare. At the hospital, they tried everything, even though, he died.

The court, recognizing Crystal's suffering, the immediate threat she faced, and her lack of intent to harm Tom, imposed probation and treatment rather than prison.

Five other women who killed and two who shot but did not kill their abusers faced similar circumstances of imminent death. These cases were all charged as murder or manslaughter because they did not meet the legal requirements for self-defense. In each case, there was only one weapon present, either a gun or a knife. If the woman had possession of the weapon, and the man was unarmed even for a moment, her lethal action could not be defined as proportionate force. From women's perspective, however, their partners clearly posed an imminent threat and they had "no doubt" that they were in danger of being killed. Their stories are all similar: he was in an angry rage; he threatened to kill her, her children, or another loved one; he kept loaded guns around the house, or insisted that she carry one for protection, and the woman used it to protect herself from him; the look on his face or in his eyes made him appear "evil," "crazy," and like "someone else." In two cases, Dorothy and Crystal, a knife was used. None of these cases involved any evidence of planning or premeditation, and testimony on the effects of battering was very helpful in explaining women's perceptions of lethal danger. As mentioned above, only one woman who defended herself in a situation of immediate threat received a prison sentence, and this was five years for manslaughter. She served two and a half years before being released on probation.

It is unclear why Dianne received a harsher sentence than any other woman. Her prior abuse was documented and her husband was known to be unstable, violent, alcoholic, and a drug abuser. On the night she shot him, she had gone out with a friend and returned home a few minutes later than he had expected. When they returned home, he was in a rage and had destroyed her furniture, plants, and other belongings. Her friend saw the destruction and heard his accusations, but Dianne told her to leave before she got hurt, so she did not actually witness the homicide. He screamed at Dianne that she was a fucking whore, hit her in the face several times, and told her to get out. At one point, he left the house and she locked all the doors. He reentered by breaking out the bedroom window and confronted her. She pulled out the loaded gun they kept in a dresser drawer, and he told her, "Go ahead and do it." Dianne was terrified and pulled the trigger. She said, "I knew he would never let me leave that house alive." She was deeply in love with her husband, devastated by his death, and said they would still be together if he were alive. However, the prosecution did not believe her life was in danger and, as mentioned in chapter 2, depicted her as tough and promiscuous, someone who could not have been a battered woman.

Other women who killed in similar circumstances shared Dianne's working-class status; two were also American Indian women. However, none of the women who received probation or had charges against them dropped had the strong, tough demeanor of Dianne. It may have been this appearance, more than her race or class status, that influenced the prosecution's and court's views that she was not a battered woman, and thus not defending herself out of fear.

Proactive Violence

Women in violent relationships develop a knowledge of their partner's moods and aggressiveness. In this respect, these battered women present as highly perceptive and sensitive social agents within broader structural matrices that evidence much violence and pain. They are not simply passive victims, but active agents in crafting responses to men's violence. The things that trigger his anger, the cues he gives about impending violence, and the look on his face are signals that forewarn women when violence is about to erupt. Although women describe much violence as arising "out of the blue," they also recognize signs that they should take precautions and prepare for the worst. In three cases where women killed their abusers and three where they shot but did not kill, women were responding proactively to a situation in which they believed severe abuse was pending. These cases were particularly problematic for the courts because they did not occur in the immediate context of an assault. The men were unarmed and women waited for them with a gun or, in three cases, actually went to their estranged partner's residences with guns. The conventional requirements for self-defense, therefore, were not in place.

In three cases where men were shot proactively, two lethally, women described a series of circumstances that predicted they were about to be seriously beaten. These cases all involved high levels of prior violence against the women by their partners. In Jane's case, described in chapter 1, her husband's pattern of raping women, then returning home to beat her, framed her perceptions that another beating was imminent. The prosecutor believed she was a cold-blooded murderer who had premeditated her husband's death. Jane had confided in a neighbor that she had considered killing him, and she had also seriously contemplated suicide because she believed there was no way out. The statement to her neighbor and the fact that she waited for her husband with a loaded gun constituted grounds for first-degree (premeditated) murder in the view of the prosecutor. Jane, however, explained how she knew that she was in for another terrible beating:

> I got to where I could feel the hostility in Daryl, I don't know how to explain it, after twelve-and-a-half years, after being through it so many times, when Daryl would get this rage in him, until he would release this rage, which usually meant beat the hell out of me, it was there, I don't know. I just didn't want him to hurt me anymore. How did I know he was gonna hurt me? I had been through it so many times. I knew he was gonna kill me, he told me before, if I ever tried to leave, he would. I heard the prosecutor say he didn't know how I knew it was gonna happen, well I *lived* it, that's how I knew, I'm not ESP, I'm not psychic.

Daryl's physical, sexual, and psychological abuse of Jane was severe, but she did not want people to know that he was the person inflicting her injuries. She loved him and wanted to protect him, and also believed that if she told anyone, he would punish her more severely. Jane was white and Daryl was black, and both of their birth families disapproved of the interracial marriage. When they married in 1978, their home state in the Deep South still had anti-miscegenation laws on the books, so they moved to another state to marry. Jane felt she was stigmatized by both whites and blacks, and that she could not return to her family because they disapproved of her choice. Daryl's constant denigration contributed to her sense that she was a bad person, unworthy of love and protection:

> I heard people, was denied service in restaurants, and I started believing what society told me. Everyone was telling me I was bad, my husband was, his family was, so I thought, that's just the way it was. . . . When I called home to tell my parents we got married, they said, "Just whatever you do, don't have any children." Daryl used that against me, I heard that for the rest of my life. . . . No, I didn't report it. No, I didn't go to the doctor and tell anybody about it. I tell a doctor my husband was doing this to me? One time he forced himself on me, sodomized me, and I bled for like three or four days, and I didn't tell anybody. I couldn't tell my mother, I couldn't tell anybody else my

husband was doing this to me. It took a long time before I told anybody. He blamed me, I thought everybody else would too. He used to tell me I deserved it.

Jane also explained why she did not think calling the police would help protect her:

I've seen women in jail taken in because of defending themselves from their husbands. I wouldn't call the police, no, uh huh, who's gonna protect me when he gets out? No one. And it's gonna be worse, I know, I been there. I think that law [mandatory arrest] is crazy. They say, "well, why didn't you call the police?" Well, what was I supposed to do? Say, "Excuse me a minute while I go use the phone"? In [country's name], he was so mad at me, he locked me in a trunk and left for the day. When he got back, I was so glad to get out of there, calling the police was the furthest thing from my mind. Then he'd say he was gonna take Chelsea and take off with her.

When Jane decided she would divorce Daryl, he held a loaded gun on her. He let her know he would never let her leave the relationship:

JANE: I told him I couldn't go on living like that. He didn't say anything, he just got up, got his gun, and sat there with his finger on the trigger. "I told you if you ever tried to leave me I'd kill you." He kept cocking the trigger, letting it go, cocking it, letting it go.

KATHLEEN: You must have been strong to endure what you did.

JANE: That wasn't strength, that was fear. I loved him, but I was afraid of him. I don't know if I would have left him, I don't think I would. I would say I was gonna leave him, but I remember one time I had gotten so far as to pack, and he met me at the door with a gun, and he said, "Where you going?" and I said "I'm leaving" and he said "Not alive," and I just went and unpacked. He stayed up all night.

Jane felt there was no exit from this relationship because Daryl threatened to kill her and her daughter if she left. She was also deeply depressed and uncertain of her own worth. Despite her fear, Jane also continued to feel love for Daryl and hope that he would change and become the charming, likable person she fell in love with:

If I could take back that night, I would. I didn't mean to shoot him, I didn't want to hurt him, I just wanted him to go away. I just didn't want him to trap me in the house. There were nights when all I could do is say, "Please, please don't hit me anymore," and he just wouldn't stop. I still miss him a lot. If it hadn't happened, if I hadn't shot him, I'd still be with him. I always thought we would grow old together, sit in rockers on the porch, thought he'd mellow out, but I feel like I just ruined everything.

Jane was sentenced to eight-and-a-half years in prison after accepting a plea to manslaughter. As mentioned earlier, she was released after four years and began to rebuild her life. She works as the director of a shelter for battered women and is reunited with her grown daughter.[30]

Dawn's story of proactive violence is similar. She also sat waiting with a loaded gun for her husband to return home. Dawn was also abused physically, sexually, and psychologically by her husband over a period of years. They had two sons who were also abused by their father. Like Daryl, Dawn's husband, Jeff, expected to be obeyed and served within his home. When he felt she was lax in her duties, or when he suspected she was flirting with men, he punished her with extreme violence, including choking, throwing, kicking, and threatening her with a knife. Forced sex, including sodomy and fellatio, were routine, as well as other degrading sexual conduct.[31] He also told her he would kill her if she tried to leave him, and threatened to take custody of their boys. She had also contemplated suicide. Dawn had no education or training and believed she would be unable to support herself and her sons on her own. She did not want to call the police because she knew it would increase Jeff's violence once she was alone with him again.

Jeff insisted that she stop working, and his own income did not cover their expenses. They fell further and further behind on bills, but Dawn was afraid to let him know the extent of their financial problems. Finally, she received a foreclosure notice from the mortgage company and knew they would lose their home. On that morning, Jeff was in a foul mood and had already hit Dawn before leaving for work. When she took him his lunch, as she always did, he was even more angry and asked her, "How would you like your ass kicked?" She was convinced that once he learned of the foreclosure, she would be severely beaten or killed. After her sons were asleep, she loaded Jeff's gun and was about to shoot herself. She then decided she would defend herself instead, and waited for Jeff to return home. When he walked in the door, she shot him and then immediately called 9-1-1 for help. Fortunately, Jeff did not die from this gunshot, although he suffered damage to his internal organs. Dawn was sentenced to probation and retained custody of her sons.

Leah (described in chapter 1), was severely abused by her partner of twelve years. They were both alcoholics, and her partner, Emory, served jail time for assaulting her. Leah never called the police, however, because she felt she would receive worse beatings once he was released. They had four children together, but Emory spent a lot of his time with other women and made no secret of his ongoing affairs. He rarely provided money to the family. They separated and reunited several times, but Emory expected her to remain faithful to him. He told her he would kill her if she ever left him. Leah had quit drinking and was working as a nurse's aide when she discovered that Emory was still involved with another woman. She told him she was going to leave him again and he became angry and started to assault her. Leah ran out of the house to their car and retrieved a shotgun she had purchased for Emory's birthday. She loaded the gun and, as he ran out of the house toward her, she shot him. As he lay on the ground, she told him she would not help him because she wanted him to know what pain felt like.

As mentioned in chapter 1, Leah considered shooting herself at this point, but her son said, "Let's go, Mom," and she got in the car and drove away. Again, in this situation, Leah had a loaded gun and Emory was unarmed. Unlike most of the women who shot their abusers, Leah left the scene and refused to obtain help for Emory. She was viewed as callous and jealous by the prosecutor and judge. The prosecution employed an expert witness who testified that Leah was definitely not a battered woman, although he had never met her and indicated he had no expertise in the field. The reason he gave for his decision that she was not battered was her confrontation with and slapping the face of her husband's mistress, as well as her habit of carrying a knife in her boot. She was found guilty of second-degree murder in a bench trial. In determining her sentence, the judge departed downward one year from the presumptive term because of Emory's prior acts of violence and one year for Leah's nonviolent record. He did not, however, believe that she was a battered woman.

The judge said that he did not see "fear, only anger and jealousy" in Leah's actions, and she was sentenced to nine years. It took thirteen months to complete the trial, during which time Leah was under her own recognizance. During this time, she was beaten twice by Emory's friends and all of her belongings were burned by his family. Through a friend who met her in prison, I learned that Leah completed her sentence and felt that she benefited from the time away and the help she received in the federal prison. I have not heard how she is doing in the last three years.

Two of the women, Mona and Lisa, pursued their estranged partners and shot them (described in chapters 1 and 3). In each of these cases, women's prior experiences of abuse were minor considerations in charging and sentencing. The injuries they inflicted were not serious, and they were charged with aggravated assault. Mona was charged as "nondangerous, nonrepetitive," but Lisa was charged as "dangerous, repetitive," resulting in an enhanced sentence. Mona was sentenced to five years, Lisa to six and a half. As mentioned earlier, Lisa's judge said that "the violence goes both way" in her marriage. The most serious penalty for both women, however, was the loss of custody of their children. Because they committed a violent crime against their children's fathers, they both lost custody of their children. Lisa's crime was motivated by her desire to protect her daughter from molestation by the child's father, and Mona was devoted to protecting her little girl. The loss of their children was the most painful punishment they could have received.

Third-party Murders

The premeditated nature of homicide is undeniable when a third party is solicited to commit the crime. Even if the planning of the offense occurs within a short time prior to its commission, when other people are involved it suggests a decision to act rather than a reaction to an emotional or dangerous situation. Three women were charged with conspiring to commit the murder of their husbands. In two cases, the men who actually committed the murders were also charged and convicted. One received the same sentence as the woman, life imprisonment; the other received three years' less, a sentence of fifteen compared to eighteen years. The third man was released due to "insufficient evidence." The woman received a twelve-and-a-half-year sentence.

Danielle's relationship to her husband was described in chapters 1 and 2. There was considerable verification that she had been battered, including testimony from a marriage counselor to whom her husband admitted violence. The counselor had also seen Danielle with a black eye and described Tony as "a monster." The prosecution used an expert witness who said that Danielle was not a battered woman. Like the prosecution's witness in Leah's trial, this expert had no specialized expertise or training in domestic violence and had never before served as an expert on battering. Danielle had separated from Tony for several months, but she was planning to move back in with him. She told me that he would never allow her to divorce him. He was a resident alien, and he let her know that he could whisk the children to another country before she even knew they were missing. On one occasion, he did hide the children from her over the weekend to prove his point. She believed that he would take her children and also that he would kill her if she tried to divorce him.

One of her coworkers, Bo, who knew of her situation, offered to beat Tony up. She did not think he was serious, but when he introduced her to a friend who wanted to follow through, she agreed that it would "show him how it feels." She still did not really believe that they would beat up her husband, and she never offered compensation. On the night before she was scheduled to move back with him, however, this man not only beat up Tony; he killed him. He also stole some of his belongings that were easily traced. Through a female undercover officer, Danielle made incriminating statements that led to her prosecution and eventual conviction. Her case was complicated by her love affair with Bo, the man who originally suggested the violence. He was twenty years younger than she and African American while she was white. He was originally charged with soliciting murder, first-degree, but he received a three-and-a-half-year sentence and was released after fifteen months. The prosecutor displayed a large photograph of Bo so that the jury could appreciate the racial and age differences between him and Danielle. In the end, the jury did not care whether Danielle was battered because they believed she conspired to have her husband murdered in cold blood. Danielle was sentenced to life in prison. And, as with Lisa and Mona, she missed out on her children's lives as they progressed through adolescence.

Shanna's case is chillingly similar. She was also approached by a coworker with an offer to "beat up" her husband. People at work saw her black eyes, and her husband, Chad, harassed her at work. The abuse had escalated and Shanna and Chad were about to move from his parents' home into their own place. Shanna was fearful that without her in-laws' presence, the violence would be even worse. She remembered that once after Chad was beaten in a bar fight, he stopped abusing her for a few months. So, she accepted her coworker's offer and planned the assault to "teach him a lesson." Shanna never disputed this agreement, which did not involve any promises of pecuniary gain. When she and her coworker met at her home, Chad was asleep in the bedroom. Shanna waited in the kitchen while her coworker went in the back to administer the beating. However, Chad awoke quickly and tried to fight back. The man "lost it" and beat Chad to death with an iron bar. He later said that he had a flashback to his stepfather sexually abusing him, and felt as if he were beating his tormenter, not Chad.

In an account that strains credibility, Shanna claimed she did not realize that Chad had been killed; she returned to work. When she returned home later and found him, she immediately called for help. The prosecutor did not believe that the plan was limited to "beating up," or that Shanna did not know Chad was being bludgeoned to death in another room. Again, the evidence of battering was not considered germane to a deliberate plan to inflict violence, especially lethal violence of such a brutal nature. She accepted a plea to second-degree murder and received an eighteen-year sentence. Her coworker was sentenced to fifteen years. As mentioned previously, Shanna's son was placed with her former brother-in-law, who brings him to the prison once a month to visit. He was three when his mother went to prison, and is now a young adult. She reports that he has done well in school and they have a close relationship. Shanna has been denied clemency in two hearings.

Finally, Eve's situation is quite bizarre and difficult to unravel. She, her husband Earl, and their two children lived in a seedy, drug-infested part of town. Earl had abused her and was heavily into alcohol and drugs. One of his drinking buddies, Jack, began hanging around the apartment and watching Eve's every move. She felt uncomfortable around him and asked Earl to make him leave. Earl became angry and told her to shut up. One day while Earl was asleep, Jack forced Eve to have sex with him. He told her that if she said anything, he'd kill her as he told her he had killed many other people and buried them in the desert. The next day, while she was at the park with her children, Jack murdered Earl with an ax and threw his body in the bathtub. When Eve returned, Jack pushed her up against the bathroom wall, showed her the corpse, and told her "If you ever tell anyone, you'll be next." Eve was in shock and did not know what to do. She tried to tell a neighbor, but Jack saw her speaking to him and became enraged. He took the body to the desert and buried it, then reported Earl's disappearance to the police.

When the body was located, both Jack and Eve were arrested. Jack, however, was released "for lack of evidence," while Eve was prosecuted. The judge and prosecution did not believe she was battered, and the changing stories she gave to police suggested she was lying. There was little corroboration of her reports of abuse, and Earl's grief-stricken family testified that he was never violent. Neighbors testified about a horrible, foul smell in the apartment for at least a week before the murder was reported. The possibility that Eve concealed the body for a week because of her fear of Jack was not credible to the court. She accepted a plea to manslaughter and is serving a twelve-and-a-half-year sentence. Jack left the state without a trace.

It is not possible for me to know the level of women's collusion in these murders. Their accounts to me were made in an effort to mitigate their responsibility and avoid prosecution. However, all three of the men who actually committed the murders were extremely violent men. When women became connected to them, either voluntarily or through coercion (as Eve claims), they were not in a strong position to control their actions. The conclusion that they deliberately and methodically colluded with these men to have their husbands killed is inconsistent with the women's beliefs about their ability to control the men. All three women had been abused physically, sexually, and psychologically for years by their husbands. None of them had criminal records for any activities, were involved in violence, or abused alcohol or drugs. All were afraid of their partners, and Danielle and Shanna believed that if the men received a beating, it would help restrain their abuse. None of them actually promised or paid any money to the killers.

It seems unlikely that these women could have controlled the violent men who killed their husbands once these men decided what they wanted to do. The women's criminal liability was based on the perception that they were manipulative liars who conspired to have men do their dirty work. Their sexuality was invoked in each case: Danielle's affair, Shanna's alleged promise of sex (which she denies and there is no evidence to support), and Eve's sex with the murderer (which she alleges was rape). They were perceived in the spirit of the devious women described by Otto Pollock, who cleverly convince men to commit crimes through their sexual charms. My testimony about their fear, entrapment, and hopelessness as a consequence of years of abuse did not undermine this perception, and they received some of the harshest sentences of any woman in this book.

The situations surrounding women's use of violence against their abusers varied, as did their motivations and the consequences they faced. Evidence of their battering was helpful in explaining why women perceived inescapable danger when others would have simply left the scene. In eleven cases, women were sentenced to probation; in three, charges were dropped. In other cases, sentences were reduced slightly based on evidence of battering. But in some cases, the experience of battering was not deemed relevant to criminal liability. In cases where women were not in immediate danger, proactively engaged in violence, or when a third party committed the murder, information about battering and its effects did not diminish sentences. Indeed, some prosecutors viewed evidence of battering as establishing motive. The acceptance of expert testimony on battering and its effects is certainly not carte blanche for killing one's husband, as some critics have worried.[32] It is, however, one approach to help contextualize women's perceptions of threat for the benefit of legal actors responsible for evaluating culpability for the death or injury of their violent partners. Apart from legal considerations and consequences, however, the death of a violent partner may protect a woman's life, but not eliminate the fear, sadness and confusion caused by his violence and abuse.

I Feel Him Inside Me: The Ghostly Traces of Violent Men

Even when he's dead, he's got me, he did what he said he's gonna do, it's like even when he's dead, he still has this control over me. I still catch myself saying, "Oh, I can't do that, Daryl won't let me do that." I feel like he's watching me still, I catch myself looking. I remember what it was like when he was beating on me, yelling at me, I just get so scared, I don't even know what I'm afraid of. —Jane

The power and control that violent men exert over their partners is reinforced by physical violence. However, it is the psychological abuse, isolation, and surveillance that install men as ubiquitous tormenters in women's minds. It is women's internalization of their partner's control—the batterer's "gaze," in postmodern terms—that produces compliance and dread of his reactions. His physical absence, through abandonment, incarceration, or death, often does not terminate this internalized gaze and its effects. As discussed in chapter 6, the authority of batterers is based on their violence *and* on women's internalization of their commands and wishes. The abuser does not have to be present to enforce his rules because women police themselves. In some cases (Nicole and Julia), women believed their living, incarcerated assailants were able to know their thoughts and inflict punishment for disloyalty, either through other people or by breaking free of guards.

Women's fear of leaving, calling the police, or telling other people about crimes against them or others is related to the internalization of men's control. I am not suggesting that every woman who is abused by her intimate partner develops this overwhelming sense of constant surveillance. The women I am describing throughout this book represent extreme cases where abuse was severe. At the same time, many women who do not commit violent crimes have described similar feelings of internalized control and the impossibility of escape. Some of the women discussed in chapter 2 who felt nothing could stop their abusers were not offenders, but only victims of men's violence. Surely many women overcome the anxiety and depression that accompany intimate partner violence once they have escaped.[33] The women in this book, however, all described the ways that men's control continued after they had separated or the man was dead.

Women's love for an abuser also continues after he is gone. For women who were still in love with their partners at the time that they killed them, grief over their loss is a painful, ongoing struggle. Many women said that they wished they would have died instead of their partners, and were contemplating suicide; only thoughts of their children or grandchildren prevented them from following through. Psychiatrists diagnosed women as severely depressed and prescribed antidepressant medication.[34] As others have documented, being placed on suicide watch in jail is a tortuous, humiliating experience.[35] The nature of the ordeal is well known among inmates, so most women tried to conceal their suicidal thoughts from jail staff. However, women expressed their suicidal thoughts to me. The ambivalent combination of love and fear that permeated women's feelings about their partners while they were alive continued in their deaths. At one level, they knew their partners were dead; at another, they felt their presence, in both positive and negative ways.

As Jane said, fear continued to dominate women's lives after men's deaths, even though they consciously knew they could no longer be beaten. This fear limited women's ability to trust others and to resume normal activities. Dorothy described her continuing fear: "Sometimes I'm just so scared, I'm scared to look around, to this day. I still have that habit. When I go somewhere, I don't wanna look around. It seems like you're just gonna be yelled at again. So, it's kinda hard for me to look at people, after all this time, it's kinda hard to talk to people too, so, mostly, I don't say anything." Beth also described how she continued to monitor her behavior to comply with her dead boyfriend's rules:

I think that if Matt had his way I would be with him, under his control. Sometimes I feel like I still am. I go to say something and I stop myself. I go to do something and I find myself going, "Matt wouldn't like that." Or the decisions that have to be made and I stop and I think, "What would Matt say?" I still feel like he's so in control of me and I think he is. I think he is. But it's got to come to an end somehow and I know that I've gotten stronger since I've been here [jail] and I know I have a long way to go.

Shanna, who is serving an eighteen-year sentence, met with me to discuss her upcoming clemency hearing. She had already been in prison for ten years, but she still suffered from nightmares and fears that her husband was going to attack her. Her bunk was up against a wall in her cell because if she were in the open, she would not sleep for fear that someone would attack her from behind. She still jumped off the chair if there was a loud noise.

Some women felt their abusers were not dead, even though months had passed since his death. Leah could not sleep or eat because she felt he was close by, laughing at her. Like Jane, Leah felt that her abuser had accomplished what he promised, to take away her children, her home, her life, and leave her alone without love. For some women, the ongoing fear was connected to the pain of physical injuries that caused permanent damage. Crystal showed me her scars and bumps and explained the effects of her husband's abuse:

> He kicked my forehead, he just kicked me, and he didn't care where, and gradually I'm losing my eyesight, on this side, I couldn't see, so, you know, it's just like, it's just on the side, I could barely see, but not that much, this side is just dark. And he didn't care what he got ahold of. He used anything that was there, he would use on my head. Right here, you can feel it (*leans over to have me feel her head, which was full of bumps*), and it just stays like that. There's sometimes I wonder, am I gonna die tonight? There's sometimes I, like, forget things, and it scares me, because I know this is all because of what I went through. But sometimes, he would just grab my hair, and you know, hit me against the wall, and I would try to protect my body, and he didn't care where he hit or where he kicked on my body. And sometimes, I would be in a pool of blood, and he would yank me up and say he's hungry, and he would use the pots and pans on me even though I'm trying to cook for him.

Crystal was losing her memory and her eyesight because of the beatings with a metal rod and a hose and the kicks to the head with steel-toed boots she had endured. She explained the pain she continued to feel and the remorse she felt for killing him:

> I never did hurt him, I never did try to fight back or anything, I loved him so much. I tried to do everything to please him and, when I think about it, I think to myself, I didn't do that, I didn't do that. No, at times I still do love him, sometimes I think I'm crazy, after all the things that I went through, all the pain. But I never hurt him. He was the one always beating me up. Even when I was pregnant. And sometimes I could just in my sleep, and now, even I can just kinda feel all those pains. And I'm scared too. Just the thought of it now. It just makes me

just cry. And why? What did I ever do? End up taking his life. I never meant to hurt him, never even wanted to hurt him. I was always there. I loved him so much. I always tried to please him in any way I could.

About one-fourth (five out of nineteen) of the women missed the men they had killed and felt lonely and isolated without them. Dorothy described her depression in trying to cope with her husband's death:

Sometimes I feel like cryin', screamin', even now, as I say that, I'm not really free. I'm still scared. I guess after about seven years of bein' scared, and not sayin' anything, just got to be a habit. I hope, sometimes, I hope maybe there's hope, you know, that things will be all right. My grandkids, maybe there's something to hope for, I think, maybe that day has come. It's so hard (*crying*). I don't miss the beating part, but it's just that I miss him. I tried so hard to make a good life, but then, it just got bad.

Sometimes I feel so alone there. Like I'm the only one in this whole world that has this problem, that there's nobody to help me. It seems like I'm cut out from the whole world, and out there by myself. I don't know, I guess right now I just don't know. Some days it's easier, some days it's worse. Mostly it's worse. At night, you know, when you're by yourself, you get lonely, you get, sometimes I miss him, sometimes, you know, like, I talk to him. Tell him, why, why, why was he like that? Why, why, like, didn't he go for treatment? Why, well, mostly I just thought it was his temper. But now lately, you know, when I have time to think about it, how he is, and, he shouldn't be losin' his temper that much, all the time. Yeah, and treatin' my family like that. Then sometimes, I think it maybe was the war. I don't know that much about that, if he really was in combat, or if it was just what he went through.

I was so scared most of the time. But I miss him a lot, I miss him. It will take time probably. . . . I have a lot of [American Indian] medicine man, they say prayers and stuff, and they do a lot of things, like to straighten your mind out, they give you smoke, they say a prayers for you, and stuff like that. But mostly I wanted to go to talk to a psychologist to see what was my problem with this thing. But once I get in their office, I can't talk to them, I don't know what to say, it seems like my mind just goes blank. I need to get some kind of help, because right now I'm just where I don't care. I want to do somethin' to myself, but then I can't do it too, when I look at the kids, there's got to be somethin' for me out there. I don't know where my life is at, at the moment.[36]

Dorothy struggled to understand why her husband was so violent and still could not make sense of it. She contemplated suicide, but did not want to hurt her grandchildren. The help she was receiving from medicine men did not take away the pain and loneliness, but she did not know how to talk to non-Indian psychologists. Although Barney hurt and scared her, she missed him and could not bear to remain in the house they had shared. Dorothy did receive help and support at a residential program run by Native women.

Beth, who was sentenced to ten years on a manslaughter plea, expressed similar feelings about the death of her partner:

He comes to me in my dreams. I think that was the first good night's sleep that I had here [in jail] then I woke up and realized . . . I slept on his chest all night long in this dream. That's where I stayed. I didn't want to wake up. He was my everything. I was attached to him completely. I wish I could change that night. I've gone over it in my head a million times. I blame myself but then I don't blame myself. I just . . . I know somebody's got to pay for what happened. I'd like to kill myself. I'd do that if it would make anybody feel better from his family. I've contemplated it time and time again. I think then there wouldn't be another boy or girl who would have to see that his mom's a convicted murderer. Maybe my mom wouldn't have to go through any more pain, being worried about me and taking care of me and maybe his family would feel like they've gotten some satisfaction and then it would be done. And I would be able to be with Matt.

Like Dorothy, however, Beth knew that if she took her own life, her son would have to deal with the consquences:

I have his little pictures plastered all over my room and it's a constant reminder of why I don't do anything stupid. One time in here I had saved up all my sleeping pills and I was going to take them all. I was just going to go to sleep. At the time that I was going to do it I saw his little face in a picture of him. I looked up and I saw that picture and I thought to myself, "You can't be selfish anymore, Beth. You have a responsibility." That responsibility is what I live every day for. If I was to kill myself, then I can't imagine the childhood I would give him.

The grief these women live with surpasses the pains of imprisonment. They wanted the abuse to end, not their partners' lives. They are also aware of the pain they have caused the other people in their partners' lives, mothers, fathers, siblings, and children. Some of these people testified against women at sentencing hearings and let them know the contempt they felt for them. At Matt's sentencing, the family brought a giant posterboard filled with photographs of Matt and lettering saying, "WE LOVE YOU" and "WE MISS YOU." They told the judge about the hole in their lives left by the loss of their loved one. Most families denied that the man was abusive, even when there was substantial evidence that he was. But even those who admitted his violence shared the feelings of the women, juries, and the court: he did not deserve to die.

The loss of men's lives at the hands of their abused partners is a tragedy. They were cruel, abusive, and dangerous but they were also people who were loved. Like the women, these men were neither angels nor demons. As children and as adults the men had experienced their own forms of victimization and struggles. Unfortunately, no one was able to stop them, intervene, and protect the women they abused. If they had not died, it is very likely that their partners and perhaps other people would have been killed.

Conclusion

When women used violence against abusers in a context of imminent threat, testimony and evidence on the effects of battering was effective in explaining their perceptions of threat and alternatives. Most women in this situation received a sentence of probation, or had charges dropped; those who were sentenced received leniency in consideration of their abuse. Because the cases discussed here began in 1983, it is not possible to assert that the anti–violence against women and battered women's self-defense efforts were responsible for the outcomes. It is possible, however, that this work has led to changes in charging practices. Over the past five years, I have had no requests for expert testimony on cases where women killed abusers in the context of an imminent threat. This absence of requests could be the result of a number of factors, such as case law limiting the scope of testimony about battering, or attorney ignorance about the relevance of expert testimony. It is also possible, however, that these cases are not being charged, given the prosecution's growing awareness of the dynamics of intimate partner violence. For example, in 1996, the chief homicide prosecutor requested that I testify about the effects of battering in a "cold case" (twenty years old) child homicide. He asked that I explain during a pre-trial hearing how battering could restrain a woman from reporting the death of her child. The judge heard my testimony and agreed that charges should not be brought against the woman. Her husband was convicted. It seems that this prosecutor was attuned to the effects of battering and did not think that justice would be served by charging a battered woman for the crime of her husband.[37]

In other cases where abusers are hurt or killed, however, the effects of expert testimony on battering are more ambiguous. In all cases where a third party committed the homicide, women were sentenced to lengthy prison terms. These cases are extremely problematic, as they provide clear indication of malice aforethought and planning. None of the three women described here felt that they had control over the person who committed the murders; in two cases, however, women did not dispute their participation in discussing plans for assaults against their husbands. Brutal crimes were committed and, in these cases, evidence of battering did not help to explain women's fear. It seemed, rather, to endorse a motive for wanting their husbands to die. In each case, women's sexuality was also invoked to suggest that the violence of men who killed their abusers was motivated by promises of sexual gratification (in Danielle's case, for the murderer's friend). It is not clear to me whether expert testimony in these cases is helpful.

When women used proactive violence against abusers, there was more sympathetic appreciation of their histories of abuse. Dawn and Sheila received probation, but Jane, Leah, and Mona all received prison sentences ranging from five (victim only injured) to nine years (victim killed). Still, these sentences were lower than they would have been without consideration of histories of abuse. Finally, when it appeared that women were acting out of anger and jealousy (such as Tina and Leah), or in order to pursue a relationship with another man (Shanna and Cindy), even if these appearances were not true, women received the harshest sentences. The two women serving life, Tina and Danielle, demonstrated their histories of abuse, but did not persuade the court that they acted out of fear. Tina was defined as acting out of an obsessive desire to reunite with a reticent partner, and Danielle's participation in a third-party murder was portrayed as an effort to get her husband out of the way so she could enjoy a new romantic partner. After spending much time with these women, and reading mounds of documents, I do not agree with these views of either woman.

None of the women who were charged with crimes against their abusers were chronic offenders with violent criminal histories. Beth and Lisa had both been arrested for domestic violence but, as discussed in chapter 2, their offenses were minor, and Lisa's was in response to her own abuse. Several women had been arrested on DUIs (driving under the influence of alcohol), but none were dangerous violent offenders. Incarceration for crimes against abusers, especially for long-term sentences, does not seem to serve a specific deterrent function for these women; it is imposed as retribution for life lost or injured. As most women had children who lost both parents as a result of the homicide and their mother's incarceration, the public interest served by this response is debatable. I return to this question in chapter 6.

Once violence became a part of these relationships, most women believed they were trapped and there was nothing they could do. Men were arrested, incarcerated, sent to counseling, participated in AA (Alcoholics Anonymous) and continued with their abuse. What could have stopped the violence and prevented their deaths? There are no individual-level solutions that will end intimate partner violence. The resources that have been developed over the past thirty years help: women *do* find refuge and support in shelters; men *are* arrested and sometimes deterred from future violence; orders of protection empower *some* women and prevent *some* violent men from harassing them. But the levels of intimate partner terrorism described here cannot be eliminated through these individual-level mechanisms alone.

All of the men who were killed by their partners demonstrated pathological jealousy and possessiveness.[38] They constantly accused women of flirting, being unfaithful, and having sex with the most unlikely partners: their close relatives, a repairman, a man phoning the house by mistake. They attempted to enforce loyalty by close surveillance and physical punishment. Their use of violence demonstrated their sense of entitlement to women's obedience, faithfulness, and adoration. When they felt deprived of these benefits, they used violence to enforce their entitlement. Women continually expressed bewilderment over men's perceptions of their transgressions. They described painstaking efforts to please their partners. Almost all of them described ways they tried to reduce conflict and accusations. Four women explicitly mentioned limiting their eye movements to avoid accusations of flirting! But it was impossible to avoid their partners' accusations and consequent punishments because it was not their behavior that men were reacting to: it was men's own beliefs about their partners and men's response to their perceptions of women's disloyalty and disrespect.

Ideas about men's entitlement and women's innate untrustworthiness are central components of patriarchal ideology (discussed in chapter 3). These ideas have been challenged and undermined in the United States and throughout much of the world. They continue to circulate within popular culture and major institutions and to inform the ways that boys learn about masculinity.[39] Individually focused interventions contribute to women's safety, and thus indirectly to the safety of abusive men and a reduction in the harmful effects of intimate partner violence on the entire community.[40] Such interventions cannot, however, end intimate partner violence unless they are accompanied by sustained, systematic efforts to dismantle the structure and ideology of male dominance inherent in patriarchy.

Men's beliefs that women should serve and obey them are also the context in which women commit crimes at the direction of their abusive partners. In the following chapter, I describe the crimes of obedience in which women became violent offenders. Their experiences of abuse are the same as those of women who killed or harmed their abusers. The consequences, however, were crimes against innocent people.

6 ~~~ Angelic Demons?: Crimes of Complicity

I didn't wanna be there, I didn't wanna be anywhere, I just wanted to die, to tell you the truth. There was no malicious intent in my heart whatsoever, I was just scared, I didn't know where to go.
> —Jennifer, convicted of manslaughter for a murder committed by her boyfriend.

When innocent people are harmed by women's crimes, it is easy to view women as demons with malicious intentions. There are women who perpetrate terrible crimes against others with little concern for the damage they inflict. I am not describing those women here. My focus is on women who participate in crimes through their relationships with violent partners. Fear, hopelessness, and confusion are the feelings most commonly described by women charged with crimes committed by or under orders from their abusers. Their crimes are not committed with "malicious intent," but through their compliance with the demands of violent partners.

In this chapter, I discuss the ways that the authority established by abusive partners frames women's participation in criminal activity. Of forty-five women interviewed, nineteen were charged with crimes against people other than their abusers. In twelve cases, the crimes were actually committed by women's intimate partners or under orders from them. In two cases, it is not possible to determine who actually perpetrated the assaults that led to the deaths of children, and one child's death was the result of neglect by both parents. In all three of these cases, women failed to obtain medical attention for their children. In one case, a homicide occurred through the accidental firing of a gun while a woman attempted to follow her partner's orders. One woman killed her children after abuse and abandonment by her partner, but her case is excluded from analysis due to its notoriety and easy identification. Although her crime was related to her own victimization, it was not a result of complying with the demands of her partner.

The crimes discussed include armed robbery, counterfeiting, mail fraud, drug purchasing, sexual assault, sexual and physical abuse of children, and homicide. Six of these women received probation; the rest were sentenced to prison (see appendix F). When innocent people are harmed, women's prior victimization is viewed as less relevant to their culpability than when they harm the person who has abused them.

Other studies on women's "pathways to crime" that have examined victimization have focused on women who are immersed in street crime.[1] These studies have demonstrated how childhood and adult victimization combines with the structural constraints of sexism, racism, and social class barriers to entrap women in criminal activity. Women participate in illegal activities as survival strategies, alternative entrepreneurialism, and to placate abusive partners. The women I have met display many of the same characteristics described in the "pathways" research: they have experienced physical, sexual, and emotional abuse from multiple offenders, within and outside their families. Often, they assume the role of caregiver to parents, siblings, and adult intimate partners. And street drugs and alcohol are used to numb the pain of loneliness, boredom, and abuse.

But the women here were not immersed in street crime. Of all forty-five women, the only prior arrests for violence were Lisa's and Beth's arrests for domestic violence against abusive partners. The vast majority, thirty-eight of forty-five (84 percent), had no prior arrests for anything. Of the nineteen women charged with crimes against people other than their abusers, four (21 percent) had prior arrests. Prior arrests included shoplifting, procuring drugs, public intoxication, permitting a child's life and morals to be endangered and DUIs (driving under the influence of alcohol), but none of the women were routinely engaged in street crime.[2] For most women, the felonious crimes they committed were anomalous events in otherwise law-abiding lives. Like the women who killed or injured their partners, for most women who committed crimes against others, their first offenses were serious felonies.

It is more straightforward to articulate the relationship between prior experiences of battering and defensive actions *against an abuser* than to explain how battering leads to crimes against others. Common understanding of self-defense forms a foundation for understanding defensive actions by battered women against abusers. The effects of battering on women who commit crimes against people other than their abusers involve explanations of the contexts in which women feel compelled to acquiesce to the demands of abusers. Known as *social framework testimony,* this form of explanation is not a special consideration extended to battered women. Evidence of the context in which crimes are committed is accepted in all types of criminal trials. The Fifth and Fourteenth Amendments to the Constitution guarantee the right to due process. This includes the right of defendants to present evidence that explains their conduct. For any criminal offense, culpability is dependent on a person's voluntary action to engage in the illegal behavior. Legal "control excuses" include duress and "volitional" tests for legal insanity.[3]

Duress is a very specific legal term with evidentiary requirements that vary among the states and the federal rules of evidence. In order to prove that a person was acting under duress, there must be evidence of immediate threat to do harm to that person greater than the criminal behavior demanded. Legal insanity is also strictly defined in state and federal rules.[4] Individuals' control over their own conduct is related to their capacity to form criminal intent; evidence of lack of control can mitigate intent. Duress or legal insanity is presented as part of a defense to explain criminal conduct or lack of intent to do harm. Social framework evidence may also be admitted to rebut evidence that a person acted with a specific mental state defined as an element of a crime charged. The level of criminal charges may be reduced, sentencing may be mitigated, or acquittal may result from consideration of a person's lack of control when he or she committed a crime.

Women's experiences of prior and current victimization inform the ways that prosecutors charge crimes, juries evaluate their conduct, and judges impose sentences. There is no special consideration given to battered women that is not extended to other defendants. Their criminal culpability is evaluated within the context of experiences with coercion and control and their fear of their intimate partners. Their perceptions of men's authority within the relationship and the consequences they face for disobedience frame their obedience to abusers. Women's failure to challenge their partner's authority and their collusion in violent crimes is consistent with what we know about the relationship among obedience, authority, and moral conscience in other contexts.

Authority and Obedience

People will often obey, despite personal moral objections, when placed in situations where legitimate authority figures command obedience to orders.[5] The famous 1961–62 obedience experiments conducted by Stanley Milgram demonstrated the effect of authority figures in overcoming an individual's moral commitments to nonviolence. In a laboratory setting, a man posing as a scientist in a white lab coat informed participants that they were involved in an experiment to test learning ability. The "scientist" instructed them to apply increasing levels of electric shocks when people (defined as "learners"), strapped to a chair in an adjoining room, provided wrong answers to questions asked by the "teachers." Despite screams, pleas to stop, and feigned fainting, two-thirds of the teachers continued to administer shocks as the scientists authoritatively told them "the experiment must continue." (The "learners" were actors; no shocks, in fact, were given.) These experiments have been criticized on both methodological and ethical grounds; in addition, almost all of the trials involved only males.[6] Nevertheless, the Milgram experiments provide some insight into the ways in which the presence of an authority figure undermines individual commitment to moral values.

One of the questions raised subsequent to Milgram's initial experiments was what *kind* of authority produces obedience in subordinates. Mario Morelli, for example, argued that Milgram did not adequately identify the basis for obedience to an authority figure and suggested a difference between people *in* authority and people *of* authority.[7] That is, Morelli suggested that subjects obeyed the scientist because they saw him as a person of authority. They believed he knew what he was doing and would not have required them to cause actual harm to another person.

Forms of Authority

Untangling the operations of authority and obedience involves broad, complicated questions about the nature of power and its social contexts. Max Weber's classic sociological formulation of types of authority has had a lasting influence on analyses of the bases of authority and the obedience it commands.[8] He defined authority as "the probability that certain specific commands (or all commands) will be obeyed by a given group of persons."[9] Weber distinguished among traditional, rational-legal, and charismatic forms of authority and argued that modern societies relied primarily on rational-legal bases for authority.[10] Put succinctly, *traditional* authority depends on customary rules and relationships, *charismatic* authority on the personal powers of individuals, and *rational-legal* on formalized, institutionalized rules. Weber found that "among the prebureaucratic types of domination the most important one by far is patriarchal domination."[11] He defined patriarchalism as "the authority of the father, the husband, the senior of the house, the sib [sibling] elder over the members of the household and sib [siblings]; the rule of the master and patron over bondsmen, serfs, freed men."[12] This form of authority extracts obedience from subjects based on traditional norms and personal relationships. According to Weber:

> In the case of domestic authority the belief in authority is based on personal relations that are perceived as natural. This belief is rooted in filial piety, in the close and permanent living together of all dependents of the household which results in an external and spiritual "community of fate." The woman is dependent because of the normal superiority of the physical and intellectual energies of the male.[13]

The perception of the hierarchal patriarchal family as "natural" was part of the legitimation of male authority within the medieval household and continues to influence relationships within nuclear families today. Writing in the early 1900s, Weber's own acceptance of the "normal superiority . . . of the male" seems to have escaped his critical analysis. The belief in the natural and normal superiority of males is still a component of the ideology that legitimates male dominance within and outside of families.

Weber argued that traditional authority waned with industrialization and the development of the capitalist mode of production, which required efficient calculation of costs and benefits.[14] While economic and political relationships are governed more by legal-rational authority, traditional authority maintains a hold within many families and intimate relationships.[15] Women in violent relationships routinely report their partners' beliefs that men are the natural authority figure within their homes, deserving of respect and service. As described above, men had expectations of their partners' unquestioning obedience and, in many cases, women tried to perform as they were told.

For many women, this traditional authority is enhanced by their perceptions of the charismatic power of their partners. Weber's definition described group relationships rather than intimate dyads; nonetheless, it mirrors disturbingly the descriptions some women gave of their partners' supernatural powers: "The term 'charisma' will be applied to a certain quality of an individual personality by virtue of which he is considered extraordinary and treated as endowed with supernatural, superhuman, or at least specifically exceptional powers or qualities."[16] The authority that derives from a charismatic personality is a public construction, not a private belief. Typical examples of charismatic authority are warrior heroes and divinely ordained rulers. But in their isolated relationships with violent men, women who believed their partners had the ability to monitor their thoughts and actions and to compel people to do their bidding expressed a similar view of charismatic authority. The ideal types of authority described by Weber were not intended to apply cleanly to all situations, and he indicated that, in practice, all three forms could operate simultaneously. Women in violent intimate relationships are influenced by tradition, the charisma of their partner, and legal regulations to accept their partner's legitimate authority. The use of brute force to exact compliance is not considered to be a *legitimate* source of authority, even if it is effective.[17] In violent relationships, physical violence is coupled with traditional, charismatic, and legal forces to establish abusive men's authority.

Premodern and Modern Forms of Power

Weber's analysis of authority informs sociological understandings of power. The patriarchalism of traditional authority that he described is consistent with Foucault's descriptions of premodern forms of power. Foucault's genealogies of power suggest that in the premodern era the power of a sovereign entity controlled people. The king, lord, or master was a distinct, recognizable authority who ruled over subjects with stern, often brutal, severity. People repressed their own desires and obeyed the will of the sovereign out of fear of punishment. Foucault described the external nature of power and authority pressing down on subjects as the "repressive hypothesis."[18] Foucault argued that in the modern era, this repressive power becomes diffused into many local and internalized sources. Rather than being controlled by an external sovereign, people become their own police and guards. Power in the modern era is less physically brutal, but more psychologically complete, as people discipline themselves.

Women who live with violent men are subject to *both* external sovereign and internalized, diffuse power. Their violent partner represents a sovereign authority who monitors their behavior and uses physical violence to enforce demands. But women also *internalize* their partners' views of what is expected, as well as the traditional rules and values that prescribe males as the legitimate authorities within families. They police their own behavior and go to extraordinary lengths to preserve the dream of a good marriage. Even after men's deaths, women described the fear and self-monitoring they continued to perform. The physical violence described throughout this book is brutal and terrifying. But it is less frequent than the constant verbal and psychological abuse that fractures women's perceptions of their worlds. Women almost always define the psychological abuse as more damaging than the physical abuse they endure. Andrea C. Westlund points out that women in violent relationships are subjected simultaneously to both premodern and modern forms of power.[19] That is, they are disciplined by the direct physical power of their partners as well as their partners' diffuse and internalized expectations and psychological manipulation.

The coercion that occurs within intimate relationships, as detailed above, involves every aspect of a woman's life. She is not only concerned about immediate consequences for failure to obey, but about the longer-term effects on her children, extended family, and her abusive partner. The tentacles of authority within abusive relationships have a much greater and more tangled reach than those of authority figures who have no intimate ties to their subjects. Gender has not been a significant consideration in studies of obedience to authority, and so women's obedience to violent intimate partners falls outside the margins of this body of research. Given our knowledge about intimate partner violence, however, the literature on obedience and crimes of obedience offers insights into the ways women are persuaded to betray their own values and beliefs.

Crimes of Obedience

When people follow the commands of an authority figure that are inconsistent with their own moral values as well as those of the larger community, they commit what Herbert C. Kelman and V. Lee Hamilton refer to as "crimes of obedience."[20] The paradigmatic example of the influence of authority figures on immoral behavior is the genocide perpetrated by ordinary people during the Jewish Holocaust. The execution of millions of innocent people by the Nazis gave rise to numerous academic arguments and studies about the conditions under which apparently normal, reasonable people would perpetrate genocide. Scholarly attention to the causes of these crimes of obedience has focused on the political, economic, social, and cultural factors that generate racist hatred and unquestioning obedience to authority.[21]

Kelman and Hamilton examine more recent examples of military and civilian crimes of obedience, including the My Lai massacre, Watergate break-in, Iran-Contra cover-up, and the Chrysler odometer case. Based on the statements made by participants in these cases, they delineate three social processes that contribute to conditions under which crimes of obedience are likely to occur: authorization, routinization, and dehumanization. Authorization is the belief that the person giving orders to commit crimes or immoral acts has the legitimate authority to prescribe the activity: "when acts of violence are explicitly ordered, implicitly encouraged, tacitly approved, or at least permitted by legitimate authorities, people's readiness to commit or condone them is enhanced."[22]

In the Milgram experiments, one of the reasons that people continued to shock the "learners" was the belief that the scientist was both a legitimate authority who understood the danger posed by the shocks and a trustworthy professional who would not permit harm to the participants. In military crimes of obedience, personnel follow orders from their superiors based on a commitment to military objectives and national security. They are trained to obey officers and respect their experience and wisdom in making tactical decisions. Military personnel are expected by law to follow the reasonable orders of commanding officers. Although military and international law explicitly *requires disobedience* to illegal orders, the actual prosecution of subordinate military personnel is rare and is mitigated by consideration of factors that would obfuscate the illegal nature of orders from a superior.

The massacre of hundreds of old men, women, and children in My Lai 4 Village is an example of a crime of obedience. My Lai was carried out by ordinary U.S. soldiers of Charlie Company C, under the command of Lieutenant Colonel Frank Barker. Many men were brought to trial for war crimes committed at My Lai, but only Lieutenant William Calley was convicted. Calley executed at least 102 unarmed villagers who were herded into a drainage ditch. These crimes were the most easily identifiable and prosecutable offenses that were committed at My Lai. The other men who engaged in acts of illegal aggression against civilians were not convicted. Calley was originally sentenced to life imprisonment, but only served three years under house arrest before being granted parole.[23]

When the context of obedience is military or political, people accept authorization; individuals may indicate that they were "simply following orders." Their conduct is often excused or mitigated in court and in popular opinion. Kelman and Hamilton found that the majority of a random sample of U.S. citizens felt that soldiers at My Lai were acting appropriately and that the prosecution of Lieutenant Calley was wrong.[24] Obedience to immoral orders of legitimate authority figures is often tolerated by the public.

Establishing Authority in Violent Relationships

The men who order women to participate in crimes do not possess an authority that is socially sanctioned as legitimate outside of the intimate relationship. In many cases, the men have criminal records that place them in opposition to legitimate authorities. Women are not obedient to these men because of their commitment to and training in a formal organization, such as the military. They are, however, socialized to accept male authority through their experiences in patriarchal institutions. Many have experienced the pain resulting from attempts to resist that authority as girls and young women. Within their intimate relationships, their partners demand that they recognize their authority and comply with their demands. For women in violent relationships, obedience to their partners is monitored by close surveillance and control. Challenging the authority of their partners risks both direct, immediate punishment (emotional and physical) and long-term consequences, such as deportation or losing custody of children. In many cases where women commit crimes related to their abuse, the perceived price of disobedience is death.

The establishment of authority within an intimate relationship depends upon isolation from other sources of support and information about the relationship. When abused women are cut off from interacting with people who would condemn the batterer's behavior and suggest alternatives, they are denied one of the most important resources for developing resistance. Economic dependency and fear of losing custody of their children also restrict women's material resources to resist their abusers' demands. Although women do resist batterers in many ways, they also comply with orders as a strategy for maintaining the "smoothness of social interaction," that is, for preventing violent eruptions.[25]

Enforcing authority through everyday interactions sets the stage for larger and more problematic orders. For example, control over what women wear, the time and content of meals, to whom she can speak, and what she can say constructs an interactional environment very similar to the military.[26] Orders must be obeyed without question, and the established rules must be followed without verbal reminders. Unlike military authority, however, abusive partners can be with women at all times or at least convince women that they are under constant scrutiny. Women describe being monitored even while showering and using the toilet. Abusive men also impose authority over their partners with little regard for accountability to rules that would regulate violence and abuse. The violence men inflict as punishment for perceived disobedience would not be tolerated systematically in other contexts of legitimate authority, such as the military or law enforcement.

Resistance to Authority

Kelman and Hamilton argue that for individuals to resist authority, they must have access to "alternative definitions of the situation and interpretations of its requirements"; further, they must "be prepared to disrupt the established social order and the smoothness of social interaction."[27] They also suggest that individuals must have the material resources both to obtain alternative information and to support themselves if they are cut off from resources as a result of their disruption. People who are able to reject demands of authorities that deviate from their own morality have a high level of autonomy. As Thomas S. Szasz says, "Autonomy is the death knell of authority."[28] Establishing autonomy within a violent relationship, however, is not only difficult, but extremely dangerous. When women resisted men's demands and attempted to assert their autonomy, they were punished. Phyllis was beat into unconsciousness for throwing soup in Billy Bob's face and Monica was hit in the head with a wrench for refusing to make supper (chapter 1). Many women faced loaded guns and vivid death threats when they mentioned leaving their partners. Women also lost jobs and friends as a result of their partner's abuse, harassment, and threats. Abusers crushed every effort to establish autonomy.

Men's violence, however, had an ironic effect on their authority. Over time, most women's respect and love for their partner was worn away by abuse. The more violent men became, the less credibility they had. As they lost credibility, women withdrew emotionally and strategized ways to escape. Men then became more violent, in a cycle that sometimes led to their deaths, as discussed in the previous chapter, or to the death of others. This cycle is what preceded women's deaths in many of the cases described by others.[29]

Sociohistorical Obstacles to Resistance

The women's acceptance of their partner's authority occurs within a sociohistorical tradition of male authority over female intimate partners, and personal contexts of isolation, prior victimization, and violence from their partners. Male partners disciplined their partners whom they treated as their servants and property.[30] Women had histories of unpunished abuse by relatives (stepfathers, uncles, brothers, mothers, and aunts) and others in authority (coaches, teachers, fathers of friends). For both men and women, the putative authority of men to order compliance with illegal acts has historical roots in law and custom, regardless of individual awareness of these roots.

The custom of obedience to husbands has lingered in religious and social practices into the twenty-first century despite formal rejection of the doctrine of coverture. Marriage vows that bound women to "love, honor, and obey" their husbands diminished, but did not disappear. In 1998, the Southern Baptist Convention revised their official statement of beliefs to include the statement that "a wife is to submit herself graciously to the servant leadership of her husband."[31] During the same period, marriage advice manuals repeated the well-worn advice to women for successful marriages: let your husband make the decisions and do not question his authority.[32] *The Surrendered Wife* was a national best seller in 1999 and spawned numerous self-help groups of women learning to "surrender" to their husband's authority. While such calls for wifely submission draw ridicule, they also find eager disciples, as evidenced by the ongoing Web-based discussion groups for *Fascinating Womanhood*, Helen Andelin's 1965 handbook on how to be the perfect wife.[33] The legal, religious, and cultural support for wives to obey husbands unquestioningly maintains influence in only a minority of families within the United States. Yet, for women and men in violent relationships, echoes of the past reverberate in men's expectations and demands and women's compliance.

Obviously, cultural and religious expectations for women's submission do not include acceptance of illegal or immoral behavior at the command of husbands. No religious authority would condone women's criminal actions because they were ordered by their husband to break the law. The cultural context endorsing obedience to husbands, however, is one piece in the framework of women's perceptions of their partners' authority, even when that authority is illegitimate in the eyes of outsiders.

Contemporary intimate relationships do not constitute an authority situation in the same manner as in the military, or even a corporate hierarchy, but the women charged with crimes of obedience perceived and referred to their partners as authorities who had to be obeyed. In Weber's terms, this authority was based on tradition, law, and, in some cases, charisma. It was reinforced by physical violence and its threat, as well as a lack of practical alternatives. In speaking of nondomestic crimes of obedience, Kelman and Hamilton note that "authorization processes create a situation in which people become involved in an action without considering its implications and without really making a decision. Once they have taken the initial step, they are in a new psychological and social situation in which the pressures to continue are powerful."[34] Once women become accustomed to relinquishing moral autonomy to their intimate partners, men's insistence on obedience is a powerful pressure to continue in spite of the objections women may have to their commands.

The crimes of obedience committed by women in violent relationships are not bureaucratized or routinized in the manner of military or corporate crimes. However, the pattern of obedience to their partner's authority is routinized by daily enforcement of minor demands, such as choices of words ("You better say what I wanna hear"), answering the telephone ("I wouldn't let any men call the house"), preparing food ("It seemed like he wanted everything perfect"), and even thought processes ("This free thinking of yours has got to stop"). Women become accustomed to following mundane orders and to accepting their partner's authority under threat of punishment; when greater, immoral, and illegal demands are made, women do not perceive a *choice*, but only another demand that must be obeyed.

The man's constant surveillance, ordering, and violence in a sense routinizes his authority and his violence so that she sees no realistic alternatives to obedience. As discussed above, when women *do* resist the authority of violent partners, they are brutally punished. At the same time, their existence is intertwined with his in multiple and intimate ways, so that there is no simple option to exit the situation. The complexity and intensity of the internal and external bonds to an abusive partner leave many women feeling that death is the only exit.

Katy tried to fulfill the subservient, unquestioning, obedient role of a traditional wife. She was devoted to serving an extremely violent, drug-addicted man—Phil—who was a member of the Dirty Dozen, an outlaw motorcycle gang. She worked two jobs, one as a maid at a hotel, the other as a repair person, and provided all the income for herself and Phil. She owned a home, paid all the bills, did all the domestic labor as well as providing all income, and supplied Phil with marijuana on demand. She knew that Phil saw other women and, after her arrest, learned that he had fathered four children with other women during the course of their ten-year relationship. Katy never had children with Phil, and they never married. In spite of his own philandering, Phil was pathologically jealous and possessive of Katy and would beat her for receiving phone calls from any men whatsoever. She purchased a pager so clients could contact her and she could return their calls rather than risk a beating if Phil knew a man called her home. She was arrested and pled guilty to drug trafficking charges for procuring and supplying Phil with marijuana. She did as she was told and knew that she would receive a beating if she disobeyed orders. When I asked how soon after she and Phil began living together the violence started, Katy explained the levels of violence and Phil's threats if she failed to meet his demands:

KATY: I was not allowed to get any phone calls from any man almost immediately. But he didn't beat me, the first time he ever beat me, we were together for like a year, a year and a half.

KATHLEEN: Do you remember what that was about?

KATY: I never knew what any of it was about.

KATHLEEN: It was just out of the blue? He just started hitting you? What would he say?

KATY: He would just call me names. I don't know what it was about. I think it was about whatever he was doin' on the side, whatever he had in his life goin' on. 'Cuz I was really good to him. I provided for him, like I was supposed to (crying).

KATHLEEN: You paid all the bills, worked two jobs.

KATY: Mmhmmm.

KATHLEEN: Would he usually be high when that would happen?

KATY: Usually, well, it was hard to say because he was so, he would, if he didn't have any pot to smoke, he'd go, I think there's somethin' wrong with him, really wrong with him, some kind of chemical imbalance. If he didn't have any drugs, he would flip out and beat me up. No matter what time of the day or night it was, and he would tell me that I had fifteen minutes to go get him that pot, whether it was two in the morning, or whatever, and he'd make me go do that. But I don't smoke pot, but I had to have those contacts too. 'Cuz he did really hurt me.

KATHLEEN: Did you ever receive medical treatment for that?

KATY: No, not really . . . I went to a chiropractor, I was gettin' real bad migraines and stuff because he used to hit me in the head . . . we moved from the house where we were living to this house I bought, and he started beatin' me like every day and I started bleeding from my ears every time he hit me, and my head was split open a lotta times, 'cuz he'd always hit me in the head, well not always, but a lotta times because he figured that wouldn't show.

Phil also broke her ribs, her fingers, and her sternum, and pistol-whipped her. Although Katy could not identify a reason for any of Phil's assaults, she did know that if she failed to obey his commands to procure marijuana for him, she would be badly hurt. Katy had no other criminal record apart from the charges for buying marijuana. Both Katy and Phil were charged with purchase and possession, and Phil was convicted at a jury trial. He spent only six months in jail, but Katy received two years because she was the primary purchaser. Her sentence was reduced because of her lack of priors and consideration of the impact of domestic violence on her actions. Although buying drugs is not a component of the traditional model of domesticity, Katy tried to adhere to that model within the framework established by her boyfriend. She worked hard at legitimate jobs and did not use drugs herself. Her crimes were not the result of a rejection of conventional morality, but of adherence to an outmoded model of obedience to her male partner's demands. She was well integrated into the social order, but bonded to a man who demanded that she violate its rules.

Social Bonding and Women's Crime

People's positions within the social order influence their perceptions of formal legal rules and possibilities for resistance. Theorists of crime and delinquency have argued that people who are strongly attached to the conventional social order and to their family and friends are most likely to adhere to the law. These theorists, known as *control theorists*, have focused on the criminal behavior of marginalized social groups.[35] Some members of the privileged race and economic class, however, although successful and highly integrated in the conventional social order appear quite comfortable violating the law. White-collar and corporate crime involving large sums of money is almost exclusively committed by successful business-people.[36] Theorists of elite deviance argue that this form of crime reflects bonding to an unjust social order, rather than failure to bond to a just system.[37]

Shifting to a critical macroperspective, consideration of elite deviance illuminates the limitations of theories of crime that focus on individual commitment to a moral order without examining the nature of that order. Highly respected and socially successful people may commit crimes because of their acceptance of a moral order that rewards economic profits over social good. C. Wright Mills referred to this as the "higher immorality."[38] When individuals commit political or corporate crime, they often rationalize their behavior as "just following orders" of their corporate superiors. They may participate in behaviors that cause loss of life, suffering, economic losses, and environmental destruction; nevertheless, they are able to rationalize their behavior because they were doing their jobs, following directives from corporate or political superiors.[39] Those ordering commission of deviant acts by people who work for them are accorded authority and considered legitimate leaders who should be obeyed. The social bonding of upper-class men and women appears to offer more opportunities to commit white-collar crime and insulation from the harshest forms of punishment.[40] People without stocks and access to positions of corporate power are not likely to violate security and exchange laws, regardless of their level of commitment to the social order, simply because they do not have the opportunity to commit such crimes.

When people live in communities where the underground economy is taken for granted, participation is normalized. In many marginalized communities, both urban and rural, drug manufacturing and trading is pervasive.[41] People are exposed to the drug trade from an early age and have few alternative avenues for earning adequate income. They may have negative personal views of the drug market, but participate in order to survive. One of the women interviewed in my and Angela Moe's study of jailed women indicated that she did not regret her drug sales because it kept her children out of a homeless shelter. Concerning her crime, Alicia said:

> I don't regret it. Because without the extra income, my kids wouldn't be fed every day. Even though I do have a good job when I work and stuff like that, it's hard raising two kids by yourself. . . . Not all of us are horrible and not all of us are threats to society, we do what we have to do to survive. I mean, I'm not justifying the fact that what I did was right but it wasn't wrong at the time. I'm not killing anybody, robbing anybody, hurting nobody. They're gonna get it [crack] from somebody.[42]

People make distinctions between breaking drug laws and actually committing crimes of violence against individuals. Women who participate in the illegal economy do not view their conduct as moral in the abstract, but consider it necessary to survival given the concrete circumstances of their lives. As Alicia said, "it wasn't wrong at the time." Like people who commit elite deviance, Alicia drifted between legal and illegal activities in the manner described by Gresham Sykes and David Matza.[43] She worked at a legitimate job when she could, but supplemented that income by selling crack. Her rationalization of her criminal activities is reminiscent of the rationalizations of high-level defense contractors who sell arms to opposing countries in armed conflict: if we don't sell to them, someone else will.[44] The huge profits and social respectability of defense contractors are in stark contrast to the social and economic marginality of Alicia and other women who participate in the underground economy. The similarities in the rationalizations for crime expressed by street-level, white-collar, and corporate offenders belies the differential approbation expressed toward their conduct. Very few white-collar or corporate offenders suffer imprisonment or the social stigma and exclusion that follow people convicted of drug offenses. Some might even argue that Alicia's dire circumstances are correlated with the diversion of tax dollars from the social welfare system to the corporate welfare system that underwrites transnational corporations. Shifting focus from street crime to elite crime raises questions about the validity and usefulness of many popular theories of crime, particularly those that assume a consensus model of social order.

Alicia's financial difficulties were related to her abuse by her children's father. She chose to live alone with her kids and to supplement their income through selling crack rather than continue her relationship with an abusive man or live in a homeless shelter. She differs from the nineteen women I discuss in this chapter because her crime was related to her *rejection* of a violent relationship. Women who commit crimes of obedience do so in the context of an ongoing commitment and bond to a violent man.

Theorists of the social bonding and control perspectives on crime and delinquency have not considered how women's high levels of integration into their family and strong bonds to abusers may shape their perceptions of crime. Although none of the women here were immersed in street crime, their relationships with violent men affected their views of the law. None believed that "killing, robbing,

hurting" others was acceptable behavior. But their eventual participation in these crimes was influenced by their perceptions of their
partner's authority and the consequences they would face for disobedience. Some women viewed their families as conventional nuclear families and were committed to maintaining that image in the
community and for themselves. Other women were bonded to their
abusers, but held an oppositional stance toward the dominant culture. Their perceptions of "victimless" and minor property crimes
and the underground economy were ambivalent. They did not view
these crimes as morally "right," but they justified their participation in them as right for their situations. The use of drugs, obtaining
liquor from bootleggers on dry reservations, and becoming intimately
involved with men they knew were criminals reflected women's
views that some laws were unreasonable or irrelevant. Their marginal status contributed to a cynical view of laws governing personal
use of drugs and alcohol or the underground economy. This moral
detachment colored their perceptions of the law as a framework for
their conduct and as a source of protection from abusers. Women
who were emotionally bonded to their abusers and had been arrested
for minor offenses viewed the law as unreasonable and placed greater
confidence in the authority of abusers than the law.

Some women's ambivalence toward the law was exacerbated by
drug addiction that overwhelmed previous beliefs about right and
wrong. For example, Phyllis was arrested several times prior to her
major felony conviction, for an open container of beer, having drug
paraphernalia, and for public intoxication. She would not press
charges against her husband, Billy Bob, even for the worst beatings.[45]
Once she became addicted to crack, she stole from her mother and
wrote bad checks at Wal-Mart to have enough money to buy drugs:
"I went to Wal-Mart to write bad checks for $20 over, do that three
times, then a buy a rock. I did that for a whole night, like three
hours, and I talked my way out of it and never got caught. It's just
how you play the game. I never been like that before, except for that
stuff, as soon as you take a hit you want another one, and your
wheels are just goin' on how you're gonna get the next one, and you
just get to the point where you don't care." Although Phyllis never
broke the law prior to her addiction to crack, once she began stealing from Wal-Mart she found it easy and she stopped caring whether
it was right or wrong. She became more attached to her husband and

less able to turn to the legal system for protection. She began to steal from her mother under Billy Bob's orders. She believed his threats to kill her mother and brother if she failed to do as she was told, but she also wanted the money for her own drug consumption:

> He told me, "You're gonna take her checkbook, you're gonna take her wallet, you're gonna fuckin' do it, or I'm gonna whip your ass, and I'm gonna kill your brother, and I'm gonna kill your mom," and all this kinda' stuff, and I was so high that I totally believed it. I didn't know what to do. He said, "I'm cuttin' the phone lines, so don't even think about callin' the police. When we get there, you're gonna do exactly what I said." He told me Mom wouldn't have to pay the credit card bills because we stole the cards. I was so easily convinced, or I had, really, no choice. I had to believe whatever he was tellin' me, and I wanted to justify it, I guess some way too.

Phyllis exemplifies the continuum of compliance to the illegal orders of abusive men. Her initial resistance was worn down by Billy Bob's extreme violence. She began using crack to please him and to cope with her physical and emotional pain. Once addicted, her own desire for the drug overcame her moral qualms about stealing from Wal-Mart, and then from her mother. Billy Bob provided rationalizations for their crimes, but also used threats of violence to ensure her compliance. Phyllis committed these crimes on her own volition, but within a context of coercive control.

The devolution of Phyllis's moral boundaries led to her involvement in the most serious offense. She was eventually involved in the murder of a man that she and Billy Bob met camping. They were rambling around the countryside when they met a man in a remote mountain campground. The three shared beer and food and stayed up late, becoming extremely inebriated. Billy Bob believed that the man was making a pass at Phyllis, and began to assault him with a hammer. As described in chapter 1, Billy Bob had previously assaulted Phyllis in the head with a hammer. Billy Bob yelled at Phyllis to get him something to tie the man up with and to "hurry up, bitch, or you'll be next." Afraid and inebriated, Phyllis picked up a shotgun she saw in the man's camper, and attempted to hand it to Billy Bob. The gun fired, hitting the man in the head and killing him. Phyllis claimed that the shotgun went off accidentally when she tried to hand it to Billy Bob, but she was not believed. She was convicted of murder and sentenced to life in prison.

Women's Responses to Abusers

The sociocultural environment affects how gender is enacted within relationships in terms of authority and obedience. But individual-level factors also shape women's responses to violent behavior and commands from abusers. As discussed in chapter 4, the majority of women described childhood backgrounds of loss and loneliness. Of the nineteen women who committed crimes against people other than their abusers, eight had experienced physical and/or sexual abuse as children. These experiences were significant factors in their decisions to leave home early and to become intimately involved with men as a way out of their parents' homes. As none of their abusers were prosecuted, childhood abuse also contributed to women's mistrust of the law as a source of protection. The middle-class women in this group had been estranged from their parents for a variety of reasons, and did not feel they could turn to them for help. Women from low-income groups did not have parents with resources to turn to. Only two women in this group had a close relationship with their parents when they committed their crimes, and both were able to return to their homes after being placed on probation.

Nine women also had previous experiences with violent partners before becoming involved with their co-defendants. Emma and Luisa had so many violent men in their lives they could not recall all the abuse documented in police reports, and Sarah also recounted a litany of violent victimization from multiple men. For women with lengthy histories of abusive relationships, it was difficult to imagine a loving relationship that did not include violence. Emma said, "All my life I've been running from men. I don't think I want a relationship any more, I just want to be left alone." Chris entered her relationship with her violent partner and co-defendant in order to be protected from her ex-husband. When her new partner became violent and insisted she participate in his counterfeiting scheme, she felt backed into a corner with no escape.

The women in this group (those nineteen who committed crimes against people other than their abusers) experienced extreme levels of physical violence, and all but one of them had been threatened with death by their abusers. This group was less likely to have on-going feelings of love toward their abusers than was the group of women who killed their partners. Only two women said that they still loved their partners, although both moved back and forth between love and hate. Phyllis continued to love her abuser after several months in jail. She expressed ambivalence, telling me, "sometimes I just hate him so much," but also admitting she still had feelings of love for him. No one doubted that she had been battered by Billy Bob, but the prosecution and the court perceived her continued involvement with him as voluntary. She received no leniency because of her battering and was held responsible for her actions, despite the context of terror in which she was trapped. The impact of battering on her perceptions of alternatives was not acknowledged, and she received the same punishment as Billy Bob. In the conclusion to this chapter, I discuss the social implications of holding women criminally responsible when their crimes are intertwined with their own victimization.

Laura's boyfriend was committing mail fraud and storing stolen mail in her car. He beat her routinely and prevented her from returning to her parents' home, threatening to kill her mother if she tried. She was only twenty-one when she was charged with the federal offense of mail fraud. When I asked her if she still loved her boyfriend at the time she was arrested, she said yes. I then asked how she felt at the time of our interview, six weeks after being incarcerated in a federal detention center. She replied, "I still know I have love for him and I hate him at the same time. And I don't wish death on anyone, but I hope he suffers for everything that he's done to me and anybody else." Laura described the common feeling among women that their abusers had exploited their love and ruined their lives.

Fear and Loathing

All of the women who committed crimes against others were afraid of their partners. The fear continued during incarceration, and combined with loathing toward the men who created that fear. As they sat in jail facing serious felony charges, women reevaluated their relationships; some felt they had been set up and used by men. Jennifer, for example, said of her partner, "As I look back on it in reflection, sometimes I think he just wanted a ride to California, and I just happened to stick around too much, or somethin'. He was just usin' me the whole time." None of the women had any desire to reunite with their abusers if and when they got out of jail or prison. Monica, for example, was arrested for failure to protect her children from sexual abuse a week after she married her husband. Although he was also in prison, she expressed the same fears that women who killed their abusers described. She was afraid he was going to come and get her and hurt her again:

> He told me that he would make me lose everything, my kids, my job, my freedom, and he's done that. He's been tellin' me that if I testify against him that I'm gonna go down with him. I feel like that's the only reason he married me was, he said, well, now you're my wife, you can't testify against me. I think he's more worried about me testifying against him, than anything. That's the only reason why he married me. It was a mistake on my part, I realize this, but in a way I feel like I didn't have a choice. I felt like, you know, that this man was gonna keep threatenin' me, call me a snitch and all this, and I felt like maybe if I married him that he would back off, and leave things alone, and that maybe if I was his wife that things would be different, but I don't know, I never found out because he ended up gettin' arrested and I ended up gettin' arrested too, so, I don't know. I've got a divorce packet in there, and I've put in two requests to talk to a legal attorney about it. 'Cuz I'm not really sure what to do. I know I can't get my kids back if I'm married to him. I want my kids back (crying hard). I'm still scared. I don't understand why I'm still scared to do that, though. He's in jail, he can't hurt me, but I still think he can.

Fear of their partners pervaded women's perceptions and was a direct influence on their participation in crimes. This fear was both specific (at the point a crime was committed), and general (the pervasive feeling that escape was impossible). Ten of the men had violent histories and made sure women knew they were capable of murder. Like women who killed their abusers, some women were given tours of the desert where men said they would be buried or pushed into snake-filled pits if they failed to obey. Some women also witnessed men's violence to others. Their threats were thus perceived as credible and women did not doubt their willingness to retaliate if they refused to obey or reported crimes to the police.

Chris had been severely battered by her husband, Rex, whose paranoid delusions were described in chapter 3. He hit her all over her body with a two-by-four board, punched her with fists, and cut her with knives. Rex also tortured her three small dogs, choking them and burning them with cigarettes while she pleaded with him to stop. She tried everything to keep him away and be safe, including calling the police, pressing charges, taking out orders of protection, trying to have him committed to a mental institution, and going into a shelter, but he kept returning to her home. Chris was also charged with failing to appear in court for a hearing on one of the assaults against her because Rex refused to let her leave the house. She spent three days in jail on a charge of failure to appear. She suffered several years of abuse before Rex finally gave up and moved out of state. The ineffectiveness of the police and orders of protection in controlling Rex influenced her perception of alternatives when her new partner, Morgan, became abusive. His violence and threats to kill her, as well as his prior murders, convinced her that she had no alternative to assisting in his counterfeiting scheme. She explained:

When he moved the press in I said, "I don't really want to do this." He said, "Well, when we talked about it, you were all for it." I said, "Well, I was only joking. At the time I was poor as a church mouse. At the time I probably could have used it, but not now. I really didn't mean it. I don't want to do it." He said, "We got to do it. This is the only way we're gonna get anywhere." I said, "No, it isn't." We argued about it. He was real nice at first and then he wasn't. He said, "You know, you made a deal with me. I expect you to stick to it. We're friends. Don't make this hard. It's gonna be very easy."

When he got out of prison, he told me about his past. I really knew nothing about it. I knew very little of it. I knew he'd been in a little trouble but I didn't know what the trouble was. He told me he had been indicted twice for murder, acquitted on both counts. He'd been a big-time drug dealer, wiretapping. I asked him, "You were found not guilty on the murder charges. You didn't do it right?" "Oh, ya', I did it." Then he told me exactly how he did it, where he buried the bodies, why he did it, and who they were, not their names, but just what their relationship was to him. He told me that they weren't the only ones. They were the only ones found or that he got caught on. He said,

> "I killed over five people. Don't doubt that I wouldn't hold you to this bargain." I didn't doubt him because he told me the two people he killed, well, one of them he killed because he backed out of a deal with him. I said, "Well, did he back out? Did he want something for it?" When they were drug dealing together, did he want him to pay him or something? "No. He wanted nothing. He just wanted out. Well I wasn't gonna let him out. We had made a pact and we were gonna stay together for like five years or something. And then he wanted out." The other one he killed because he testified against him at his murder trial. There was two counts but, like I said, he killed more than two people.

Chris's clean record and Morgan's prior convictions, including one for counterfeiting, contributed to the state's conclusion that her participation in Morgan's scheme was not voluntary. She accepted a plea and was placed on probation. Although Chris did not have to spend time in prison, she lost her home and all her belongings and had a felony conviction on her record. She had to start her life over again with no money and no job.

Blood In, Blood Out

Men's threats were often combined with demands that women commit felonies to prove loyalty and demonstrate that they would not "snitch" on their partners. Sarah's childhood and adult victimization was described in previous chapters. After a series of chaotic, violent relationships, she became involved with Cliff, who had just been released from prison. Cliff demanded that she help him steal her ex-husband's motorcycle, and told her committing felonies would help prove that she wasn't a snitch:

> Either I was gonna prove that I wasn't a snitch and he wasn't gonna have to kill me, by goin' and doin' as he told me, three in, blood in, blood out, or some shit like that, three felonies, he told me, "we're gonna go commit three felonies before I can trust you and even then it's iffy 'cuz you're a bitch," you know. "Or I can take you to California and tell my brothers [Hell's Angels], and they'll kill ya." . . . He goes, "You're a snitch, you got me in trouble, I'm gonna go back to prison. You've ruined my life, just as I'm tryin' to start over, and if you're not a snitch, you're gonna go along with me, and otherwise, I'm gonna bury you right here."

Jennifer was also told that she needed to prove loyalty by committing felonies. Her partner forced her to shoot the dead body of the man he had killed so she would be implicated in the murder. He also threatened that if she told anyone what happened, she would be labeled a "rat" and retaliated against in jail:

> You know I'm so terrified to testify. I don't know if you know much about jail, but they get to, girls don't like that much, when you rat, or whatever. And he's threatened me, he goes, "You don't wanna go to jail with a rat jacket on," to me that's a definite threat, that he's gonna put the word out and have me hurt. But I have to do what's best for me, and I have to listen to the attorneys, and my family and what they want. I'm terrified and it keeps me awake at night.

The men had prior records and knew more about the law than the women, most of whom had never spent a day in jail before their felonies. They threatened women before being arrested, and while incarcerated tried to influence them through letters and other people. Women knew they were being manipulated and that they needed to be truthful about what happened, but continued to feel afraid of what their abusers could do or have done to them.

The Sexualized Context of Coercion

Women's sexual relationships with men who coerced them into crimes put them at high levels of risk. Not only were they violated sexually by the men they were initially attracted to; their sexuality was interpreted as deviant and as evidence of their culpability for the crimes committed. Sexual attraction to abusive men was often the pretext for the initiation of relationships. Women described being immediately attracted to the men and drawn to their charismatic charms. However, as the relationship became more abusive, men forced women to have sex as a method of terrorizing and intimidating them. After crimes were committed, the prosecution and the media focused on women's sexuality in constructing images of women as deviant predators. Abusive men, prosecutors, and the media invoked sexist double standards regarding women's so-called promiscuity. The sexual conduct of abusive men was never mentioned in court or newspaper accounts, despite their multiple partners and violent sexuality. By contrast, women's sexuality was a prominent factor in evaluating their character and culpability for crimes.

Sarah had worked in a sexualized profession—exotic dancing—prior to her charges. As discussed in chapter 1, Sarah had internalized expectations for women's sexual subordination and servitude through her experiences with childhood sexual abuse, work as an exotic dancer, and identification as a biker chick. She explained how her efforts to conform to the expectations of biker culture clashed with the reality of her partner's abuse:

> I decided if these girls knew how to act right, they wouldn't be knocked around. I'll just show 'em how to do it. I'll be the best bitch they ever seen. Wrong. I'd find the most psychotic one and decide that's the one I like, you know, so I ended up with this guy, Hunter, and I was workin' at Les Girls and the guy who was the bouncer was my buddy, no one would mess with me. Well, now [Hunter decided] I was a slut, "You're holdin out on money, you're doin' dope with him, you're doin this, you're doin that," you know, "I can't talk to any of my brothers anymore, 'cuz they're all laughin' at me behind my back, 'cuz you're sleepin' with all of em," you know. So he cuffs me up to his bike in the dining room, and kicks me, and pisses on me, and rapes me in front of his brothers. Not a pretty sight.

Sarah eventually got away from this man, but she was sold, passed around from "brother to brother," because "they like to keep ya in the family, ya know. Go from brother to brother, just once you're around, you tend to learn things you're not supposed to know, and they don't want you just wanderin' around tellin' people shit."

While riding on the back of one of the "brother's" cycles, Sarah was in an accident that resulted in the loss of one leg. Her legs had been her trademark and identity as a dancer. The settlement from the accident allowed her to purchase a home, and she settled down with a man and gave birth to a daughter. The marriage did not last, but she was trying to establish a normal life for herself and her daughter when she became enmeshed in strange events that "made the Hell's Angels look like the good guys." Her account of her life in the year leading up to her crime was convoluted, frightening, and bizarre. She felt that her neighborhood was the center of a pornography and drug ring, and she was talking with an FBI agent about busting it. There was a series of strange people and events that she believed were designed to get control of her house as an operations post. She became involved with a man who believed he was Jesus Christ and threatened to throw her into a fiery pit because she was a whore. Then another who told her he was an "alien vampire" who had sacrificed women and children in the desert. Both men spoke of making human sacrifices. I do not know whether Sarah's descriptions of these strange people were accurate, but they were similar to accounts of several other women who talked about the bizarre, cultlike behavior of the people they were surrounded by. Sarah felt she was in the middle of a nightmare that she could not share with anyone reliable: "I just, you know, after all this stuff goin' on, I'd wake up in the mornin' and I'd have to check to see if I was actually awake 'cuz I couldn't believe anything any more, you know. . . . I was startin' to think I was insane, but I wasn't hallucinatin' this stuff. I don't think I'll ever get rid of these people, so it doesn't really matter." Sarah had just gotten rid of the "alien vampire," when she met Cliff:

SARAH: So, he took off. And, lo and behold, came along Cliff. Fresh out of prison. Absolutely gorgeous.

KATHLEEN: Seemed very caring . . .

SARAH: Oh yeah, he was my biker hero. He'd never beat a woman, you know, took the rap for his mom [for growing marijuana], 'cuz that's the kinda son he was, even tho' it was a family business that she had put him in, he was a Hell's Angel.

KATHLEEN: You said it was like a week that he was around being nice, helping you . . .

SARAH: Oh, he slept on a couch on the front porch. I was thinkin', "God, this guy's gorgeous, how come he doesn't want anything to do with me?"

After becoming involved with Cliff, Sarah discovered that he was not a Hell's Angel and he had gone to prison for grand theft auto, not his mother's marijuana. As mentioned above, he insisted that she commit felonies to prove her loyalty to him. Sarah was charged with armed robbery, and a dangerous crime against children, because she did what Cliff told her to do. Cliff decided to steal her ex-husband's dilapidated motorcycle, stored at the home of Sarah's ex-brother-in-law and his wife, as payment for unpaid child support. He told Sarah that he would kill her and the entire family unless she helped him steal the bike. Following his instructions, Sarah pointed an unloaded handgun at her ex–in-laws and their twelve-year-old daughter while Cliff loaded the motorcycle into the back of his truck. While Cliff was outside, she gave the couple the name and number of an FBI agent and told them to call him, but they did not. After loading the bike into his truck, Cliff told Sarah to get into the cab and he threw her artificial leg into the truck bed. He hit her repeatedly while driving south to Mexico from Phoenix and told her he would bury her in the desert if she betrayed him. They were caught at the border and both placed in Mexican jails. Extradited back to Phoenix, Sarah was sentenced to three years in prison, but Cliff fled the country undetected.

Sarah felt she had no alternatives, that he would kill her if she disobeyed, and that she had nowhere else to go except prison:

> I don't know what the hell I was supposed to do, you know, and then, people are like, "You know, you coulda got away from him." Yeah, I coulda got away from him. For what? Now I had nowhere to go. I couldn't go home. I was facin' goin' to prison for the rest of my life. 'Cuz he forced me to go commit felonies with him so he could trust me, you know. Yeah, come back, turn yourself in, go to prison for a good part o' your life.

Like Sarah's experience with Cliff, Jennifer was initially very attracted to Jared and said she "fell head over heels" for him. After a few weeks together, the sex between them became coercive and frightening. After he raped her, she became more terrified of what he could do to her: "I was just ready to die, that night was just the hardest night for me. I even got to the point where I took his gun, and I was gonna shoot myself, and then he raped me that night, and that was horrible, 'cuz, um, I mean, sex had always been different between us, but it had never been forced, you know, without consent, you know what I'm sayin? I asked him, why are you doing this, are you torturing me? And he said, 'yeah.'"

The press compared Jennifer to Mallory Knox, the main female character in Oliver Stone's 1994 film *Natural Born Killers*. Mallory Knox was a sociopathic young woman who, with the help of her boyfriend, killed her abusive father then went on a killing spree for fun. The film was exceptionally violent and the Knox character highly sexualized. Jennifer did not kill anyone and was terrified by the circumstances surrounding her crimes.

Jennifer was a student at a small, liberal arts college. She had been sexually abused by her swimming coach, and a friend's father. Prior to her crime, she was in counseling and believed she had been sexually abused by one of her two stepfathers. In jail, however, she said she did not know what the truth was about this sexual abuse and that her life had become "too serious" to worry about it. Her mother was diagnosed with cancer when Jennifer was seventeen, and Jennifer cared for her during her last year of life. Jennifer had been hospitalized for depression and alcohol dependency; at the time she met Jared she was taking antidepressants and seeing a counselor. Jared swept her off her feet and told her he was moving to Mexico to escape from his gang ties in Los Angeles. Jennifer fell in love with him and, after knowing him only two weeks, left her small town to travel to Mexico. She quickly learned, however, that he had no intention of going to Mexico, and they began rambling pointlessly around the country. He convinced her that he had special powers and that they were soul mates: "I fell head over heels for this guy. I mean, the soul mate thing came up, and I mean just really weird spiritual stuff, like 'I remember you from a past life,' you know. 'Look in my eyes and stare at me, and see what you see. Don't look away, I'm your mirror.'" Jennifer had recently been through a "treatment" from a purported American Indian shaman, and Jared told her that he was American Indian.[46] His Indian identity, claims of supernatural powers, and being her soul mate made sense to her and were a strong attraction.

While traveling around the country, Jared decided to rob people who were camping. The first robbery turned into a murder. Jared ordered a man to kneel and then shot him in the head. He also shot the man's dog. He then told Jennifer that she had to shoot the dead body so that he could trust her not to report the murder. Jennifer complied. Two days later, Jared again tried to rob a camper, but the man escaped and reported the incident to the police. Jared and Jennifer were apprehended later that night.

His eyes got really big, and he said, "Get in the car," and then we started driving, and he said, "You better tell me what I wanna hear or I'm gonna run this car right off the road." I'm thinkin' my life's over, I really thought he was gonna kill me. I was terrified. I shake when I think about it. Then he ended up not. And he dropped me at the campsite and took off. For like about half an hour, twenty minutes I didn't know if he was comin' back or not. And I was out among the coyotes and, you know, like he said would happen, there was no campfire or anything, I was freezing, so that night I basically thought if I said no, or did anything that the same thing would happen, and he would go crazy and maybe even kill me this time. I honestly believed that, 'cuz, um, I don't know.

Jennifer initially took the blame for the murder committed by Jared; when the forensic evidence contradicted her version of the incident, however, she acknowledged that Jared initiated and carried out the crime. On the other hand, Jared continued to place the blame on Jennifer. She accepted a plea bargain for ten and a half years for manslaughter, and Jared pled to first-degree murder and a life sentence to avoid the death penalty. Once they were both incarcerated, Jennifer learned that Jared was from Wisconsin, not Los Angeles, and he was married with a young daughter. He had a prison record and several aliases. The name and biography he gave to Jennifer were entirely fabricated. The state's parole board recommended Jennifer for clemency, but the governor rejected their recommendation.

Nicole's childhood sexual abuse was also described in chapter 4. Nicole was initially attracted to Mark and said, "Sex was really good with Mark, he of course is half crazy, that's why." But as their relationship progressed, he made sexual demands that were excessive. When I asked if he ever forced her to have sex, she said no, but then recalled times when she felt forced to perform oral sex: "This is hard to say, it seemed like he would want me to have oral sex on him all the time, not all the time, almost constantly, you know. That was the thing. One time he, you know, kinda forced me, like, this is really awful, we had gone to Tucson for something, from Tucson almost from the time we left until we drove into Phoenix, he, I had to perform oral sex on him almost the whole time."

Prior to her involvement with a violent man, Nicole was employed and married with two young children. Her stable, middle-class lifestyle showed no indication of her troubled childhood. Her sexual abuse by her stepfather began at age four, and her uncle and grandfather also sexually abused her prior to age thirteen. Despite this abuse, she was a successful student and completed two years of college. In her early thirties, however, she began sharing crystal meth with her neighbor. She rapidly developed an addiction that led to the abandonment of everything important in her life. She started shoplifting and stealing from her husband to support her habit, and she met and fell in love with a violent ex-con, Mark. Her husband kicked her out and she lost custody of her children.

She moved to a remote ranch with Mark and they lived by selling their cars and other goods and spent their days using crystal meth. Mark became increasingly paranoid, and began to accuse Nicole of infidelity. He listened in on all of her phone conversations and limited her contact with people to his friends. As punishment for not following his rules to his satisfaction, he took her keys and locked the gates to the compound. She lost touch with her family and friends and had no money or transportation of her own. There were numerous people coming and going from this house, and Nicole did not know exactly who they were. Like Sarah, Nicole heard strange tales from these people about pornography rings and child abductions and was unsure about the truth of these stories.

Mark believed that Nicole stole from him and chased her through the fields, shooting at her with a pellet gun. He was extremely violent and beat several men in front of her, threatened to kill her, and stabbed her cat to death. The dead cat was found inside Nicole's purse in the freezer after their arrests. Mark insisted that Nicole try to win custody of her children back and wanted her to kidnap them. When she refused, he beat her. Nicole gave up meth in her effort to prove to the courts that she was a good mother and was tested weekly. She thought Mark had stopped using as well. But it soon became apparent that he had not. Mark killed two men on separate occasions in Nicole's presence.

Prior to the murders, Mark's paranoia had increased and become obvious to those around him. One of the neighbors who was interviewed by Nicole's attorney reported:

> Well, I can give you a real short-term summary of what was running through his mind, that was, he was a hit man for the CIA, Mark was, and that he had refused to do a job, and now they were sending someone out to infiltrate [*sic*] him, and to take him out, and to have his phones tapped, and his vehicles tapped, they had his house tapped, all this other stuff. And he's telling me all this while we're riding in his truck, which is supposedly tapped. I see him tear apart a cellular phone and take out a regular standard brand that's made by Motorola, transistor, and tell me that he knew who made that bug. He knew the technician who put that together. He just, he'd lost it.

The men who spent time at the ranch were also afraid of Mark and obeyed his commands. One man interviewed after the murders said that Mark threatened to kill his whole family and make him watch as he peeled his children's skin off. Mark's displays of violence and terrorizing threats caused everyone around him to become fearful and obedient. His control over Nicole was more complete because he was always with her or monitoring her behavior. With Mark's intense paranoia, Nicole never knew if he would decide that she was his enemy and needed to be eliminated as well. Mark also told her that they were soul mates and that he had superhuman powers. Nicole was uncertain about his claims to special powers, but did believe he was fully capable of killing her.

She told me that when they were both in detention waiting to be arraigned he was taken past the room she was in and he called her name in a singsong manner as one would call a child, "Nicole, Nicole." When he saw her, he said, "Hello, soul mate," in a deep, snarling voice. Although they were both in custody, Nicole was terrified that he would find a way to escape and come after her. She felt a mixture of love and fear toward Mark that contributed to her inability to evaluate the truthfulness of what he told her. Apart from the period when she gave up drugs as part of her custody battle, Nicole was using crystal on a daily basis. Nicole's isolation and the secrecy enforced by Mark combined with her drug use to create a situation in which "reality" was elusive. Even after she was in jail, she was afraid that he would "get her."

> I remember when we would talk, he would tell me that we were always gonna be together and that I could never leave him. I told you before that I thought that he had superhuman powers, 'cuz he just built himself up that way, and when the cops arrested me, I still thought he was gonna come. I remember when I was first here in jail, thinkin' he was gonna break out of jail, and I could just imagine him grabbing a pencil and using it to get his way out o' there, and he was gonna break out and come and get me, and I was so afraid . . . and at night I couldn't even sleep, 'cuz I knew he was gonna come.

The first murder Mark committed was of a young man who had been living at the ranch with them. Roy had recently been released from jail, and Mark was convinced that he was stealing from him and was a member of the "Sick Puppy Club" that abducted young

women for enslavement in the porn industry. Mark told Nicole and
Roy that they were wasting his airspace, and they were going for a
ride and he wasn't sure who was coming back. He injected Roy with
a horse tranquilizer, gave him beer and Valium and ordered him into
the toolbox on the back of his pickup. Roy complied, and Nicole sat
in the front of the truck while Mark drove to a deserted canal bank.
When he got Roy out of the toolbox, he made him kneel on the
ground. Nicole made the following statement to the grand jury:

> He wanted me to shoot Roy. He told me—he said—before, obviously,
> he killed him, he wanted me to kill him and he put this black gun in
> my hand and he had his hands over my hands and he said, "Show me
> how much you love me." And I couldn't. I couldn't do that. He had it
> pointed to the back of Roy's head and I—I couldn't shoot him. I have
> no reason to shoot Roy. I didn't want to kill Roy. I didn't want Roy
> dead. I thought Mark was going to kill me that night too and, at that
> point, I wanted to die. I really did. I had tried to commit suicide before
> and I didn't succeed. I was taken to a hospital, but I didn't succeed in
> that. I wanted to die, but I didn't want to do it myself. That's basically
> why I didn't put up a struggle with Mark that day. Anyway, he killed
> Roy by hitting him in the head with a meat tenderizer and I feel like I
> was as much—I'm not—I was a victim of Mark just like Roy was. The
> only difference was I didn't die.[47]

After Mark killed Roy and threw his body in the canal, he told
Nicole she could never leave him and that he would kill her if she
told anyone what happened. Nicole described it thus:

> I heard this gurgling and then this splash, and then he came up behind
> me, and he kinda lifted me up, and I thought, it's my turn too now, and
> that's when he told me that he loved me, and that he'd never let me
> live without being with him, he said, because now you know what I'm
> capable of. And, I couldn't believe that he had killed somebody . . . he
> told me that if I ever told anybody that he would rip my heart out and
> that I could see the last bit of blood. So, he was tellin' me all kinds o'
> things. Not to leave, not to tell anybody, and then, one o' the things
> that, I just pretend like nothing happened. I didn't tell anybody, and I
> know, I can't, it was not real to me.

Nicole distanced herself mentally from the murder and continued
to live with Mark without telling anyone what happened. After two

months, Mark insisted that Nicole find a job. She had a hot, exhausting day of job hunting and stopped for gas on her way home. She had no money, so the gas clerk had to phone Mark for permission to put gas on his tab. While Nicole waited, she was approached by a man who struck up a conversation and told her he could help her find a job. He gave her his business card and then asked, "What's a guy gotta do to get a blow job around here?" Nicole was offended by the man's suggestion that she was a prostitute, and also afraid that someone would tell Mark that she was speaking to a man. When she got home, she told Mark what happened. He insisted that she contact the man and convince him to come to the ranch so that Mark could teach him a lesson. She did as she was told and, when the man arrived, Mark and his friend were waiting for him. They took him into a shed and spent the night taking turns beating him to death with a baseball bat and locking him in a car trunk between beatings. Two days later, Mark took his body to the national forest where he beheaded it and removed the hands and feet. He injured himself in the process, and when he went to the hospital for treatment, he was arrested. A few hours later, Nicole and two other accomplices were apprehended in the city.

After the second murder, Mark would not let Nicole speak to anyone, and told her, "This free thinking of yours has got to end. When I come back here, you're gonna have no friends and you're gonna do what I say when I say." She was convinced that he was watching and listening to her every moment, and her fear of his surveillance lasted months after she was incarcerated. Her participation in luring the man to the ranch and her failure to contact the police were the grounds for the murder charges against her. All the people involved in this man's murder used crystal meth throughout the night. Four people were charged and sentenced to prison: Mark is on death row, and Nicole was sentenced to twenty-five years in prison for these murders.

Nicole's sexuality was a focus for the prosecution. Testimony was given by two witnesses who said that Nicole was "turned on" by violence. Nicole adamantly denies this accusation. One witness later said her statement was not true and Nicole's attorney tried to have the testimony removed from the record. Another witness testified that Nicole watched while Mark beat him and that she "appeared to be having an orgasm." This testimony, from people who were drug addicts and criminal offenders, was used to portray Nicole as a sadist. Her luring the second murder victim to their home to "party," was thus construed as a deliberate plan to satisfy Nicole's sexual interest in watching violence. Although one witness retracted her statement and neither witness was credible, the prosecution maintained their view of Nicole. The facts of her abuse by Mark were thus considered less relevant in evaluating her culpability for the murders.

In all these cases, women were immersed in a world where their own perceptions were ridiculed or undermined and the abuser asserted his own view of reality. The men simultaneously threatened that unless the women demonstrated loyalty through following orders, they would be killed. None of the women had prior criminal records for violent or serious crimes, but all of the men did. The violent offenses women were finally charged with were either actions performed or ordered by their abusers. The women did as they were told to avoid being killed themselves. Their actions were not the consequence of intentional plans to hurt others, of a malicious heart, but reactions to situations that were bizarre and terrifying. Their violence, or failure to intervene in their abusers' violence, was a consequence of obedience to authority in a situation where they saw no other alternatives.

Child Abuse

It is hard to withhold harsh judgment on women who do not protect their children from their violent partners. Mothers are expected to defend their children, regardless of the danger they may face.[48] In a widely publicized national case, Hedda Nussbaum witnessed Joel Steinberg beat their daughter into a coma and failed to intervene or obtain medical attention. Many people, including one of the intellectual founders of the antirape movement, Susan Brownmiller, argued that no amount of battering could explain her moral paralysis.[49] But for women trapped in violent relationships, the inability to protect their children is framed by a context of coercive compulsion from their abuser and concrete social obstacles to escape. Like the women described above, women whose children were harmed had ambivalent feelings of love and hate toward their abusers. They experienced high levels of physical violence; they were threatened with harm if they tried to leave or call the police, and subjected to psychological manipulation by their partners. In addition, all the women faced extraordinarily difficult economic circumstances that were mitigated by men's financial contributions. Lack of realistic alternatives combined with emotional and physical battering to lock women in situations where they did not protect their children. As Andrea Dworkin wrote, this entrapment does not equate with innocence.[50] It means that women's moral judgments are framed by what they view as possible in the context of terror and economic dependence.

Some women do not acknowledge that their children are being abused. Women who say their children lie about abuse, just to get attention or for some unknown reason, replicate the responses to their own victimization as children and adult women.[51] Women are frequently disbelieved because they do not have sufficient documentation or evidence, or because their reports are delayed or change in detail over time. One woman told me that her boyfriend was not prosecuted for assaulting her with a hammer because she was unable to identify which one of three hammers was the assault weapon. As discussed in chapter 4, many women who were sexually assaulted as children were not believed when they told caretakers. When these children become mothers whose boyfriends and husbands abuse their children, they sometimes repeat their own experience by disbelieving their children's complaints.

The emotional and financial bonds that some women have with abusive partners may make them reluctant to accept the validity of reports of abuse and to intervene. It is difficult for any woman to accept and believe that the man she loves and shares an intimate relationship with is sexually abusing her children. The difficulty of acknowledging and intervening to stop the abuse is magnified when the man is also physically and emotionally abusive to her. If her financial stability and ability to provide for her children depends on this man's income and housing, recognition of the abuse threatens the existence of them all. Additionally, men may convince women that if they leave the relationship or report the abuse, the *women* will lose custody.[52] They will then be completely unable to protect their children from their father's abuse. Women may not be passively accepting abuse, but doing their best to protect their children in an untenable situation.[53]

Women also abuse alcohol and drugs as a response to current and

prior victimization. "Self-medication" appears to be voluntary behavior that increases the chances that their children will be abused
or neglected. Simply being drunk or using illegal drugs in the presence of children is criminal and damaging to kids. But when inebri-
ation or drug use prohibits protection of children from violent and
predatory male partners, women's self-destructive coping mechanisms take on a more malevolent character. Mothers too drunk or
high to detect abuse and to intervene violate fundamental expectations of maternal care. Yet often their drug or alcohol use is an effort
to cope with their own lack of care as children and the ongoing pain
of abuse in their intimate relationships.

Fathers are rarely held accountable for failure to protect children
from abuse, even murder, by their mothers. I can find no statistics
on this issue, but in several high-profile maternal filicides, such as
those committed by Andrea Yates, fathers who failed to intervene
have been portrayed as tragic victims rather than criminal offenders.
Rusty Yates knew that his wife was suffering from postpartum psy-
chosis and had tried to commit suicide twice. She believed her children were doomed to hell because of her own sins and she heard
voices, yet he left her alone to care for five small children whom she
drowned in the bathtub. But Rusty Yates was not charged for failure
to protect his children.[54] In contrast, Kimberly Novy was the first
woman to be convicted of first-degree murder for failure to protect a
child in the death of her stepson. Despite evidence of his abuse of
both the boy and Kimberly, Keith Novy, the child's biological father,
was not charged.[55] Fathers, especially stepfathers, are more likely to
perpetrate physical and sexual violence against children than mothers or stepmothers, but mothers are more likely to be charged with
the neglect of children.[56] When fathers fail to protect children from
maternal abuse or neglect, however, social and legal sanctions reflect
cultural assumptions regarding the responsibility for care of children.
Mothers, not fathers, are expected to protect children from the inad-
equacies of the other parent at all costs.[57] Neil Websdale's analysis of
child protection files in Florida cases of child homicides found evidence that workers often blamed mothers for failure to protect children from abusive male partners. He found no "comparable discourse
of blame" toward fathers in the files of children killed by women.[58]

Of the women discussed here, three were charged with child sexual abuse because their partners perpetrated abuse against their chil-

dren. Two women, Marcie and Monica, experienced high levels of physical violence and emotional abuse from their partners. The other woman, Toni, refused to discuss anything with me and insisted that she did not know what happened to her children. Toni was an African American woman with seven children who worked at a photo-finishing store. She had spent fifteen years with her partner, and he provided income to the family while moving in and out of the household. I sat with Toni in her attorney's office and watched the video of the two-hour interview of her daughters describing the sexual abuse they suffered from their father. One little girl was seven years old; the other, eleven. At the end of the interview, Toni maintained that she still did not know what happened, and that the children were lying. All of Toni's children were placed in foster homes after the two girls reported sexual abuse to a neighbor. The girls said their father beat their mother, but when I asked Toni if there had been any domestic violence in their relationship, she laughed and said, "No, I never thought that way." Repeated attempts to elicit information about any aspect of the relationship were met with one-word answers and "I don't know." Toni emphasized that she was too busy taking care of her children to think about anything else and that she did not understand what was happening, even after watching the video.

KATHLEEN: So you think that the kids have made up this story they're telling? About the abuse?
TONI: It's lies, I think. Yes, mmhmm. Domestic violence, yes.
KATHLEEN: But what about the sexual abuse?
TONI: I don't know. I don't know anything about that.
KATHLEEN: You don't believe it happened?
TONI: I don't know nuthin'. I don't know anything. Like I said, I was working, staying at home, taking care of the kids, I don't know.

It was clear that Toni did not trust me, a white stranger, and would not offer any information that could be used in the criminal cases against herself or her partner. She did not trust her attorney, a Latino man, either, and our efforts to explain the importance of her participation in her defense only met with silence. Toni had no reason to trust either one of us. I do not know whether her partner abused her. He was convicted of the sexual abuse of the girls and the charges against Toni were dropped.

The other two women, Monica and Marcie, were white, working-class women married to white, working-class men who had prior arrests, were alcoholics, and seemed obsessed with sex. Monica did not believe her children's reports of sexual and physical abuse either. Her severe physical abuse by her partner and her subsequent marriage to him was described in chapter 3 and earlier in this chapter. Monica was addicted to crystal meth and was on probation when she met Dick. She was trying to support herself and her three children, but had difficulty maintaining a household. She moved in and out of her mother's home, but moved in with Dick after dating him for several months. Dick was an alcoholic and meth addict, addicted to gambling and pornography. His first wife described him as a sex addict who paid for the services of prostitutes at least twice a week. He also beat her throughout their marriage until she finally was able to divorce him. He began to beat Monica as soon as she moved into his home, and also sexually molested her nine- and fourteen-year-old daughters and physically assaulted her eleven-year-old son. The girls reported the abuse to their grandmother, who called child protective services (CPS). About three weeks after Dick broke Monica's skull open with a pipe wrench, she married him in a civil ceremony. Monica returned to work after the ceremony and there was no celebration. Dick disappeared and was arrested the following day, and Monica was arrested within a week. As noted above, Monica believed the marriage was simply Dick's scheme to prevent her from testifying against him. While they were incarcerated, Dick wrote her letters every day, saying how much he loved her, referring to her as his wife, and warning her to keep her mouth shut. The following excerpt from one of his letters illustrates Dick manipulations:

I would choose you over my kids. If they were going to split them up I don't know. Your mom's probably already drawing welfare on them. I'm going to have to charge you rent for staying in my head all the time. . . . I've had some terrible thoughts about you and I hope I'm completely wrong. Don't you think it would be nice just the two of us traveling around and then come spend a few weeks here so you could be with your kids some? I don't think I need to be around them anymore. I know I was mean to them some times. They were mean to me a lot of times and this is really uncalled for. You'll never know how much I've been thinking of ending it. I thought you had snitched on me and did all the wrong things. I do hope that I'm very wrong on those thoughts. Be truthful. Beautiful, I sincerely love and miss you very much. I think by now you should know that. Take care of my favorite person and always keep me in mind. I'll get you some money, unless you tell me otherwise. Love, Your Husband

In this as well as many other letters, Dick lets Monica know that, if she testifies against him, he will define it as a betrayal. He never writes that he will kill her, but he threatens suicide in all of his letters. While expressing his sincere love and longing, he also admits he has "terrible thoughts" about her. He offers her money and reminds her that she was nothing when he "found" her and provided her with a home, food, and security for her children. In this and other letters, he undermines her relationship with her mother, who had care of her children, and implies she only had the kids in order to collect money from welfare. He pits her love for him against her love of her children, denies he has harmed them, and indicates he would always put her before his own children. Of course, Monica expressed ongoing fear of Dick and confusion about their relationship. By the time I met her in jail, she knew that her children's complaints were true and she felt horribly guilty about failing to protect them. At the same time, she felt that her options were extremely limited and she did not know how to get Dick out of her life and establish a life of her own with her children. After spending several months in jail, Monica was sentenced to probation and treatment. She returned to live with her mother and children. Dick was sentenced to two years in prison for assault on a plea bargain that dropped the sexual abuse and crimes against children charges.

The letters Monica received in jail document a pattern of manipulation that all women described. Abusers profess love and commitment, but simultaneously threaten violence and a cessation of economic support if women report violence against themselves or their children or testify against them. These threats from a person already charged with a crime constitute witness tampering and are chargeable offenses. However, none of the men who threatened the women described here were ever charged with witness tampering or intimidation. Women were threatened with such charges by detectives who warned them they could not discuss pending charges with their children, but I do not know of any cases where charges were actually filed. In most cases, men's threats occur prior to their criminal charges, as a way to keep women from reporting their abuse.

Marcie described her experiences of intimidation by her husband who assaulted her and their daughter. As mentioned briefly in chapter 1, Marcie had a mental condition that limited her ability to work. She could not keep up the pace demanded by most employers and had lost several jobs prior to being classified as disabled by Social Security. She had been married to Lou for eighteen years and they had seven children ranging in age from five to eighteen. Marcie's mother died when Marcie was fourteen, and her father was an alcoholic who could not care for her. He died several years later, leaving Marcie on her own. She married Lou at age eighteen, and she felt she was more his maid than his wife. Like Dick, Lou spent a great deal of time at topless bars and with prostitutes. He also used pornography every day, demanding that Marcie watch with him and perform the acts he saw in the videos. When their oldest daughter was eleven, Lou began to watch her in the shower, take photographs of her, and fondle her. Over several years, the abuse escalated to include rape of Marcie while Lou fondled their daughter. Both Marcie and Lou were regular churchgoers, and Lou provided some income to the family.

> We went into a marriage of him cheating on me and he was a very controlling, very hardheaded person. He always wanted it his way. Women are always in the kitchen cooking and cleaning and taking care of the kids. And I was kind of his maid for eighteen years, not his wife . . . he tells me that he has been out in bars and magazines and movies and he's always using "the Lord" to back it up. You know? "The Lord is going to heal me of this, the Lord is going to take care of this, the Lord is going to forgive me for this. It will be okay. I'm going to get over this." You know and then he would go for like three to six months without doing anything and then he would get back into it. Eventually it would get worse and worse.

Marcie spoke with her minister about their problems. He tried to work individually with Lou, but did not report the abuse to authorities. Marcie says she cannot understand why nobody in her neighborhood intervened because she screamed, yelled, and cussed loudly for help. Our interview took place in her trailer home that was no more than fifty feet from adjoining units, so it seems unlikely that no one heard her screams. When Marcie tried to call the police, Lou ripped the phone out of the wall. His most effective method of control, however, was to tell Marcie that she would be unable to support her children and would lose custody if she reported him. When Marcie first suspected abuse, she asked her daughter if there was a problem and tried to obtain help:

> I asked her because me and Lou's relationship was sort of dwindling and I didn't know why and she came up and told me that dad was trying to do things to her in the wrong way and so I went and had a talk with Lou and that's when he started filling my head with all of these lies about if I told anybody I would get in trouble and I'd lose my kids and I wouldn't be able to support the family, so let's keep it hush-hush. And I tried to tell my pastor at church. I knew that as far as she told me, he was taking pictures and watching her through the bathroom window taking showers and watching her undress. So I told my pastor all of that and he said there's not enough evidence to do anything about it right now. So he didn't report it. And every time I try to pick the phone up and call the police he would yank it out of the wall and throw it at me and start filling my head with a bunch of lies. "I told you that you can't support these kids by yourself."

Lou was telling the same story to their daughter to prevent her from reporting the abuse. As in the cases of child murders discussed below, when external authorities, such as Marcie's pastor, fail to identify the danger to children and to take decisive steps to intervene, women get the message that nothing can be done. Marcie doubted her own judgment, partly because of her disability and because of Lou's abuse, and placed her faith and trust in her pastor's opinion.

Eventually, Lou became concerned that someone would report the abuse and he moved the family to another state to avoid detection. There, their daughter reported her father's abuse at a revival meeting and he was arrested. The police interviewed Marcie as part of Lou's case and told her she would not be prosecuted. However, when she returned to Arizona to live with her sister, these interviews were used to file charges against her and she was placed in jail.

> [In the other state] I was not on probation but I was on some kind of where the CPS would watch for six months and make sure I can handle my kids and make sure everything was all right in the family

after he left. They cleared my charge and I was fine and taking care of my kids the way a normal parent should do. There was no abuse physically or mentally or anything. So they told me I was okay to move to Arizona with my sister. But in the meantime, I didn't know the detectives from Phoenix came to question me and I thought they were questioning me on behalf of Lou. And I asked them twice, "Am I going to get arrested for this?" and they said, "No" and after I moved out here about three or four months later, an officer came to my house and arrested me and took me to jail. So, they lied to me. . . . My attorney tells me I should pick going to trial, the worse that could happen is you can go to jail for two years. I said, "Well, I can't go to prison. I will lose all my benefits, I will lose my kids."

Marcie accepted a plea offer and was sentenced to probation and seven months of weekends in jail. Her sister helped with the children while Marcie served her time. Lou was sentenced to twenty-two years in Arizona and six years in the other state. Lou's brothers cause problems for Marcie because they blame her for their brother's incarceration:

Lou's brothers are giving me trouble because they don't understand the whole story from eighteen years to now. They're blaming me for putting him in prison and they lost a brother and they can't really cope with it. Because Lou was always a Christian, good father, providing for his family outside of the home in front of everybody, but at home he was a monster, you know. They didn't see the monster part of him, they just saw the Christian man he was.

Unfortunately, the church acted as camouflage for Lou rather than an effective control. Marcie put her faith in the church to help stop the abuse, believing that if she involved the police, she would lose her children. Her fears almost came true, but her defense attorney was eventually able to convince the prosecution that, without Lou in the home, Marcie was a good mother. Her incarceration would have resulted in the dispersion of her six youngest children to foster homes. Although they are poor, living on the miserly TANF (Temporary Assistance to Needy Families) payments in Arizona—$636 per month for six children in 2000—and Marcie's disability payments, the family is together and safe from abuse.

The Death of Children

Nationally, at least fifteen hundred child deaths were attributed to maltreatment or neglect in 2003.[59] The FBI Supplementary Homicide Reports identified five hundred children who were the victims of murder or nonnegligent mansaughter in 2002.[60] In Arizona, thirty-seven children died of maltreatment and forty-two were victims of homicide in 2003.[61] The state and national data on the domestic killings of children are probably underestimates. Child deaths resulting from parental abuse or familicides are often not classified as homicides. In Websdale's analysis of child fatalities in Florida, he found that many children killed in familicides or homicide/suicides were not recorded in CPS files or police files as domestic deaths.[62] A report from the U.S. Advisory Board on Child Abuse and Neglect also documents the underreporting and misidentification of child homicides. In Missouri, a concerted effort by the Child Fatality Review Team found that only 38.8 percent of 121 cases of verified fatal mistreament were identified as homicides by the FBI.[63]

In cases that are identified as maltreatment fatalities or as child homicides, male caretakers are the most common perpetrators. Women are more likely to be labeled as the perpetrator in child deaths resulting from neglect. As in nonfatal maltreatment, gendered assumptions of responsibility for children's care influence the attribution of guilt for child neglect deaths to mothers more often than to fathers.[64]

It is not possible to know how many of these deaths can be linked to the abuse of mothers by male intimate partners. The nexus between intimate partner abuse and child fatalities has not been a systematic focus of research and data collection efforts. There are no national or state statistics on the proportion of children killed by parents whose mothers were being abused. Statistics, even when available, could not describe the lived experience of women who are abused and unable to protect their children from their partners.

Websdale's research on domestic homicides is one of the few studies that illuminates the connections between intimate partner violence and child homicides. Through a detailed examination of the case files of eighty-three children killed in domestic homicides, Websdale identified seven themes: a history of child abuse; a history of domestic violence in the parental or caretaker relationship; prior contact with agencies; poverty, inequality, and unemployment; a criminal history on the part of the perpetrator; the use of drugs and/or alcohol; and the easy availability of weapons.[65] All of these themes, except the availability of weapons, were present in the four cases where women's abusive partners killed their children.[66] Children were killed with men's fists and feet, by a wooden paddle, or through neglect rather than guns or knives. There was a history of child abuse that had been investigated by child protective services in three cases. In two cases, children had been removed from their mother's care due to maltreatment and parental drug or alcohol use. The children's deaths occurred shortly after their return to mothers by child protective services (CPS): three weeks in one case, five months in the other. In one other case, CPS investigated after the woman's former mother-in-law reported seeing bruises on the two children. They decided no abuse was occurring, which provided reassurance to their mother that her boyfriend was not harming her daughters. Two months later, on the day CPS closed the case, he beat the youngest child to death.

Child protective services was not the only agency to fail these families. In all four cases, police, medical personnel, neighbors, coworkers, extended family members, or welfare workers knew that domestic violence was being committed against the mother. In three cases, mothers' alcoholism or drug addictions were known to these extended networks. All four men who abused the women and their children had prior criminal records and had served time in prison or jail for violent crimes, drug abuse, or theft. Two men were on probation. These prior records and current probation requirements were considerations in men's reactions to the abuse of children. Men informed their partners that if they told anyone about the abuse, the men would go back to prison. In the context of physical and emotional abuse of women, the warnings issued to "keep your mouth shut" prevented women from contacting authorities who might have helped their children.

In addition to the themes noted by Websdale, I found common themes in these four cases. All four women were low-income women of color: three Latinas and one American Indian woman. They had all experienced prior sexual abuse as children, although one, Salina, was a bystander to her sister's long-term abuse rather than a direct victim. Two of the women, Emma and Luisa, had lifelong histories of violence and rejection by parents. These women were abused physically, sexually, and emotionally by a series of men and women from the time they were toddlers. No one ever protected them from abuse despite the knowledge of other family members, teachers, and social workers. The women all began having children at fifteen or sixteen and engaged in no efforts to control their fertility. These families were living at the extreme end of poverty, and all four women were under pressure to provide income, housing, food, and medical care to their children. Three of the families were large or very large: Teresita, age 20, had five children, including a set of special-needs twins; Emma, age 39, had eleven children, with a twelfth born shortly after she was incarcerated (she had lost custody of eight of them prior to the death of her daughter); Luisa, 29, had six children, including special-needs twins, and gave birth to a seventh while incarcerated. Salina, 23, had two children and also gave birth shortly after her incarceration. The size of these families created enormous pressure on women. Only Salina had completed high school, and none had jobs beyond minimum-wage waitress, cleaning woman, or clerk at Wal-Mart. The men they lived with did not have good jobs or educations either, and three of the four were surviving on welfare and food stamps. Emma was living in a tiny one-room shack without running water, insulation, or electricity. It was the best home she had had in many years and it belonged to her boyfriend's father. This was the environment to which CPS returned two of her children.

It is well documented that living with domestic violence creates problem behaviors in children, including aggression, enuresis, depression, fear, and excessive worry about separation from mothers.[67] These behaviors create stress in any mother. When they occur in the context of extreme poverty and violence and threats from male partners, women face extraordinary challenges to successful mothering.

Three children were beaten to death and women failed to obtain medical attention for them. The other child died of neglect and starvation. All of the children were three years of age or younger; three were girls and one was a boy. In two of the beating deaths, women had used inappropriate physical discipline with the children. Their male partners admitted assaulting the children, and their stories fluctuated between accepting blame and blaming the women. All three women whose children were beaten to death were sentenced to life in prison. One of the male perpetrators was sentenced to death; another, to life in prison; one man accepted a plea bargain and is serving a five-and-a-half-year sentence. In the neglect case, both the woman and her male partner accepted plea bargains for second-degree murder and received sentences of ten years to life. In the three beating cases, the men were not the biological fathers of the children and had expressed resentment toward them. This pattern is consistent with other research on child homicides, uxoricides, and familicides: the presence of a stepchild or unrelated child is strongly correlated with male-perpetrated homicides within the family.[68] Some research reports approximately equal numbers of biological parents and stepfathers or mothers' boyfriends perpetrating child homicides.[69] The child who died of neglect was living with both of her biological parents.

In all cases, male partners routinely made denigrating comments about the children and women's parenting abilities. They complained that women were too indulgent and did not know how to discipline the children appropriately. Men perceived the attention that women gave to children as detracting from their own pleasure and satisfaction. Children, especially those with special health needs, were viewed by the men as a nuisance. Men expected women to keep the children quiet and unobtrusive, but to do so without diminishing the attention and service men demanded. Women felt they were juggling the demands of their adult partners with those of their children in situations where there was not enough energy or money to meet anyone's needs. When women abused alcohol or drugs, their ability to cope with this extraordinary stress was compromised even further.

Teresita's eighteen-month-old daughter died from lack of care. Her partner and the baby's biological father, Primo, was a crack addict who abused Teresita physically, sexually, and emotionally. She had four other children under the age of five to care for, and all of them were sick the weekend that her daughter died. She had believed Primo when he told her he was taking care of the baby and she focused on the other sick children. Teresita accepted responsibility for her failure to challenge Primo and to insist on taking care of the child herself, but she also hoped that people would understand the effect that his abuse had on her:

I just hope that they see where I'm coming from. Where they see I'm not this monster that everybody's making me out to be. . . . I'm not trying to blame that, you know what I'm sayin'? Cause that's what people are going to be like, "Oh domestic violence, oh yeah, right." You know, it does, though. No one realizes how much it can mess you up in life. It seriously does. He had me in a hole to where I couldn't go anywhere. He had me trapped. Just being scared, you know, it's hard. It's hard not knowin' if today is going to be a good day, not knowing if you're gonna die this day, you know. If he's gonna trip out and really beat you bad that day. It's like you never know.

Like women who committed crimes against people other than their abusers, women whose children died did not think intimate partner violence was an excuse. Rather, they felt trapped, afraid, and confused in circumstances they were unable to control. They wanted people to understand that they were not demons who callously allowed their children to be beaten or starved to death. They were overwhelmed with demands that they could not meet, afraid to challenge their partners, and unable to escape their circumstances. Three women whose children died are sentenced to life in prison, and Teresita's sentence is ten years to life. It is a tragic irony that none of the social services or law enforcement agencies that were involved in women's lives prior to children's deaths were able to provide the support that would have protected them and their children from men's violence. Yet after the death of children, the government mobilized the resources to prosecute and to incarcerate women at the cost of approximately twenty thousand dollars per year for at least the next twenty-five years.[70] (This figure, of course, does not include the cost of caring for their surviving children, placed with relatives or in foster care.) The death of a child, and the failure of a mother to protect that child, is a horrible tragedy that reflects on the deterioration of entire communities. I do not accept, however, that lifelong incarceration of these children's mothers and the lifelong "sentences" to be served by their remaining children, is the appropriate or just response.[71]

Conclusion

As Andrea Dworkin wrote, battered women who commit crimes of complicity are not innocent. They do what they must do each day to survive.[72] It is easy to judge them. The more relevant challenge is to understand what their lives are like and why they become enmeshed in criminal contexts from which escape seems impossible. The women described here were known in their communities as victims of intimate partner violence. The men they lived with had committed crimes of violence prior to beginning relationships with the women, and they had all perpetrated severe acts of violence against the women. Most threatened to kill women if they "snitched"; some also threatened to kill women's relatives or themselves. Protection from these men seemed impossible to achieve, and women's fear continued after men were incarcerated. The feelings of love and sexual intimacy that first attracted women to these men were mixed with fear and loathing after women became implicated in men's crimes. Some women continued to feel a mixture of hate and love toward men. Most women felt only anger, fear, and hate toward the men who they believed used them then abandoned them to the criminal processing system.

The harshest sentences of any of the forty-five women were given to women involved in crimes against people other than their abusers. In nonfatal crimes, consideration of the impact of battering sometimes helped mitigate both charges and sentences. In these cases, women were able to continue providing care for their children. With their partners incarcerated, women were able to improve their lives and feel safe. On the other hand, when people died as a result of women's obedience to violent male partners, there was little consideration of the effects of battering in charging, determination of guilt, or sentencing. Women who were with men who killed others suffered some of the most extreme abuse from their male partners. Although prosecutors, juries, and judges believed the abuse occurred, they did not accept its influence on women's actions. Unlike soldiers, or even corporate executives, women who followed the immoral and illegal orders of violent male partners were held fully accountable for their actions. In the epilogue, I consider the social ramifications of this approach to women's crimes committed in the context of victimization.

Epilogue

I have described women's experiences with victimization and offending to elaborate the complicated webs of pain that frame their behavior. The structures of feeling that permeate childhood and adult
family life reproduce women's pain and contribute to their entrapment in violent relationships. These structures of feeling are not individual, psychological states. They are patterns of emotions formed
by material conditions. Women had hopes that romantic love would
fill the void of loneliness, boredom, and meaninglessness that began
in early childhood. These hopes reflected the disappointments in
their families, their limited occupational and educational horizons,
and gendered cultural prescriptions for women. Some women described their abusive partners in positive terms and emphasized the
"good parts" of their relationships. Other women found that hopes
for fulfillment in an intimate partnership were extinguished by physical, emotional, and sexual violence and by fear and worry about
their own and their children's safety. For both groups of women,
their partners' violence and the limitations of their social contexts
constrained their efforts to construct safe and meaningful lives.

The anti–violence against women movement has been successful
in transforming awareness of intimate partner violence and the resources available to women who are victimized. As I completed this
book, the U.S. Congress reauthorized the Violence Against Women
Act (VAWA), allocating approximately $3.9 billion over the next five
years for shelters and law enforcement. This third version of VAWA
addresses some of the limitations of the earlier legislation, particularly for immigrant and trafficked women.[1] Federal, state, and local
funding for shelters, hotlines, and criminal justice programs have
provided women with many more options than were available at the

beginning of the movement in 1970. The success of the movement is an example of the possibilities for social change inherent in the concerted dedication and effort of the community.

At the same time, many people who have participated in this movement recognize the limitations of an individualized response to intimate partner violence. Activists in the early years of the movement viewed the criminal justice system and the creation of shelters as limited, short-term remedies for a problem rooted in the larger relations of gender, race, and class structures.[2] Over the past twenty-five years, the challenge and success of achieving changes in the criminal justice system and in developing shelters has eclipsed the more radical demand for social justice. Funding for criminal justice interventions has expanded while many of the progressive social gains of the 1960s and 1970s have been rolled back.

The stories I have recounted portray the horrific pain and long-term consequences of intimate partner violence for individual women and their families. It is important to help women who have been abused; it is also important to prevent the abuse from happening. Women who are both victims and offenders offer us subjugated knowledge that illuminates why and how individualized responses to intimate partner violence fail. Their knowledge also suggests possible alternatives.

Limitations of the Crime Control Model

Women in this book did not have a positive relationship with the criminal processing system. Some women complained about the failure of police to arrest and courts to hold men in jail or prison. This complaint is the same as that raised in the early 1970s, prompting activists then to file civil suits and advocate for equal protection of battered women.[3] The extent to which all of the work that has gone into improving the criminal justice response to battering has been successful in enhancing women's lives is still a question. It is clear that this response remains problematic and uneven, and I am skeptical about the possibility of eliminating these problems.

Most women in this book did not view the police or the courts as appropriate avenues of support and protection. As mentioned in chapter 2, only 45 percent of the women had police involvement in their relationships; for several of these, police had been called only by other people. Similar to women reporting in national surveys, these women felt the police could not help and would only exacerbate their problems. Because this group is composed solely of women whose victimization led to their own criminal offenses, by definition it is skewed toward cases where police involvement did not end their abuse. The excerpts I have included from women who were *not* offenders (in chapter 2), illustrate the ineffectiveness of police intervention for some women. On the other hand, there are unknown numbers of women who have found safety through appropriate actions by police and the courts. That there are many women who do not desire police intervention or are dissatisfied with the criminal justice response, does not mean that there should be a retreat from the efforts to provide police protection. It does mean, however, that there are significant limitations to this form of intervention.

Of course, for all the women described in this book, crime control efforts were directed at *them,* either for crimes against their abusers or against others. On the one hand, the criminal processing system sends a message that women are agents responsible for their decisions when they are prosecuted and incarcerated for crimes committed against abusers (outside a context of immediate self-defense) or against others in compliance with abusers' orders. If women "choose" to remain in violent relationships, they will be held to the same standard of criminal responsibility as all others. Women, perhaps, would be deterred from remaining in these dangerous situations if they knew that the coercive nature of their relationships would not mitigate their responsibility for crimes.

This approach, however, does not take into account the multiple factors that structure women's "choice" in a context of intimate partner violence. I have attempted to demonstrate the ways that the matrix of domination limits women's opportunities to resist and escape abusive relationships. Women developed strategies to deal with men's violence that kept them alive, but these strategies involved negotiating surreal conditions, acquiescing to men's demands, and keeping silent. Many women were convinced that a more direct challenge to a partner or an attempt to leave him would be punished with death. It is not easy for women to defy partners who inflict the kinds of abuse described in this book. Women's agency is circumscribed by the matrix of domination. Unless this matrix is addressed, crime control of intimate partner violence will be of limited value to many women, particularly women who are both victims and offenders.

The crime control model also tends to concentrate resources within the criminal processing system. Over the past twenty-five years, the federal government and many state and local governments have reduced funding for a range of human needs from education and child care to housing and cash assistance.[4] Research has demonstrated that supporting women with practical resources, such as jobs, housing, child care, and transportation, is more effective in preventing violence than trying to control their abusers.[5] When people focus on controlling individual men through the criminal processing system, they tend to overlook other ways that violence can be condemned and abusers held accountable. For example, Allen's recent research on domestic violence coordinating councils found that they focus on criminal justice reforms and are less effective in achieving goals that transcend this arena.[6] In countries where there is not such a strong emphasis on policing domestic violence, people have developed grassroots strategies for confronting violent men. For example, Andrea Smith cites an organization in India—Masum—that organizes women to engage in nonviolent demonstrations outside the homes where men are abusing women. The community supports Masum because they also provide services such as microcredit, health care, and education.[7] I agree with Smith that focusing on the "criminal justice system has limited our imagination with regard to strategies to combat domestic violence."[8]

Building on Women's Strength

Women in this book struggled with internal and external obstacles to creating safety and happiness in their lives. These obstacles were sometimes extraordinarily brutal physical and emotional violence; they often included the more impalpable pain of loneliness, confusion, and fear. Sometimes women's behavior was also brutal to others. Women acknowledged the pain they had caused through their crimes and did not want people to think they were denying all responsibility for their actions. I am not suggesting that the strength they demonstrated in multiple ways erases the harm they have caused to others. These women are not angelic heroes. The strength women have demonstrated, however, could become the genesis for an approach to intimate partner abuse that transcends the paradigm of individual control.

Women showed strength in developing multiple strategies of resistence to men's abuse. They gained nuanced knowledge of men's moods, facial expressions, tone of voice, and actions. This knowledge allowed them to shape their behavior in ways that minimized the possibilities of harm to themselves and others. It was not an infallible strategy for these women, as all were hurt and also participated in crime. For the majority of women who experience intimate partner abuse but do *not* become criminal defendants, such strategies provide a modicum of safety for themselves and their children. Women's ability to craft resistance in a context of abuse is an example of how women are experts on their own abuse. If services are to be of use to women, their expert knowledge must be an integral, ongoing component of planning and implementation. When the criminal justice system is involved, women's knowledge of men's behavior should be recognized and acted upon.

It is remarkable that more than half of the women (twenty-four) were able to maintain paid employment during the period of severe abuse that led up to their crimes. Several women were producing all the income for their families, working two minimum-wage jobs. Women lost or quit jobs because of their partner's abuse or their own alcohol or drug use, but others were able to maintain employment. Those who have been given the opportunity to work in prison have performed well, received promotions, and saved money.[9] Yet the number and types of jobs for women and men in the United States has been dwindling over the past twenty years. The number of people without advanced education and training far exceeds the number of unskilled jobs available that pay wages adequate to support a family.[10] Proposals that address the minimum-wage standard as well as the creation of jobs and the responsibility of multinational corporations to workers would contribute to an economic environment supportive of women's autonomy. VAWA 2005, Title vii, includes recommendations to enhance women's economic security, but focuses on women who are already victims of violence. Broader changes that address economic conditions for all women—including the lack of affordable child care—would reduce women's vulnerability to violent and controlling partners.

Jobs are not enough, however. The twenty-four women who held
jobs while they were abused (and especially those who supported
their partners financially) suggest that having a job is not sufficient
to protect women from abuse. The willingness and ability of women
to work hard should be matched by efforts to encourage girls to pursue careers, not just jobs. Careers provide more than the minimum
wage plus benefits, and they also offer goals and purpose that make
life interesting. Only two women had careers that they found satisfying. A career is not a guarantee against abuse, but it offers women
both practical and emotional resources for self-support.

The blurred boundaries between women's own self-interest and
the interests of those they love suggest that social policies must recognize the context of women's decisions about their lives. Women
will stay in abusive situations if they believe that their children and
other family members will suffer *more* if they leave. Abusive men
who warn women, "you can't make it without me" are abetted by
the ideology that any "man in the home" is better than none. Divorce rates are high and it is not difficult *legally* to dissolve a marriage. There are, simultaneously, many cultural stories about the
harm to children in single-mother families that circulate widely in
the popular media and faith communities. The increased chances of
poverty, lack of health care, and diminished educational opportunities for children in female-headed households, however, are facts
that women contemplate in deciding what to do about their partners' violence. These facts can only change through changes in the
resources and opportunities for women.

Toward a Liberatory Approach

The women described in this book have been left behind by the anti-
violence movement. There is no simple solution that would address
the complicated problems that led to their victimization or their offense. Most did not use the shelter system, and police and orders of
protection did not deter their abuser. People in their families, as well
as official state actors, clergy, and neighbors, were aware of the abuse
women suffered. Some tried to intervene, but no one provided the
kind of support women needed to end the abuse in their lives.

It is not possible to respond successfully to abuse without addressing the larger context in which abuse occurs. Crime control and service provision do not alter the emotional and financial poverty that forms the background for intimate partner violence. This poverty is not only the result of low-wage, service-sector jobs, high unemployment levels, and lack of socialized services such as child and health care. It also results from a culture that does not provide sufficient opportunities for each person to feel securely loved, valued, and respected. Although not all of the women in this book were economically poor, all were deprived of this sense of meaning and belonging. I did not talk to the men who abused them, but from the women's accounts, the men were also bereft of these essential components of human life.

This lack cannot be remedied through policies that increase surveillance and control—even those that provide social services if at the same time they disregard the nature of life in families, schools, workplaces, and communities. The transformation of these social contexts requires that the ultimate worth of each individual be at the center of analysis and action. Policies that focus on punishment cannot accomplish this. All people need the opportunity to recognize their own and others' value and to contribute to social change. Basic material well-being is foundational to this opportunity, and it is out of reach for nearly 20 percent of the people in the United States.

A liberatory response to intimate partner violence would expand the vision of safety and well-being beyond protection from a violent individual. It would be linked to other movements for social justice. In order to make these links, the anti-violence movement needs to focus less on punitive control and more on imagining and creating the conditions under which violence against an intimate partner would be unthinkable.

Appendixes

Appendix A

Pseudonym, Race/Ethnicity, Charges, Relationship to Victim(s) and Role in Offense

Pseudonym (Race/Ethnicity)	Original charge	Final charge	Relationship to victim(s)	Alleged role in offense
Dawn (white)	attempted murder	aggravated assault	wife	primary offender
Kelly (white)	aggravated assault	none	wife	primary offender
Rhonda (American Indian)	1st degree murder	manslaughter	wife	primary offender
Doreen (white)	1st degree murder	manslaughter	wife	primary offender
Lynne (white)	1st degree murder	none	wife	primary offender
Sue (white)	1st degree murder	manslaughter	wife	primary offender
Anne (white)	1st degree murder	manslaughter	girlfriend	primary offender
Abby (white)	1st degree murder	manslaughter	wife	primary offender
Dianne (white)	1st degree murder	manslaughter	wife	primary offender
Beth (white)	1st degree murder	2nd degree murder	wife	primary offender
Mona (white)	attempted murder	aggravated assault	wife	primary offender
Jane (white)	1st degree murder	1st degree murder	wife	primary offender
Michelle (American Indian)	1st degree murder	manslaughter	wife	primary offender
Crystal (American Indian)	1st degree murder	manslaughter	wife	primary offender
Dorothy (American Indian)	1st degree murder	manslaughter	wife	primary offender

Pseudonym (Race/Ethnicity)	Original charge	Final charge	Relationship to victim(s)	Alleged role in offense
Leah (American Indian)	1st degree murder	2nd degree murder	wife	primary offender
Shanna (white)	conspiracy, 1st degree murder, robbery	same	wife	accomplice
Cindy (white)	1st degree murder	2nd degree murder	wife	primary offender
Tina (white)	1st degree murder	same	girlfriend	primary offender
Carrie (American Indian)	1st degree murder	same	sister	primary offender
Carol (American Indian)	1st degree murder	same	mother	primary offender
Ronnie (African American)	attempted 1st degree murder	aggravated assault	girlfriend	primary offender
Danielle (white)	conspiracy, 1st degree murder, aggravated assault, robbery	same	wife	accomplice
Lisa (Latina)	aggravated assault	same	wife	primary offender
Angie (white)	attempted murder	unknown	girlfriend	primary offender
Sheila (white)	attempted murder	same	girlfriend	primary offender
Eve (white)	1st degree murder	manslaughter	wife	failed to report/ facilitated

Pseudonym, Race/Ethnicity, Charges, Relationship to Victim(s) and Role in Offense (continued)

Pseudonym (Race/Ethnicity)	Original charge	Final charge	Relationship to victim(s)	Alleged role in offense
Marcie (white)	failure to protect child, sexual abuse	same	wife of offender/ mother of victim	failed to report
Salina (Latina)	1st degree murder	same	girlfriend of offender/ mother of victim	failed to report, false report of missing child
Monica (white)	failure to protect child, sexual abuse	same	girlfriend/ wife of offender/ mother of victim	failed to report
Chris (white)	counterfeiting	same	public	accomplice
Laura (white)	mail fraud	same	public	accomplice
Nicole (white)	double 1st degree murder	manslaughter	acquaintance and stranger	failed to report/ facilitated
Sarah (white)	armed robbery, dangerous crime against child	armed robbery	ex–sister-in-law	equal participant with boyfriend
Jennifer (white)	1st degree murder, armed robbery	manslaughter	strangers on two separate offenses	failed to report/ facilitated
Myrna (white)	armed robbery	unknown (probation granted)	bank	primary offender

Pseudonym (Race/Ethnicity)	Original charge	Final charge	Relationship to victim(s)	Alleged role in offense
Katy (white)	drug trafficking	unknown (probation granted)	public?	accomplice
Bonnie (white)	armed robbery	same	bank	accomplice
Teresita (Latina)	1st degree murder	2nd degree murder	mother	accomplice
Julia (white)	sexual assault, armed robbery	simple assault	stranger	accomplice
Phyllis (white)	1st degree murder, armed robbery	same	stranger	primary offender
Luisa (Latina)	felony murder, child abuse	same	mother	unknown; boyfriend involved
Emma (American Indian)	felony murder, child abuse	same	mother	accomplice, failed to report or obtain medical attention
Toni (African American)	failure to protect, child sexual abuse	child sexual abuse dropped	mother	failed to report
Margaret (white)	2nd degree murder	manslaughter	wife	primary offender

Appendix B

Abuse of Drugs and Alcohol

Pseudonym	Drug abuse by abuser?	Drug abuse by woman?	Alcohol abuse by abuser?	Alcohol abuse by woman?
Dawn			X	
Kelly			X	X
Rhonda			X	X
Doreen	X		X	
Lynne			X	
Sue			X	
Anne				
Abby	X		X	
Dianne	X		X	X
Beth	X	X	X	X
Mona	X		X	
Jane			X	
Michelle			X	X
Crystal			X	
Dorothy			X	X
Leah			X	X
Shanna	X		X	
Cindy			X	
Tina			X	X
Carrie	X	X	X	X
Carol				
Ronnie	X	X	X	X
Danielle	X		X	
Lisa	X	X	X	X
Angie				
Sheila	X	X	X	X
Eve	X		X	
Marcie	X		X	
Salina	X		X	
Monica	X		X	
Chris	X		X	
Laura	X	X	X	X
Nicole	X	X	X	X
Sarah	X	X	X	X
Jennifer	X	X	X	X

Pseudonym	Drug abuse by abuser?	Drug abuse by woman?	Alcohol abuse by abuser?	Alcohol abuse by woman?
Myrna	X		X	
Katy	X		X	
Bonnie	X	X	X	X
Teresita	X	X	X	X
Julia	X	X	X	X
Phyllis	X	X	X	X
Luisa	X	X	X	X
Emma	X		X	X
Toni				
Margaret			X	

Appendix C

Women Who Killed Their Husbands/Partners

Pseudonym	Relationship	Weapon	Sentence	Living With?
Rhonda	common-law husband	ran over with truck	5 years	Y
Doreen	husband	shot with gun he gave her	probation	Y
Lynne	husband	shot with gun he threw at her	not charged	Y
Sue	husband	shot with gun he put in her hands	probation	Y
Anne	boyfriend	shot with gun he gave her	probation	N
Abby	husband	shot with his gun	probation	Y
Dianne	husband	shot	5 years	Y
Beth	husband	stabbed	10 years	Y
Jane	husband	shot	8.5 years	Y
Eve	husband	axe, third party	12.6 years	Y
Michelle	common-law husband	lead pipe	probation	N
Crystal	common-law husband	knife	probation	Y
Dorothy	common-law husband	knife	probation	Y
Leah	common-law husband	shot	9 years	Y
Shanna	husband	third party, lead pipe	18 years	Y
Cindy	husband	shot	16 years	Y
Tina	boyfriend	shot	life	N
Danielle	husband	third party, shot	life	N
Margaret	husband	shot	unknown	Y

Appendix D

Context of Violence against Husbands/Partners

Pseudonym	Context	Action/Location	Feelings about abuser
Rhonda	Accident	hit with car /public place	not in love, not afraid
Doreen	imminent threat	shot and killed/bedroom	not in love, terrified
Lynne	imminent threat	shot and killed/bedroom	not in love, terrified
Sue	imminent threat	shot and killed/bedroom	in love, terrified
Anne	imminent threat	shot and killed/street	not in love, terrified
Abby	imminent threat	shot and killed/living room	not in love, terrified
Dianne	imminent threat	shot and killed/living room	in love, terrified
Beth	accident during fight	stabbed and killed/doorway between living room and bedroom	in love, terrified
Jane	proactive	shot and killed/front yard	in love, terrified
Eve	third party	axed to death/in house	not in love, not afraid
Michelle	argument	hit in head with pipe, field	not in love, afraid
Crystal	imminent threat	stabbed and killed/in car	in love, terrified
Dorothy	imminent threat	stabbed and killed/bedroom	in love, terrified
Leah	proactive	shot and killed/front yard	not in love, terrified
Shanna	third party	hit in head with metal bar; died/bedroom	in love, terrified
Cindy	don't know	shot and killed by somebody/ kitchen	not in love, terrified
Tina	don't know/ says imminent threat	shot and killed/garage	in love, terrified
Danielle	third party	shot and killed/in house	not in love, terrified
Margaret	proactive	shot and killed/in house	not in love, terrified
Dawn	proactive	shot and injured/front room	not in love, terrified
Kelly	imminent threat	shot and injured/bedroom	not in love, terrified
Mona	proactive	shot and injured/outside apt.	not in love, terrified
Sheila	proactive	shot and injured/bedroom	not in love, terrified
Ronnie	aggressive	stabbed and injured/ outside apt.	not in love, afraid
Lisa	aggressive	shot and injured/front yard	not in love, terrified
Angie	imminent threat	shot and injured/bedroom	not in love, terrified

Appendix E

Police Involvement, Children, Work, Abused as Child, Parental Absence

Pseudonym	Prior police involvement?	Children	Work	Abused as child	Parental absence?
Dawn	N	Y	husband forbade	unknown	unknown
Kelly	Y	N	car sales	unknown	unknown
Rhonda	Y	Y	N	unknown	unknown
Doreen	Y	Y	clerical (fired)	unknown	unknown
Lynne	Y	Y	bar and domestic	unknown	unknown
Sue	Y	N	product operator	Y	Y
Anne	N	Y	bar	unknown	unknown
Abby	N	Y	cashier	N	N
Dianne	Y	N	domestic	N	Y
Beth	Y	Y	bar (forced to quit)	Y	Y
Mona	N	Y	sales	N	N
Jane	Y	Y	N	N	N
Michelle	Y	Y	N	N	Y
Crystal	N	Y	N	N	N
Dorothy	Y	Y	N	N	N
Leah	Y	Y	N	Y	Y
Shanna	Y	Y	clerical	N	Y
Cindy	N	N	hairdresser	N	Y
Tina	N	N	waitress	Y	Y
Carrie	Y	Y	N	Y	Y
Carol	N	Y	N	Y	Y
Ronnie	N	Y	mail carrier	Y	Y
Danielle	N	Y	sales	Y	N
Lisa	Y	Y	N	N	N
Angie	N	N	grocery stocker	N	Y
Sheila	Y	Y	bar	Y	Y
Eve	N	Y	N	N	N
Marcie	N	Y	N	N	Y
Salina	N	Y	waitress	N	Y
Monica	Y	Y	clerical	N	Y
Chris	N	N	med. tech.	Y	Y
Laura	N	N	waitress	N	N
Nicole	N	Y	N	Y	Y
Sarah	N	Y	N	Y	Y
Jennifer	N	N	N	Y	Y
Myrna	N	Y	N	N	N
Katy	N	N	bar and pharmacy	N	N

Pseudonym	prior police Involvement?	Children	Work	Abused as child by caretaker?	Parental absence?
Bonnie	N	N	fast food	Y	Y
Teresita	Y	Y	N	stranger rape	Y
Julia	N	N	N	N	N
Phyllis	Y	Y	lost job	N	N
Luisa	Y	Y	N	Y	Y
Emma	Y	Y	N	Y	Y
Toni	N	Y	photofinisher	N	N
Margaret	N	Y	nurse	N	N

Appendix F

Women Who Committed Crimes against Others

Pseudonym	Offense	Victims	Sentence	Abuser's Sentence
Marcie	Child abuse and sexual abuse	oldest daughter	probation	28 years
Salina	felony murder, child abuse	oldest daughter	35 years	death
Monica	child sexual abuse	son and daughter	probation	2 years
Toni	child sexual abuse	daughters	charges dismissed	unknown
Chris	counterfeiting	public	probation	unknown
Laura	mail fraud	public	probation	unknown
Nicole	murder, kidnapping	unknown male	22 years	death
Sarah	armed robbery	ex-husband	3 years	fled country
Jennifer	manslaughter	unknown male (camper)	10.5 years	life
Myrna	armed robbery	bank	probation	unknown
Carol	murder	own children	life	not involved
Katy	drug purchase	public	2 years	6 months
Bonnie	armed robbery	bank	10.5 years	life
Teresita	murder, child abuse	youngest child	10 years to life	10 years to life
Julia	sexual assault, kidnapping	unknown woman	2 years plus probation	life
Phyllis	murder	unknown man (camper)	life	life
Luisa	murder, child abuse	son	35 years	5.5 years
Emma	murder, child abuse	daughter	life	life

Appendix G

A Note on Method

I collected the interviews that form the basis of this book over a twenty-three-year period. I followed a loose, interactive style, allowing women to tell their stories in terms of what they thought was most important. Rather than ask women directly if they had been physically abused by their partners, I cued women to talk about childhood and adolescence, relationships with parents and caretakers, any experiences of abuse by family members or strangers, their intimate relationship(s), and any criminal conduct. Some women were interviewed on several occasions. Most interviews were audiotape-recorded, ranging in length from one hour to four hours, and transcribed verbatim.

In sixteen cases, I was able to interview women in my university office, their homes, or the office of their attorneys, as they were not detained prior to trial. The other interviews were conducted in county jails or federal detention centers. One woman was only interviewed by telephone, as she lived three hundred miles away and the charges against her were dropped after our phone interview. The first four interviews of battered women who killed their abusers, which took place between 1983 and 1988, were not tape-recorded. I stopped tape-recording two years ago because of concerns about the confidentiality of tapes. For conversations that were not taped, I took detailed notes.

In some cases, I interviewed friends or family members, and in most cases I read transcriptions of collateral interviews conducted by investigators. Videotaped interviews by police and forensic investigators were available for about one-fourth of the cases. I also reviewed police reports, the probation officer's presentence report, medical records, psychological evaluations, autopsy reports, and other available documents, such as school and child protective records. In some cases, these documents filled two or three large cardboard storage boxes. Five women wrote detailed descriptions of their relationships with their partners. In several cases, I have exchanged letters with the women and visited them in jail and prison. I also observed the sentencing hearing for one co-defendant. I observed and participated in clemency hearings for two women sentenced for the death of their abusers. One woman went through two hearings, but both women remain in prison. I observed and participated in a clemency hearing for a woman charged for the murder and armed robbery committed by her intimate partner. The board unanimously recommended her for clemency, but the governor rejected their recommendation. I participated in one other clemency hearing for a woman who shot but did not kill her abuser. She was also recommended for release by the board, but the governor chose not to follow their recommendation.

Notes

Introduction *(pp. 1–9)*

1. Collins 2000, 70–72.
2. In the instance of "victimless crimes," such as certain forms of drug use or sexual conduct, the social fabric is the assumed victim of behavior deemed destructive to the moral status quo.
3. Facella 2000.
4. Ibid., 72.
5. The "Angel in the House" image was adapted from the popular 1854 poem of that name by Coventry Patmore.
6. Collins 2000, 72–84. According to Collins, although working-class white women could not meet all the requirements for "angels of the house," they nevertheless benefited from the binary contrast of black women as mammies, matriarchs, welfare queens, and jezebels.
7. Woolf 1984 [1931].
8. Thus, the Hollywood dramatization of the life of executed serial killer Aileen Wournos was titled *Monster.*
9. Whitcombe 2000.
10. Ibid.
11. Caputi 1993. In some medieval Christian writing, discussions of women did not distinguish between good and bad; all women (except the Virgin Mary) were evil. Conrad of Marchtal, an abbot of the French Premonstratensian Order, wrote in the twelfth century: "We and our whole community of canons, recognizing that the wickedness of women is greater than all the other wickedness of the world, and that there is no anger like that of women, and that the poison of asps and dragons is more curable and less dangerous to men than the familiarity of women, have unanimously decreed for the safety of our souls, no less than for that of our bodies and goods, that we will on no account receive any more sisters to the increase of our perdition, but will avoid them like poisonous animals." Quoted in K. Anderson 1991, 58; Blamires 1992.
12. Myers and Wright 1996.

13. See Bumiller 1990 for an examination of this binary in the representation of rape victims in legal culture.

14. Greenfeld and Snell 1999; American Correctional Association 1990; Harlow 1999.

15. Greenfeld and Snell 1999; Harlow 1999.

16. Browne, Miller, and Maguin 1999; Ross 1998; Leonard 2002.

17. Meda Chesney-Lind has published widely on the criminalization of girls' victimization. See Chesney-Lind 1997 and 2002, and Chesney-Lind and Sheldon 2003.

18. Chesney-Lind 2002.

19. The Sentencing Project 2005.

20. Ibid.

21. Harrison and Beck 2005, 5.

22. U.S. Department of Health and Human Services 2005b.

23. Greenfield and Snell 1999.

24. Rennison 2003, 1.

25. Tjaden and Thoennes 2000, iv.

26. DeVault 1990; D. Smith 1990a and 1990b; Spender 1980.

27. D. Smith 1990a and 1990b.

28. DeVault 1990.

29. Gordon 1996.

30. See Parrish 1996 for a review of the history of legal testimony on battering.

31. For excellent analyses of same-sex intimate partner violence, see Girshick 2002; Ristock 2002; Renzetti 1992.

32. The man who killed his male roommate adamantly denied any intimate connection between them.

33. DeVault 1990.

34. Research that has documented men's accounts of their violence includes Adams, forthcoming; Ptacek 1988; Dobash and Dobash 1998; Bancroft 2002; Jacobson and Gottman 1998.

Chapter 1. Blurred Boundaries and the Complexities of Experience
(pp. 10–45)

1. Dobash and Dobash 1979; Ferraro 1989a and 1996.

2. Pleck 1987, 4.

3. Spender 1980 explains the ways that man-made language shapes our ways of thinking and endorses the myth of male superiority.

4. Lemkin 1944, 79–95.

5. D. Smith 1990a describes the "conceptual practices of power" in a man-

ner that informs my own investigation of the discourses of intimate partner violence. Smith stresses the role of social sciences and bureaucracies in enforcing abstract categories that "make worlds that exist only in texts" (12).

6. Smart 1995 provides a concise overview of this position.

7. Harding 2004 points out that standpoint theory originated in the work of Marxists describing the "standpoint of the proletariat." The epistemological assumptions of standpoint theory are grounded in a historical materialist perspective. For feminist analyses of standpoint, see Harding 1986, 1992, and 2003; Hartsock 1983 and 1998; Jaggar 1983; D. Smith 1987, 1990a, and 1990b.

8. Collins 1991, 234.

9. Ibid.

10. Foucault 1980, 82. Quoted in Collins 1991, 18.

11. Scott 1991, 797.

12. See the exchange between Clough 1993, Smith 1993, and Benhabib et al. 1995.

13. INCITE! Women of Color Against Violence was organized in 2000 by women who viewed the mainstream anti–violence against women movement as a depoliticized movement that did not recognize the experiences of women of color or the connections among violence against women, racism, colonialism, militarism, the prison industrial complex, and transnational capitalism. The 2005 conference theme was "Stopping the War on Women of Color." Visit their Web site for information. http://www.incite-national .org/about/index.html.

14. Ferraro 1996.

15. Websdale and Johnson 1997 demonstrated that providing women with these basic resources was the most effective way of reducing violence in their lives.

16. See Ariès 1962.

17. Rebecca Emerson Dobash makes this point in her response essay, Dobash 2003.

18. Quinney 1970.

19. Lukács 1972.

20. Walker 1979.

21. Schneider 2000 makes a similar point in chapter 4 of her *Battered Women and Feminist Lawmaking*.

22. Yllo and Bograd 1988.

23. Johnson and Leone 2005; Johnson and Ferraro 2000.

24. Dobash and Dobash 1979; Pleck 1987.

25. Ferraro 1979 and 1983.

26. The Arizona Coalition Against Domestic Violence (2002) estimates about ninety domestic violence fatalities each year in Arizona. By mid-

September 2005, some 176 people died trying to cross the border from Mexico to Arizona. See Rolstein 2005.

27. War crimes tribunals are an example of efforts to assign criminal responsibility for violence by one group against another. The determination of responsibility in such cases is extremely complicated and difficult; see Kelman and Hamilton 1989.

28. The "modernist project" is "a belief in the possibilities opened up by modernity involving a commitment to social progress through a rational and reasoned engagement with the world." See Bilton et al. 1997, 18.

29. For a discussion of epistemological debates and sociological methods, see Alcoff and Potter 1992; Longino 2002; Denzin and Lincoln 2005, esp. chapter 8.

30. The revised version of the CTS expands the items to include emotionally abusive behaviors and some physically violent behaviors excluded from the original version, as well as measures of the consequences of behaviors. It is available online at: http://pubpages.unh.edu/~mas2/text%20 form-CTS.htm. Some adaptations of the CTS do not frame the survey in terms of resolving conflicts, recognizing that much intimate partner violence is not a response to a specific conflict. See Johnson and Sacco 1995.

31. Straus 1979; Straus, Gelles, and Steinmetz 1980. The Conflict Tactics Scale has been the subject of a great deal of research and debate. It has been revised since its original formulation, but remains tethered to assumptions that it is possible to bracket and measure intimate partner violence objectively. See Ferraro 2000.

32. When I worked with a group of people to open a shelter in 1978 in Scottsdale, Arizona, behavioral health funding officials told us they did not think wife beating occurred frequently enough to justify public funding. We used national statistics to help make our case. As of 2005, there are forty-one shelters in Arizona and, in 2004, some sixteen thousand women and children were turned away.

33. For example, the survey data generated by Straus and Gelles have been twisted to support fathers' rights and men's rights groups that argue that women are as abusive as men in relationships. See Gelles n.d. Gelles has consistently argued that this is an invalid interpretation of their data because serious injuries and death are much more likely to be inflicted on women by men.

34. Martin 1976.

35. O'Brien 1971.

36. Ferraro 1983.

37. Schneider 2000, chapter 5; Renzetti 1999.

38. Sykes 1992; Dershowitz 2000.

39. O'Dell 1997.

40. Benedict 1992; Lamb 1999; Madriz 1997.

41. Konradi 1996.

42. Haraway 1989.

43. Schechter 1982.

44. Ferraro 1997.

45. Walker 1979.

46. DeVault 1990, 102.

47. Barnett and LaViolette 1993 review some of the work that analyzes women's love of their abusive partners.

48. See Ferraro 1997.

49. Walker 1979. In Walker's study, 50 percent of men did not apologize for violence once it became an established part of their relationships.

50. M. Dutton 1992.

51. Buehl 2001.

52. Foucault 1990.

53. In several instances, I violated the neutrality expected of researchers by telling women that men's behavior was not "normal." As one of the few, or only, people they had told about their experiences, I felt it was important to help shift their self-blame by saying that most people would not agree with their partner's definitions of "normality."

54. See Rosen 2004 for a discussion of this phenomenon among adolescent mothers.

55. Salina's case is discussed more thoroughly in chapter 6.

56. Chesney-Lind 2004; Bortner and Williams 1997; Gaardner and Belknap 2002; Belknap, Holsinger, and Dunn 1997.

57. Bergen 2000.

58. Websdale 1999; U.S. Advisory Board on Child Abuse and Neglect 1995.

59. Stark and Flitcraft 1996, 107.

60. Ferraro 2000.

61. Gelles and Straus 1988.

62. Dobash and Dobash 1998.

63. Scheppele 1992, 144.

64. Scheppele 1992, 143; Scheppele and Bart 1983, 79.

65. Ferraro and Johnson 1983.

66. See Faith 1993, 1, for an analysis of the construction of the category "unruly women," and the ways in which this concept has been reinforced by "class-based, racist and heterosexist myths."

67. See A. Smith 2005a and 2005b; Richie 1996 and 2000; Ritchie 2005; Dasgupta 2002.

*Chapter 2. Irreconcilable Differences: Women's Encounters
with the Criminal Processing System (pp. 46–70)*

1. I follow Dasgupta's (2003), use of the term "criminal processing system" as a way to avoid the word "justice," which seems inapplicable to many women's experiences of this system.

2. Kim Lane Scheppele 1992 provides an excellent analysis of these criteria for cases of sexualized violence. She relies on the transcriptions of the Anita Hill–Clarence Thomas hearings and several other sexual harassment cases to describe how the criteria are employed and the ways women's credibility is undermined by failure to conform to them. See also, Mack 1993.

3. Ferraro 1989a.

4. Ferraro and Pope 1993.

5. The National Clearinghouse for the Defense of Battered Women and the Battered Women's Justice Project (BWJP) are dedicated to advocacy, training, education and support for battered women who interact with the criminal and civil justice systems. See the BWJP Web page (*www.bwjp.org/*) for information about their important work. These organizations, as well as many advocates within state domestic violence coalitions, offices of state attorney generals, victim witness programs in city and county prosecutors' offices, and law enforcement agencies have advanced significant progress in making the criminal processing system more accessible and relevant for battered women. Also, the development of safety audits through the work of Ellen Pence at the Domestic Abuse Intervention Project in Duluth, Minnesota, has helped to identify gaps and problems in the systems designed to protect battered women.

6. This transcript was part of a separate study of the prosecution of interpersonal assaults. See Ferraro and Boychuk 1992.

7. See summaries of the research on the effectiveness of orders of protection in American Bar Association 1998; Buzawa and Buzawa 1996; and Fagan 1996. A recent study by the California Attorney General's Office (2005) found that even when judges issued orders, they were not logged in the state system, that is, the Domestic Violence Restraining Order System. In some counties, there were zero orders logged into the system, despite more than one hundred expected orders, based on convictions requiring the issue of orders. In Riverside County, while there were an expected 2,906 orders, only 130 orders were listed in the system. If orders are not logged, police officers have no way of knowing the issues are in effect. This study also found that the legal requirement to prohibit possession of firearms by people under criminal protective orders was not being followed in significant proportions of cases. In the summer of 2005, the U.S. Supreme Court ruled that Jessica Gonzales could not sue the Castle Rock, Colorado, police depart-

ment for failing to enforce a restraining order against her ex-husband. Police failed to respond after many requests for help from Gonzales, and her husband shot and killed their three daughters. He was shot by police after he went to the station and opened fire, using a handgun he had purchased that day. See Family Violence Prevention Fund 2005.

8. Durose et al. 2005, 26.

9. Ferraro 1989b.

10. See Websdale 1999.

11. Campbell 1992; Hardesty 2002; Websdale 1999.

12. Setty and Kaguytan 2002; Raj and Silverman 2002.

13. Unfortunately, some law enforcement officers are not aware of VAWA either. In 2002, a shelter director in Nogales, Arizona, was placed under house arrest by the local sheriff for her refusal to cooperate in the deportation of an undocumented battered woman residing in her shelter. She communicated this story at the Legal Committee Meeting of the Arizona Coalition Against Domestic Violence. .

14. Asian and Pacific Islander Institute on Domestic Violence 2002; Coker 2004; Crenshaw 1993.

15. Edelson 1999; Fantuzzo, Boruch, Beriama, et al. 1997.

16. The Greenbook Initiative, 2005.

17. *Nicholson v. Williams*, 205 FRD 92, 95, 100 [ED NY 2001].

18. Ferraro and Moe, 2003a.

19. In *DeShaney v. Winnebago County Department of Social Services*, 489 U.S. 189, 193 (1989), the Seventh Circuit Court of Appeals ruled that the Winnebago County Department of Social Services could not be held responsible for violating Joshua DeShaney's due process rights. The decision was upheld by the U.S. Supreme Court. In 1984, Joshua DeShaney was beaten into a permanent coma by his father following two years of involvement of the Department of Social Services. Joshua was removed from custody, and returned, admitted to the hospital twice for injuries that appeared to be caused by abuse, and visited more than twenty times by a caseworker. The court ruled that the county was not responsible because they did nothing to place Joshua in a situation worse than he would have faced had they never intervened at all. This decision has been invoked by courts to justify decisions that victims of child abuse and woman battering have no constitutional right to expect protection by police or child protective services. See Jones 1994, chap. 2, for a discussion of this and other relevant court decisions.

20. See Roberts 1993, for a discussion of other cases where women have been prosecuted for failure to protect their children from their abusive partners.

21. Several of the incarcerated women interviewed by Ferraro and Moe (2003a), had lost custody of their children because their abusive partners

moved back into their homes. One of the women resumed her alcoholism after losing custody and was in jail on a DUI. Ferraro and Moe 2003a.

22. Roberts 2003.

23. Websdale 2001; Raphael 2000; Richie 1996; Roberts 1994; A. Smith 2005a.

24. A. Smith 2003 and 2005a; Razack 1994.

25. Websdale 2001, chap. 4.

26. Websdale 2001; Ferraro and Moe 2003a; Dasgupta 2002; Chesney-Lind 2002.

27. Ritchie 2005.

28. See Razack 1994, for a discussion of this issue in a Canadian context.

29. A. Smith 2003, 123, quotes a report by the International Human Rights Association of American Minorities "documenting the involvement of mainline churches and the federal government in the murder of over 50,000 Native children through the Canadian residential school system." Widespread physical and sexual abuse has also been documented. See Razack 1994; *Sherwyn Zephiers, et al. v. United States* lawsuit on behalf of children abused in Indian boarding schools in the United States. http://www.dlncoalition.org/dln_issues/complaint.pdf. Accessed June 12, 2005.

30. Platt 1969.

31. Justice Policy Institute 2002; J. Miller 1996.

32. Websdale 2001, 139–41.

33. Greenfield, Rand, et al. 1998.

34. The Major Crimes Act (Title 18 U.S. Code, sect. 1152) specifies that seven major felonies that occur on reservations are under the jurisdiction of the federal government. According to the FBI Web site (2005), "the 1994 Crime Act expanded federal criminal jurisdiction in Indian Country in such areas as guns, violent juveniles, drugs, and domestic violence. Under the Indian Gaming Regulatory Act, the FBI has jurisdiction over any criminal act directly related to casino gaming." Tribal courts do not have jurisdiction over non-Indians committing crimes on the reservation. This is a tremendous problem for American Indian women, who are most likely to be violently victimized by non-Indian men. See Harjo 2005.

35. McGillivray and Comaskey 1999.

36. U.S. Census Bureau 2004b.

37. U.S. Census Bureau, 1995, 3.

38. Cockburn 1997.

39. A. Smith, 2005b.

40. The Navajo Peacekeeping process has been developed as a way of responding to intimate partner violence that is said to be more consistent with traditional Navajo culture than the dominant criminal processing system. There is tremendous criticism of this process, though. There is also a

wider movement to adopt alternative conflict resolution for intimate partner violence. There is considerable controversy over the appropriateness of conflict resolution for these crimes. See the special issue of *Violence Against Women* (May 2005), edited by James Ptacek, for analyses of this controversy.

41. A. Smith 2003, 2004, 2005a, and 2005b; Ritchie 2005; and Richie 1996 and 2000.

42. Renzetti 2001.

43. S. Miller 1989 and 2000; Dasgupta 2002.

44. Chesney-Lind 2002, 83.

45. Ibid.

46. Dasgupta 2002, 1382 n. 4.

47. S. Miller 2005.

48. N. Miller 2004.

49. Dasgupta 2002.

50. Quoted in Sickler 2002, 1–2.

51. Ferraro 2003.

52. See Dasgupta 2002, for a review of research documenting women's use of self-defensive violence and its failure to stop men's violence.

53. S. Miller 2005, also reports that women's use of violence against intimate partners rarely is successful in controlling the behavior of abusers.

54. The typology developed by Michael P. Johnson identifies situational couple violence as most likely to involve gender symmetry and both intimate partners' use of low-levels of violence. Mutual violent control is where both partners use violence as one tactic in the effort to control and dominate the other person. This form of intimate partner violence is the rarest and least studied; see Johnson and Leone 2005.

55. In thirty years of working with intimate partner violence, I have met one man who was terrorized by his female intimate partner. This was an unusual case in which the woman had been given legal guardianship over the man, who was twenty years her junior. He used violence in self-defense, but her violent behavior, as well as emotional abuse, control, isolation, and jealousy, was like that of the men described by women abused by their partners.

56. Stark 2004; Pence 2005.

57. Stark's analysis of this suggestion (2004) is clear and compelling.

Chapter 3. Negotiating Surreality (pp. 71–107)

1. Maslow 1970.

2. Garfinkle 1988 and 1964.

3. Bancroft and Silverman 2002; Pence and Paymar 1993.

4. There are more of these counternarratives than it is possible to list. Some sources of counternarratives are Minh-ha 1989; Modisane 1963; Zinn 2003; Galeano 1991 and 1992; Stannard 1992; A. Smith 2005b.

5. See Danner 2004.

6. Bloke Modisane (1963) tells how the history he learned in school was an alibi for the subjugation and dispossession of black people of South Africa and that he learned to parrot this history to survive.

7. Mynra showed the bank teller a note saying it was a robbery and she had a gun; she did not actually have a gun. She told me, "I did not have no weapon, even though, in the letter it said I had a weapon, but when the cops came in the bank, they checked me over and they said she don't have a gun. I don't own a gun, I don't really believe in 'em, except for protection." Bank personnel rang the alarm and locked the doors and Myrna simply sat down and waited to be taken to jail. She said the responding officer asked her, "Are you nuts?" and she replied, "Yeah, I know. Stupid."

8. See Herman and Chomsky 2002.

9. See, for example, the discussion about reactions to Hedda Nussbaum in Jones 1994.

10. Jaggar 1983, 33.

11. See, for example, see the anthologies edited by Findlen 2001 and Hernández and Rehman 2002 and the "Postfeminist Forum" at http://www .altx.com/ebr/ebr3/forum/forum.htm.

12. Schlafly 2003; Graglia 1998; Belkin 2003.

13. Walby 1990, 20.

14. Walby 1990; Jaggar 1983; Benhabib et al. 1995.

15. Dobash and Dobash 1979, 43–44.

16. Center for American Women in Politics (June 2005).

17. Homophobia may channel women's erotic and emotional desire into heterosexual relationships and foreclose the possibilities for more egalitarian relationships with other women as intimate partners. Unfortunately, lesbian relationships are not immune from the influence of patriarchal culture. See Renzetti 1992; Girshick 2002; Ristock 2002.

18. Friedman 1993; Dobash and Dobash 1979.

19. Friedman 1993, 213.

20. Rowe 1988, 151–52.

21. Friedman 1993, 214.

22. In Arizona, the duress statute reads: "it shall be a mitigating circumstance where '[t]he defendant was under unusual and substantial duress, although not such as to constitute a defense to prosecution.'" The law presumes every defendant has free will and is held accountable for his actions. *State v. Raymond Tison II,* 129 Ariz. 546, 633 P.2d 355 (1981). To rebut the presumption, the defendant must show that someone "coerce[d] or induce[d]

[him] to do something against his free will." *State v. Brewer,* 170 Ariz. 486, 826 P.2d 783 (1993). Duress has been defined as "any illegal imprisonment, or legal imprisonment used for an illegal purpose, or threats of bodily or other harm, or other means amounting to or tending to coerce the will of another, and actually inducing him to do an act contrary to his free will." Id. In sum, the defendant must persuade the court that his will was over-whelmed by threats or provocation outside himself. *Raymond Tison II;* see *State v. Wallace* (Wallace II), 154 Ariz. 362, 728 P.2d 232 (1986) (no duress from evidence showing murder not prompted by threats or provocation). http://www.supreme.state.az.us/courtserv/CrtProj/capsentguid/G2Duress.htm. Accessed June 14, 2005.

23. Bourgois 1995.

24. Rush 1980. Jacobson and Gottman (1998) provide examples of this process on 129–32.

25. Bancroft and Silverman 2002, 10–11.

26. See Raphael 2000.

27. Lloyd 1997.

28. Gelles and Loseke 1993; Bancroft 2002.

29. Toch and Adams 1994.

30. Jacobson and Gottman 1998.

31. The Domestic Violence and Mental Health Policy Initiative in Chi-cago addresses the mental health needs of domestic violence survivors and their children. Their Web page, www.dvmhpi.org, publishes summaries of research on this topic. Numerous studies have found rates of alcohol abuse from 50 to 85 percent in families experiencing domestic violence. See the Center for Alcohol Studies at Rutgers, www.rci.rutgers.edu/~cas2 as well as the chapter by Zubretsky and Digirolamo 1996. Although alcohol abuse does not *cause* domestic violence, it is associated with abuse incidents for men who drink heavily. See Fals-Stewart 2003. The relationship between abuse of certain types of drugs, such as methamphetamine, crystal, and "ice" and violent behavior is strong. The infiltration of these drugs into communities has increased rates of violence in homes and in the streets. See *Honolulu Star-Bulletin* 2003.

32. D. Smith, 1990a.

33. Niehoff 1999, 207–208 provides an overview of the research on the biological and social interactions that produce the effects of cocaine and methamphetamine.

34. See Laing 1968; Scheff 1984; D. Smith 1990a.

35. See Lundgren 1998.

36. See Erdoes and Ortiz 1984. The creation stories of many tribes de-scribe human descent from the Great Sun, the Great Mystery, a First Woman impregnated by a sunbeam, a salmon, or the west wind. Some spirits have a

sex, like Glooscap (male) or White Buffalo Woman, while others are beyond sex, like Takuskanskan, the White River Sioux name for the power of motion. American Indian people do not define either sex as divinely ordained as superior to the other, and human beings are not superior to other aspects of the world.

37. Yarrow et al. 1955.

38. Szasz 1961; Scheff 1984; D. Smith 1990a; Laing 1968.

39. Ferraro and Johnson 1983.

40. Ptacek 1988; Dobash and Dobash 1998.

41. Ferraro 1983 and 1996.

42. Websdale 1999.

43. Faith 2001.

44. Jones 1994.

45. An injunction against harassment is a civil order requiring a person to stay away from the petitioner. It is used like an order of protection in cases where people are unmarried.

46. Her attorney's assistant saw Doreen at a store and passed along this report of her well-being.

47. Haaken 1998.

48. Haaken 1998, chap. 1 for an account of the competing narrations of incest in the Freyd family. Jennifer Freyd is the cognitive psychologist who publicly described her recovered memories of childhood sexual abuse. Pamela and Peter Freyd are Jennifer's parents. They not only deny Jennifer's accusations; they founded the False Memory Syndrome Foundation (FMSF). FMSF is a self-help group for parents who believe they have been falsely accused of sexually abusing their children. See also Alisen 2003 for a personal account of recovered memories and the experience of siblings who do not share the same memories.

49. Laub 1992, 57.

50. Briere 1992, 36.

51. Berliner and Brier 1999.

52. J. Herman 1997.

53. Beattie and Shaughnessy 2000.

Chapter 4. The Social Reproduction of Women's Pain (pp. 108–157)

1. D. Dutton 2000; Haapasalo and Aaltonen 1998; Heyman and Smith Slep 2002; Widom and Maxfield 2001; English, Widom, and Brandford 2003. See M. Johnson and Ferraro 2000, 957–58 for a critique of the research on "intergenerational transmission."

2. Williams 1977, quoted in Nenga 2003.

3. "It is that we are concerned with meanings and values as they are actively lived and felt. We are talking about characteristic elements of impulse, restraint, and tone; specifically affective elements of consciousness and relationships: not feeling against thought, but thought as felt and feeling as thought: practical consciousness of a present kind, in a living and inter-relating continuity"; Williams 1977, 132–34.

4. I use the term "ethereality of violent experiences" to convey the invisible, potentially volatile and deadly, nature of violence. Ether, the root of ethereal, is a highly volatile, flammable liquid that is colorless. Ancient philosophers once believed that ether filled the upper regions of space; thus, its association with heaven. "Ethereality" connotes invisible, volatile, and complicated phenomena, such as the intimate partner and family violence I describe.

5. Widom and Maxfield 2001.

6. Pfohl 1994; Dobash and Dobash 1979.

7. See M. Johnson and Ferraro 2000.

8. Schechter 1982.

9. Schwartz 1988.

10. Philippe Bourgois 1995 and 1998, describes how children become violent in a barrio in New York City where violence and illegal drug use is inescapable. His rich ethnographic description highlights the limitations of cycle of violence models that ignore the context of children's experiences.

11. Rubin 1976, 46.

12. Alisen 2003; Haaken 1998.

13. For example, Lisa's description of her childhood as "average" does not capture the struggles her parents must have experienced raising seventeen children on the wages of a farm laborer.

14. Kaufman and Zigler 1987; Widom and Maxfield 2001; English, Widom, and Brandford 2003.

15. Widom 2003.

16. Angier 1999.

17. Chesney-Lind 2004.

18. Collins (2000) outlines four domains of power in the matrix of domination: structural, disciplinary, hegemonic, and interpersonal (276–88).

19. See Stannard 1992, 256–58; A. Smith 2005b.

20. In categorizing social class, I relied on parents' occupations and educations. I defined as *middle class* those working in professional occupations with at least some postsecondary education.

21. One woman whose relatives paid for private legal representation wrote to me from prison that she had not had good experiences with attorneys, who she felt tended to drain your bank accounts, not keep promises, or return phone calls or letters. In some ways, women who hired private

counsel felt more exploited because their families stretched to pay their fees. Women who had court-appointed or public defenders did not incur these costs and, in most cases, had very good representation.

22. One woman has been able to continue her profession as hairdresser while in prison and the other was working in a prison telemarketing company. Within the prison, these are good jobs. In contrast, other women have difficulty obtaining the funds for soap and shampoo.

23. Kurz 1995.

24. Lareau 2003.

25. Ariès 1962.

26. Ibid., 414–15.

27. W. Wilson 1987; Bowles, Gintis, and Osborne-Groves 2005; Shipler 2005; Annie E. Casey Foundation 2005. I am focusing on childhood in the United States. For a comparative perspective, see Scheper-Hughes and Sargent 1998.

28. Lareau 2003, refers to the middle-class preoccupation as "concerted cultivation," and the working-class view of childhood goals as "the accomplishment of natural growth" (1–3).

29. Bourgois 1995; Hays 2003; Kurz 1995.

30. Children's Defense Fund 2004, xxx.

31. Kochanek and Smith 2004, 23.

32. Children's Defense Fund 2004, 88.

33. See Boocok and Scott 2005; James, Jenks, and Prout 1998.

34. Brewer 1988; Collins 2000; E. Anderson 1990; W. Wilson 1987 and 1996.

35. Bourgois 1998, 333–34.

36. Bureau of Labor Statistics 2005.

37. Ibid., 334.

38. Raphael 2000; Bourgois 1995.

39. Amott and Matthaei 1996; Rubin 1976 and 1994.

40. L. Gordon 1988.

41. Hays 2003; Ehrenreich 2001.

42. In 2003, the median income of white households was $47,957; for black households it was $29,987; for Hispanic households, it was $33,913; and for American Indians / Alaska Natives it was $33,024. In 2003, the poverty rate among black and Hispanic youth was more than three times the rate of whites. U.S. Census Bureau, 2004a.

43. Kurz 1995, 89.

44. Raphael 2000; Kurz 1995; Ferraro and Moe 2003a.

45. Kurz 1995; Hays 2003. See Goldstein 2003 for a description of mothering under conditions of absolute poverty in Brazil.

46. Kurz (1995, 78, 87–90) notes that middle-class women experienced

the most drastic cuts in standard of living following divorce, even though their reduced standard exceeded that of postdivorce working-class and poverty-level women.

47. Howell (1976) coined the terms *hard living* and *settled living* to describe lifestyles in the low-income community he studied. Hard-living men were often absent from their families, engaged in illegal drug use, alcoholism, violence, and the underground economy. Settled-living families tried hard to adhere to conventional morality.

48. J. Jacobs 1990.

49. Sennett and Cobb 1972.

50. Rubin 1976 and 1994; Skeggs 1997; Steedman 1987; Zandy 1994; Tea 2003.

51. Sennett and Cobb 1972, 170–71; emphasis in original.

52. Jacobson and Gottman 1998.

53. Friedan 1963.

54. Spellman 1988.

55. All American Indian women were married to American Indian men, officially or "common law" and lived on their reservation. The Harvard Project on American Indian Economic Development (2005) reports that poverty and unemployment for single-race American Indians decreased faster between 1990 and 2000 than for other racial/ethnic groups in the United States. This decrease was true for gaming and nongaming nations. Despite the improvement, both poverty (23.8 percent) (U.S. Census Bureau, 2005) and unemployment (46 percent) (Center for Community Change, 2005) remain much higher than the national averages (12.5 percent poverty; 5 percent unemployment).

56. See Wesely 2003, for a discussion of women's ambivalent feelings about work as exotic dancers.

57. See Ferraro 2003 for a discussion of how the images of passivity and helplessness connected to the "battered woman's syndrome" distort perceptions of women's agency.

58. In contrast to Danielle's enjoyment of her work at Wal-Mart, see the ethnographic account of working at Wal-Mart in Ehrenreich 2001.

59. Rubin (1976, chap. 4) reported this finding for both young men and women in her interviews with working-class families. In her more recent study (1994), Rubin indicates that working-class men and women are delaying marriage and focusing more on careers. I did not find marriage deferral among most of the women I met.

60. Pearson 1997; Baskin and Sommers 1997.

61. Pipher 1997.

62. See Kurz 1995; Bourgois 1995. Bancroft 2002 describes the role of addictions as an excuse for violence (chap. 8).

63. See also Wesely 2003.

64. Richie 1996; Ross 1998.

65. According to the National Household Survey on Drug Abuse, American Indians or Alaska Natives were nearly twice as likely to report past-year dependence on or abuse of alcohol or other illicit drugs in 2001: 13.9 percent versus 7.3 percent. However, heavy and binge use of alcohol was similar for American Indians, whites, and Hispanics. National Household Survey on Drug Abuse Report 2003, 2–3.

66. American Indians in the United States have "a life expectancy of 47 years . . . [a] tuberculosis rate . . . 533 percent higher than the national average; the accident mortality rate 425 percent higher; the infant mortality rate 89 percent higher; the sudden infant death syndrome rate 310 percent higher; the alcoholism rate 579 percent higher; the diabetes rate 249 percent higher; and the suicide rate 190 percent higher than the national average." A. Smith 2004, 116. See also Ross 1998.

67. Obviously, Sarah was not old enough to drive legally, but she nevertheless assumed this responsibility as there was no one else available to help.

68. Rubin 1996 describes fantasy as a positive response to trauma in childhood that contributes to "transcendence" over victimization.

69. Her father is serving a twelve-year sentence for child abuse.

70. J. Herman 1997, chap. 5.

71. J. Herman 1997, 111 and 112.

72. J. Herman 1997, 105. "The malignant sense of inner badness is often camouflaged by the abused child's persistent attempts to be good. In the effort to placate her abusers, the child victim often becomes a superb performer."

73. Stories of people who succeed in spite of their backgrounds of abuse are presented by Rubin 1996.

74. Chodorow 1999.

75. See Ferraro and Moe 2003a; Moe and Ferraro (forthcoming).

76. See Moe and Ferraro (forthcoming); Ferraro and Moe 2003a; Sharp and Eriksen 2003; Henriques 1982; and Bloom 1992, for analyses of incarcerated women's mothering.

77. Rubin 1976, chap. 5, describes how working-class women *and men* have fantasies of marriage as a haven of love and how disillusioned they become with its realities. See also Jacobson and Gottman 1998, 51–52; Barnett and LaViolette 1993, 16–17.

78. Richie 1996 describes the abuse and abandonment endured by most of the imprisoned women in her study. The experiences of African American battered women were markedly different from those of white battered women or nonbattered African American women. The battered African

American women "worked the hardest and the longest and, indeed, with the most conviction, to create and maintain a hegemonic nuclear family, even when the violence began and they became involved in illegal activities" (67). In Richie's sample, the six white battered women were more realistic about their partners' abuse, and were "less disappointed because they were less satisfied initially and had lower expectations" (74). These lower expectations were not true of the women I interviewed of any race. All of the women I have interviewed were extremely sad and disappointed that their relationships were unsuccessful. I only interviewed two African American women, however, and one was unwilling to provide much information. My sample of white battered women is larger than Richie's, included women who were not incarcerated, and took place in the Southwest rather than in New York City. The differences in samples may account for the different characteristics and experiences of the women interviewed.

Chapter 5. Demonic Angels?: Violence against Abusers (pp. 158–195)

1. The first book to analyze women's intimate partner homicides and report this pattern was by Browne (1987).
2. Jones 1980; Browne 1987; Gillespie 1989; Gagné 1998; Leonard 2002. The film *The Burning Bed*, based on the life of Francine Hughes and starring Farrah Fawcett, has been played repeatedly on television since its release in 1984. In 1987, the National Clearinghouse for the Defense of Battered Women was established in Philadelphia by Sue Osthoff and Barbara Hart. The clearinghouse maintains information on criminal and civil cases involving battered women and provides legal consultation to attorneys working on self-defense and other cases; the clearinghouse has worked on a broad range of issues related to criminal prosecution and civil cases, as well as clemency and prison conditions. The battered women's clemency movement has focused on such cases where battered women killed abusers.
3. Durose et al. 2005, 17.
4. Bureau of Justice Statistics 2004a.
5. Bureau of Justice Statistics 2004b. Between 1976 and 2002, women were 11.4 percent of homicide offenders and 23.6 percent of victims.
6. See H. Allen 1987 for a discussion of the presumption of women's harmlessness in the prosecution of violent crimes. Although her discussion is nearly twenty years old, it describes a tendency to portray women's violence as harmless and women as incapable of planning and intending harm.
7. Bumiller 1990.
8. In some cases, the difference between homicides and sublethal assaults was determined by the availability of medical assistance. Victims who re-

ceived prompt attention were more likely to survive than those in poor and remote locations who had to wait up to an hour for medical attention.

9. Von Hentig 1941; Wolfgang 1958; Luckenbill 1977. Luckenbill draws on Erving Goffman's work to describe criminal homicide as a "character contest," "a confrontation in which at least one, but usually both, attempt to establish or save face at the other's expense by standing steady in the face of adversity" (177). The notion of "character contest" seems particularly ill-suited for female-perpetrated intimate homicide, as I discuss in this chapter.

10. Luckenbill 1977. Luckenbill's study of homicide included many cases in which the offender and victim were intimate partners. His pathbreaking analysis was published prior to the emergence of contemporary scholarship on intimate partner homicide. Luckenbill did not foreground the dynamics of battering relationships in exploring the ways that men perceived an "offense to face." His examples of precipitating offenses included men's perception that women disobeyed them, persisted in "never-ending flirtation," or showed "a refusal, under threat of violence, to conciliate a failing marriage." He acknowledged that the perceptions of offenders may have had little to do with the intentions of victims, but did not consider the context of abuse that framed these perceptions. See Polk 1994 for a critique of Luckenbill and a gendered analysis of confrontational homicide.

11. Browne 1987; Websdale 1999; Leonard 2002.

12. Luckenbill 1977, 179.

13. Luckenbill illustrates this with a case of a father who killed his infant because the baby continued to cry after being told to shut up (ibid., 180).

14. These three contexts are similar to those identified by S. Miller (2005) in her study of women arrested for domestic violence. Her categories include generalized violent behavior, frustration response behavior, and defensive behavior. The vast majority of women in her study engaged in the latter two categories, and about 5 percent engaged in generalized violent behavior toward people other than their abusive partners.

15. This is consistent with the research of Browne 1987; Maguigan 1991; and Websdale 1999.

16. Forced marriage is a topic deserving of further attention. A woman I met through my expert testimony in her civil suit, and one of the women described in the next chapter, told me that they had literally been forced to marry their husbands. Both women are Mexican. See Asian and Pacific Islander Institute on Domestic Violence 2002 for brief discussions of forced and arranged marriages among Asian and Pacific Islander women.

17. See Schneider 2000.

18. Ibid., 146.

19. Parrish 1996.

20. Gordon 1996.

21. Ibid.; Ferraro 2003.

22. In 2004, activists in Free Battered Women were successful in getting the California legislature to revise the criminal, family, and civil code to replace "battered woman syndrome" with "intimate partner violence and its effects." S.B. 1385, http://info.sen.ca.gov/pub/bill/asm/ab_0201–0250/ab_220_cfa_20050404_103710_asm_comm.html. Accessed July 22, 2005.

23. The list of such critiques is long. A sample of articulate critiques includes Jones 1994 and Schneider 2000.

24. Websdale 1999, 124 and 126.

25. Wilson and Daly 1993; H. Johnson and Hotton 2003; Websdale 1999; Campbell 1992; Campbell et al. 2003a and 2003b.

26. Campbell et al. 2003a.

27. Browne 1987; Websdale 1999; and Leonard 2002 report similar findings.

28. I learned about Sue's successful remarriage through her defense attorney's legal assistant who met her by chance in the grocery store.

29. Campbell et al. 2003b.

30. At a presentation at a National Domestic Violence Fatality Review Initiative conference, I used a quote from Jane. Two women in the audience recognized the quote as something Jane would say, and after the session, asked me if she was the person I quoted. They worked with Jane in another state and informed me of her whereabouts and well-being.

31. Campbell et al. 2003a report a 9.9-fold increase in lethality for prior choking by abusers, and a 7.6-fold increase for women forced to have sex.

32. See Parrish 1996, 7: "Of the battered women defendants' appeals (152 state court decisions) analyzed here, 63 percent resulted in affirmance of the conviction and/or sentence, even though expert testimony on battering and its effects was admitted or found admissible in 71 percent of the affirmances. This is strong evidence that the defense's use of or the court's awareness of expert testimony on battering and its effects in no way equates to an acquittal on the criminal charges lodged against a battered woman defendant."

33. See Goetting's (1999) excellent book on women who successfully escaped violent relationships.

34. Overmedication of incarcerated women is a significant problem. See Davies and Cook 1999; Ross 1998.

35. Ferraro and Moe 2003b, 77, cite one of their interviewees, Orca: "I was on suicide watch for 48 hours. If I wasn't suicidal, that'll drive you to it."

36. I have not forced Dorothy's quote into standard, white English because it would alter her meaning and I wish to preserve her words. For example, among her tribe many people use plural and singular nouns differently than whites. They are not typos, they are Dorothy's words.

37. On the other hand, the cases of women charged in the deaths of their

children described in chapter 6 suggest that not all prosecutors share this view. Unfortunately, I do not have data on charging patterns for cases where battered women kill their abusers.

38. Again, according to Campbell et al. 2003a, pathological jealousy is highly correlated with femicide.

39. Bancroft 2002 explains this process and its connection to intimate partner violence in Chapters 13 and 15.

40. Between 1976 and 2000, the number of men murdered by intimate partners dropped by 68 percent. In the same time period, the number of women murdered by intimate partners dropped only 22 percent (Rennison 2003). See Dugin, Nagin, and Rosenfeld 2003 for a discussion of the relationship between services and the decline in intimate partner homicides.

Chapter 6. Angelic Demons?: Crimes of Complicity (pp. 197–245)

1. Gilfus 1992; K. Daly 1994; Comack 2005.

2. Permitting a child's life and morals to be endangered was charged several times against a woman who appeared drunk in public with her children. It is not a violent crime.

3. Morse 1994, 1.

4. Katz, Moore, and Morse 1999.

5. Milgram 1974; Kelman and Hamilton 1989.

6. A. Miller 1986 and 2004; Blass 2000.

7. Morelli 1983, quoted in Blass 2000.

8. The English translation of Weber's *Wirtschaft und Gesellschaft: Grundriss der verstehenden Soziologie* uses "authority" and "domination" interchangeably. The chapter title where the typology of forms of authority appears is "The Types of Legitimate Domination," but within the chapter, "authority" is used to describe the three forms. The translator, Guenther Roth, explains various opinions about the terms "authority," "domination," "imperative control" and "leadership" as translations of the German *Herrschaft* (61 n. 31). See Weber 1978, chap. 3.

9. Weber 1978, 212.

10. Ibid., 215.

11. Ibid., 1006.

12. Ibid., 296.

13. Ibid., 1007.

14. Ibid., 240.

15. This point was raised by Dobash and Dobash 1979, 273–74 n. 66, and Websdale 1998, 130.

16. Weber 1978, 241.

17. See Websdale 1998, 160, for a brief discussion of debates over Weber's descriptions of the state's monopoly on legitimate coercive violence.

18. Foucault 1980.

19. Westlund 1999.

20. Kelman and Hamilton 1989, 46.

21. Adorno 1950; Fromm 1973; Browning 1992; Arendt 1966.

22. Kelman and Hamilton 1989, 16.

23. Kelman and Hamilton 1989, 1–12.

24. Kelman and Hamilton 1989.

25. Ferraro and Moe 2000.

26. While interviewing corroborating witnesses in a child custody dispute, one woman coworker of an abusive man told me: "I felt like I was a Marine and he was my drill sergeant."

27. Kelman and Hamilton 1989, 138.

28. Szasz 1983, 200.

29. Websdale 1999; Campbell et al. 2003a.

30. See Bancroft and Silverman, 2002, 7–9 and 11–13, for an overview of the characteristic entitlement and possessiveness batterers display in their relationships.

31. The statement of faith also states that husband and wife are equal in the eyes of God. The full statement, sect. xviii, reads: "The husband and wife are of equal worth before God, since both are created in God's image. The marriage relationship models the way God relates to His people. A husband is to love his wife as Christ loved the church. He has the God-given responsibility to provide for, to protect, and to lead his family. A wife is to submit herself graciously to the servant leadership of her husband even as the church willingly submits to the headship of Christ. She, being in the image of God as is her husband and thus equal to him, has the God-given responsibility to respect her husband and to serve as his helper in managing the household and nurturing the next generation." Taken from the Southern Baptist Conference Web page: http://www.sbc.net/bfm/bfm2000.asp#xviii. Accessed June 28, 2005.

32. Andelin 1965; Doyle 1999; Slattery 2001; Barnes 1998.

33. Andelin's suggestions for a happy marriage focus on performing femininity in a way that fulfills a husband's needs and makes him happy, shielding him from stress, and concealing one's own needs, opinions, and even bodily functions. For example, women are warned against blowing their nose in public. The Fascinating Womanhood Web page boasts a 2005 photo of a Fascinating Womanhood class in Virginia and recent letters thanking Andelin for her help. http://www.fascinatingwomanhood.net/.

34. Kelman and Hamilton 1989, 17.

35. Hirschi 1969.

36. Simon 2005.

37. Simon 2005; Simon and Eitzen 1993.

38. "The higher immorality is a systematic feature of the American elite; its general acceptance is an essential feature of the mass society"; Mills 1956, 343.

39. Kellman and Hamilton 1989, 308–315.

40. In 2003, five people were sentenced to prison in the federal system for violating antitrust laws. By contrast, 23,776 people were sentenced to federal prison for drug trafficking.

41. Maher 1995; Bourgois 1995.

42. Alicia was interviewed at the Pima County Detention Center, Tucson, Arizona, as part of a study of jailed women's experiences of violence conducted by myself and Angela M. Moe. See Ferraro and Moe 2003b.

43. G. Sykes and Matza 1957.

44. Eitzen and Baca Zinn 2006; Berrigan and Hartung 2005.

45. Expanded arrest power does not require a victim of domestic violence to "press charges." Rather, the state prosecutes offenders, and it is not up to the victim to decide whether charges will be brought. However, if victims refuse to participate in prosecution, or testify that their injuries were not caused by the defendant, it is difficult to prosecute successfully. It is not impossible, however, with careful police and prosecution work. Prosecution policies that include careful consideration of victims' needs and wishes are most successful at protecting women; see Ford and Regoli 1993.

46. Particularly in the Southwest, false claims to spiritual power linked to a dubious American Indian identity are common. Any hotel in Sedona, Arizona, for example, provides glossy brochures on opportunities for spiritual healing or readings from purported American Indians. This phenomenon is one aspect of the theft and commercialization of indigenous culture. See Meyer and Royer 2001, and also, "Cultural Theft and Misrepresentation," posted on the Web page of the Hopi tribe, http://www.hopi.nsn.us/view_article.asp?id=20&cat=1. Accessed June 18, 2005.

47. This quote is taken from the official grand jury transcript, but I have changed the names to protect anonymity.

48. M. Jacobs, 1998.

49. Susan Brownmiller, antirape feminist icon, argued that Nussbaum should not be exonerated of guilt in the death of her illegally adopted daughter. Andrea Dworkin wrote a response to Brownmiller critiquing her logic. See Dworkin 1993.

50. Dworkin 1993.

51. Shipler 2005, 161–63, discusses the inability of some mothers to understand their children's need for attention as these women were never

given attention or nurturance themselves. He describes programs that work with women to help understand and meet their children's developmental needs.

52. The possibility that abusive men will obtain custody of children in family court is real and substantial. See Kernic et al. 2005; N. Johnson et al. 2005.

53. Meyer and Oberman 2001, make this point (164).

54. Roche 2002.

55. Discussed in M. Jacobs 1998, 613–14. Jacobs mentions that three states—Iowa, Minnesota, and Oklahoma—have affirmative defenses for parents at risk of death or serious bodily injury if they try to protect a child (619).

56. U.S. Department of Health and Human Services, 2005a.

57. See Jacobs 1998, esp. 587–93.

58. Websdale 1999, 174–75.

59. U.S. Children's Bureau 2005.

60. Durose et al. 2005, 17.

61. Arizona Department of Health Services 2004.

62. Websdale 1999, 167.

63. U.S. Advisory Board on Child Abuse and Neglect, 1995, xxvui and 19.

64. Ibid., 13–14.

65. Websdale 1999, 173.

66. Due to the small number of women's prosecutions for child deaths, and the media attention to them, my discussion of these cases will be general and lack the detail that could lead to identification of the women.

67. Bancroft and Silverman 2002; Jaffe, Lemon, and Poisson 2003; American Bar Association 1994.

68. U.S. Department of Health and Human Services 2005a; Wilson and Daly 1998, 226–30; Daly and Wilson 1988, 83–93; Campbell et al. 2003a and b.

69. Websdale 1999; U.S. Advisory Board on Child Abuse and Neglect 1995.

70. Arizona State Legislature 2004.

71. All of the women discussed here are poor women of color. There are no national data on the sentences of women whose partners killed their children. I did find a recent case in Nebraska where a middle-class white woman was not even charged in the beating death of her daughter based on the fact that she was a "classic sufferer of battered woman syndrome." Cooper 2005. For analyses of the problems of incarcerated mothers and their children, see Bortner 2002 and Ferraro and Moe 2002.

72. Dworkin 1993.

Epilogue (pp. 246–252)

1. VAWA 2005 was passed by Congress on December 17, 2005. For information on the reauthorized legislation see Legal Momentum's Web site, www.legalmomentum.org.

2. See Ferraro 1996 for an analysis of the transformation of early feminist demands to a crime control model of domestic violence.

3. Ferraro 1989a.

4. Hays 2003.

5. Websdale and Johnson 1997.

6. Allen 2006.

7. A. Smith 2005b, 430.

8. Ibid., 431.

9. Most prison jobs pay about fifty cents per hour, out of which women must pay for toiletries, paper, stamps and envelopes, and commissary food.

10. Wilson 1996.

References

Adams, David. Forthcoming. *Why Do They Kill? An Investigation of Men Who Kill Their Intimate Partners.* Nashville, Tenn.: Vanderbilt University Press.

Adorno, Theodor W. 1950. *The Authoritarian Personality.* New York: Harper.

Alcoff, Linda, and Elizabeth Potter. 1992. *Feminist Epistemologies.* New York: Routledge.

Alisen, Paige. 2003. *Finding Courage to Speak: Women's Survival of Child Abuse.* Boston: Northeastern University Press.

Allen, Hilary. 1987. "Rendering Them Harmless: The Professional Portrayal of Women Charged with Serious Violent Crimes." In *Gender, Crime and Justice,* edited by P. Carlen and A. Worrall, 81–94. London: Open University Press.

Allen, Nicole E. 2006. "An Examination of the Effectiveness of Domestic Violence Coordinating Councils." *Violence Against Women* 12, no. 1:46–67.

American Bar Association. 1994. *The Impact of Domestic Violence on Children* [A Report to the President of the American Bar Association]. Washington, D.C.: American Bar Association.

———. 1998. *Legal Interventions in Family Violence: Research Findings and Policy Implications.* Research Report, Washington, D.C.: U.S. Department of Justice, Bureau of Justice Statistics, NCJ 171666.

American Correctional Association. 1990. *The Female Offender: What Does the Future Hold?* Washington, D.C.: St. Mary's.

Amott, Teresa, and Julie Matthaei. 1996. *Race, Gender, and Work: A Multicultural Economic History of Women in the United States.* Boston: South End.

Andelin, Helen. 1965. *Fascinating Womanhood.* Santa Barbara, Calif.: Pacific.

Anderson, Elijah. 1990. *Streetwise: Race, Class and Change in an Urban Community.* Chicago: University of Chicago Press.

Anderson, Karen. 1991. *Chain Her By One Foot.* London: Routledge.

Anderson, Michael A, Paulette M. Gillig, Marilyn Sitaker, Kathy McCloskey, Kathleen Malloy, and Nancy Grisby. 2003. "Why Doesn't She

Just Leave? A Descriptive Study of Victim Reported Impediments to Her Safety." *Journal of Family Violence* 18:151–57.

Angier, Natalie. 1999. *Woman: An Intimate Geography.* New York: Houghton Mifflin.

Annie E. Casey Foundation. 2005. *Kids Count Data Book.* Baltimore, Md.: Annie E. Casey Foundation.

Arendt, Hannah. 1966. *The Origins of Totalitarianism.* New York: Harcourt, Brace and World.

Ariès, Phillippe. 1962. *Centuries of Childhood: A Social History of Family Life.* Translated by R. Baldock. New York: Knopf.

Arizona Coalition Against Domestic Violence. 2002. *Arizona Domestic Violence Fatality Review: A Review of 2000 and 2001 Murder Suicides.* Phoenix, Ariz.: Arizona Coalition Against Domestic Violence. http://www.azcadv.org/PDFs/DVFatalityRevue.pdf. Accessed May 20, 2005.

Arizona Department of Health Services. 2004. *Arizona Child Fatality Review Program, 11th Annual Report.* Phoenix, Ariz.: Arizona Department of Health Services. http://www.azdhs.gov/phs/owch/pdf/cfr2004.pdf. Accessed September 18, 2005.

Arizona State Legislature. 2004. *Fiscal Year 2004, Appropriations Report.* http://www.azleg.state.az.us/jlbc/04app/doc.pdf. Accessed September 24, 2005.

Asian and Pacific Islander Institute on Domestic Violence. 2002. *Domestic Violence in Asian and Pacific Islander Communities National Summit 2002: Proceedings.* Arlington, Va.: LCG, Inc.

Bancroft, Lundy. 2002. *Why Does He Do That? Inside the Minds of Angry and Controlling Men.* New York: Berkley.

Bancroft, Lundy, and Jay G. Silverman. 2002. *The Batterer as Parent.* Thousand Oaks, Calif.: Sage Publications.

Barnes, Bob. 1998. *What Makes a Man Feel Loved.* Eugene, Oreg.: Harvest House.

Barnett, Ola W., and Alyce D. LaViolette. 1993. *It Could Happen to Anyone: Why Battered Women Stay.* Newbury Park, Calif.: Sage Publications.

Baskin, Deborah R., and Ira B. Sommers. 1997. *Casualties of Community Disorder: Women's Careers in Violent Crime.* Boulder, Colo.: Westview.

Beattie, L. Elisabeth, and Mary Angela Shaughnessy. 2000. *Sister in Pain: Battered Women Fight Back.* Lexington: University of Kentucky Press.

Belkin, Lisa. 2003. "The Opt-Out Revolution." *New York Times Magazine.* (October 26), sect. 6, p. 42.

Belknap, Joanne. 2001. *The Invisible Woman: Gender, Crime and Justice.* 2nd ed. Belmont, Calif.: Wadsworth.

Belknap, Joanne, Kristi Holsinger, and Melissa Dunn. 1997. "Understanding

Incarcerated Girls: The Results of a Focus Group Study." *Prison Journal* 77, no. 4:381–404.

Benedict, Helen. 1992. *Virgin or Vamp: How the Press Covers Sex Crimes.* New York: Oxford University Press.

Benhabib, Seyla, Judith Butler, Drucilla Cornell, and Nancy Fraser. 1995. *Feminist Contentions: A Philosophical Exchange.* New York: Routledge.

Bergen, Raquel Kennedy. 2000. "Rape Laws and Spousal Exemptions." In *Encyclopedia of Women and Crime,* edited by N. H. Rafter, 223–25. Phoenix, Ariz.: Oryx.

Berliner, Lucy, and John Brier. 1999. *Trauma and Memory.* Thousand Oaks, Calif.: Sage Publications.

Berrigan, Frida, and William D. Hartung. 2005. *U.S. Weapons at War 2005: Promoting Freedom or Fueling Conflict?* New York: World Policy Institute. http://www.worldpolicy.org/projects/arms/reports/wawjune2005 .html. Accessed September 8, 2005.

Bilton, Tony, Kevin Bonnett, Pip Jones, David Skinner, Michelle Stanworth, and Andrew Webster. 1997. *Introductory Sociology.* 3rd ed. London: Macmillan.

Blamires, Alcuin. 1992. *Women Defamed and Women Defended: An Anthology of Medieval Texts.* New York: Oxford University Press.

Blass, Thomas. 2000. *Obedience to Authority: Current Perspectives on the Milgram Paradigm.* Mahwah, N.J.: Lawrence Erlbaum Associates.

Bloom, Barbara. 1992. "Incarcerated Mothers and Their Children: Maintaining Family Ties." In *Female Offenders: Meeting the Needs of a Neglected Population.* Laurel, Md.: American Correctional Association.

Boocock, Sarane Spence, and Kimberly Ann Scott. 2005. *Kids in Context: The Sociological Study of Children and Childhoods.* Lanham, Md.: Rowman and Littlefield.

Bortner, M. A. 2002. "Controlled and Excluded: Reproduction and Motherhood among Poor and Imprisoned Women." In *Women at the Margins: Neglect, Punishment and Resistance,* edited by J. Figueira-McDonough and R. C. Sarri, 253–69. New York: Haworth.

Bortner, M. A., and Linda M. Williams. 1997. *Youth in Prison: We the People of Unit Four.* New York: Routledge.

Bourgois, Philippe. 1995. *In Search of Respect: Selling Crack in El Barrio.* Cambridge: Cambridge University Press.

———. 1998. "Families and Children in Pain in the U.S. Inner City." In *Small Wars: The Cultural Politics of Childhood,* edited by N. Scheper-Hughes and C. Sargent, 331–51. Berkeley and Los Angeles: University of California Press.

Bowles, Samuel, Herbert Gintis, and Melissa Osborne-Groves. 2005. *Un-*

equal Chances: Family Background and Economic Success. Princeton, N. J.: Princeton University Press.

Brewer, Rose. 1988. "Black Women in Poverty: Some Comments on Female-Headed Families." *Signs* 13 (Winter):331–39.

Briere, John. 1992. *Child Abuse Trauma: Theory and Treatment of the Lasting Effects.* Newbury Park, Calif.: Sage Publications.

Browne, Angela. 1987. *When Battered Women Kill.* New York: Free Press.

Browne, Angela, Brenda Miller, and Eugene Maguin. 1999. "Prevalence and Severity of Lifetime Physical and Sexual Abuse Among Incarcerated Women." *International Journal of Law and Psychiatry* 22, nos. 3–4: 301–22.

Browning, Christopher R. 1992. *Ordinary Men: Reserve Police Battalion 101 and the Final Solution in Poland.* New York: HarperCollins.

Buehl, Sarah. 2001. Keynote address at Arizona Governor's Summit on Domestic Violence. Mesa, Arizona.

Bumiller, Kristin. 1990. "Fallen Angels: The Representation of Violence Against Women in Legal Culture." *International Journal of the Sociology of Law* 18:125–42.

Bureau of Justice Statistics. 2004a. *Homicide Trends in the U.S.: Intimate Homicide.* Washington, D.C.: U.S. Department of Justice. http://www.ojp.usdoj.gov/bjs/homicide/intimates.htm. Accessed July 25, 2005.

———. 2004b. *Homicide Trends in the U.S.: Trends by Gender.* Washington, D.C.: U.S. Department of Justice. http://www.ojp.usdoj.gov/bjs/homicide/gender.htm. Accessed July 25, 2005.

Bureau of Labor Statistics. 2005. *Employment Characteristics of Families in 2004.* Washington, D.C.: U.S. Department of Labor. http://www.bls.gov/. Accessed July 13, 2005.

Buzawa, Eve S., and Carl G. Buzawa. 1996. *Do Arrests and Restraining Orders Work?* Thousand Oaks, Calif.: Sage Publications.

California Attorney General's Office. 2005. *Keeping the Promise: Victim Safety and Batterer Accountability: Report to the California Attorney General from the Task Force on Local Criminal Justice Response to Domestic Violence.* Sacramento, Calif.: California Attorney General's Office. http://www.safestate.org/documents/dv_report_ag.pdf. Accessed September 4, 2005.

Campbell, Jacquelyn C. 1992. "'If I Can't Have You, No One Can': Power and Control in Homicides of Female Partners." In *Femicide: The Politics of Woman Killing,* edited by J. Radford and D. E. H. Russell, 99–113. New York: Twayne.

Campbell, J. C., D. Webster, J. Koziol-McLain, C. R. Block, D. Campbell, M. A. Curry, et al. 2003a. "Risk Factors for Femicide in Abusive Relationships: Results of a Multi-site Case Control Study." *American Journal of Public Health* 93, no. 7:1089–97.

———. 2003b. *Assessing Risk Factors for Intimate Partner Homicide.* Washington, D.C.: National Institute of Justice. NCJ 196547.

Caputi, Jane. 1993. *Gossips, Gorgons and Crones.* Santa Fe, N.Mex.: Bear and Co.

Center for American Women in Politics. 2005. *Fact Sheet: Women in Elective Office.* Center for American Women in Politics. New Brunswick, N.J.: Rutgers, The State University of New Jersey. http://www.rci.rutgers .edu/~cawp/Facts/Officeholders/elective.pdf. Accessed July 2, 2005.

Center for Community Change. 2005. "Issues: The Native American Project: Socio-Economic Information." http://www.communitychange.org/ issues/nativeamerican/background/. Accessed July 19, 2005.

Chesney-Lind, Meda. 1997. *The Female Offender: Girls, Women and Crime.* Thousand Oaks, Calif.: Sage Publications.

———. 2002. "Criminalizing Victimization: The Unintended Consequences of Pro-Arrest Policies for Girls and Women." *Criminology and Public Policy* 2, no. 1:81–91.

———. 2004. *Girls and Violence: Is the Gender Gap Closing?* VAWnet Applied Research Forum.

Chesney-Lind, Meda, and Randall G. Shelden. 2003. *Girls, Delinquency, and Juvenile Justice.* 3rd ed. Belmont, Calif.: Wadsworth.

Children's Defense Fund. 2004. *The State of America's Children, 2004.* Washington, D.C.: Children's Defense Fund.

Chodorow, Nancy J. 1999. *The Reproduction of Mothering: Psychoanalysis of the Sociology of Gender.* Updated ed. Berkeley and Los Angeles: University of California Press.

Clough, Patricia T. 1993. "On the Brink of Deconstructing Sociology: Critical Reading of Dorothy Smith's Standpoint Epistemology." *Sociological Quarterly* 34, no. 1:169–82.

Cockburn, Alexander. 1997. "Big Mountain Land-Grab: Theft of Indian Lands Exposes Sham of Indian Sovereignty Under U.S. Laws." *Los Angeles Times* (Orange County edition), April 27, Commentary section. Reprinted on www. worldfreeinternet.net/news/nws32.htm. Accessed, January 24, 2005.

Coker, Donna. 2004. "Race, Poverty, and the Crime-Centered Response to Domestic Violence." *Violence Against Women* 10, no. 11:1331–335.

Collins, Patricia Hill. 1991. *Black Feminist Thought: Knowledge, Consciousness, and the Politics of Empowerment.* New York: Routledge.

———. 2000. *Black Feminist Thought: Knowledge, Consciousness, and the Politics of Empowerment.* 2nd ed. New York: Routledge.

Comack, Elizabeth. 2005. "Coping, Resisting, and Surviving: Connecting

Women's Law Violations to Their Histories of Abuse." In *In Her Own Words: Women Offenders' Views on Crime and Victimization,* edited by L. F. Alarid and P. Cromwell, 33–43. Los Angeles: Roxberry.

Cook, Sandy, and Susanne Davies, eds. 1999. *Harsh Punishment: International Experiences of Women's Imprisonment.* Boston: Northeastern University Press.

Cooper, Todd. 2005. "Mother of Slain Child Also Was a Victim. Battered Woman Syndrome Blamed; Situation was Complex." *Omaha World-Herald,* February 5. Taken from the National Center on Domestic and Sexual Violence Web site, http://www.ncdsv.org/images/MotherSlain Child.pdf. Accessed October 11, 2005.

Coser, Lewis A. 1977. *Masters of Sociological Thought: Ideas in Social and Historical Context.* 2nd ed. New York: Harcourt Brace Jovanovich.

Crenshaw, Kimberle. 1993. "Mapping the Margins: Intersectionality, Identity Politics, and Violence Against Women." *Stanford Law Review* 43: 1241–99.

Danner, Mark. 2004. *Torture and Truth: America, Abu Ghraib, and the War on Terror.* New York: New York Review of Books.

Daly, Kathleen. 1994. *Gender, Crime and Punishment.* New Haven, Conn.: Yale University Press.

Daly, Martin, and Margo Wilson. 1988. *Homicide.* New York: Aldine de Gruyter.

Dasgupta, Shamita Das. 2002. "A Framework for Understanding Women's Use of Nonlethal Violence in Intimate Heterosexual Relationships." *Violence Against Women* 8, no. 11:1364–89.

———. 2003. *Safety and Justice For All: Examining the Relationship Between the Women's Anti-Violence Movement and the Criminal Legal System.* New York: Ms. Foundation. www.ms.foundation.org/user-assets/ PDF/Program/safety_justice.pdf. Accessed October 3, 2005.

Davies, Susanne, and Sandy Cook. 1999. "Neglect or Punishment? Failing to Meet the Needs of Women Post-Release." In *Harsh Punishment: International Experiences of Women's Imprisonment,* edited by S. Cook and S. Davies, 272–90. Boston: Northeastern University Press.

Denzin, Norman K., and Yvonna S. Lincoln. 2005. *Sage Handbook of Qualitative Research.* 3rd ed. Thousand Oaks, Calif.: Sage Publications.

Dershowitz, Alan M. 1994. *The Abuse Excuse.* New York: Little Brown.

DeVault, Marjorie L. 1990. "Talking and Listening from Women's Standpoint: Feminist Strategies for Interviewing and Analysis." *Social Problems* 37, no. 1:96–116.

Dobash, R. Emerson. 2003. "Domestic Violence: Arrest, Prosecution and Reducing Violence." *Criminology and Public Policy* 2, no. 2:313–18.

Dobash, R. Emerson, and Russell P. Dobash. 1979. *Violence Against Wives.* New York: Free Press.

———. 1992. *Women, Violence and Social Change.* London: Routledge.

———. 1998. "Violent Men and Violent Contexts." In *Rethinking Violence Against Women,* edited by R. E. Dobash and R. P. Dobash, 141–68. Thousand Oaks, Calif.: Sage Publications.

Dobash, R. Emerson, Russell P. Dobash, Katherine Cavanagh, and Ruth Lewis. 2004. "Not an Ordinary Killer—Just an Ordinary Guy: When Men Murder an Intimate Woman Partner." *Violence Against Women* 10, no. 6:577–605.

Dodge, Mary, and Edith Greene. 1991. "Juror and Expert Conceptions of Battered Women." *Violence and Victims* 6, no. 4:271–82.

Doyle, Laura. 1999. *The Surrendered Wife: A Practical Guide to Finding Intimacy, Passion and Peace with a Man.* New York: Fireside.

Dugan, Laura, Daniel S. Nagin, and Richard Rosenfeld. 2003. *Do Domestic Violence Services Save Lives?* Washington, D.C.: U.S. Department of Justice. NCJ 196548.

Durose, Matthew R., Caroline W. Harlow, Patrick A. Langan, Mark Motivans, Ramona R. Rantala, and Erica L. Smith. 2005. *Family Violence Statistics.* Washington, D.C.: U.S. Department of Justice. NCJ 207846.

Dutton, Donald G. 2000. "Witnessing Parental Violence as a Traumatic Experience Shaping the Abusive Personality." *Journal of Aggression, Maltreatment and Trauma* 3:59–67.

Dutton, Mary Ann. 1992. *Empowering and Healing the Battered Woman.* New York: Springer-Verlag.

———. 1996. *The Impact of Evidence Concerning Battering and its Effects in Criminal Trials Involving Battered Women.* Washington, D.C.: National Institute of Justice and National Institute of Mental Health. NCJ 160972. http://www.ncjrs.gov/pdffiles/batter.pdf. Accessed June 14, 2005.

Dworkin, Andrea. 1993. *Letters From a War Zone.* Brooklyn, N.Y.: Lawrence Hill Books.

Edelson, Jeffrey L. 1999. "Children's Witnessing of Adult Domestic Violence." *Journal of Interpersonal Violence* 14, no. 8:839–71.

Ehrenreich, Barbara. 2001. *Nickel and Dimed: On (Not) Getting By in America.* New York: Metropolitan.

Eizten, Stanley, and Maxine Baca Zinn. 2006. *Social Problems.* 10th ed. Boston: Allyn and Bacon.

English, Diana J., Cathy Spatz Widom, and Carol Brandford. 2003. *Childhood Victimization and Delinquency, Adult Criminality, and Violent Criminal Behavior: A Replication and Extension.* Final Report. Washington, D.C.: U.S. Department of Justice. Document No. 192291.

Erdoes, Richard, and Alfonso Ortiz. 1984. *American Indian Myths and Legends*. New York: Pantheon.

Facella, Carol A. 2000. "Madonna/Whore Dichotomy." In *Encyclopedia of Women and Crime*, edited by N. H. Rafter, 153–54. Phoenix, Ariz.: Oryx.

Fagan, Jeffrey. 1996. *The Criminalization of Domestic Violence: Promises and Limits*. Series: NIJ Research Report. January. http://www.ncjrs.org/txtfiles/crimdom.txt. Accessed May 21, 2005.

Faith, Karlene. 1993. *Unruly Women: The Politics of Confinement and Resistance*. Vancouver: Press Gang.

———. 2001. *The Long Prison Journey of Leslie Van Houten: Life Beyond the Cult*. Boston: Northeastern University Press.

Fals-Stewart, William. 2003. "The Occurrence of Partner Physical Aggression on Days of Alcohol Consumption: A Longitudinal Diary Study." *Journal of Consulting and Clinical Psychology* 71, no. 1:41–52.

Family Violence Prevention Fund. 2005. "Gonzales Ruling a 'Serious Blow' to Victims of Violence Who Need Police Protection." July 27. http://endabuse.org/newsflash/index.php3?Search=Article&NewsFlashID=628. Accessed October 11, 2005.

Fantuzzo, J., R. Boruch, A. Beriama, et al. 1997. "Domestic Violence and Children: Prevalence and Risk in Five Major U.S. Cities." *Journal of the American Academy of Child and Adolescent Psychiatry* 36:116–22.

Federal Bureau of Investigation Home Page. 2005. http://www.fbi.gov/libref/factsfigure/indian.htm. Accessed May 24, 2005.

Ferraro, Kathleen J. 1979. "Physical and Emotional Battering: Aspects of Managing Hurt." *California Sociologist* 2, no. 2:134–49.

———. 1983. "The Rationalization Process: How Battered Women Stay." *Victimology* 8, no. 34:203–214.

———. 1989a. "The Legal Response to Battering in the U.S." In *Women, Policing and Male Violence: International Perspectives*, edited by M. Hanmer, J. Radford, and E. Stanko, 155–84. London: Routledge.

———. 1989b. "Policing Woman Battering." *Social Problems* 36 no. 1:61–74.

———. 1996. "The Dance of Dependency: A Genealogy of Domestic Violence Discourse." *Hypatia* 11, no. 4:77–91.

———. 1997. "Battered Women: Strategies for Survival," In *Violence Between Intimate Partners: Patterns Causes and Effects*, edited by A. Carderelli, 124–40. Boston: Allyn and Bacon.

———. 2000. "Woman Battering: More Than a Family Problem." In *Women, Crime and Justice: Contemporary Perspectives*, edited by L. Goodstein and C. Renzetti, 135–53. New York: Roxbury.

———. 2003. "The Words Change, but the Melody Lingers: The Persistence of the Battered Woman's Syndrome in Criminal Cases Involving Battered Women." *Violence Against Women* 9, no. 1:110–29.

Ferraro, Kathleen J., and Tascha Boychuk. 1992. "The Court's Response to Interpersonal Violence: A Comparison of Intimate and Nonintimate Assault." In *Domestic Violence: The Criminal Justice Response*, edited by E. Buzawa, 209–26. Westport, Conn.: Greenwood.

Ferraro, Kathleen J., and John M. Johnson. 1983. "How Women Experience Battering: The Process of Victimization." *Social Problems* 30, no. 3:325–39.

Ferraro, Kathleen J., and Angela M. Moe. 2000. "Resistance, Compliance, and Battered Women's Participation in Violence." Paper presented at the annual meeting of the Society for the Study of Social Problems, Washington, D.C., August 11–13.

———. 2003a. "Mothering, Crime, and Incarceration." *Journal of Contemporary Ethnography* 32, no. 1:9–40.

———. 2003b. "Women's Stories of Survival and Resistance." In *Women in Prison: Gender and Social Control*, edited by B. Zaitzow and J. Thomas, 65–94. Boulder, Colo.: Lynne Rienner.

Ferraro, Kathleen J., and Lucille Pope. 1993. "Irreconcilable Differences: Police, Battered Women, and the Law." In *Legal Responses to Wife Assault*, edited by N. Z. Hilton, 96–126. Newbury Park, Calif.: Sage Publications.

Findlen, Barbara. 2001. *Listen Up! Voices from the Next Feminist Generation*. 2nd ed. Seattle: Seal.

Ford, David, and Mary Jean Regoli. 1993. "The Criminal Prosecution of Wife Assaulters: Process, Problems, and Effects." In *Legal Responses to Wife Assault*, edited by N. Z. Hilton, 127–64. Newbury Park, Calif.: Sage Publications.

Foucault, Michel. 1980. *Power/Knowledge: Selected Interviews and Other Writings, 1972–1977*. Edited by C. Gordon. New York: Pantheon.

———. 1990. *The History of Sexuality: An Introduction*. Vol. 1. New York: Vintage.

Friedan, Betty. 1963. *The Feminine Mystique*. New York: Norton.

Friedman, Lawrence M. 1993. *Crime and Punishment in American History*. New York: Basic.

Fromm, Erich. 1973. *The Anatomy of Human Destructiveness*. New York: Holt, Rinehart, and Winston.

Gaardner, Emily, and Joanne Belknap. 2002. "Tenuous Borders: Girls Transferred to Adult Court." *Criminology* 40, no. 3:481–517.

Gagné, Patricia. 1998. *Battered Women's Justice: The Movement for Clemency and the Politics of Self-Defense*. New York: Twayne.

Galeano, Eduardo. 1991. *The Book of Embraces*. Translated by Cedric Belfrage with Mark Schafer. New York: Norton.

———. 1992. *We Say No: Chronicles, 1963–1991*. Translated by Mark Fried et al. New York: Norton.

Garfinkle, Harold. 1964. "Studies of the Routine Grounds of Every-Day Activities" *Social Problems* 11, no. 3:225–49.

———. 1988. "Evidence for Locally Produced, Naturally Accountable Phenomena of Order, Logic, Reason, Meaning, Method, etc., in and as of the Essential Quiddity of Immortal Ordinary Society: An Announement of Studies." *Sociological Theory* 6, no. 1:103–109.

Gelles, Richard J. N.d. *Domestic Violence: Not an Even Playing Field.* http://thesafetyzone.org/everyone/gelles.html. Accessed September 25, 2005.

Gelles, Richard J., and Donileen R. Loseke. 1993. *Current Controversies on Family Violence.* Newbury Park, Calif.: Sage Publications.

Gelles, Richard J., and Murray A. Straus. 1988. *Intimate Violence.* New York: Simon and Schuster.

Gilfus, Mary. 1992. "From Victims to Survivors to Offenders: Women's Routes of Entry and Immersion Into Street Crime." *Women and Criminal Justice* 4, no. 1:63–89.

Gillespie, Cynthia. 1989. *Justifiable Homicide.* Athens, Ohio: Ohio State University Press.

Girshick, Lori B. 2002. *Woman-to-Woman Sexual Violence: Does She Call it Rape?* Boston: Northeastern University Press.

Goetting, Ann. 1999. *Getting Out: Life Stories of Women Who Left Abusive Men.* New York: Columbia University Press.

Goldstein, Donna M. 2003. *Laughter Out of Place: Race, Class, Violence, and Sexuality in a Rio Shantytown.* Berkeley and Los Angeles: University of California Press.

Gordon, Avery. 1996. *Ghostly Matters: Haunting and the Sociological Imagination.* Minneapolis: University of Minnesota Press.

Gordon, Linda. 1988. *Heroes of Their Own Lives: The Politics and History of Family Violence.* New York: Viking.

———. 1995. *Pitied But Not Entitled: Single Mothers and the History of Welfare.* Cambridge, Mass.: Harvard University Press.

Gordon, Malcolm. 1996. *Validity of the "Battered Woman Syndrome" in Criminal Cases Involving Battered Women.* Washington, D.C.: National Institute of Justice and National Institute of Mental Health. NCJ 160972. http://www.ncjrs.org/pdffiles/batter.pdf. Accessed July 22, 2005.

Gowdy, Voncile B. 1998. "Adult Female Offenders." Chapter 1 in *Women in Criminal Justice: A 20-Year Update.* Washington, D.C.: U.S. Department of Justice.

Graglia, F. Carolyn. 1998. *Domestic Tranquility: A Brief Against Feminism.* Dallas, Tex.: Spence.

Greenbook Initiative. 2005. http://www.thegreenbook.info/. Accessed May 21, 2005.

Greene, Edith, Allan Raitz, and Heidi Lindblad. 1989. "Jurors' Knowledge of Battered Women." *Journal of Family Violence* 4, no. 2:105–25.

Greenfeld, Lawrence A., and Tracy L. Snell. 1999. *Women Offenders.* Washington, D.C.: U.S. Department of Justice. Bureau of Justice Statistics. NCJ 175688.

Greenfield, Lawrence A., Michael R. Rand, Diane Craven, Patsy A. Klaus, Craig A. Perkins, Cheryl Ringel, Greg Warchol, Cathy Maston, and James Alan Fox. 1998. *Violence by Intimates: Analysis of Data on Crimes by Current or Former Spouses, Boyfriends, and Girlfriends.* Washington, D.C.: U.S. Department of Justice. Bureau of Justice Statistics. NCJ-167237.

Haaken, Janice. 1998. *Pillar of Salt: Gender, Memory, and the Perils of Looking Back.* New Brunswick, N.J.: Rutgers University Press.

Haapasalo, Jaana, and Terhi Aaltonen. 1998. "Mothers' Abusive Childhood Predicts Child Abuse." *Child Abuse Review* 8:231–50.

Haraway, Donna J. 1989. *Primate Visions.* New York: Routledge.

Hardesty, Jennifer L. 2002. "Separation Assault in the Context of Postdivorce Parenting: An Integrative Review of the Literature." *Violence Against Women* 8:579–625.

Harding, Sandra. 1986. *The Science Question in Feminism.* Ithaca, N.Y.: Cornell University Press.

———. 1992. "Rethinking Standpoint Epistemology: What is 'Strong Objectivity?'" In *Feminist Epistemologies,* edited by L. Alcoff and E. Potter 49–82. New York: Routledge.

———. 2003. *The Feminist Standpoint Theory Reader: Intellectual and Political Controversies.* New York: Routledge.

———. 2004. "A Socially Relevant Philosophy of Science? Resources from Standpoint Theory's Controversiality." *Hypatia* 19, no. 1:25–47.

Harjo, Suzan Shown. 2005. "Congress: Make the Streets Safe for Indian Women Too!" *Indian Country Today,* April 28. Online version: http:// www.indiancountrytoday.com. Accessed May 24, 2005.

Harlow, Caroline Wolf. 1999. *Prior Abuse Reported by Inmates and Probationers.* Washington, D.C.: Bureau of Justice Statistics, U.S. Department of Justice. NCJ 172879.

Harrison, Paige M., and Allen J. Beck. 2005. *Prison and Jail Inmates at Midyear 2004.* Washington, D.C.: Bureau of Justice Statistics, U.S. Department of Justice. NCJ 208801.

Harrison, Paige M., and Jennifer C. Karberg. 2003. *Prison and Jail Inmates at Midyear, 2003.* Washington, D.C.: Bureau of Justice Statistics, U.S. Department of Justice. NCJ 203947.

Hartsock, Nancy. 1983. "The Feminist Standpoint: Developing the Ground for a Specifically Feminist Historical Materialism." In her *The Feminist Standpoint and Other Essays,* 105–32. Boulder, Colo.: Westview.

———. 1998. "The Feminist Standpoint Revisited." In her *The Feminist Standpoint and Other Essays*, 227–48. Boulder, Colo.: Westview.

Harvard Project on American Indian Economic Development. 2005. "The U.S. Census Data on American Indians: 1990 v. 2000: Report Compiles Economic and Social Indicators for Decade." http://www.ksg.harvard.edu/press/press%20releases/2005/hpaied_report_010505.htm. Accessed July 19, 2005.

Hays, Sharon. 2003. *Flat Broke With Children.* Oxford: Oxford University Press.

Henriques, Zelma W. 1982. *Imprisoned Mothers and Their Children.* Lanham, Md.: University Press of America.

Herman, Edward S., and Noam Chomsky. 2002. *Manufacturing Consent: The Political Economy of the Mass Media.* New York: Pantheon.

Herman, Judith. 1997. *Trauma and Recovery.* New York: Basic Books.

Hernández, Daisy, and Bushra Rehman. 2002. *Colonize This!: Young Women of Color on Today's Feminism.* New York: Seal.

Heyman, Richard E., and Amy M. Smith Slep. 2002. "Do Child Abuse and Interparental Violence Lead to Adulthood Family Violence?" *Journal of Marriage and the Family* 64, no. 4:864–71.

Hirschi, Travis. 1969. *Causes of Delinquency.* Berkeley and Los Angeles: University of California Press.

Honolulu Star-Bulletin. 2003. "Violence in the Home Tops Problems of Drugs." *Honolulu Star-Bulletin*, Tuesday, September 16.

Howell, Joseph T. 1976. *Hard Living on Clay Street.* Garden City, N.Y.: Anchor.

Jacobs, Janet Liebman. 1990. "Reassessing Mother Blame in Incest." *Signs* 15, no. 3:500–514.

Jacobs, Michelle S. 1998. "Requiring Battered Women Die: Murder Liability for Mothers Under Failure to Protect Statutes." *Journal of Criminal Law and Criminology* 88, no. 2:579–660.

Jacobson, Neil S., and John M. Gottman. 1998. *When Men Batter Women: New Insights into Ending Abusive Relationships.* New York: Simon and Schuster.

Jaffe, Peter G., Nancy K. D. Lemon, and Samantha E. Poisson. 2003. *Child Custody and Domestic Violence: A Call for Accountability and Safety.* Thousand Oaks, Calif.: Sage Publications.

Jaggar, Allison. 1983. *Feminist Politics and Human Nature.* Totowa, N.J.: Rowman and Allenheld.

James, Allison, Chris Jenks, and Alan Prout. 1998. *Theorizing Childhood.* New York: Teachers College Press.

Joe, Karen A., and Meda Chesney-Lind. 1995. "'Just Every Mother's Angel': An Analysis of Gender and Ethnic Variations in Youth Gang Membership." *Gender and Society* 9, no. 2:408–30.

Johnson, Holly, and Tina Hotton. 2003. "Homicide Risk in Estranged and Intact Intimate Relationships." *Homicide Studies* 7, no. 1:58–84.

Johnson, Holly, and Vincent Sacco. 1995. "Researching Violence Against Women: Statistics Canada National Survey." *Canadian Journal of Criminology* 37, no. 3:281–304.

Johnson, Michael P., and Kathleen J. Ferraro. 2000. "Research on Domestic Violence in the 1990s: Making Distinctions." *Journal of Marriage and the Family* 62:948–68.

Johnson, Michael P., and Janel M. Leone. 2005. "The Differential Effects of Intimate Terrorism and Situational Couple Violence." *Journal of Family Issues* 26, no. 3:322–49.

Johnson, Myke. 1994. "Wanting to be Indian: Cultural Appropriation in White Feminist Spirituality." *Sinister Wisdom* 52:79–88.

Johnson, Nancy, Dennis P. Saccuzzo, and Wendy J. Koen. 2005. "Child Custody Mediation in Cases of Domestic Violence: Empirical Evidence of a Failure to Protect." *Violence Against Women* 11, no. 8:1022–1053.

Jones, Ann. 1980. *Women Who Kill.* New York: Fawcett Columbine.

———. 1994. *Next Time She'll Be Dead.* Boston: Beacon.

Justice Policy Institute. 2002. *Cellblocks or Classrooms? The Funding of Higher Education and Corrections and its Impact on African American Men.* http://www.justicepolicy.org/article.php?id=275. Accessed June 10, 2005.

Katz, Leo, Michael S. Moore, and Stephen J. Morse. 1999. *Foundations of Criminal Law.* Oxford: Oxford University Press.

Kaufman, Joan, and Edward F. Zigler. 1987. "Do Abused Children Become Abusive Parents?" *American Journal of Orthopsychiatry* 57, no. 2:186–292.

Kelman, Herbert C., and V. Lee Hamilton. 1989. *Crimes of Obedience: Toward a Social Psychology of Authority and Responsibility.* New Haven, Conn.: Yale University Press.

Kendall, Kathleen. 1998. "Evaluation of Programs for Female Offenders." In *Female Offenders: Critical Perspectives and Effective Interventions,* edited by R. Zaplin, 361–79. Gaithersburg, Md.: Aspen.

Kernic, Mary A., Daphne J. Monary-Ernsdorff, Jennifer K. Koepsell, and Victoria L. Holt. 2005. "Children in the Crossfire: Child Custody Determinations Among Couples With a History of Intimate Partner Violence." *Violence Against Women* 11, no. 8:991–1021.

Kessler-Harris, Alice. 2003. *Out to Work: A History of Wage-Earning Women in the United States.* Twentieth anniversary ed. Oxford: Oxford University Press.

Klein, Dori. 1973. "The Etiology of Female Crime: A Review of the Literature." *Issues in Criminology* 8, no. 3:3–30.

Kochanek, Kenneth D., and Betty L. Smith. 2004. *Deaths: Preliminary Data for 2002*. National Vital Statistics Report 52(13). Atlanta, Ga.: Centers for Disease Control and Prevention.

Konradi, Amanda. 1996. "Preparing to Testify: Rape Survivors Negotiating the Criminal Justice Process." *Gender and Society* 10:404–452.

Kurz, Demie. 1995. *For Richer, For Poorer: Mothers Confront Divorce*. New York: Routledge.

Laing, R. D. 1968. *The Politics of Experience*. New York: Ballantine Books.

Lamb, Sharon. 1999. "Constructing the Victim: Popular Images and Lasting Labels." In *New Versions of Victims*, edited by S. Lamb, 108–138. New York: New York University Press.

Lareau, Annette. 2003. *Unequal Childhoods: Class, Race, and Family Life*. Berkeley and Los Angeles: University of California Press.

Laub, Dori. 1992. "Bearing Witness or the Vicissitudes of Listening." In *Testimony: Crises of Witnessing in Literature, Psychoanalysis, and History*, edited by S. Felman and D. Laub, 57–74. New York: Routledge.

Lemkin, Raphael. 1944. *Axis Rule in Occupied Europe: Laws of Occupation—Analysis of Government—Proposals for Redress*. Washington, D.C.: Carnegie Endowment for International Peace.

Leonard, Elizabeth Dermody. 2002. *Convicted Survivors: The Imprisonment of Battered Women Who Kill*. New York: State University of New York Press.

Lloyd, Susan. 1997. "The Effects of Domestic Violence on Women's Employment." *Law and Policy* 19, no. 2:139–67.

Longino, Helen E. 2002. *The Fate of Knowledge*. Princeton: Princeton University Press.

Luckenbill, David. 1977. "Criminal Homicide as a Situated Transaction." *Social Problems* 25, no. 2:176–86.

Lukács, Georg. 1972. *History and Class Consciousness*. Cambridge, Mass.: MIT Press.

Lundgren, Eva. 1998. "The Hand That Strikes and Comforts: Gender Construction and the Tension Betweeen Body and Symbol." In *Rethinking Violence Against Women*, edited by R. Emerson Dobash and Russell P. Dobash, 169–98. Thousand Oaks, Calif.: Sage Publications.

Mack, Kathy. 1993. "Continuing Barriers to Women's Credibility: A Feminist Perspective on the Proof Process." *Criminal Law Forum* 4, no. 1:327–53.

Madriz, Esther. 1997. *Nothing Bad Happens to Good Girls*. Berkeley and Los Angeles: University of California Press.

Maguigan, Holly. 1991. "Battered Women and Self-Defense: Myths and Misconceptions in Current Reform Proposals." *University of Pennsylvania Law Review* 140:379–486.

Maher, Lisa. 1995. *Sexed Work: Gender, Race and Resistance in a Brooklyn Drug Market*. Oxford: Oxford University Press.

Martin, Del. 1976. *Battered Wives.* San Francisco, Calif.: Glide.

Maslow, Abraham. 1970. *Motivation and Personality.* 2nd ed. New York: Harper and Row.

Mason, Mary Ann. 1994. *From Father's Property to Children's Rights: The History of Child Custody in the United States.* New York: Columbia University Press.

McGillivray, Anne, and Brenda Comaskey. 1999. *Black Eyes All of the Time: Intimate Violence, Aboriginal Women, and the Justice System.* Toronto: University of Toronto Press.

Meyer, Carter Jones, and Diana Royer. 2001. *Selling the Indian: Commercializing and Appropriating American Indian Culture.* Tucson: University of Arizona Press.

Meyer, Cheryl L., and Michelle Oberman. 2001. *Mothers Who Kill Their Children.* New York: New York University Press.

Milgram, Stanley. 1974. *Obedience to Authority: An Experimental View.* New York: Harper and Row.

Miller, Arthur G. 1986. *The Obedience Experiments: A Case Study of Controversy in Social Science.* New York: Praeger.

———. 2004. *The Social Psychology of Good and Evil.* New York: Guilford.

Miller, Jerome G. 1996. *Search and Destroy: African American Males in the Criminal Justice System.* Cambridge: Cambridge University Press.

Miller, Neal. 2004. *Domestic Violence: A Review of State Legislation Defining Police and Prosecution Duties and Powers.* Alexandria, Va.: Institute for Law and Justice. http://www.ilj.org/publications/dv_Legislation-3.pdf. Accessed June 12, 2005.

Miller, Susan L. 1989. "Unintended Side-effects of Pro-arrest Policies and Their Race and Class Implications for Battered Women: A Cautionary Note." *Criminal Justice Policy Review* 3:299–317.

———. 2000. "The Paradox of Women Arrested for Domestic Violence: Criminal Justice Professionals and Service Providers Respond." *Violence Against Women* 7, no. 12:1339–76

———. 2005. *Victims as Offenders: The Paradox of Women's Violence in Relationships.* New Brunswick, N.J.: Rutgers University Press.

Mills, C. Wright. 1956. *The Power Elite.* New York: Oxford University Press.

Minh-ha, Trinh T. 1989. *Woman, Native, Other: Writing Postcoloniality and Feminism.* Bloomington: Indiana University Press.

Modisane, Bloke. 1963. *Blame Me On History.* London: Thames and Hudson.

Moe, Angela M., and Kathleen J. Ferraro. Forthcoming. "Criminalized Mothers: The Value and Devaluation of Parenthood from Behind Bars." *Women and Therapy.*

Moraga, Cherríe, and Gloria Anzaldúa. 1983. *This Bridge Called My Back.* San Francisco, Calif.: Kitchen Table–Women of Color Press.

Morash, Merry, Timothy S. Bynum, and Barbara A. Koons. 1998. *Women Offenders: Programming Needs and Promising Approaches.* Washington, D.C.: U.S. Department of Justice.

Morelli, Mario F. 1983. "Milgram's Dilemma of Obedience." *Metaphilosophy* 14:183–89.

Morse, Stephen J. 1994. "Acts, Choices and Coercion: Culpability and Control." *University of Pennsylvania Law Review* (May), 142:1587–1619.

Myers, Alice, and Sarah Wright. 1996. *No Angels: Women Who Commit Violence.* San Francisco, Calif.: HarperCollins.

National Household Survey on Drug Abuse Report. 2003. *Substance Use Among American Indians or Alaska Natives.* National Household Survey on Drug Abuse Report. May 16, 2003. *http://oas.samhsa.gov/2k3/ AmIndians/AmIndians.pdf.* Accessed January 4, 2006.

Nenga, Sandi Kawecka. 2003. "Social Class and Structures of Feeling in Women's Childhood Memories of Clothing, Food and Leisure." *Journal of Contemporary Ethnography* 32, no. 2:167–99.

Niehoff, Debra. 1999. *The Biology of Violence: How Understanding the Brain, Behavior, and Environment Can Break the Vicious Circle of Aggression.* New York: Free Press.

O'Brien, John. 1971 "Violence in Divorce-Prone Families." *Journal of Marriage and the Family* 33:692–98.

O'Dell, Lindsay. 1997. "Child Sexual Abuse and the Academic Construction of Symptomatologies." *Feminism and Psychology* 7 no. 3: 334–39.

Oliver, Pamela E. 2001. "Racial Disparities in Imprisonment: Some Basic Information." *Focus* 21, no. 3:28–31.

Osthoff, Sue. 1996. Preface to *Trend Analysis: Expert Testimony on Battering and its Effects.* Washington, D.C.: National Institute of Justice and National Institute of Mental Health. NCJ 160972. *http://www.ncjrs.gov/ pdffiles/batter.pdf.* Accessed April 4, 2005.

Osthoff, Sue, and Holly Maguigan. 2005. "Explaining Without Pathologizing." In *Current Controversies on Family Violence,* edited by D. R. Loseke and R. J. Gelles, 225–40. 2nd ed. Thousand Oaks, Calif.: Sage Publications.

Owen, Barbara. 2004. "Women and Imprisonment in the United States: The Gendered Consequences of the U.S. Imprisonment Binge." In *The Criminal Justice System and Women: Offenders, Prisoners, Victims, and Workers,* edited by N. J. Sokoloff and B. R. Price, 195–206. New York: McGraw Hill.

Parrish, Janet. 1996. *Trend Analysis: Expert Testimony on Battering and its Effects.* Washington, D.C.: National Institute of Justice and National Institute of Mental Health. NCJ 160972. *http://www.ncjrs.gov/pdffiles/ batter.pdf.* Accessed April 4, 2005.

Patmore, Coventry. 2004. *The Angel in the House.* Whitefish, Mont.: Kessinger.

Pearson, Jessica. 1997. *When She Was Bad: How and Why Women Get Away With Murder.* New York: Viking.

Pence, Ellen. 2005. "Did the Battered Women's Movement Really Fail? What Would Piven and Cloward Say?" Paper presented at the annual meeting of the Society for the Study of Social Problems, Philadelphia, Pennsylvania, August 12–14.

Pence, Ellen, and Melanie Paymar. 1993. *Education Groups for Men Who Batter: The Duluth Model.* New York: Springer-Verlag.

Pfohl, Stephen. 1994. *Images of Deviance and Social Control: A Sociological History.* 2nd ed. New York: McGraw-Hill.

Pipher, Mary. 1997. *Reviving Ophelia: Saving the Lives of Adolescent Girls.* New York: Ballantine.

Platt, Anthony M. 1969. *The Child Savers: The Invention of Delinquency.* Chicago: University of Chicago Press.

Pleck, Elizabeth. 1987. *Domestic Tyranny.* New York: Oxford University Press.

Polk, Kenneth. 1994. "Masculinity, Honour, and Confrontational Homicide." In *Just Boys Doing Business?* edited by T. Newburn and E. A. Stanko, 166–88. London: Routledge.

Pollak, Otto. 1950. *The Criminality of Women.* Philadelphia: University of Pennsylvania Press.

Ptacek, James. 1988. "Why Do Men Batter Their Wives?" In *Feminist Perspectives on Wife Abuse,* edited by K. Yllo and M. Bograd, 133–57. Newbury Park, Calif.: Sage Publications.

Quinney, Richard. 1970. *The Social Reality of Crime.* Boston: Little, Brown.

Rafter, Nicole Hahn, and Elizabeth Stanko. 1982. *Judge, Lawyer, Victim, Thief: Women, Gender Roles and Criminal Justice.* Boston, Mass.: Northeastern University Press.

Raj, Anita, and Jay Silverman. 2002. "Violence Against Immigrant Women: The Roles of Culture, Context, and Legal Immigrant Status on Intimate Partner Violence." *Violence Against Women* 8, no. 3:367–98.

Raphael, Jody. 2000. *Saving Bernice: Battered Women, Welfare, and Poverty.* Boston: Northeastern University Press.

Raven, B. H. 1992. "A Power/Interaction Model of Interpersonal Influence: French and Raven Thirty Years Later." *Journal of Social Behavior and Personality* 7:217–44.

Razack, Sherene. 1994. "What is to be Gained by Looking White People in the Eye? Culture, Race, and Gender in Cases of Sexual Violence." *Signs* 19, no. 4:894–923.

Rennison, Callie Marie. 2003. *Intimate Partner Violence, 1993–2001.* Washington, D.C.: Bureau of Justice Statistics, U.S. Department of Justice. NCJ 197838.

Renzetti, Claire. 1992. *Violent Betrayal: Partner Abuse in Lesbian Relationships.* Newbury Park, Calif.: Sage Publications.

———. 1999. "The Challenge to Feminism Posed by Women's Use of Violence in Intimate Relationships." In *New Versions of Victims: Feminists Struggle with the Concept,* edited by S. Lamb, 42–56. New York: New York University Press.

———. 2001. " One Strike and You're Out: Implications of a Federal Crime Control Policy for Battered Women." *Violence Against Women* 7, no. 6:685–97.

Richie, Beth. 1996. *Compelled to Crime: The Gender Entrapment of Black, Battered Women.* New York: Routledge.

———. 2000. "A Black Feminist Reflection on the Anti-Violence Movement." *Signs* 25, no. 4:1134–38.

Ristock, Janice L. 2002. *No More Secrets: Violence in Lesbian Relationships.* New York: Routledge.

Ritchie, Andrea. 2005. "Police Violence Against Women of Color in the Context of Domestic Violence." Paper presented at the annual meeting of the Society for the Study of Social Problems, Philadelphia, Pennsylvania, August 12–14.

Roberts, Dorothy. 1993. "Motherhood and Crime." *Iowa Law Review* 79: 95–141.

———. 1994. "Deviance, Resistance and Love." *Utah Law Review* no. 1: 179–91.

———. 1998. *Killing the Black Body: Race, Reproduction and the Meaning of Liberty.* New York: Vintage.

———. 2003. *Shattered Bonds: The Color of Child Welfare.* New York: Basic.

Roche, Timothy. 2002. "Andrea Yates: More to the Story." *Time On-Line Edition,* March 18. http://www.time.com/time/nation/article/0,8599, 218445,00.html. Accessed September 17, 2005.

Rolstein, Arthur H. 2005. "Feds Say They're Slowing Illegal Immigration through Arizona." *San Diego Union,* online version, September 22. http://www.signonsandiego.com/news/nation/20050922–1608-wst-border crackdown.html. Accessed September 23, 2005.

Rosen, Daniel. 2004. "I Just let Him Have His Way." *Violence Against Women* 10, no. 1:6–28.

Ross, Luana. 1998. *Inventing the Savage: The Social Construction of Native American Criminality.* Austin, Tex.: University of Texas.

Rowe, G. S. 1988. "*Femes Covert* [*sic*] and Criminal Prosecution in Eighteenth-Century Pennsylvania." *American Journal of Legal History* 32: 138–56.

Rubin, Lillian Breslow. 1976. *Worlds of Pain: Life in the Working-Class Family.* New York: Basic.

———. 1994. *Families on the Fault Line.* New York: HarperCollins.

———. 1996. *The Transcendent Child.* New York: Basic.

Rush, Florence. 1980. *The Best Kept Secret: Sexual Abuse of Children.* New York: Prentice-Hall.

Saunders, Daniel G., Ann Lynch, Marica Grayson, and Daniel Linz. 1987. "The Inventory of Beliefs about Wife Beating: The Construction and Initial Validation of a Measure of Beliefs and Attitudes." *Violence and Victims* 2, no. 1: 39–57.

Schechter, Susan. 1982. *Women and Male Violence.* Boston: South End.

Scheff, Thomas J. 1984. *Being Mentally Ill: A Sociological Theory.* New York: Aldine.

Scheper-Hughes, Nancy, and Carolyn Sargent. 1998. *Small Wars: The Cultural Politics of Childhood.* Berkeley and Los Angeles: University of California Press.

Scheppele, Kim Lane. 1992. "Just the Facts, Ma'am: Sexualized Violence, Evidentiary Habits, and the Revision of Truth." *New York Law School Law Review* 37:123–72.

Scheppele, Kim Lane, and Pauline Bart. 1983. "Through Women's Eyes: Defining Danger in the Wake of Sexual Assault." *Journal of Social Issues* 39, no. 2:63–80.

Schlafly, Phyllis. 2003. *Feminist Fantasies.* Dallas, Tex.: Spence.

Schneider, Elizabeth M. 2000. *Battered Women and Feminist Lawmaking.* New Haven, Conn.: Yale University Press.

Schuller, Regina. 1990. "The Impact of Expert Testimony Pertaining to The 'Battered Woman Syndrome' on Jurors' Information Processing and Decisions." Ph.D. diss., University of Western Ontario.

Schwartz, Martin D. 1988. "Ain't Got No Class: Universal Risk Theories of Battering." *Contemporary Crises* 12:373–92.

Scott, Joan W. 1991. "The Evidence of Experience." *Critical Inquiry* 17 (Summer): 773–97.

Sennett, Richard, and Jonathan Cobb. 1972. *The Hidden Injuries of Class.* New York: Knopf.

Sentencing Project. 2005. *New Incarceration Figures: Growth in Population Continues.* www.sentencingproject.org. Accessed October 1, 2005.

Setty, Sudha, and Janice Kaguytan. 2002. *Immigrant Victims of Domestic Violence: Cultural Challenges and Available Legal Protections.* VAWNET online publication. http://www.vawnet.org/DomesticViolence/Research/vawnetDocs/AR_immigrant.pdf. Accessed May 21, 2005.

Sharp, Susan F., and M. Elaine Eriksen. 2003. "Imprisoned Mothers and Their Children." In *Women in Prison: Gender and Social Control,* edited by B. Zaitzow and J. Thomas, 119–36. Boulder, Colo.: Lynne Reiner.

Shipler, David K. 2005. *The Working Poor: Invisible in America*. New York: Vintage.

Sickler, Larry. 2002. "Woman Enters Plea Agreement in Shooting." *Arizona Daily Sun*, October 24, pp. 1–2.

Simon, David R. 2005. *Elite Deviance*. 8th ed. Boston: Allyn and Bacon.

Simon, David R., and Stanley Eitzen. 1993. *Elite Deviance*. 4th ed. Boston: Allyn and Bacon.

Skeggs, Beverly. 1997. *Formations of Class and Gender: Becoming Respectable*. Thousand Oaks, Calif.: Sage Publications.

Slattery, Julianna. 2001. *Finding the Hero in Your Husband: Surrendering the Way God Intended*. Deerfield Beach, Fla.: Health Communications.

Smart, Carol. 1976. *Women, Crime, and Criminology: A Feminist Critique*. London: Routledge and Kegan Paul.

———. 1995. *Law, Crime and Sexuality*. London: Sage.

Smith, Andrea. 2003. "Not an Indian Tradition: The Sexual Colonization of Native Peoples." *Hypatia* 18, no. 2:70–85.

———. 2004. "Beyond the Politics of Inclusion: Violence Against Women of Color and Human Rights." *Meridians* 4, no. 2:120–25.

———. 2005a. "The Anti-Violence Movement as an Alibi for the State in American Culture." Paper presented at the annual meeting of the Society for the Study of Social Problems, Philadelphia, Pennsylvania, August 12–14.

———. 2005b. *Conquest: Sexual Violence and American Indian Genocide*. Boston: South End.

Smith, Dorothy E. 1987. *The Everyday World as Problematic: A Sociology for Women*. Boston: Northeastern University Press.

———. 1990a. *The Conceptual Practices of Power*. Boston: Northeastern University Press.

———. 1990b. *Texts, Facts, and Femininity: Exploring the Relations of Ruling*. New York: Routledge.

———. 1993. "High Noon in Textland." *Sociological Quarterly* 34, no. 1:183–92.

Snell, Tracy L., and Danielle C. Morton. 1994. *Women in Prison: Survey of State Prison Inmates 1991, Bureau of Justice Statistics Special Report*. Washington, D.C.: U.S. Department of Justice, Bureau of Justice Statistics. NCJ 145321.

Spector, Jill. N.d. Brief for *Amicus Curiae* in Commonwealth of Pennsylvania v. Beth Ann Markman, in the Supreme Court of Pennsylvania, No. 371 Capital Appeal Docket. Philadelphia, Pa.: National Clearinghouse for the Defense of Battered Women.

Spellman, Elizabeth. 1988. *Inessential Woman*. Boston: Beacon.

Spender, Dale. 1980. *Man-Made Language*. London: Routledge and Kegan Paul.

Stanko, Elizabeth A. 1990. *Everyday Violence*. London: Pandora.

Stannard, David E. 1992. *American Holocaust: The Conquest of the New World*. Oxford: Oxford University Press.

Stark, Evan. 2004. "Insults, Injury, and Injustice," *Violence Against Women* 10, no. 11:1302–30.

Stark, Evan, and Anne Flitcraft. 1996. *Women at Risk: Domestic Violence and Women's Health*. London: Sage.

Steedman, Carolyn Kay. 1994. *Landscape for a Good Woman*. New Brunswick, N.J.: Rutgers University Press.

Straus, Murray A. 1979. "Measuring Intrafamily Conflict and Violence: The Conflict Tactics (CS) Scales." *Journal of Marriage and the Family* 41, no. 1:75–89.

Straus, Murray A., Richard J. Gelles, and Suzanne K. Steinmetz. 1980. *Behind Closed Doors: Violence in the American Family*. Garden City, N.Y.: Anchor/Doubleday.

Sudnow, David. 1965. "Normal Crimes: Sociological Features of the Penal Code in a Public Defender Office." *Social Problems* 12, no. 3:255–76.

Sykes, Charles. 1992. *A Nation of Victims*. New York: St. Martin's.

Sykes, Gresham M., and David Matza. 1957. "Techniques of Neutralization: A Theory of Delinquency." *American Sociological Review* 22, no. 6: 667–70.

Szasz, Thomas S. 1961. *The Myth of Mental Illness: Foundations of a Theory of Personal Conduct*. New York: Dell.

———. 1983. "The Control of Conduct: Authority vs. Autonomy." In *Compliant Behavior: Beyond Obedience to Authority*. edited by Max Rosenbaum, 199–206. New York: Human Sciences Press.

Tea, Michelle. 2003. *Without a Net: The Female Experience of Growing up Working Class*. Emeryville, Calif.: Seal.

Tjaden, Patricia, and Nancy Thoennes. 2000. *Extent, Nature and Consequences of Intimate Partner Violence*. Washington, D.C.: National Institute of Justice and Center for Disease Control. NCJ 181867.

Tierney, Kathleen. 1982. "The Battered Women Movement and the Creation of the Wife Beating Problem." *Social Problems* 29, no. 3:207–20.

Toch, Hans, and Kenneth Adams. 1994. *The Disturbed and Violent Offender*. Washington, D.C.: APA Books.

United States Advisory Board on Child Abuse and Neglect. 1995. *A Nation's Shame: Fatal Child Abuse and Neglect in the United States*. Washington, D.C.: Department of Health and Human Services.

United States Census Bureau. 1995. *Housing of American Indians on Reservations*. Washington, D.C.: U.S. Department of Commerce.

———. 2004a. *Current Population Survey, 2002 to 2004 Annual Social and Economic Indicators*. Washington, D.C.: U.S. Census Bureau.

———. 2004b. *State and County Quick Facts*. http://quickfacts.census.gov/qfd/states/46000.html. Accessed January 23, 2005.

━━━. 2005. Historical Poverty Tables. http://www.census.gov/hhes/www/poverty/histpov/hstpov24.htm. Accessed July 19, 2005.

United States Children's Bureau. 2005. *Child Maltreatment 2003*. U.S. Department of Health and Human Services, Administration on Children, Youth and Families. Washington, D.C.: Government Printing Office, 2005. http://www.acf.hhs.gov/programs/cb/publications/cm03/index.htm. Accessed September 18, 2005.

United States Department of Health and Human Services. 2005a. *Male Perpetrators of Child Maltreatment*. Washington, D.C.: Government Printing Office. http://aspe.hhs.gov/hsp/05/child-maltreat/report.pdf. Accessed September 17, 2005.

━━━. 2005b. *Women's Health USA 2005*. Rockville, Md.: U.S. Department of Health and Human Services.

United States Sentencing Commission. 2003. *Sourcebook of Federal Sentencing Statistics*. Table 12. Washington, D.C.: United States Sentencing Commission. http://www.ussc.gov/ANNRPT/2003/SBTOC03.htm. Accessed September 15, 2005.

Vidmar, Neil J., and Regina A. Schuller. 1989. "Juries and Expert Evidence: Social Framework Testimony." *Law and Contemporary Problems* 52: 133–76.

Von Hentig, Hans. 1941. "Remarks on the Interaction of Perpetrator and Victim." *Journal of Criminal Law, Criminology, and Police Science* 31: 303–309.

Walby, Sylvia. 1990. *Theorizing Patriarchy*. Oxford: Basil Blackwell.

Walker, Laurens, and John Monahan. 1987. "Social Frameworks: A New Use of Social Science in Law." *Virginia Law Review* 73:459–60.

Walker, Lenore. 1979. *The Battered Woman*. New York: Harper and Row.

Weber, Max. 1948. *From Max Weber: Essays in Sociology*. Edited by Hans Gerth and C. Wright Mills. London: Routledge and Kegan Paul.

━━━. 1978. *Economy and Society: An Outline of Interpretive Sociology*. Edited by Guenther Roth and Claus Wittich. Berkeley and Los Angeles: University of California Press.

Websdale, Neil S. 1998. *Rural Woman Battering and the Justice System*. Thousand Oaks, Calif.: Sage Publications.

━━━. 1999. *Understanding Domestic Homicide*. Boston: Northeastern University Press.

━━━. 2001. *Policing the Poor: From Slave Plantation to Public Housing*. Boston: Northeastern University Press.

Websdale, Neil S., and Byron Johnson. 1997. "Reducing Woman Battering: The Role of Structural Approaches." *Social Justice* 24, no. 1:54–81.

Wesely, Jennifer. 2003. "Exotic Dancing and the Negotiation of Identity: The Multiple Uses of Body Technologies." *Journal of Contemporary Ethnography* 32:643–69.

Westlund, Andrea C. 1999. "Pre-modern and Modern Power: Foucault and the Case of Domestic Violence." *Signs* 24, no. 4:1045–66.

Whitcombe, Christopher L. C. E. 2000. "Lilith and Eve." In *Eve and the Identity of Woman*, chapter 7. http://witcombe.sbc.edu/eve-women/7evelilith.html. Accessed October 4, 2005.

Widom, Cathy Spatz. 2003. *Child Abuse and Neglect and Later Criminal Behavior.* Center of Excellence for Early Childhood Development, Montreal. Online presentation accessed on July 12, 2005. http://www.excellence-earlychildhood.ca/documents/Spatz-Widom.pdf.

Widom, Cathy Spatz, and Michael G. Maxfield. 2001. "An Update on the 'Cycle of Violence.'" Washington, D.C.: U.S. Department of Justice.

Williams, Raymond. 1977. *Marxism and Literature.* London: Oxford University Press.

Wilson, Margo, and Martin Daly. 1993. "Spousal Homicide Risk and Estrangement." *Violence and Victims* 8, no. 1:3–16.

———. 1998. "Lethal and Nonlethal Violence Against Wives and the Evolutionary Psychology of Male Sexual Proprietariness." In *Rethinking Violence Against Women*, edited by R. E. Dobash and R. P. Dobash, 199–230. Thousand Oaks, Calif.: Sage Publications.

Wilson, William Julius. 1987. *The Truly Disadvantaged: The Inner City, the Underclass, and Public Policy.* Chicago: University of Chicago Press.

———. 1996. *When Work Disappears: The World of the New Urban Poor.* New York: Vintage.

Wolfgang, Marvin E. 1958. *Patterns of Criminal Homicide.* Philadelphia: University of Pennsylvania Press.

Woolf, Virginia. 1984. "Professions for Women." In *The Virginia Woolf Reader*, edited by M. Leaksa, 276–82. Orlando, Fla.: Harcourt.

Yarrow, Marion Radke, Charlotte Green Schwartz, Harriet S. Murphy, and Leila Calhoun Deasy. 1955. "The Psychological Meaning of Mental Illness in the Family." *Journal of Social Issues* 11, no. 4:12–24.

Yllo, Kersti, and Michel Bograd. 1988. *Feminist Perspectives on Wife Abuse.* Beverly Hills, Calif.: Sage Publications.

Zaitzow, Barbara H., and Jim Thomas. 2003. *Women in Prison: Gender and Social Control.* Boulder, Colo.: Lynne Rienner.

Zandy, Janet. 1994. *Liberating Memory: Our Work and Our Working-Class Consciousness.* New Brunswick, N.J.: Rutgers University Press.

Zinn, Howard. 2003. *A People's History of the United States: 1492–The Present.* New York: Perennial Classics.

Zubretsky, Theresa M., and Karla M. Digirolamo. 1996. "The False Connection Between Adult Domestic Violence and Alcohol." In *Helping Battered Women*, edited by A. R. Roberts, New York: Oxford University Press.

INDEX

abandonment, 117, 123, 131–32,
141–42, 154–55
Abby, 66, 165
abortion, 65, 81
African Americans: "angel" symbol
and, 2, 267n6; anti-violence movement and, 269n13; battered woman
discourse and, 45; child protective
custody and, 56; interracial marriage, 179; sustained commitment
to abusive relationships, 282–83n78;
women's incarceration rate, 4. *See
also* Ronnie; Toni
alcohol: National Household Survey
on Drug Abuse, 282n65; role in
partner violence, 85–87, 134–35,
164, 277n31; social reproduction
of pain and, 135–38, 198; table of
alcohol abuse by victims and partners, 258–59 (Appendix B); victimization compromised by, 44–45,
64, 65–66
Alicia, 212–13
Allen, Hilary, 283n6
Allen, Nicole E., 249
American Indians: cultural theft,
288n46; delusions and social location, 88, 89; economic status,
280n42, 281n55; effects of colonization, 117–18, 136–37, 142;
health problems among, 142,
282n65–66; legal jurisdiction of
tribal vs. U.S. courts, 274n34;
matrilineal authority, 58, 117;
Navajo Peacekeeping process,
274–75n40; racial oppression of,
57–59, 274n29. *See also* Carol;

Carrie; Crystal; Dorothy; Emma;
Leah; Michelle; Rhonda
Andelin, Helen, 208, 287n33
"angel" symbol: Beth compared with,
63; class status and, 127; culpability in violence and, 44–45; cultural
origin and scope of, 1–2; in non-
conventional contexts, 36; rape
victim typology and, 19–20; source
of, 267n5
Angie, 27, 68–69, 160–61
Anne, 95–98, 165, 171
anti-violence movement: Arizona
Coalition Against Domestic
Violence, 269–70n26; Battered
Women's Justice Project (BWJP),
272n5; cycle of violence and, 111;
Domestic Abuse Intervention
Project, 272n5; domestic violence
coordinating councils, 249; impact
on public views of abuse, 10;
INCITE!, 59, 269n13; ineffectiveness for some victims, 251; liberatory approach to, 252; National
Clearinghouse for the Defense
of Battered Women, 166, 272n5;
National Violence Against Women
Survey, 4; resource awareness
initiative of, 246; theoretical
problems with, 12–13. *See also*
feminism
Arizona Coalition Against Domestic
Violence, 269–70n26
authority. *See* obedience; power
autonomy, 206–7, 250. *See also*
economic dependence/
independence

Barney (Dorothy's partner), 173–74, 192
Baskin, Deborah, 134
battered woman discourse: ambivalence not accommodated by, 24–25; development of, 14–15; domestic violence laws and, 167, 285n22; effect on prosecution/sentencing, 187, 245; expert testimony and, 166–68; influence on public opinion, 18–22; perceptions of women's agency in, 129, 281n57; "pure victim" bias in, 44–45; social framework legal approach and, 199; "tough woman" image and, 66–68, 177–78, 182–83. See also binary categories; victimization
battered woman syndrome, 24, 166–67, 285n22, 285n32
Battered Women's Justice Project (BWJP), 272n5
Bauman, Kimberly, 52
Beautiful Mind, A (film), 90
Belinda, 71, 72–73
Belknap, Joanne, 29
Beth: awareness of partner's threatening demeanor, 161; biographical sketch, 61–64; child sexual abuse of, 143; continued feelings for partner, 189, 192; feeling of entrapment of, 170; on nonconsensual sex, 30, 61; parent alcohol/drug abuse, 139–40; partner's jealousy, 84; on physical vs. emotional abuse, 16; prior abuse arrest of, 60–61, 198; sentencing of, 164
Billy Bob (Phyllis's partner), 84, 104–5, 130, 132, 214–16, 217
binary categories: angel vs. demon, 44; complexity obscured by, 26; victimless crime and, 267n2; victim/offender category pair, 1; victim/offender vs. "mutual combat," 8, 60, 64–65, 70, 275nn54–55. See also "angel" symbol; battered woman discourse; victimization
Blackgoat, Roberta, 58
Bo (Danielle's lover), 184–85

Bobby (Julia's partner), 92–93
Bonnie, 138
boredom, 128–29
Bortner, M. A., 29
Bourgois, Philippe, 120, 279n10
Brian (Lisa's partner), 64, 130, 163
Brownmiller, Susan, 231, 288n49
Bruce (Anne's partner), 95–98
Buehl, Sarah, 26
Burning Bed, The (film), 21, 283n2

Campbell, Jacquelyn, 173
Carol, 143, 154
Carrie, 141–42, 155
Chad (Shanna's partner), 185
charisma, 202
Chesney-Lind, Meda, 3, 29, 60, 116
Child Fatality Review Team, 240
childhood: "childhood" as cultural concept, 13, 119–23; circumstances of sexual abuse, 142–43; communal responsibility for children, 156–57; dissociation/fantasies as resource for, 101, 145, 150, 282n68; maternal physical violence, 140; parent alcohol/drug abuse, 135–37, 139–42; social class and, 121–28; table of childhood abuse/parental absence, 262–63 (Appendix E); of women in study, 114–15
child protective services (CPS), 54–56, 140, 238–39, 240–42, 273n19. See also custody of children
children (of victims): attempts to protect mother, 34–35; child fatalities, 240–44; child protective services (CPS), 54–56, 140, 238–39, 240–42, 273n19; partner threats against, 32–33, 180, 184; sexual abuse of, 28, 218, 232–39; table of victims with children, 262–63 (Appendix E); victims' concern for, 30–33, 153–54, 251. See also custody of children; failure-to-protect-children charge
child sexual abuse (of adult victims): overview, 114; betrayal of reality

and, 74; circumstances leading to, 142–47; dissociation/fantasy response to, 150; effect on adult sexuality, 27–29, 61–62, 149, 222; empathic caretaker response to, 151, 282n72; intergenerational cycle model of, 108–9, 110–13, 123; memory of, 100–107, 113–15, 145–49; as precursor to marriage, 132–33, 143; rarity of prosecution for, 143, 216; scholarship on, 3; statute of limitations and, 46

Chodorow, Nancy J., 153

Chris: on betrayed reality, 74; childhood experiences, 109, 151; effort to resist abuse, 219; empathic caretaker response to abuse, 151–52, 156; history of abusive relationships of, 216; partner's controlling behavior, 93–95

Cindy, 164, 194

class: "angel" symbol and, 2, 267n6; definitions of, 279n20; divorce experience and, 280–81n46; employment status of victims, 128–29; epistemology of marginalized women, 11–12; gender expectations and, 36; good/bad women opposition and, 1–2; "hidden injuries of class," 125–28; impact on childhood experiences, 116–19; prison sentence severity and, 118; social construction of childhood, 119–20; social control of desire and, 110; structures of feeling and, 108–9, 118–19, 125–28; theories of crime and, 211–12, 288n38, 288n40. *See also* economic dependence/independence

Cliff (Sarah's partner), 220, 223–24

Clinton, Bill, 59

Cobb, Jonathan, 125–27

Collins, Patricia Hill, 11–12, 267n6, 279n18

Comach, Elizabeth, 60

Comaskey, Brenda, 57

communal responsibility for children, 156–57

Conflict Tactics Scale (CTS), 18, 40, 270nn29–30

control theory, 211–12

corporate crime, 212, 288n38, 288n40

counterfeiting, 95, 152, 219–20

criminal justice. *See* criminal processing system; law

criminal processing system: abuse victim testimony in partner murder trial, 36, 60–61; American Indians and, 58–59; as anti-violence activism concern, 12–13; arrests of women victims, 60–61; battered woman discourse and, 20–21; "criminal justice" term vs., 272n1; exaggeration/minimization in victim testimony, 22; expert witness testimony, 6, 67–68, 118, 166–68, 184, 193–94; failure-to-protect-children sentencing costs, 244; homicide studies, 159–60; housing eviction policies and, 59; legal counsel, 118, 279–80n21; marginalized groups' distrust of, 49–51, 55–59; marriage counselor testimony, 184; no-drop prosecution policies, 70; orders of protection, 19–20, 50–53, 272–73n7; proper victim behavior in, 46–47, 66–69; rarity of child abuse prosecution, 143, 216; social causes of crime, 3–4, 10; use of victim survival strategies, 250; witness tampering, 236–37. *See also* expert witness testimony; failure-to-protect-children charge; law; police

criminology: control theory, 211–12; homicide studies, 159–60; National Crime Victimization Study, 51–52; "pathways to crime" studies, 198

Crystal: abuse experiences, 37–38, 174–76, 190; continued fear after partner's death, 190–91; decision not to resist violence, 37–38; on "good parts" of relationship, 23; isolation from parents, 117; violence against abusive partner by, 174–76, 177 custody of children: abusive men as custodians, 289n52; child protective services (CPS), 54–56, 140, 238–39, 240–42, 273n19; custody threats as control device, 33, 118, 171, 181, 232, 238; as issue in marriage decision, 218; as problem for incarcerated women, 153–55, 183, 195, 239, 244, 273–74n21, 289n71. See also children (of victims)

cycle of violence: overview, 9, 108, 110–13; child normalcy of future victims, 134; cycle models of social behavior, 26; cyclical pattern in abusive relationships, 22–24; gender, race, and class and, 115–19; intergenerational cycle model of, 108–9, 110–15; "pathways to crime" studies, 198, 286n1; social reproduction of pain and, 113, 126–28, 143, 156–57, 279n10; structures of feeling and, 108–9, 116, 122

Danielle: attempted suicide, 33; desire to keep abuse private, 35–36; feelings of entrapment of, 170; feelings about sexuality, 27–28; feelings toward partner, 34–35, 165; marriage as means of independence, 131; on orders of protection, 51–52; partner's controlling behavior, 128–29; prison sentence of, 163, 184–85, 194–95; on the unexpectedness of partner violence, 43; violence against abusive partner, 184–85, 187

Daryl (Jane's partner), 179–80

Dasgupta, Shamita Das, 60, 64, 272n1

Dawn, 161, 181–82, 194

demons, 2

DeVault, Marjorie, 5, 7, 23

devious woman cultural type, 187

Dianne: awareness of partner's threatening demeanor, 161; childhood, 124–25; on "good parts" of relationship, 24; partner's delusions, 89–90; prison sentence of, 162, 177; response to jealousy, 39; "tough woman" discourse and, 66–68, 69, 177–78

Dick (Monica's partner), 235–36

discipline. See obedience; power

dissociation, 101, 105–7, 145, 149, 150, 229

Dobash, Rebecca, 41, 78–79, 269n17

Dobash, Russell, 41, 78–79

Domestic Abuse Intervention Project, 272n5

Domestic Violence and Mental Health Policy Initiative, 277n31

domestic violence coordinating councils, 249

Domestic Violence Restraining Order System, 272–73n7

"domestic violence" term, 10, 14, 15. See also intimate partner violence

domination. See obedience; power

Doreen, 83, 98–99, 101

Dorothy: autobiographical narrative by, 285n36; avoidance-of-abuse strategies, 38–39; continued feelings for partner, 189, 191–92; on "good parts" of relationship, 23; on the unexpectedness of partner violence, 44; violence against abusive partner by, 173–74, 177

drugs: abuse victims as drug crime accomplices, 40–41, 209–11; difficulty negotiating surreal experience and, 74, 88–89; drug induced delusions, 88, 89, 94, 98–99, 227–28; forced or triggered by abuse, 86–87, 123, 149; marginalized groups and, 212–14; National Household Survey on Drug Abuse, 282n65; One-Strike and You're Out policy, 59; reproduction of pain and, 123, 134–35, 232–33; role in partner violence, 85–86, 133, 134–35, 227, 277n31; socioeconomic context for, 123; table of drug abuse by victims and part-

ners, 258–59 (Appendix B); victimization compromised by, 44, 65–66
Dutton, Mary Ann, 26
Dworkin, Andrea, 232, 244–45, 288n49
dysfunctional families, 108, 111–12

Earl (Eve's partner), 185–86
economic dependence/independence: career/job opportunities, 121–22, 250–51; dependence as control mechanism, 165, 171, 181, 206–7, 232, 238; drug crimes and, 212–13; independence as trigger of violence, 84–85; middle-class victims, 118, 128–29, 133, 151, 216, 225–26; race/ethnicity and, 122, 280n42; standard of living following divorce, 280–81n46; table of jobs of victims, 262–63 (Appendix E). *See also* class
Emma, 141–42, 216, 241–42
Emory (Leah's partner), 182–83
epistemology. *See* knowledge
ethnomethodology, 71
Eve, 163, 185–86
experience: battered woman discourse and, 19; categories of bounded experience, 13, 45, 112; knowledge and, 12; structures of feeling and, 108–9
expert witness testimony: construction of victimization and, 67–68; effect on conviction/sentencing, 166–68, 187, 194, 285n32, 285–86n37; historical development of battered woman testimony, 166–67, 268n30; recent decline in use of, 193–94; use by middle-class victims, 118; use by prosecution, 6. *See also* criminal processing system

failure-to-protect-children charge: detrimental effects of sentencing for, 244; as factor in reporting violence, 238–39; fathers not often accountable for, 233–34; legal responsibility of nonabusive parent,

54–55; prosecution of abuser and, 103–4, 218; public drunkenness as substance for, 286n2; sentences of abusers, 243. *See also* criminal processing system; custody of children; law
False Memory Syndrome Foundation (FMSF), 278n48
families: as complex social/emotional environment, 108; domestic authority and, 201, 205–8; dynamics of violence in, 111–12; familicide, 32; hard-living/settled-living families, 123, 281n47; victim's family as support resource, 169–70, 216
Fascinating Womanhood (book), 208, 287n33
Fatal Attraction (film), 164
FBI Supplementary Homicide Reports, 240
feminism, 5, 11–12, 15, 78, 269n7. *See also* anti-violence movement
fighting back, 37–40, 68–70. *See also* resistance
flirtation, 66–68
Flitcraft, Anne, 33
foster care system, 56
Foucault, Michel, 12, 27, 202–3
Frankie (Mona's partner), 103
Free Battered Women, 285n22
Freyd, Jennifer, 278n48
Friedan, Betty, 128
Friedman, Lawrence M., 80

Gaardner, Emily, 29
Gaslight (film), 82–83
gaslighting, 82–83
gaze (of batterer), 188
Gelles, Richard, 18, 41, 270n33
gender: blame for abuse and, 124; daughter-as-caretaker role, 139–40, 144, 282n67; failure-to-protect-children charge and, 233–34; gender neutrality issue, 14–15, 60; intimate partner violence and, 18–19; social class experience and, 36, 125–28; victimization and, 158–59, 283n6

Goffman, Erving, 284n9
good/bad women opposition, 1–3,
    44–45
Gordon, Avery, 5
Gordon, Linda, 122
Gottman, John M., 85
Greenbrook Initiative, 55

Hamilton, V. Lee, 204–5, 206–7,
    208–9
Harding, Sandra, 11
Hart, Barbara, 283n2
Hartsock, Nancy, 11
Hays, Sharon, 120
Herman, Judith, 150, 151, 282n72
Hispanics. *See* Latinas/os
homicide studies, 159–60, 284n9–10,
    284n13
homophobia, 276n17
Howell, Joseph T., 281n47
Hughes, Francine, 283n2

identity: battered woman discourse
    and, 19–20; class status and,
    126–27; complex personhood, 5;
    dissociation, 101, 105–7, 145, 149,
    150, 229; historical grounding of,
    12; partner's false identity, 72,
    95–98, 223; personality vulnerabil-
    ities of child abuse victims,
    150–51; remembering as identity
    construction, 100–101; self-blame
    as means of self-control, 42–43;
    self-deception, 66; self-doubt, 65;
    self-esteem, 14. *See also* individu-
    alism; surreality; victimization
immigrant women, 54
incest. *See* child sexual abuse
INCITE!, 59, 269n13
individualism: battered woman dis-
    course and, 19, 166–67; criminal
    responsibility and, 17, 270n27;
    cycle of violence and, 26, 112, 153;
    free-will decisions and, 81–82,
    248–49; group violence, 3–4, 10,
    16–17, 270n27; liberal democracy
    and, 77–78; liberal philosophy and,
    3–4; solutions to partner violence

and, 195, 247; treatment programs
    and, 111. *See also* identity
intimate partner terrorism: burial site
    displays and threats, 65, 186, 218,
    220, 223; control/intimidation
    tactics, 15–16, 38–41, 92–93;
    domestic authority and, 205–6;
    "going back" as fear response, 47,
    180; incarceration ineffective in
    preventing, 53; internalization of
    partner's control, 188–93, 218; by
    partner's family, 57, 183, 239;
    threats to children and property,
    32–33, 96–97, 218; threats to take
    custody of children, 33, 118,
    153–54, 171, 180, 190, 232, 238;
    threats to victim's extended
    family, 160, 245; turning family
    against victim, 170. *See also* inti-
    mate partner violence; surreality;
    violence against abusers
intimate partner violence: child fatal-
    ities from, 240–44; consequences
    of resistance, 37–38, 39–40, 68–70;
    emphasis on physical assault,
    15–16, 21; ethereality of violent
    expressions, 109, 156, 279n4;
    forced abortion, 65; forced drug
    use, 86–87; homicide as "character
    contest," 284n9–10; lack of tradi-
    tional research on, 19; language of,
    13–18; by men vs. women, 4, 158;
    as once-accepted normal behavior,
    10, 15; origin of term, 10, 15; by
    partner's family, 57, 183, 239; risk
    factors for fatality, 173; role of
    weapons in, 173–75; triggers for,
    40, 42–43, 169, 178; unexpected-
    ness of, 43, 44, 178; victim self-
    blame for, 42, 271n53. *See also*
    intimate partner terrorism; rape;
    violence against abusers
intimate relationships: aggressive
    intimacy in, 165–66; ambivalence
    as unanticipated feeling in, 25–26;
    arguments/conflict not linked
    with violence, 40; childhood pain
    and, 123; forced marriage, 284n16;

"good parts" of abusive relationships, 23–24, 25–26, 171, 246; marriage as means to prevent testimony, 218; marriage counselors, 35, 184; "moderate chastisement" once accepted in, 10, 15; as romantic utopia, 131–34, 141, 281n59, 282n77; "soul mate" paradigm for, 92–93, 146, 225, 228. *See also* leaving a relationship
intimidation tactics, 40–41. *See also* intimate partner terrorism

Jack (Eve's co-defendant), 186
Jacobson, Neil S., 85
James (Dianne's partner), 67
Jane: biographical sketch, 43–44, 178–81; concern for daughter, 32, 33; contemplated suicide, 33–34, 178–79; continued fear after partner's death, 189; custody of child of, 155; on "good parts" of relationship, 23; predictability of partner's violence, 38, 43–44, 161, 179; sentencing of, 194
Jared (Jennifer's partner), 145–46, 225–26
jealousy: as betrayal of shared reality, 73–74; correlation with femicide, 195–96, 286n38; distortion of reality and, 83–84; economic independence as trigger of, 84–85, 129; efforts at accommodation of, 38, 209–10; as factor in abuse, 39; flirtatious conduct accusation and, 66–68; possessiveness of partner and, 66, 84–85, 195, 210
Jeff (Dawn's partner), 181–82
Jennifer: on betrayed reality, 74; biographical sketch, 224–26; childhood abuse memories of, 113, 145; crimes of obedience of, 221; post-conviction feelings about partner, 217–18
jobs. *See* class; economic dependence/independence
Johnson, Michael P., 15, 275n54
Julia, 92–93

Katy, 25, 209–11
Kelman, Herbert C., 204–5, 206–7, 208–9
knowledge: binary categories, 1; experience and, 12; masculinist bias, 11; modernist project, 17, 270n28; partner's false identity, 72, 95–98, 223; reification, 14; scientific "coding" of experience, 17–18; situated knowledge, 12, 45; social context of "truth," 74–76; truth in delusional fantasies, 98; "truth" of partner violence and, 45; women's expert knowledge of partners, 51–54, 178, 250. *See also* memory; surreality
Konradi, Amanda, 19
Kurz, Demie, 120, 122, 280–81n46

Laing, R. D., 90
language, 5, 12, 13–15, 17–19. *See also* translation
Lareau, Annette, 119–20
Latinas/os, 4, 59, 280n42. *See also* Lisa; Luisa; Salina; Teresita
Laub, Dori, 100–101
Laura, 217
law: battered woman discourse in, 167, 285n22; corroborating evidence requirements, 46; *DeShaney v. Winnebago County Department of Social Services* ruling and, 273n19; Doctrine of Coverture, 80–81; duress as legal defense, 81–82, 199–200, 276–77n22; injunctions against harassment, 97, 278n45; legal counsel, 118, 279–80n21; malicious intent and, 197; mandatory arrest policies, 60, 70, 288n45; mandatory sentencing laws, 4; murder vs. self-defense, 81, 166, 167–68, 173, 176, 283n2; orders of protection, 50–53, 272–73n7; premeditation and, 159, 167–68, 179, 183–84; recognition of battered women's perspective, 166–68, 268n30, 285n32; social framework testimony, 199. *See also* criminal processing system;

law (continued)
   expert witness testimony; failure-
   to-protect-children charge
Leah: abuse of, 182; biographical
   sketch, 131; contemplated suicide,
   34; continued fear after partner's
   death, 190; marriage as means of
   independence, 131; parent alcohol/
   drug abuse, 141; sentencing of,
   183, 194; violence against abusive
   partner by, 182–83; violence by
   abuser's family of, 183
"learned-helplessness," 14, 166–67
leaving a relationship: ambivalence
   toward, 24–25; American Indian
   difficulty with, 58; as criminal
   processing system issue, 168–69;
   economic dependency as obstacle,
   168, 169, 170–71, 232; feeling of
   entrapment, 169–71; patriarchy as
   limit to independent resources, 80;
   public misconceptions about, 47,
   167, 168; rationalizations for staying, 91–92; "separation assault"
   and, 53–54, 169; standard of living
   following, 280–81n46; study of
   successful leaving, 285n33. See
   also intimate relationships; resistance; survival strategies
Lemken, Raphael, 10
lesbian partner violence, 7, 268n31,
   276n17
liberatory approach to, 252–53
Lisa: abuse of, 64–65; biographical
   sketch, 64–66, 130; custody of
   children of, 154, 185; nonviolent
   first husband of, 129–30; prior
   abuse arrest of, 60–61, 64, 198;
   violence against abusive partner
   by, 64, 163, 183
Lloyd, Susan, 84–85
loneliness, 109, 115, 117, 123–28,
   135, 155–56, 198
Lou (Marcie's partner), 237–39
Luckenbill, David, 162, 284n9–10,
   284n13
Luisa, 140–41, 216, 241–42
Lynne, 172–73

madonna symbol, 1
mandatory arrest policies, 60, 70,
   288n45
mandatory sentencing laws, 4
Marcie, 28, 33, 233–35, 237–39
marginalized groups: dominant
   cultural narratives and, 75; drugs
   and, 212; obstacles to safety from
   abuse, 82; perspective on domination, 11–12; relationship with
   authorities, 54–56; views of
   victimless crime in, 214
marital rape, 10, 27, 30
Mark (Nicole's partner), 226–30
marriage. See intimate relationships
Masum, 249
Matt (Beth's partner), 30, 62–64, 139,
   161, 189, 192, 193
Matza, David, 213
McGillivray, Anne, 57
memory: difficulty remembering
   abuse, 102–4; dissociation and,
   150; normalization of abuse in
   childhood and, 141–43; recovered
   memory controversy, 113–15,
   278n48; trauma and, 73, 100–102;
   uncertainty of memories of childhood sexual abuse, 145–46. See
   also knowledge; narrative
men: as abuse victims, 70, 270n33,
   275n55, 286n40; complex personhood and, 7–8; fabricated identities
   and, 72, 74; failure-to-protect-
   children charge and, 233–34; guns
   and, 173; hard-living/settled-living
   lifestyles, 123, 281n47; masculine
   entitlement, 36, 41, 80, 83–84,
   195–96; patriarchal disarray,
   121–22; patriarchy, 78–80; sexual
   double standard and, 221–22;
   social reproduction of pain and,
   126–27. See also patriarchy
mental illness, 87–88, 90–91, 96–98
methodology, 6–7, 265–66 (Appendix
   G), 271n53, 279n20, 285n36,
   289n66
Michelle: childhood experiences, 109;
   friends' encouragement to fight

back, 69–70; parent alcohol abuse,
135–37, 139; sentencing of, 164;
trauma memories of, 106
middle class. *See* Chris; Cindy;
class; economic dependence/
independence; Nicole; Ronnie
Milgram, Stanley, 200, 204
Miller, Susan L., 60, 284n14
Mills, C. Wright, 212, 288n38
mind games, 72, 82–85. *See also*
surreality
modernism, 17, 270n28
Moe, Angela, 56, 212, 285n35
Mona: ambivalent feelings, 31;
battered woman discourse and,
20–21, 24–25; biographical sketch,
20; concern for daughter, 32; concern for drugs in the house, 40–41;
custody of children of, 185; prison
sentence of, 162–63; refusal to
obey partner, 39–40, 41–42; sentencing of, 194; trauma memories
of, 101–3; violence against abusive
partner by, 20, 183
Monica: failure-to-protect-children
charge, 233–36; post-conviction
feelings about partner, 217–18;
refusal to obey partner, 39–40,
41–42; trauma memories of,
103–4
Monster (film), 267n8
Morelli, Mario, 200
Morgan (Chris's second partner), 95,
219–20
Myrna, 76–77, 276n7

narrative: complexities of victimization reflected in, 5–6; identity
construction and, 100–101; problems with narrative coherence, 65,
101; as reflection of social reality,
74–76; trauma memory and, 101–3.
See also memory
National Clearinghouse for the
Defense of Battered Women, 166,
272n5, 283n2
National Crime Victimization Study,
51–52

National Household Survey on Drug
Abuse, 282n65
National Violence Against Women
Survey, 4
Natural Born Killers (film), 224
Navajo Peacekeeping process,
274–75n40
Nicholson v. Williams (2004), 55
Nicole: attempted suicide, 33, 229;
biographical sketch, 226–31; child
sexual abuse of, 148–50; on drug
use, 88; "struggling relationship"
characterization by, 24; trauma
memories of, 106–7
Novy, Kimberly and Keith, 233
Nussbaum, Hedda, 95, 231, 288n49

obedience: crimes of obedience,
204–5, 207–9, 210, 214–15, 216–20,
223–24, 230–31; duress as legal
defense and, 199–200, 276–77n22;
economic dependency and, 84–85,
165, 171, 181, 206–7, 209–10; fear
for personal safety and, 249; forced
marriage and, 284n16; forms of
authority, 200–202; gendered behavior and, 36–37, 80–81; as intimidation tactic, 40–41, 93, 204–5,
208–9; military as model for, 89,
204–6, 208, 287n26; social bonding
and, 211–12, 288n38; surveillance
and, 188, 206, 209; views of
victimless crime and, 214. *See
also* power; resistance
One-Strike and You're Out policy, 59
orders of protection, 50–53, 272–73n7
Osthoff, Sue, 283n2

pain: alcohol and, 136, 137, 139–41;
normality and, 113–14, 115; social
reproduction of, 113, 122–23,
126–28, 143, 156–57, 279n10;
structures of feeling and, 109–10
parenting. *See* childhood
"pathways to crime" studies, 198
patriarchy: definition, 78; domestic
authority and, 201, 205–6; feminist
discourse and, 78–80; as focus

patriarchy (*continued*)
of anti-violence initiatives, 196,
286n40; law and custom as foundation for, 207–9; patriarchal
disarray, 121–22; structure and
ideology of, 79–80. *See also* men
Pearson, Jessica, 134
penalties. *See* sentencing
personal responsibility. *See* individualism
Phil (Katy's partner), 209–11
Phyllis: abuse of, 37, 69, 104; drug use
of, 88, 214–16; loyalty to partner,
104–5, 217; nonviolent first husband of, 130; partner's demands,
37, 84, 215; physical resistance
by, 37, 39–40, 69, 207; sentencing,
216; upbringing, 132
Pipher, Mary, 134
police: actions against victim by, 56,
59, 60, 64; ineffectiveness in protecting victim, 50–53, 57–60, 64,
172, 180–82, 219, 247–48; National
Crime Victimization Study treatment of, 52; victims' use of, 61,
262–63 (Appendix E); violence
against abusers and, 60–61
Pollock, Otto, 187
possessiveness. *See* jealousy
power: conceptual practices of power,
268–69n5; forms of power, 202–3;
knowledge structure and, 11–12;
matrix of domination and, 279n18;
patriarchy and, 78–79. *See also*
obedience
prevention. *See* treatment programs
Primo (Teresita's partner), 29–30,
132–33, 170, 243–44
prostitution, 61–62, 81
psychology. *See* knowledge; mental
illness

race/ethnicity: commitment to abusive relationships and, 282–83n78;
decision to report and, 59; economic opportunities and, 122;
epistemology of marginalized
women and, 11; "people of color"

concept, 119; social control of
desire and, 110; of victims in
study, 254–57 (Appendix A).
See also African Americans;
American Indians; Latinas/os
rape: betrayal of reality and, 71, 73;
forced sodomy, 28, 179; marital
rape, 10, 19, 27, 29–30, 181; rape
victims as cultural type, 19–20;
teen rape as precursor to marriage,
133. *See also* sexuality
reification, 14
relationships. *See* intimate relationships
religion: Christian family structure,
117, 208, 287n31; church as moral
camouflage for abuse, 237, 239;
drug induced delusions and, 89–90;
gender in American Indian cos-
mologies, 89, 277–78n36; women
in Jewish and Christian religious
texts, 2, 267n8
reporting violence: financial necessity
of abusers and, 143; internalization of partner's control and, 188;
police actions against victim,
52–53, 54–59, 64, 180; race as
factor in, 54, 59; reasons for not
reporting assault, 30, 51–57, 61,
248–49
resistance: autonomy and, 206–7;
counternarratives to abusers' reality, 76; fighting back, 37–40, 68–70;
threats as self-defense, 63–64;
victimization and, 37–41, 68–70.
See also leaving a relationship;
obedience; reporting violence;
survival strategies
restraining orders. *See* orders of protection
Rex (Chris's first partner), 94–95, 219
Rhonda, 164
Richie, Beth, 59, 282–83n78
Ritchie, Andrea, 56, 59
Ronnie: attempted suicide, 33; biographical sketch, 133; on marital
sexuality, 27, 30; violence against
abuser-partner, 163–64

Rubin, Lillian, 113, 125–26, 281n59, 282n68
Rush, Florence, 82

Salina: child sexual abuse memories, 29, 146–48, 150; custody of child of, 154; decision not to report violence, 59; dissociation response of, 150; fatality of child of, 150, 241–42
Sam (Doreen's partner), 98–99
Sarah: biographical sketch, 36, 222–24; child sexual abuse of, 143–45; crimes of obedience of, 220, 223–24; as daughter-caretaker, 133, 144, 282n67; history of abusive relationships of, 216; marriage as means of independence, 133–34; surreality experience of, 222–23, 227
Scheff, Thomas J., 90
Scheppele, Kim Lane, 42, 272n2
Scott, Joan W., 12
Seeley, Kathryn, 52
self-blame, 42–44, 271n53
self-defense, 64, 166, 167–68, 173, 176, 283n2
self-esteem, 14
Sennett, Richard, 125–27
sentencing: accidental death claim and, 63, 164; for accomplice status in crime, 104, 138, 147, 220, 224, 226, 230, 236, 239, 242–43, 245; for child fatalities, 242–43; clemency hearings, 6, 118, 185, 226, 265–66 (Appendix G), 283n2; community service at women's shelter, 172; custody of children in, 154–55, 182–83, 195; for failure-to-protect-children, 29, 55, 147, 234, 236, 239, 242–44; male vs. female sentences, 147, 163, 184–85, 186, 211, 217, 224, 239, 264 (Appendix F); mandatory sentencing laws, 4; proactive violence and, 162–63, 181, 182–83, 194; probation/treatment, 68, 99, 162, 164, 176, 182, 192, 194; prohibition of intimate relationships, 172; reversal of blame and, 94–95; self-defense and, 63–64, 68, 81, 166, 167–68, 173, 176–77, 283n2; situational contexts for violence and, 162–64, 176, 178–79, 261 (Appendix D); table of crimes-against-others sentences, 264 (Appendix F); table of sentences for women who killed abusers, 260 (Appendix C); for third-party assaults, 183–84, 194; visitation by children, 154–55, 185
separation assault, 53–54
sexual harassment, 10, 272n2
sexuality: in abusive relationships, 27–30; accusations of sexual infidelity, 37–39, 72, 83–84; attraction to abusive men, 221, 224; childhood abuse, 28–29; as factor in prosecution/sentencing, 187, 194–95, 221, 230–31; normal sexuality, 27–30, 271n53; promiscuity, 149, 221; repulsion, 27–28; sexual modesty as virtue, 1–2; women as sexual property, 39. *See also* rape
Shanna: continued fear after partner's death, 189–90; parents' involvement in partner violence, 170; prison sentence of, 163; prison visits by children, 154–55, 185; sentencing of, 194; violence against abusive partner, 185, 187
Sheila: biographical sketch, 137–38; childhood experiences, 109; economic independence of, 171; sentencing of, 138, 194
shelters for battered woman, 19, 172, 251, 270n32, 273n13
Sista II Sista, 59
Skeggs, Beverly, 125–26
Smith, Andrea, 59, 142, 249, 274n29
Smith, Dorothy, 5, 90, 268–69n5
social framework testimony, 199
social reality. *See* surreality
sodomy, 28, 65
Sommers, Ira, 134
soul mate paradigm, 92–93, 146, 225, 228, 288n46

stalking, 10
standpoint feminism, 11–12, 269n7
Stark, Evan, 33
statute of limitations, 46
Steedman, Carolyn, 125–26
Steinberg, Joel, 95, 231
Straus, Murray, 18, 41, 270n33
structures of feeling, 116, 118–19,
    122, 125–28, 246; defined, 108–9,
    279n3
subjugated knowledges, 12
Sue, 171–72, 173
suicide, 33–34, 178–79, 189, 191–92,
    285n35
surreality: betrayal of reality and,
    72–74; distortion of reality and,
    8–9, 72, 76–77, 83–84; everyday
    social reality and, 71–72, 74;
    gaslighting, 82–83; as limit to free
    will, 81–82; mind games, 72,
    82–85; partner's delusions and,
    90–91, 92–100, 222–23, 227–28;
    partner's false identity, 72, 95–98,
    223; rationalization of violent
    behavior, 91–92; reversal of blame,
    42–44, 72, 94–95; trauma memory
    and, 100–107; women's credibility
    and, 46–51, 82–83. *See also* inti-
    mate partner terrorism; knowledge
Surrendered Wife, The (book), 208
surveillance, 92–93, 188, 203, 206,
    209
survival strategies: avoidance-of-
    abuse strategies, 38–39; criminal
    processing system and, 46–54;
    importance to criminal processing
    system initiatives, 250; ineffective-
    ness of police and, 50–53, 57–60,
    64, 172, 180–82, 219, 247–48; min-
    imization of abuse, 22; obedience
    as survival strategy, 39–40; protec-
    tion of children, 30–33, 183;
    weapons as precautionary mea-
    sure, 22; women's efforts to create
    safety, 8, 31, 167, 249–50; women's
    intimate knowledge of partners,
    51–54, 178, 250. *See also* leaving a
    relationship; reporting violence;
    resistance; victimization
Sykes, Gresham, 213
Szasz, Thomas S., 90, 207

Tea, Michelle, 125–26
Teresita: childhood sexual assault
    of, 132–33; desire to keep abuse
    private, 34; fatality of child of,
    242–44; on "good parts" of rela-
    tionship, 23–24; on her partner's
    jealousy, 83; on nonconsensual
    sex, 29–30; parents' involvement
    in partner violence, 170; on separa-
    tion from her children, 153
Tina, 164, 194–95
Tom (Crystal's partner), 174–76
Toni, 234
Tony (Danielle's partner), 34–36, 52,
    131, 170, 184–85
tough women, 66–68, 177–78
translation, 5, 14. *See also* language
"transmission" of violence. *See* cycle
    of violence
traumatic bonding, 24
treatment programs, 111
truth. *See* knowledge

unruly women, 44–45
U.S. Advisory Board on Child Abuse
    and Neglect, 240

VAWA (Violence Against Women
    Act), 54, 246–47, 250, 273n13
victimization: concern for family,
    30–33, 36; criminal histories and,
    195; criminalization of, 3; feelings
    of failure/shame, 31; fighting
    back and, 37, 68–70; gender and,
    158–59; individualism and, 16–17;
    "learned-helplessness," 21, 166–67;
    legitimate obedience and, 208,
    211; loyalty to partner, 34–35,
    104–5, 165, 188–89; men's victim-
    ization, 7–8, 286n40; "mutual
    combat" contrasted with, 8, 44,
    60, 64–65, 70, 275nn54–55; "path-

ways to crime" and, 198; victim/offender binary opposition, 1; women's credibility and, 46–51, 82–83, 186–87. *See also* identity; reporting violence; survival strategies

victimless crime, 214, 267n2

violence against abusers: continued love for partner after, 165, 181, 190–92; defensive vs. offensive violence, 161–62; fatality in, 159, 283–84n8; feeling of entrapment and, 171–78; feelings about abusers and, 165–66, 261 (Appendix D); premeditation and, 159, 167–68, 179, 183–84, 283n6; proactive violence, 178–83, 194; protection of children as motive, 183; situational contexts for, 162–64, 176, 178–79, 261 (Appendix D), 284n14; statistics for, 158, 286n40; table of, 260 (Appendix C), 261 (Appendix D); third-party murders, 183–87, 194

violence against innocent people, 197–98, 264 (Appendix F), 285–86n37

Violence Against Women Act (VAWA), 54, 246–47, 250, 273n13

Walker, Lenore, 22–23, 166. *See also* cycle of violence

Weber, Max, 200–202, 208, 286n8

Websdale, Neil, 169, 233, 240–41

Westlund, Andrea C., 203

Widom, Cathy Spatz, 116

Williams, Linda M., 29

Williams, Raymond, 108–9, 279n3

women who killed their husbands/partners. *See* violence against abusers

Woolf, Virginia, 2

Wournos, Aileen, 267n8

Yarrow, Marion Radke, 90

Yates, Andrea and Rusty, 233

Zandy, Janet, 125–26